"Susan Eastman has done it again. In this learned and provocative commentary, which integrates rigorous exegesis with pastoral and theological reflections, readers will find a riveting analysis of Paul's gospel to the Romans. Building upon years of teaching, preaching, and writing about Romans, Eastman leads the reader through the epistle, lifting up the power and beauty of Paul's words for his day and for our own contemporary moment. In this excellent commentary, Eastman delineates the literary, rhetorical, and theological features of the missive, enabling readers to 'enliven [their] imagination' and to hear the 'living voice of Paul.' She invites us to take a seat among the members of the Roman house churches and to listen to the letter's message afresh. Scholars, students, church leaders, laity, and all those interested in Paul's most famous letter would do well to accept this invitation."

—Lisa Bowens, Associate Professor of New Testament,
Princeton Theological Seminary

"For two thousand years, Paul's Epistle to the Romans has been a remarkable treasure chest by which Jesus has been encountered, lives have been changed, and deep theological truths have been grounded. Now, in this wonderful addition to the Interpretation Bible Commentary series, Susan Eastman provides fresh learnings for all who want to hear the apostle Paul's voice anew and deepen their own relationship with the living God."

—Bishop Michael Curry, XXVII Presiding Bishop
of The Episcopal Church and author of *Love Is the Way*

"With pacey momentum, Susan Eastman's *Romans* offers a dynamic interpretation of that powerful text, with a resolute determination to benefit today's interpreters. Drawing on deep wells of academic experience and pastoral wisdom, Eastman displays theological proficiency at every turn, without a wasted word. For those in the trenches of theological interpretation and pastoral exposition, Eastman's passionate presentation of Paul's discourse in Romans will prove to be a welcome, insightful, and stimulating companion."

—Bruce Longenecker, W. W. Melton Chair of Religion, Baylor University

"Susan Eastman loves preaching, and she loves preachers. Her commentary on Romans holds treasures for both. Her exposition of the gospel through the text of Romans provides sure-footed guidance and breathtaking views. But I particularly appreciate her pastoral wisdom for preachers themselves. This is a commentary that does more than teach the steps of grace's dance; it draws preachers into its sway. Whether engaging the weight of broken nations or whispers of broken hearts, Eastman points her readers to Romans's trust in a saving God."

—Jerusha Matsen Neal, Associate Professor of Homiletics, Duke University Divinity School

"In this very readable commentary on Romans, Susan Eastman has produced a pitch-perfect voicing of the main goal of the Interpretation series: to express the best, most exacting biblical scholarship in ways that energize the work of preachers and teachers. Time and again she taps the tuning fork of a profound passage in Romans and allows it to resonate with the needs and hungers of the church and the world. Eastman shows powerfully why this great text once mattered and still matters today. Those who preach and teach Romans will treasure this commentary."

—Thomas G. Long, Bandy Professor Emeritus of Preaching, Candler School of Theology, Emory University

"Romans is an enactment in writing of Paul's desire 'to preach the gospel also to those who are in Rome' (Rom. 1:15). Susan Eastman's commentary on this letter attends to and participates in this proclamation. At once historically informed, theologically engaged, and pastorally wise, this reading of Romans hears Paul's declaration of the gospel, joins the apostle in the apocalypse of both human bondage and divine mercy, and gives the reader this same good news so that they can speak again (and again) 'the gospel of [God's] Son' that is 'the power of God unto salvation'" (1:9, 16).

—Jonathan A. Linebaugh, Anglican Chair of Divinity and Professor of New Testament and Christian Theology at Beeson Divinity School, Samford University

"In the crowded landscape of literally hundreds of Romans commentaries, Eastman's work is a standout. Drawing from a distinguished career of Pauline scholarship, she deftly exposits Paul's magisterial text, identifies its theological riches, and offers wise counsel for preaching and teaching Romans as a powerful word of God for the present. For pastors and students who are put off by dull, esoteric, and jargon-laden academic commentaries, this will be a breath of fresh air."

—Nijay K. Gupta, Julius R. Mantey Professor of New Testament, Northern Seminary

"Few contemporary Pauline scholars can match Eastman's breathtaking range. In this volume of a much-loved (and now reimagined) series, her unique combination of historical and literary insight, theological vision, and pastoral sensitivity are all on display in her dynamic reading of Romans. Preachers, teachers, scholars, and students are all in Eastman's debt for this fresh encounter with the scope and power of Paul's gospel."

—Jamie Davies, Tutor in New Testament and Director of Postgraduate Research, Trinity College Bristol

Romans

An Interpretation Bible Commentary

Interpretation Bible Commentary

Volumes in the Series

Old Testament

Genesis 1–11
Genesis 12–50
Exodus
1 Samuel
Esther
Psalms
Isaiah 1–39
Isaiah 40–66
Ezekiel
Daniel
Hosea–Malachi

New Testament

Matthew
Mark
Luke
John
Acts
Romans
1 Corinthians

Romans

An Interpretation Bible Commentary

SUSAN G. EASTMAN

First edition
Published by Westminster John Knox Press
Louisville, Kentucky

25 26 27 28 29 30 31 32 33 34—10 9 8 7 6 5 4 3 2 1

Cover and design by Allison Taylor

Library of Congress Cataloging-in-Publication Data is on file
at the Library of Congress, Washington, DC.

ISBN: 978-0-664-26433-8

For Beverly Gaventa

CONTENTS

THE CONCLUSION OF THE LETTER
Travel Plans and Greetings
Romans 15:14–16:27

SERIES FOREWORD

The work of biblical interpretation is ever-changing because the art of reading and understanding is profoundly shaped by the lives of interpreters and their communities. The original Interpretation series was designed to meet the needs of clergy, teachers, and students as a resource that integrates literary, historical, theological, and pastoral insights. The decision to extend and reframe that series as the Interpretation Bible Commentary reflects awareness of the vast historical, cultural, and ecclesial changes that have occurred since the last volume of the previous series was published in 2005. These new volumes reflect the major changes in interpretative strategies as well as a keen awareness of a dramatically changing contemporary context.

Prominent among the significant changes in the interpretive landscape is the expanded range of voices in biblical scholarship. Biblical interpretation has always been a diverse, vibrant undertaking, but that breadth has not been reflected in publications. The diversity of contributors in this renewed series reflects respect and appreciation for a broad array of witnesses.

The primary focus of the Interpretation Bible Commentary series remains unchanged from its predecessor: to invite its readers into the lively work of careful biblical interpretation for the purpose of faithful exposition. Preachers and teachers seeking reflective guidance from the biblical texts will find these volumes an illuminating and highly accessible resource. This Interpretation Bible Commentary series will tend to the needs of its twenty-first-century audience while maintaining the priorities of its creators. The words of the original editors—James Mays, Patrick Miller, and Paul Achtemeier—still ring true: "What is in mind is the work of an interpreter who brings theological and pastoral sensitivity to the task and creates an interpretation which does not stop short with judgments about the text but is engaged in a dialogue of seeing and hearing with it as a contemporary believer."

Emphasizing both sound critical exegesis and strong theological sensibilities, these new volumes employ innovative approaches that allow for fresh readings of biblical texts, including difficult passages.

The series empowers readers to engage God's creation and our place in it with fresh eyes. Through their engagement with Scripture, the commentaries illumine our relationship with God, each other, and creation so that readers are propelled with new understanding and energy for fulfilling God's claims upon us in our rapidly changing global context.

Using several interpretive methodologies that are appropriate for the varying biblical texts, these volumes promise a compelling interpretation for the church and world today. Each exposition will situate the respective biblical books historically, theologically, literarily, and socially, providing a rich resource for unleashing the homiletical and formational potential of the text.

The text on which the commentary is based is the New Revised Standard Version Updated Edition (NRSVue). Because this translation is widely available, the printing of a text in the commentary itself is unnecessary. Each commentary is divided into sections appropriate to the particular book. Instead of offering a verse-by-verse interpretation, the commentary deals with passages as a whole. Thematic topics that are especially pertinent or have great bearing on the biblical book are addressed in excursuses. A "For Further Reading" section provides resources that are instructive for broadening the reader's hermeneutical horizons and diversifying the reader's understanding of how to approach the text.

The writers and editors hope these volumes will explain and apply the meaning and significance of the biblical texts while addressing key contemporary issues. The Interpretation Bible Commentary series is intended to draw the reader into an interpretative community where, collegially, reader and interpreter can more fruitfully engage these ancient texts for present living.

The Editors

PREFACE

The late, marvelous Johannine scholar Moody Smith once told me that he had been "marinating in the Gospel of John" for forty years and was looking forward to reading the rest of the New Testament after he retired. I have been marinating in Romans for a considerable time and while I am not yet pickled, perhaps I am well-seasoned by soaking up Paul's gospel preaching. Like fine wine, Paul's good news ages well. For this reason, writing this commentary has been a tremendous gift to me, and I am profoundly grateful to the editorial board of Westminster John Knox for inviting me to participate in the new edition of the Interpretation commentary series. Completion of this work has been delayed by many events, both personal and professional. Throughout, the series editors Brian Blount and Beverly Gaventa have been unfailingly gracious and supportive. I also deeply appreciate the cordial and collaborative editorial work of Julie Mullins and Dan Braden, and the meticulous copyediting by Tina Noll, which has saved me from many errors. Any mistakes that remain are my own.

A brief word about my approach to this commentary may be helpful. Because it is written primarily for pastors and laypeople, it is heavy on pastoral and theological reflections, and relatively light on scholarly disputes about Romans. Neither space nor formatting guidelines allow for engagement with different interpretations, nor—alas!—for adequately crediting the enormous debt I owe to others' scholarly work. Works explicitly cited are noted in parentheses in the main text, along with sources of some key arguments. For further information, the reader may consult the recommendations for further research, along with the list of works cited, in the bibliography.

The commentary is based the NRSVue translation of Romans, with reference to the Greek. For the sake of simplicity, I have opted to use the historically anachronistic but familiar term "Christians" as well as "believers" to refer to Paul's audience, whom he names variously as "saints," "brothers and sisters," "in Christ," "baptized," and not least, "beloved." Throughout, I have kept my focus on the goals of preaching and pastoring in light of Paul's gospel; excursuses at the end of each section offer theological reflections and examples designed for preachers.

Authors frequently acknowledge their "debts" to others in the writing of their books; here I name some of the many "gifts" I have received, without which it would have been impossible to complete the manuscript. I say "gifts" because they far surpass any prior worth on my part, and yet they also contributed to my growth as a teacher and scholar. When I began work on this book, I was teaching at Duke University Divinity School, where one of my great joys was studying Romans with bright, engaged students; I remain grateful for that gift. A preretirement sabbatical in 2022 allowed me to spend a winter at the Collegeville Institute in Collegeville, Minnesota. Special thanks are due to the institute for their extraordinary welcome in the middle of a Minnesota winter, and for the gift of time, space, beauty, and encouragement I received there. The bulk of the commentary first draft was written during that time.

Now that I am retired, I am thankful also for the opportunity to teach a class on Romans at my local church, St. Matthew's Episcopal Church in Hillsborough, North Carolina, where the enthusiasm of the participants reminds me that Romans is always provocative and always a word in season for all people in all walks of life, not just clergy and academics.

Because the Interpretation commentary series offers a welcome opportunity to integrate exegesis with theological and pastoral reflection, this commentary has taken shape in both academic and pastoral contexts, and especially in the everyday struggles and joys of life. People from many walks of life have contributed to it, both directly in conversation and indirectly through the gift of their friendship and experience. There are far too many to name, but here I particularly thank friends and colleagues who have taught me much about the power and love of God. They comprise a circle of grace and trust, ever shifting and widening, and extending beyond death. That circle includes but is not limited to Alexandra Brown, Andrew Grove, Angela Eastman, Ann Jervis, Beverly Gaventa, Chris Anderson, David and Helen Marshall, Danny, Lia, and Elladan An, Dorothea Bertschmann, Dustin and Sherri Ellington, Eddie Eastman†, Ellen Davis, Fleming Rutledge, Jamie Davies, John Barclay, Jono Linebaugh, Laceye Warner, Liz Dowling-Sendor, Lou and Dorothy

Martyn†, Marcia Pally, Marj Oines, Phoebe Potter, Richard Hays†, Robert Fruehwirth, Shelly Matthews, Susan Smith, Thea Portier-Young, and many others.

As ever, my gratitude to and for my family knows no bounds: for Angela, Danny, Lia, and Elladan, and in memory of Eddie. Your love fills my life with warmth, joy, and laughter. The adventure continues.

Finally, this commentary is dedicated to Beverly Gaventa, with immense gratitude for her deep friendship and generous collegiality over many years.

Introduction

When I regularly hear the epistles of the blessed Paul read . . . I rejoice and enjoy the heavenly trumpet, and I am aroused and warmed by desire. I recognize the voice I love; I almost feel his presence and see him speaking.

—*John Chrysostom,* Argumentum

HOW TO READ ROMANS

It is appropriate to begin this commentary on Paul's Letter to the Romans with a quotation from John Chrysostom, the fourth-century archbishop of Constantinople who was famous for his preaching ("Chrysostom" means "golden mouth" in Greek). The present commentary is written with preaching in mind; our foremost concern is the gospel proclamation we hear in Romans and its effects on Paul's original listeners, on us, and on those with whom we minister. Chrysostom reflects on the effects of Paul's letters on him—what the letters *do to* him. Paul's words are "the heavenly trumpet"—they are a clarion call, an awakening, an impetus to action. To hear them is an event that awakens desire, warms the heart, and fires up the will. His words communicate Paul's voice, a voice that Chrysostom has learned to love; indeed, they almost make Paul present in the flesh. They speak as a living voice, not dead letters.

Similarly, the goal of the present commentary is to enliven our imaginations and clarify our understanding so that, like Chrysostom, we also hear the "heavenly trumpet" when we hear and read Romans. Like Jews who dance with the Torah on Simchat Torah, the annual festival celebrating the reading of the entire Torah cycle, we aim to dance with this text as with a beloved partner. In Marilynne Robinson's classic novel, *Gilead*, the main character is an elderly pastor named John Ames; the book unfolds as his letter to his son. In one scene, Ames recounts waltzing alone in his study; he ponders the possibility of dying of a heart attack while he is dancing and concludes that he would like to die with a book in his hand. He meditates on possible books: "Donne, or Herbert, or Barth's *Epistle to the Romans,* or Calvin's *Institutes,* Vol. 1" (Robinson 2004, 115). For Ames, these are books to live with and die with, books that should be commended even in death. How much more then is Paul's own Letter to the Romans just such a book, for life and in death.

So as we read through the Epistle to the Romans, we will listen for the living voice of Paul, warming our hearts and firing our wills, not simply instructing the Roman Christians or introducing himself but announcing and rendering the presence of the God who keeps promises, who remains faithful to the historic people of Israel, and who in Jesus Christ has acted decisively on behalf of all humanity. We will watch for the Lord who conquers sin and death, who frees humanity for service to God and one another, and who continues to live and move among believers and into the world with transforming power. Our goal is not a kind of analysis that objectifies the body of the text, leaving it dissected and dying on the operating table, but rather a dynamic encounter with the living Lord of the gospel, who liberates the listener from delusions and compulsions into the life that really is life.

Along the way, we will see and hear Paul's own struggles and passions as much as possible in the context of his time, but also speaking to ours. Such understanding requires work that draws fruitfully on scholarly historical and literary analysis. On the one hand, because the Letter to the Romans is so familiar and has such a long and complex history of interpretation, it is easy to be deaf to the trumpet, to miss the good news. On the other hand, we are reading mail from roughly two thousand years ago, from a time and place radically different from today. To read this text, as to read all ancient texts, is an exercise in cross-cultural communication, which requires bracketing our own cultural assumptions and attending with humility and care to a voice speaking out of a very different social world. Thus learning about the situation of Christians in Rome in the first century and pondering Paul's own missionary challenges will inform our imaginative engagement with the text and aid in the practice of making analogies to contemporary situations and challenges.

WHY DID PAUL WRITE ROMANS?

Commentaries on Paul's Letter to the Romans frequently begin with this question, perhaps because the answer is anything but clear. Why did Paul write a lengthy and ultimately very influential "letter" to a fledgling community of believers, most of whom he had never met, in a city to which he had never been? What was his purpose? What was his motivation? Why?

"Why" is a question worth asking because it makes us pay close attention to the content and shape of Romans, and to its author and his addressees, who were real people in difficult and complicated circumstances that may in turn make us reflect on our own situations as Paul's listeners today. I will turn to some theories about the purposes of Romans shortly. But first it is worth noting that why is a query that leads into mystery: we rarely know fully why we ourselves do anything, let alone why someone else does. Why did I send that email that I now regret? Why did you say yes to that job, or no to that person? Why did John Donne write poetry? Why did Toni Morrison write *Beloved*? There may be answers to these questions, but the answers lead to more questions. Why? can be interrogated only through an examination of history and plans and motives that goes ever deeper into the mystery of human intention and agency, and within and beyond those human intentions, into the mystery of God's purposes and actions. Paul surely leads his listeners on a journey into the mystery of God's power and grace. Beyond that mystery, the why of Romans is a question that will never be answered fully, just as the effects of this remarkable document continue across millennia and across cultural variations up to the present day.

Nonetheless, asking the question is worthwhile because it mandates careful attention to the structure and narrative details of the letter. Such attention yields *three key observations. First,* Romans begins and ends as a letter, with a lengthy personal introduction at the beginning and lengthy personal greetings to people in Rome at the end. In between is a tripartite exposition of the good news of Jesus Christ as the powerful revelation of God's righteousness: through the deliverance of all humanity from sin and death (chaps. 1–8), through God's mercy for Israel and the gentiles (chaps. 9–11), and through the shared fellowship of Jewish and gentile believers in Rome (chaps. 12–15).

Second, toward the end of the letter Paul tells the Romans of his upcoming travel plans: first to Jerusalem, to take funds from his gentile churches to the impoverished community of Jewish believers in the mother city (15:22–32); after that, to Spain by way of Rome, to continue his evangelistic mission to the known world (15:24, 28–29). Both planned trips are fraught with danger, and Paul particularly asks for prayers that the trip to Jerusalem will be peaceful and his financial gift will be accepted (15:30–31). He also hints that he hopes to receive financial support from the Roman churches when he visits there, to speed him on his way to Spain (15:24). Therefore on one level it is likely that he writes to the church in Rome to introduce himself and his gospel prior to coming for a visit, particularly if he hopes his hosts will give him shelter and food as well as support for his further mission to Spain.

These observations drawn from the letter's closing chapters offer clues as to some of Paul's goals in this lengthy missive to the churches in Rome. But they do not fully explain the extensive theological discourse that forms the bulk of the document, nor the distinctive features of that discourse in comparison with his other letters. For that we turn to the *third* observation, which will provide the guiding principle for this commentary's approach to Romans. Although Paul has not been to Rome, he has heard of their faith, for which he praises them (1:8; 15:14). Yet he wants to share the gospel with them and "reap some harvest among" them, as if they still need to hear the good news about Jesus, or at least Paul's version of that news (1:8–15). In fact, early in the letter, Paul's most emphatic statement of his reason for writing is this: "I long to see you so that I may share with you some spiritual gift so that you may be strengthened" (1:11). Shortly thereafter, he declares his "eagerness to proclaim the gospel to you also who are in Rome" (1:15). The concluding doxology reiterates Paul's goal of strengthening his listeners through gospel proclamation: "Now to God who is able to strengthen you according to my gospel and the proclamation of Jesus Christ" (16:25). This doxology provides a guide to reading the letter beyond the situation in Rome, leading even up to the present day: Paul's gospel proclamation is intended to "strengthen" his audience; the Greek word means "to set on a solid foundation." Paul wants to establish his listeners firmly in the faith, so that they will grow ever more deeply into "the obedience of faith" (1:5; 16:26). His pastoral goal will also guide our approach to Romans, as we seek to discern the varied ways Paul's message functions to strengthen his listeners' trust in God. As we shall see, that proclamation centers around the good news of God's Son in the flesh (1:3; 8:3; 9:5), whose person and work enact God's power to save and reveal God's righteousness. Paul preaches Christ's solidarity with all humanity, in his saving death and resurrection, as the power of God for salvation for both Jews and gentiles.

To hear this message afresh, we will sit with the Roman Christians and listen as the letter unfolds. But in order to listen imaginatively to the letter together with its first auditors, we need to attend to the particular situation of the churches in Rome, especially regarding the relationship between Jews and gentiles.

THE CHURCHES IN ROME

Jewish and Gentile Believers

Romans is the only extant letter Paul wrote to a church that he did not establish. Indeed, we do not know how the churches in Rome began; we can only make somewhat educated guesses. What we do know is that by the time Paul wrote Romans, probably from Corinth around 56–57 CE, there were numerous house churches in the city of Rome and the neighboring district of Puteoli (Acts 28:13–15). The main trade route into Rome from the east ran through Puteoli, and parts of both Rome and Puteoli had substantial Jewish populations. Many new religious cults made their way to Rome via the eastern trade routes; perhaps Christianity was yet another. It seems likely that Christian traders, perhaps Jewish followers of Jesus, first brought the fledgling faith to Rome. Initially, at least, it would have been seen as Jewish and taken hold among members of the synagogues, perhaps among gentile God-fearers as well as Jews. Jewish followers of Jesus, most notably Prisca and Aquila, are among the numerous Roman believers whom Paul greets by name near the end of the letter (16:3; see commentary).

In 41 CE the emperor Claudius forbade Jews to hold public meetings, presumably because they were causing public disturbances of some sort. According to the Roman historian Suetonius, in roughly

49 CE Claudius issued an edict expelling some Jews from the city: "Claudius expelled from Rome the Jews constantly making disturbances at the instigation of Chrestus" (*Claud.* 25). Later in Rome Christians were called by the name "Chrestians" (Tertullian, *Apol.* 3; Tacitus, *Ann.* 15.44). According to Acts 18:2 the Claudian expulsion included "a Jew named Aquila . . . [and] his wife Priscilla," who ended up in Corinth, where they welcomed Paul on his first journey there. Possibly Priscilla (also called Prisca) and her husband Aquila were leaders among the Jewish believers in Rome and became leaders among the Christians in Corinth until they returned to Rome, presumably after Nero came to power in 54 CE.

The expulsion of at least some of the Jewish believers from Rome in 49 CE may have led to a gradual split between the Jewish synagogue and the new followers of Jesus, although this is speculation. What is clear is that by the time Paul writes Romans, the churches have become predominantly gentile, disconnected from the synagogues; by the time of Nero's persecutions of Christians in 64 CE, the Roman authorities distinguish between Jews and Christians. What has happened in Roman churches that were once primarily composed of Jewish Christians? Clues in Romans hint at gentile arrogance toward Jews (11:13–21) and at tensions between those who practice observance of Sabbath and kosher food laws and those who do not (14:5–6). These clues may signify the existence of Roman house churches that are primarily gentile but also include a minority population of Jewish adherents of Jesus, a proposal that is strengthened by the existence of Jewish names in the long list of people whom Paul greets at the end of the letter (16:1–23).

Writing to churches with a complex and perhaps painful recent history, Paul instructs the Roman Christians on issues in their faith and fellowship. In this, he is embarking on a delicate and potentially offensive venture, instructing those over whom he has no established teaching authority. Perhaps for this reason he emphasizes his long-standing desire to meet the Christians in Rome (1:13; 15:23) and his personal relationships with many of them (16:3–15). Clearly Paul longs to strengthen Christian fellowship in which Jew and gentile together "glorify the God and Father of our Lord Jesus Christ" (15:6). Indeed, this is the goal and crowning glory of the gospel that Paul preaches and, as such, essential to our understanding of the letter.

Wealth and Poverty

Clues in Romans itself as well as Acts imply that the Christians in Rome were not generally of the upper classes. Archaeological evidence suggests that the majority of Christians were located in the poorest areas of the city, where immigrants settled—Trastavere and Porta Capena. These areas were densely populated, with abysmal living conditions in crowded five-story tenements. Thus most Roman believers were likely quite poor and of low status. Indeed, we know that many Christians were crucified during the intense persecution by Nero in 64 CE. It was illegal to crucify a Roman citizen, since this form of execution was reserved for enslaved persons and criminals; thus the implication is that many of the Roman Christians were not Roman citizens, and likely were or had been enslaved.

Rome was a highly stratified society, and Paul is notable in exhorting his listeners to an unusual mutuality between upper and lower classes (Rom 12:3–13). Evidently some members of the Roman house churches had enough means to share with their neighbors in Christ (12:8, 13). The fact that Paul thinks it necessary to encourage his listeners to such generosity, even when he has not yet met them and might appear presumptuous, indicates the degree to which he thinks Christian fellowship should be a truly radical inversion of Roman social norms. We have further evidence of fluid and diverse social status in the Roman congregations from the letter of 1 Clement, written late in the first century. Clement writes that many Roman Christians sold themselves into slavery so that the money thus gained could be used to feed fellow impoverished believers. This happened after Paul wrote Romans, of course, and likely after Paul himself perished in Nero's persecution. But it evidences the generally poor, lower-class, noncitizen makeup of most of the Roman Christian communities, as well as the strong solidarity among at least some Roman believers.

PAUL'S WRITING STYLE: GRECO-ROMAN RHETORIC AND PROPHETIC SPEECH

As this commentary will focus on the potential effects of the letter on its original listeners and on readers today, it will be important to pay close attention to Paul's language. In a variety of ways, Paul takes his audience on an experiential journey of discovery, even as that journey also discloses the experiences of the early Christians. Paul's rhetoric operates on many levels, from appeals to logic to appeals to emotion and experience. Insofar as the letter both makes its author present to his listeners and communicates a gospel gift to strengthen them, it must speak in a holistic way to the Roman house churches, addressing their minds, hearts, and bodily interactions with each other and their cultural context. Paul uses a number of rhetorical devices toward this end.

At key points, Paul uses the style of the *diatribe,* a lively pattern of questions and answers that involves the audience in the thought progression of the text. Sometimes he speaks directly to an imagined conversation partner by using the second-person singular pronoun "you" (2:1–5, 17–27; 14:4, 10); sometimes his argument progresses through a series of questions and answers that anticipate objections to his message. For contemporary readers of Paul, this style of writing has pitfalls, as it is easy to ascribe to Paul the very views against which he is arguing. Thus it is crucial to read his complex discourses all the way through, to avoid the danger of taking any verse or verses out of context. His first-century Roman audience, however, would recognize his diatribe style as a familiar way of speaking in contemporary Greco-Roman rhetoric, so that they could enjoy the repartee of question and answer as if watching a play. Furthermore, such interaction between speakers in the text also invites the listeners to see themselves in the performance and to examine their own lives. This stylistic device is particularly prominent when Paul challenges human judgmentalism and stereotyping (2:1–3:9; 14:1–4, 10–12) and when he considers Israel's unique place in God's salvation (9:1–11:36).

Paul also involves his listeners by employing performative first-person speech. Usually when Paul says "I" he simply means "I, Paul" (1:1, 8–15; 7:1; 8:18; 9:1; 10:2, 18, 19; 11:1, 11, 13, 15; 12:1, 3; 14:8, 14–32; 16:1, 17, 19). But the apostle also speaks with a performative "I" in 7:7–25, which is more like the "I" of the psalms, who invites the listeners into the experience of the psalmist. Scholars debate whether this should be categorized as speech-in-character, a technical device in Greco-Roman rhetoric, but the important point is that Paul's language draws his hearers into the experience of the speaker.

In addition to employing stylistic devices from Greco-Roman rhetoric, Paul draws extensively on the language, narratives, and motifs of Israel's Scripture. He quotes explicitly and allusively from the Psalms and the Prophets (particularly Isaiah and Hosea) as well as from Genesis and Deuteronomy. This reliance on Scripture is especially evident in regard to God's foundational calling of Israel and God's self-disclosure throughout the history of Israel (chaps. 9–11). Paul quotes from the Greek translation of Israel's Scripture, the Septuagint (LXX), which occasionally varies from the Hebrew text.

THEOLOGICAL AND PASTORAL THEMES

In such a long, complex, and intensely studied document as Romans, there are sure to be a variety of opinions on the primary theological themes of the letter. A lengthy tradition of interpretation focuses on the first eight chapters as setting forth Paul's distinctive gospel of grace. Within those chapters, some have found the center of gravity in chapters 1–4, with an emphasis on human culpability for sin and Christ's atoning sacrifice. Others point to chapters 5–8, where the themes of freedom from sin and new life in Christ dominate Paul's exposition of the gospel. In the wake of the Holocaust, however, many scholars focus on chapters 9–11, where Paul affirms the continued place of Israel in God's salvation. Then again, close attention to the potential struggles in the Roman house churches, which may have involved not only conflict regarding Jewish and gentile practices, but also differences between wealthy and poor believers, leads some to find the climax of the letter in 15:7: "Welcome one another, therefore, as Christ has welcomed you."

These debates about the theological center of Romans highlight its richness and enduring relevance. Each section of the letter contributes to Paul's gospel proclamation, and none of them could be omitted without grievously impoverishing the message. But what ties them together? This commentary argues that the good news of Jesus Christ as God's Son in the flesh, in solidarity with both Jews and gentiles, is the theme of the letter; its theological heartbeat is the revelation of God's righteousness, which is displayed above all in God's abundant, overflowing grace toward all creation.

The Good News of Jesus Christ, Incarnate, Crucified, Raised

Paul begins his letter by introducing himself only in relationship to the gospel. This gospel is the theme of the letter. It is God's gospel, God's good news, authored and enacted by God. The content of this news is God's Son, the incarnate, resurrected Lord. Twice Paul describes Jesus as God's Son in the flesh: first in 1:3–4, as born of David's seed according to the flesh and designated Son of God in power according to the Spirit of holiness; second, in 8:3, as sent by God in the likeness of sin-owned flesh, therein becoming the place where God condemned sin in the flesh. Again, in 9:5, Paul says that from the Jews according to the flesh comes the Christ according to the flesh. Thus, the identity and work of Jesus Christ in the flesh frame Romans 1–8 and introduce Romans 9–11. This Christ, in fleshly solidarity with both Jews and gentiles under sin's power, is the content of Paul's gospel proclamation in the first section of the letter and grounds his vision for God's redemption of both Israel and the gentiles in chapters 9–11. In Romans 12–15, it is the indwelling Spirit of Christ, who is equally the indwelling Spirit of the God who raised Jesus from the dead, who dwells among those in Christ, generating patterns of human interaction characterized by unmerited gifts and mutual welcome. This is the gospel that Paul longs to share in person with the Roman churches, and indeed proclaims in his lengthy letter to them.

The Revelation of God's Righteousness

In 1:16–17 Paul expands further on the character of the gospel as God's power for salvation, for in it God is apocalyptically revealing God's righteousness. God's saving power and God's righteousness are revealed in and enacted by God's action in Christ. Later Paul will speak of God's righteousness, truthfulness, and faithfulness as intertwined divine attributes of the God who entrusted God's words to Israel (3:1–7). As he thinks through the revelation of God in Israel's calling, Paul highlights God's power to harden hearts and to have mercy, and ends with praise to God as the source of all that is. Just as light reveals its colors when it passes through a prism, so the divine abundance, righteousness, trustworthiness, and truthfulness revealed in Israel's history come into sharpest focus through the prism of Christ's gracious self-giving for all humanity.

The Theological Heartbeat of the Gospel

The central doxology that concludes the first two sections of the letter's central discourse anticipates the ethical exhortations in the final section: "Who has given a gift to him, to receive a gift in return? For from him and through him and to him are all things. To him be glory forever. Amen" (11:35–36). This revelation of God as the gracious giver to whom nothing can be repaid, the source of all creation, and the one who through Christ has gifted salvation to both Jew and gentile characterizes God's dealings with all humanity (chaps. 1–8 and 9–11) and grounds the community of Jewish and gentile believers who are instructed to extend to one another the gracious welcome that God has given them (chaps. 12–15). This divine gift is bound up in the person and work of Jesus Christ, in a pattern of solidarity and exchange between Christ and humanity.

In chapters 1–8 Paul highlights the commonality of Jew and gentile "under sin," and God's saving power enacted through Jesus as God's Son in solidarity with David's heirs (1:3) and with all humanity in the grip of sin and death (8:3). Revealing God's righteous will to save God's creation, this divine participation in the plight of derelict humanity enacts God's victory over sin and death and catalyzes a reciprocal participation in Christ by believers. In chapters 9–11 Paul further develops the interpersonal dynamics of this gift of grace through a pattern of solidarity and exchange in God's redemption of Jews and gentiles together: Jews and gentiles take turns as those who have been imprisoned in disobedience and must rely on God's undeserved mercy. In chapters 12–15, such interpersonal grace is displayed by the mutual giving and receiving that shape the character of fellowship in Christ, such that all may "welcome one another, therefore, just as Christ has welcomed you, for the glory of God" (15:7). Along the way, Paul's understanding of sin and redemption discloses a picture of human beings as participants in larger relationships that shape them, and of sin as a deceptive and lethal enslaving power from which humanity is liberated by Christ.

THE STRUCTURE OF THE LETTER

Taken as a whole, the letter may be divided into the following broad outline:

The Opening of the Letter
1:1–15 Greetings and personal introduction

The Body of the Letter
Part 1: 1:16–8:39 The good news of liberation from sin and death
Part 2: 9:1–11:36 God's grace and mercy for both Jews and gentiles
Part 3: 12:1–15:13 Grace and mercy enacted in the new humanity in Christ

The Conclusion of the Letter
15:14–16:27 Concluding travel plans and greetings

The opening and conclusion of Romans are what scholars call its "epistolary frame," which simply means that they consist of greetings and information identifying Romans as a letter. The main body of the letter is Paul's tripartite proclamation of the gospel for both Jews and gentiles. The table of contents provides an overview of the main sections and subsections within this broad outline. Detailed analysis of the structure of each subsection will follow in the commentary.

The Opening of the Letter

Romans 1:1–15

Greetings and Purpose in Writing

Romans 1:1–15

Writing a letter to a church he has neither founded nor visited, Paul begins in an expected way: he introduces himself. But what quickly becomes clear is that this personal introduction is anything but routine. In Greco-Roman letters, greetings tended to be brief and to the point, whereas in Romans it takes Paul seven verses to get to his standard salutation: "Grace to you and peace from God our Father and the Lord Jesus Christ" (1:7). Why such an extended introduction? The answer is that Paul cannot introduce himself without first introducing the God who has called and commissioned him and whose purpose henceforth guides Paul's destiny. Paul's identity is enfolded in the identity and action of God; he is co-constituted by the active presence of God in Christ.

After his lengthy introduction, Paul tells the Romans why he hopes to visit them. Thus this section of the letter may be divided into two subunits: introductions (1:1–7) and purpose in writing (1:8–15).

ROMANS 1:1–7
Introducing the Main Characters in the Drama of Salvation

1:1–2. Paul

Here is what the Roman readers first learn about Paul, in his own words (1:1): first, he is a *slave of Christ Jesus*. The NRSVue uses the term "servant," but the Greek word is slave (*doulos*). Paul is placing himself within the prophetic tradition of Israel: Moses, Joshua, David, and the prophets also are called slaves of God (Josh 14:7; Judg 2:8; 2 Kgs 17:13, 23; Jer 7:25; 25:4). To be an enslaved person means that one's body, thoughts, emotions, and relationships are all in the hands of the master, whose status in turn may—or may not—raise the status of the one enslaved. To be a slave of God is very high status indeed. But as Paul's Roman audience knew very well, although some enslaved persons gained high status through their masters, many others had a degraded and brutally short life. Paul's preferred designation of himself as a slave of Christ (cf. Phil 1:1) perhaps displays this paradox; he has immeasurable worth through belonging to Christ, yet in the eyes of society he is a nobody (cf. 1 Cor 4:9–13; 2 Cor 11:24–29). Already we have a hint of what the apostle will tell his Roman listeners later in the letter: they too are "slaves," either of sin, which leads to death (6:6, 16–17, 20), or of God, who bestows life (6:16–17, 22). There is no place to stand or to live outside of this structure of belonging, which includes all human beings regardless of their social class.

Second, Paul is *called to be an apostle* (cf. 1 Cor 1:1; 2 Cor 1:1; Gal 1:1). Called by whom? we might ask. The answer is implicit in Paul's immediate focus on God. Like the prophets, Paul has been called by God (Jer 1:5; Isa 49:1). In Galatians he also emphasizes this divine call to the exclusion of any other merely human calling or authorization (Gal 1:1, 11–12). Paul is uniquely authorized by God, and therefore so is the message that he preaches.

The word "apostle" means "one who is sent out." For that reason, apostleship is a matter not so much of status or office, but of authorized activity in the service of God. Apostleship implicitly involves displacement from one's point of origin, "getting on the road with Jesus." That certainly is what Paul has done throughout the eastern Mediterranean world. Paul's calling as an apostle has made him a migrant on land and sea, traversing much of the same territory that displaced victims of war and oppression travel today.

Third, Paul is *set apart for the gospel of God*. In Galatians 1:15 Paul names God as the one who "set me apart before I was born and called me through his grace"; here again Paul's language echoes the call narratives of Jeremiah (Jer 1:5) and the Servant in Isaiah 49:1. To be "set apart" also has a cultic sense: the firstborn were to be "set apart" for God (Exod 13:12), as were the firstfruits (Num 15:20) and the Levites in their divine service (Num 8:11). By using this terminology, Paul depicts himself as "consecrated" to God for the particular purpose of proclaiming God's message of salvation. The phrase "the gospel of God" occurs elsewhere in Paul's letters only at Romans 15:16; 2 Corinthians 11:7; and 1 Thessalonians 2:2, 8, 9, and accords with the theocentric focus of Romans as a whole, in which the word "God" (*theos*) appears some 153 times. God is the main actor, the origin, and the author of the good news that Paul proclaims.

This good news fulfills the promises God made "through his prophets in the holy scriptures"—that is, through the sacred writings of Israel (1:2). Paul thus signals two aspects of the gospel that thread through the letter: the inseparable connection between Jesus Christ and God's faithfulness to Israel, and the witness of Israel's Scripture to Christ. This twofold connection grounds Paul's first depiction of Jesus in the next two verses.

1:3–4. Jesus Christ, God's Son and David's Offspring

In 1:3–4, Paul introduces Jesus Christ as the protagonist of the good news: he is God's Son (repeated in both verses), descended from the seed (*sperma,* not translated in NRSVue) of David according to the flesh, declared the Son of God with power according to the Spirit of holiness, by the resurrection of the dead; he is Jesus Christ our Lord. The activity of God, the Son, and the Spirit are bound into one; God is the origin of the good news, the content of that news is God's Son, Jesus Christ, and the Spirit witnesses to Christ's divine identity through the resurrection.

Several aspects of this brief introduction of Jesus are unique to Romans, prompting some commentators to see here a quotation of a pre-Pauline creedal statement. Whether or not this is the case, Paul introduces Christ in distinctive ways that anticipate key themes in the rest of the letter: In no other undisputed letter does Paul mention David, but David appears three times in Romans—as Christ's progenitor (1:3), as a quintessential sinner praising God for God's mercy (4:6), and as a witness to the hardening of Israel (11:9). The terms "Christ (Messiah)," "son," "seed," and "David" suggest that recognized messianic texts lie behind this description of Jesus (2 Sam 22:51; Ps 18:50; 2 Sam 7:12–14; Isa 11:10), some of which Paul cites explicitly in 15:9–12. Thus, right at the beginning of the letter, and again at the end, Paul emphasizes Jesus's identity as Israel's messiah, although he does not mention Israel by name until 9:6.

Paul's choice of terms for signifying Christ's Jewish identity is puzzling, however. Christ is descended from David "according to the flesh" (*kata sarka*) and declared Son of God "according to the Spirit [*kata pneuma*] of holiness." The question is how to interpret "according to the flesh." On the one hand, Paul uses the same phrase elsewhere in Romans to denote physical kinship, with reference to Abraham (4:1), Paul's own Jewish kin (9:3), and Jesus as Israel's Messiah (9:5). Surely that straightforward meaning applies here in 1:3 as well.

On the other hand, in the great majority of Paul's uses of the term, "flesh" (*sarx*) has a pejorative sense as a sphere of embodied existence under the power of sin and death (7:5, 14, 18; 8:3–13). Furthermore, in 8:4–5, 12–13 Paul explicitly contrasts living "according to the flesh [*kata sarka*]" with living according to the Spirit or in the Spirit. In all these places, "flesh" signifies living in the realm or thrall of sin. Particularly striking is 8:3, where, as in 1:3, Paul names Christ as God's Son in the flesh, but qualifies "flesh" as "sinful flesh"—that is, flesh in the grip of sin (see commentary). Is this association between flesh and sin also in view in Paul's depiction of Christ as God's Son in the flesh in 1:3? The question is not whether Jewish flesh per se is sinful; Paul never says this. The question is whether Christ's fleshly solidarity with David's physical descendants is encompassed in his fleshly solidarity with all humanity in the throes of sin and death. As the letter unfolds, it becomes clear that such is the case; indeed, David himself exemplifies the sinner who rejoices in God's undeserved mercy (4:6–8).

Thus right from the start of the letter Paul affirms Jesus's full humanity and historical particularity as a Jew and at the same time his divine identity, which is made known through his resurrection from the dead. These are events in time and space, not simply timeless truths. They enact God's purposes and promises to Israel and God's redemptive rule over all creation. God reigns specifically in human lives, beginning with Paul and the Roman believers, for whom Jesus Christ is not only "Son of God" but is for them personally, "our Lord."

Within the action of God, the Spirit witnesses to the identity of Jesus, who is "declared to be Son of God with power according to the Spirit of holiness." In 8:5–17, 23, 26–27, Paul has more to say about the Spirit's role in the community's life. There he names the Spirit interchangeably as "the Spirit of Christ" and "the Spirit of God" (8:9, 14). Here in 1:4, uniquely in all his letters, he uses the term "the Spirit of holiness." "Spirit of holiness" may put stress on the sanctifying role of the Spirit; the parallel construction of "according to the flesh" (1:3) and "according to the Spirit" (1:4) certainly emphasizes both the human and divine aspects of Jesus's identity. Christ's resurrection from the dead is the linchpin in the revelation of his divine identity; the link between the life-giving Spirit and the resurrection anticipates the Spirit's role in 8:9–11.

1:5. Paul's Apostleship

Toward the end of a very long sentence, in 1:5 Paul returns to his own calling and expands it in three ways: "we have received grace and apostleship to bring about the obedience of faith among all the gentiles for the sake of his name." As in 1:1, Paul echoes Jeremiah 1:5 and Isaiah 49:1, 5–6, which extend the prophetic message to the nations (Gk., gentiles). There are other apostles, such as Peter, who have a calling to take the gospel to the Jews (Gal 2:7–8), but Paul understands his vocation as focused distinctively on gentiles (yet also anticipating the salvation of his Jewish kinsfolk; cf. 11:13–14).

Paul speaks in the first-person plural: "*We* have received grace and apostleship." Who is this "we"? At first glance one might think Paul is including the Roman Christians, but the next phrase excludes that possibility. Probably, as in his other letters, Paul includes his fellow missionaries, including Phoebe, the emissary who carried his letter to Rome (16:1–2), and others who send greetings along with Paul (16:21–23). Indeed, the earliest use of "apostle" in Paul's letters is plural, as Paul speaks of himself, Sylvanus, and Timothy as apostles of God's message for the Thessalonians (1 Thess 2:6). Paul views his vocation to the gentiles as God-given but not exclusive; he is not a go-it-alone missionary.

The goal of Paul's vocation is "the obedience of faith among all the gentiles for the sake of his name." In the context, "his name" refers to Christ's name. The letter's closing doxology repeats "the obedience of faith" (16:26). Through joining "obedience" and "faith," Paul signals from the beginning that faith, which is central to the gospel, issues in transformed lives. He is confident that the Roman

Christians themselves already know this: their "faith is proclaimed throughout the world" (1:8), just as their "obedience is known to all" (16:19). "Faith" and "obedience" thus bookend the entire letter, all within the context of the gift of grace (1:5).

The meaning and content of "faith" (*pistis*) will develop as the letter progresses, but already it clearly includes dispositions, actions, and relationships. To understand faith simply as mental assent to a set of propositions is inadequate at best, and in fact quite misleading. Rather, "faith" is a relational term widespread in Greco-Roman discourse, with the foundational meanings of "trust" and "trustworthiness" as desirable characteristics of every facet of human interaction: political, familial, financial, personal, and public. Trust and trustworthiness are the basic meanings of *pistis.* Such trust naturally involves knowledge and belief about that which one trusts, but it also involves emotions, motivations, and actions. This fulsome description of faith is crucial for understanding Paul's varied uses of the term *pistis* throughout the letter. In this context, "the obedience of faith" does not mean that faith is reducible to obedience, nor that obedience and faith are the same thing, but rather that the obedience at which Paul aims expresses a relationship of trust.

1:6–7a. The Roman Believers

What of the Roman believers to whom Paul is writing? Who are they? In 1:6–7a Paul gives them a theological description in parallel with his own self-understanding, but also distinct from it. Like him, they are "called," but not as apostles. Rather, their calling is twofold: they are "called to belong to Jesus Christ," thereby sharing in Paul's status as a slave of Jesus Christ (1:6), and they are "called to be saints" (1:7). As those who belong to Christ, they acknowledge Christ as their master and Lord. As saints (*hagiois*) they demonstrate the work of the Spirit of holiness (*hagiōsunēs*); that is, they are sanctified through Jesus Christ and set aside for his service. The Greek could equally well be translated simply as "called saints." That is, sanctification is God's doing; God has called them into a new life sanctified to God, and God's calling creates their identity as saints. As the ambiguity of translation shows, however, such divine action does not preclude human action, but rather catalyzes it. The "obedience of faith" signifies living into that divinely gifted identity.

1:7b Greeting

Finally, Paul formally addresses the recipients of his letter: "To all God's beloved in Rome." He locates these saints very specifically in a dual identity that is easy to gloss over: first and most importantly, they are "God's beloved." As such, they can join with Paul in saying, "God's love has been poured into our hearts through the Holy Spirit that has been given to us" (5:5). Such love is reciprocal, but clearly in Paul's introductory greeting it first comes from God; it is the foundation of the Roman Christians' life together. Secondly, they are "in Rome." Their beloved life together does not float above the ground; it is acted out in a specific time and place, in the heart of the Roman Empire.

The very last clause of this exceedingly long sentence is the greeting Paul uses in all his letters: "Grace to you and peace from God our Father and the Lord Jesus Christ" (1:7b; see 1 Cor 1:3; 2 Cor 1:2; Gal 1:3; Phil 1:2; 1 Thess 1:1). Paul typically begins his letters by introducing himself, and sometimes his companions, and addressing his listeners as "saints." But the length of the introduction in Romans is unique, perhaps because he has not yet been to the churches in Rome. The curtain rises on the drama of salvation and the major players take a bow, identified by their key attributes: God as the one who makes and keeps promises; Jesus Christ as the fleshly son of David and crucified and resurrected Son of God, who fulfills God's promises in history; the Spirit of holiness as the one who witnesses to the identity of Jesus, and whose role in sanctification is highlighted here. But there are human players also; Paul, his fellow workers in the gospel, and the Roman believers are all caught up together into God's drama of redemption.

ROMANS 1:8–15
Paul's Purpose in Writing

1:8. Thanksgiving and Praise

As is his practice, Paul first thanks God for the letter's recipients and affirms something about them (1 Cor 1:4–8; Phil 1:3–5; 1 Thess 1:2–10). In this case, since Paul has not yet been to Rome, he affirms their reputation: "Your faith [*pistis*] is proclaimed throughout the world." What is this "faith"? It would appear to be their trust in Christ, although this is not unambiguous. It could also be their trust in God, or even simply their trustworthiness. When Paul says, "Your *pistis* is proclaimed throughout the world," he indicates that this faith is a way of life that is embodied, socially embedded, and therefore public. It is a faith that can be a source of encouragement to Paul, as also his faith will encourage the Romans (1:12), because to speak of someone's trust and trustworthiness is immediately to speak of that person in relationship with others.

1:9–15. Hopes and Plans for Future Visit

Paul's praise of the Romans' faith introduces the catalyst for the letter, which is his eager yearning to visit the churches in Rome. Paul stresses the intensity of his interest in visiting the Roman believers in several ways: he prays for them "without ceasing" (v. 9); he longs to see them (v. 11); he has often intended to visit (v. 13); he declares his "eagerness to proclaim the gospel to you also who are in Rome" (v. 15). In the very next sentence that is precisely what Paul begins to do, as he launches into an exposition of "the gospel" as "the power of God for salvation" (1:16 NRSV). If one thing is clear in the letter, it is that Paul's purpose in writing is precisely to preach the gospel, in a particular way and for particular ends.

But why? If the faith of the Roman Christians already is proclaimed throughout the world, why do they need to hear the gospel from Paul? They already are saints, already called, already God's beloved who belong to Christ. Paul obviously is aware of the incongruity of his desire to preach to fellow believers in established communities that he had no part in founding. If we back up to the previous verses, we gain a bit more clarity; Paul wants to strengthen the Roman Christians by giving them some spiritual gift (v. 11); he wants to reap some harvest (*karpos,* fruit) among them as among the rest of the gentiles (v. 13); in fact, he is under obligation to preach to everyone, across all cultural boundaries (v. 14). This language seems to put Paul in the position of benefactor and proclaimer, and the Romans in the position of needy recipients. He is keenly aware of the power dynamics in such a benefactor relationship, and so he inserts a crucial self-correction: that is, "that we may be mutually encouraged by each other's faith, both yours and mine." Nonetheless, that language of mutuality does not stop him from proclaiming the gospel at length, as he understands it.

Does Paul think the Roman Christians have not received the true version of the good news? Perhaps. If so, he has a delicate task, to honor their faith and also to correct it. Or does Paul think his listeners have heard distortions of his own preaching and want to make sure they know what he really thinks before he gets there, to avoid any misunderstandings or surprises? Perhaps. The conversational diatribe style that he occasionally uses allows him to name potential objections to, and perhaps distortions of, his message, suggesting that sometimes he is correcting misrepresentations of his preaching (see, for example, 6:1–2). Possibly Paul is clarifying his argument in Galatians about the law of Moses. Possibly Paul wants to set forth his gospel as a testament of faith, in preparation for his upcoming trip to Jerusalem (15:30–32). Perhaps.

These are all possibilities relying on hints, not outright statements, in the letter itself. What is clear from Paul's own opening greetings, however, is that he wants to preach the gospel to the Christians in Rome even though he knows they are already believers. Toward the end of the letter, he reiterates that this is what he has done, again praising and affirming the Roman Christians: "I myself feel confident about you, my brothers and sisters, that you yourselves are full of goodness, filled with all knowledge, and able to instruct one another. Nevertheless, on some points I have written to you rather boldly by way of reminder, because of the grace given me by God to be a minister of Christ Jesus to the gentiles" (15:14–15). Paul's gospel proclamation to the Romans is "by way of reminder," reminding them of the good news they share together. And why not? Even when writing to churches he founded and knows well, Paul begins by "repreaching" the gospel in order to establish the common ground on which he and his listeners stand. This gospel is news that never gets old and always bears repeating. In fact, as we shall see in the spiral structure of chapters 1–8, Paul repeatedly rephrases the news of God's action in Christ from different angles.

EXCURSUS

Reflections for Preaching and Teaching

The greetings and plans with which Paul begins his Letter to the Romans set out a series of intertwined introductions: Paul's introduction of himself, of the gospel he preaches, of the triune God who is the acting subject of that good news, and of the Roman Christians themselves, whom Paul narrates in terms of their belonging to Christ. Thus the letter begins by disclosing the identities of all the actors in the drama of salvation. These identities are bound together because Paul and his listeners cannot know who they are apart from the presence and redeeming action of God. They are who they are by virtue of being called and graced by God, albeit in different ways: Paul is called as an apostle; the Roman believers are called to be saints. Despite the differences in their calling, however, they are members of the same large household of God under the lordship of Christ. This shared belonging in Christ is the basis of the unity that Paul will enjoin throughout the letter, and it is the basis of all unity in the church to the present day.

At least four aspects of Paul's depiction of himself and the Roman Christians offer opportunities for preaching and teaching.

Solidarity with the Displaced

First, Paul is a displaced person, an itinerant preacher dependent on the hospitality of others. He sees his ministry as the culmination of Israel's prophetic tradition, but like many of the prophets, his vocation makes him a stranger among his own people. His calling entails crossing ethnic, social, and geographical boundaries, and he is convinced that such boundary crossing is at the heart of the gospel message, not least because it communicates the displaced Lord who crossed the chasm between God's righteousness and human dereliction. If Paul were a missionary today, he might well be walking with migrants around the Mediterranean or with the people at the southern border of the United States. We live in a time of massive global migrations, with all the confusion and suffering involved in profound displacement. Paul's peripatetic vocation requires solidarity with such displacement and, at the same time, a grounding of identity in God, deeper than any social or geographic sources of the self. Traveling with Jesus means openness to displacement; it also means that wherever we find ourselves, God accompanies us on the road.

In Christ and in Rome

Second, Paul locates his listeners in a double way, as belonging to Jesus Christ and as living in Rome. Paul may be on the move, but the Roman Christians are not. Rather, their calling is to live out the obedience of faith on their home turf. This calling has its own challenges. Paul's answer to those challenges, in Romans as in all his letters, is to repreach the gospel. It is good advice for preachers and pastors, even as it takes many different forms, because we, like the Roman Christians, live in a world that is deeply at odds with the good news of God in Christ. To be reoriented into the obedience of faith is to find oneself out of kilter with our social environment, whether or not we have actually moved.

In C. S. Lewis's science fiction trilogy, some of the main characters are heavenly messengers called Eldila. An Eldil can take any form, but sometimes it appears as a column of light. The odd thing is that when an Eldil is in a room, the floor appears slanted; everything seems off-kilter. This is because the Eldil's center of gravity is much stronger than that of Earth; the presence of the Eldil reveals how the earth itself is out of alignment with the grain of the universe. To have Christ as our center of gravity is to find ourselves out of sync with social mores and to have a radically reoriented vision of reality. But that reorientation of vision does not mandate or excuse escapism; just as the Roman believers are to live out their faith in their context, so are we called to live out God's decentering grace in ours, in ways that reveal just how off-kilter our own social and political contexts are.

Repreaching the Gospel

Such radical re-visioning does not happen easily, however; it requires constant reinforcement. It is not a one-time occurrence. For this reason, Paul repeats and reminds his listeners of the content of God's good news. He is convinced that repreaching this gospel is the way he can strengthen his listeners for the tough realities of belonging to Christ as Lord amid complex and often fearful social conditions. In the rest of the letter, we will see what such "strengthening" looks like. Paul's hope encourages teachers and preachers to preach the gospel day in and day out; Paul never takes it for granted that his listeners know the basics of the faith, nor should we.

At the same time, Paul uses the language of giving and receiving: "that I may share with you some spiritual gift . . . that we may be mutually encouraged . . . that I may reap some harvest among you." This language of giving and receiving suggests a two-way relationship between pastor and people that is crucial for the strengthening of the faith through gospel preaching. Paul displays and thereby encourages a combination of pastoral authority and vulnerable sharing of his own need to receive from, as well as give to, his listeners. Such acknowledgment of reciprocity may serve to encourage mutuality in churches today, without abdicating the responsibility of authoritative proclamation of the gospel message. It is at the least a matter of building trust and mutual respect and winning the right to be heard.

The Witness of Scripture

Finally, writing primarily to gentile Christians, Paul immediately reminds them that the good news they have received was promised by God in the "holy scriptures." Throughout Romans, Paul shows us how Israel's sacred writings testify to the God and Father of our Lord Jesus Christ, and thereby encourages us to do the same. Christianity is not a cut-flower religion but the deep-rooted revelation of the Lord of all time and all creation, who acts in and through the particularities of history. There has always been a temptation within Christian preaching to neglect the Judaism of Jesus and Paul, whether from a desire to make the message simpler and more "relevant" or from outright anti-Judaism, but to do so renders Romans unintelligible. As the letter unfolds, it becomes clear that there is no good news without God's enduring faithfulness to the promises to Israel—there is no salvation without the Jews. Nor can gentile Christians know who they are apart from God's dealings with Israel: rather, drawing on Israel's Scriptures to illuminate the meaning of faith (Rom 4), the identity of Jesus as the second Adam (Rom 5), and the faithfulness of God (Rom 9–11), Paul gives us new ways to narrate who we are in the midst of our shared life in the present day.

The Body of the Letter

Romans 1:16–15:13

The Gospel of Jesus Christ

God's Saving Power, the Revelation of God's Righteousness

Romans 1:16–15:13

The extensive discourse that comprises the main body of the letter proceeds in three stages: in 1:16–8:39 Paul proclaims God's righteousness for all humanity under sin, both Jew and gentile, through Christ's gracious death and resurrection. In chapters 9–11 he develops that theme of gracious redemption specifically in relationship to the salvation of Israel, which is bound up with the salvation of the gentiles. In 12:1–15:13 Paul depicts human relationships transformed through and in Christ. Each of these three stages in Paul's proclamation expands on the theme of the letter: the gospel as God's saving power through the world-shattering and re-creating revelation of God's righteousness in and through Jesus Christ (1:16–17).

Part One: The Good News of Liberation from Sin and Death

Romans 1:16–8:39

Romans 1:16–8:39 forms the first major section of the body of the letter, in which Paul sets forth an understanding of the good news of Jesus Christ in relationship to human culpability *for* sin and human bondage *to* sin. This section contains two major subsections, yet Paul's rhetoric also includes transitional sections that defy such neat divisions. In 1:16–4:25 Paul presents a first draft, so to speak, of his gospel preaching. It begins with an announcement of the gospel as the power of God for salvation, proceeds through an exposé of human sin and divine judgment, restates the good news, and presents Abraham and David as examples of trust in the God who justifies the ungodly and gives life to the dead. In the second main subsection, 5:12–8:39, Paul presents Christ as the one who rectifies Adam's wrong and liberates humanity from the powers of sin and death. Romans 5:1–11 is a transitional passage linking these two subsections of the letter. Along the way Paul limns his vision of new life in Christ, enclosed by God's love and therefore grounded in hope (5:5; 8:39).

To lay out these chapters in a purely sequential fashion is misleading, however, because they overlap thematically and linguistically. These overlaps create a spiral structure in this section of Romans, as Paul restates both the human plight and God's deliverance. As the letter progresses, it addresses human experience from different angles and on deepening levels: human accountability before God and the role of the law of Moses in witnessing to that accountability; human bondage to sin as a suprahuman power opposed to human flourishing; objective, cosmic, and corporate renewal through the action of God in Christ; and the experience of conflict between the intended good and the damaging outcomes of personal action. Paul's argument is thus both cosmological and anthropological; he is concerned with the certain reality of God's action in Christ, and he also is concerned with the effects of that action for personal and communal experience. To address these complex realities on the temporal human plane, he creates a narrative that arcs toward the future in hope but circles back to the past and catches it up into God's salvation.

The interpretation of these chapters is complicated further by three additional factors. First, Paul frequently deploys the rhetorical styles of the diatribe and occasionally personification and impersonation, sometimes making it difficult to be sure who is speaking and to whom. Second, his use of Scripture sometimes supplies an elusive subtext to the letter that illuminates its meaning but is difficult to discern. Third, two different narratives about sin, humanity, and salvation are interwoven in these chapters: the theme of human culpability for sin and enmity toward God, requiring reconciliation with God (1:18–4:25), and the theme of human bondage to sin, requiring liberation by God (5:12–8:39). The history of interpretation can be traced with reference to which theme dominates understandings of Paul's gospel; indeed, some interpreters see them as incompatible. But in fact, they are closely intertwined: the theme of bondage to sin occurs as early as 1:24, with the repeating refrain, "God gave them over" (1:24, 26, 28), and again in the bald statement that "all, both Jews and Greeks, are under the power of sin" (3:9); conversely, the theme of deliverance from condemnation for sin reappears in 8:1, 31–34. Paul's later interpreters may see human culpability and human bondage as mutually exclusive, but Paul does not.

Packed into these dense, complex, and challenging chapters is radical good news for all humanity under the dominion of sin and death. To read and reread and begin to understand them is to be habituated into hope.

ROMANS 1:16–4:25
Human Culpability and Christ's Faithfulness

This subsection of 1:16–8:39 begins with a compressed statement of the gospel as the power of God for salvation and the apocalypse of God's righteousness (1:16–17). This is followed by the apocalypse of God's wrath (1:18–32). In 2:1–3:20 Paul invites his listeners to self-examination in light of the vast difference between human judgment and God's impartial judgment upon both Jew and gentile. In 3:21–31 Paul restates and amplifies the gospel as God's grace for all; in 4:1–25 he calls on Abraham, David, and Sarah as witnesses to God's gracious justification of the ungodly and God's faithfulness to the promises. Because each of these sections is exceedingly rich, we will discuss each in depth.

1:16–17. God's Saving Power

In 1:15 Paul says he is eager to preach the gospel to the Roman Christians, and this is why he yearns to visit them. But apparently, he cannot wait for a visit, because in 1:16–17 he immediately plunges into the topic at hand. With brevity and force, he proclaims the key elements of the message that he will unfold in the rest of the letter: the gospel as power; salvation; faith; the apocalypse of God's righteousness; all "for the Jew first and also for the Greek"; all supported by the witness of Scripture. Thus, despite their brevity—or perhaps because of it—these verses require in-depth analysis; they situate everything that follows in the context of God's cataclysmic deliverance breaking into human history in Jesus Christ.

We begin by noting briefly the structure of 1:16–17. The subject of these verses is "the gospel," which Paul has introduced as "the gospel of God . . . concerning his Son" (1:1–3). Paul expounds on this good news about Jesus Christ through two parallel clauses linking God's power to save with the revelation of God's righteousness. This good news encompasses both Jews and Greeks and is intimately linked with faith.

1:16. The Gospel as God's Power for Salvation

Commentators have long puzzled over Paul's announcement in 1:16 that he is "not ashamed," asking why he makes such an apparently defensive statement. But a brief consideration of other occurrences of "shame" in Romans, as well as of Paul's letters and his life to this point, may clarify his words in two ways. First, Paul's claim that he is "not ashamed" of the gospel draws on traditions in the psalms and the Prophets, in which the speaker entreats God, "Let me not be put to shame" (e.g., Pss 22:5; 25:20; Isa 28:16 LXX). In Romans 9:33 Paul quotes Isaiah 28:16 verbatim: "Whoever trusts in him will not be put to shame"; in Romans 10:11 he adds the word "everyone" (*pas*), which reads in the Greek: "Everyone who believes in him will not be put to shame." This inclusive emphasis recalls 1:16, where Paul also emphasizes *all* who believe. Indeed, the cluster of words and themes in 1:16–17 recurs in 10:9–13: not ashamed, belief, salvation, all/everyone, Jew and Greek. Similarly, in 5:5 Paul proclaims a hope of God's glory that "does not put us to shame." For this reason, Paul's denial of shame belongs with the verses that follow; deliverance from shame is tied into the content and source of Paul's good news.

Second, Paul's proud claim that he is "not ashamed" may stem in part from his own experience. By the time Paul writes Romans, he has been whipped, beaten, and stoned; he has been shipwrecked; he has suffered "danger from rivers, danger from bandits, danger from my own people, danger from gentiles"; he has been homeless, hungry, and exposed to the elements (2 Cor 11:24–27). He is not handsome or persuasive; he is covered with ugly scars. To bear scars on one's back was shameful in Roman society because they were evidence of beatings reserved for enslaved persons and low-status folks such as mimes, or injuries suffered by soldiers fleeing battle (Glancy 2004). Everything about Paul's body and life experience looks weak, not strong, and weakness was a reason for shame in Roman society. Paul knows this well, but he turns his scars and weakness into a proclamation of the power of the cross, a bodily enactment of Jesus (2 Cor 4:8–11; cf. 1 Cor 4:9–13; Gal 6:17). In fact, claims Paul, "God chose what is weak in the world to shame the strong" (1 Cor 1:27). Given this paradoxical combination of weakness and power in Paul's own experience, which is an instantiation of the power of the gospel in the death and resurrection of Christ, it seems logical for him to say boldly, "I am not ashamed of the gospel; it is God's saving power." Paul is not ashamed because the gospel conveys God's saving power; at the same time, he recognizes that the gospel's power is hidden in weakness and appears shameful to Roman values.

The opening caveat thus provides a tip-off regarding the gospel as God's power for salvation through God's Son, Jesus Christ. The Greek word for power is *dynamis*, from which we get the words "dynamite" and "dynamic." Paul certainly thinks of the power of the gospel as world-changing, even cataclysmic, but in counterintuitive and often hidden ways, precisely because God's power works with and through human weakness (4:19–21; 5:6; 8:26; cf. 2 Cor 4:7; 12:9–10). God's power is paradoxical in the extreme, revealed in and through human shame and weakness, not least in the crucifixion of Christ.

At the same time, Paul's affirmation of the gospel's power expresses his confidence in the generative force of the divine word, which created the world (Gen 1:1–27), accomplishes God's saving purposes for all creation (Isa 55:10–11), and enacts divine judgment (Jer 23:29). Just as throughout Israel's Scripture the divine word is powerful because it is the word *of God,* so the good news Paul preaches is powerful because it is the gospel *of God.* It is through the dynamic presence and action of God that the gospel proclamation delivers and rescues God's people. Indeed, it is by proclaiming the power of God's good news that Paul wants to give the Roman believers a gift that will "strengthen" them (1:11). The flip side of this claim is that unless God "shows up," the gospel message makes no sense whatsoever.

Paul expresses that empowering reality with the term "salvation." The power of God is not diffuse, generally operative in the world, a kind of life force immanent in nature. It is God's specific action in time leading to a particular goal: salvation. *Salvation* means, in the first instance, rescue from a terrible catastrophe. Later in Romans Paul says that the death of Christ will save us from wrath (5:9), presumably at the day of judgment. Through that deliverance, the promised day of the Lord will be one of salvation eagerly anticipated, rather than judgment to be feared (13:11). Including individual believers but extending to the whole cosmos, this salvation is linked to the promise that "the God of peace will shortly crush Satan under your feet" (16:20). In this sense, salvation is future and cosmic, assuring God's final victory over the powers of evil, which also means God's final rescue of all creation from those powers.

But salvation also reaches into the present, as an immediate reality that funds future hope for believers (8:24–25) and transforms their actions now. For example, when writing from prison to the Philippians, Paul can speak very personally of his confidence that his dire circumstances will become an occasion for present salvation (Phil 1:19), publicly displayed by Christ's glorification in Paul's own body, "whether by life or by death" (1:20). The Philippians would understand this use of the word "salvation" as signifying a restoration to health and freedom, but Paul extends its meaning with reference to Christ. He hopes for personal deliverance in the present, but he frames such hope in terms that transcend death. Thus salvation is paradoxical in that it is not fully accomplished, yet it is already at least partially present. And it is paradoxical in that it is both cosmic and intensely personal. This melding of the salvation of all humanity—in fact, all creation—and the salvation of individuals is typical of Paul. He does not conceive of salvation for some individuals only, leaving everything else to rot in sin and death. No, the good of the part and the good of the whole belong together. At the same time, the hope of salvation never becomes simply cosmic and universal in an abstract way; it grounds personal hope in particular circumstances, as it did for Paul in prison (Phil 1:19).

Paul's claim that salvation is "for everyone who believes, for the Jew first and also for the Greek," establishes the scope of salvation. The little word "everyone" (*pas,* which also can be translated "all") carries considerable freight throughout the Letter to the Romans, occurring no fewer than seventy-five times. At four significant points Paul repeats the phrase "*all* who believe" (3:22; 4:11; 10:4, 11). In context, that global inclusion testifies to God as the God of both Jews and gentiles (3:29). Thus, in 4:11 Abraham is the father of "all who believe," whether circumcised or not; in 10:4, 11, again Paul clearly intends "everyone" to signify both Jew and gentile. But even when this qualification is not present, the insistent stress on inclusion—*all*—makes clear that Paul has no patience with fellowships that would include some believers and exclude others. The letter is to "*all* God's beloved in Rome" (1:7). At the same time, Paul emphasizes the priority of the Jews in God's salvation, which is a polemical pastoral correction for gentile believers who might consider themselves superior to the Jews. He develops this theme further in chapters 9–11.

What then of the qualification, "who believes"? As in the earlier three occurrences of the noun (*pistis*) denoting human trust (1:5, 8, 12), here in the first occurrence of the verb, "to believe, to trust, to be faithful" (*pisteuō*), Paul refers to human trust. The object of trust is left unstated and perhaps intentionally ambiguous: is it God,

Christ, or the gospel itself? Insofar as God's good news is about Jesus Christ, the difference may be moot. In 3:22, "for all who believe" again appears, but there it links the human act of trust to God's action in Christ. In 4:3, 5 Abraham trusts God as "the one who justifies the ungodly." Indeed, throughout Romans, the verb sometimes takes God as the explicit or implicit object of faith (4:4, 5, 17, 24; 10:10–11); sometimes the preaching of Christ is the content of what is believed (4:18; 6:8; 10:9, 14–17); sometimes, as in 1:16, the object of faith is not named (3:22; 13:11; 15:13). Nowhere is Christ explicitly named as the object of faith, although he is implied by the context (see 3:22; 10:17; cf. Gal 2:16; Phil 1:29). Nonetheless, the ambiguity is striking. At the least, it implies that faith is not simply a set of cognitive propositions about Jesus or God, but rather that it arises out of and expresses a relationship of trust in the good news of God's Son as "God's saving power."

1:17. The Gospel as the Revelation of God's Righteousness from Faith to Faith

Three elements of verse 17 invite further discussion: the righteousness of God, the verb translated "revealed," and the phrase "through faith for faith."

"The righteousness of God" parallels the power of God in verse 16, such that both divine righteousness and divine power are inseparably linked to the gospel: the gospel is the power of God for salvation; the righteousness of God is being revealed through it. What is this righteousness? Here the little preposition "of" is pivotal. It signifies that righteousness belongs to God, comes from God, and characterizes God's being and action. In 3:3–7 Paul depicts God's righteousness in terms of God's trustworthiness (v. 3) and God's truthfulness (v. 7). Together with divine righteousness, these attributes emphasize God's redeeming action in the world, through which grace reigns (5:21). This picture of God's redemptive work has roots in the psalms (e.g., Pss 71:15–19; 143:2, 11–12) and the prophets, particularly Isaiah (e.g., Isa 51:4b–5 LXX). Paul develops it in relationship to Christ, who "is our righteousness" (1 Cor 1:30) and in whom we "become the righteousness of God" (2 Cor 5:21). Thus "the righteousness of God" is a relational term denoting God's powerful, saving, and transforming will for all humanity, acting decisively in and through Jesus Christ. In social systems, this divine righteousness is manifested as justice.

God's righteousness as God's saving power unleashed in the world is emphasized by the verb "is revealed," which translates the present passive participle form of the Greek verb *apokalyptō,* from which we get the word "apocalypse." To get at the dynamic sense of the word, we might translate it as "being apocalypsed." In New Testament Greek, the passive voice of the verb often implies that God is the unstated subject of the verb; this is called a "divine passive." So here, God is the one doing the action, and that action is happening *now* through the proclamation of Jesus Christ.

Apokalyptō literally means "unveiled"; hence the translation "is revealed." But Paul also uses another verb for "being revealed" or "made manifest"—*phanerō* (1:19; 3:21). Sometimes he seems to use *phanerō* and *apokalyptō* interchangeably, since "apocalypsed" includes the sense of "revealed" (3:21). But to leave it at that is to miss the dynamic power implied in Paul's language, which is evident in the immediate context of 1:16–17, in the language of apocalypse elsewhere in Paul's letters, and in the eschatological expectation associated with this word in Jewish literature.

The verb *apokalyptō* and the noun *apokalypsis* occur in Jewish apocalyptic literature to speak of both the revelation of divine mysteries in the present (Dan 2:22, 28–29, 47) and the future Day of the Lord. This sense appears in the New Testament also (1 Pet 1:5, 7, 13; 5:1; 2 Thess 1:7; Eph 3:3; Rev 1:1). In Paul's letters "apocalypse" refers to a special revelation (1 Cor 14:26, 30; 2 Cor 12:1; Gal 2:2), the future revelation of works at the day of judgment (1 Cor 3:13), and the future coming of the Lord Jesus Christ (1 Cor 1:7). For Paul, the content of what is and will be "apocalypsed" is inseparable from Jesus Christ. God "apocalypsed" God's Son to Paul (Gal 1:16), and the "coming of faith" through the coming of Jesus Christ is also the "apocalypse" of faith (3:23–25). In these verses, the verbal form of "apocalypse" means "to come on the scene." So also in Romans 1:17, through the proclamation of the good news of Christ, the righteousness of God is "coming on the scene."

The puzzling phrase "through faith for faith" (*ek pisteōs eis pistin*) is based on the quotation from Habakkuk 2:4 that immediately follows in Romans 1:17b, linking God's righteousness with faith, trust, and trustworthiness. It seems best, therefore, to discuss it briefly, and then in more depth after looking at Paul's use of Habakkuk 2:4. "Through faith for faith" is one possible translation of the Greek phrase here; "from faith to faith" is an equally valid translation that clarifies Paul's meaning in two possible ways. Either it describes God's faithfulness or trustworthiness as the source of human faith, or it simply describes an increase in human faith. The second option would mean that through the gospel preaching, the inbreaking of the divine righteousness is progressing throughout the world, so that human faith in Christ is "on the march" (cf. 1:8). The first option emphasizes divine trustworthiness generating human trust in God: "from God's faithfulness to human faith." Given Paul's interweaving of "the righteousness of God," which elsewhere parallels the "faithfulness of God" (3:3–7), with the reference to human trust in 1:16, this option seems more persuasive. As the early patristic interpreter Ambrosiaster put it:

> What does "from faith to faith" mean? Divine faith consists in God's making a promise; human faith is placed in the God who makes this promise. Thus the righteousness of God is revealed by the fidelity of God who promises, and in the faith of the one who believes the promise. (*Commentary*, in Burns 2012, 24)

In support of his meaning, Paul immediately quotes Habakkuk 2:4. Here again, as indicated in the footnote to the NRSVue, different translations are possible. In the Greek sentence, "by faith" comes between "is righteous" and "will live" and could modify either clause. If "by faith" modifies "is righteous," it describes the way in which one becomes righteous, and the sentence should be translated, "The one who is righteous by faith will live." On the other hand, if "by faith" modifies "will live," the sentence should be translated, "The righteous one will live by faith (or faithfulness)." In this case, "the righteous one" could be a messianic title, with an oblique reference to Jesus as the Messiah. For example, in 1 Enoch 38, "the righteous one" refers to a figure closely associated with God who appears at the end of time to judge sinners; in Acts 7:52 and 22:14, "the Righteous One" is a title for Jesus. If Paul reads Habakkuk 2:4 as a messianic prophecy, Jesus is the righteous one who lives—indeed is resurrected—on the basis of his own trustworthiness. This is an appealing proposal. The problem is that it does not explain how Habakkuk 2:4 relates to "everyone who believes" in 1:16 and the immediately preceding clause, "from faith to faith."

Furthermore, when Paul quotes Habakkuk 2:4 in Galatians 3:11, he clearly intends the first interpretation: "the one who is righteous by faith (not by the law) will live" (see Gal 3:10–12). This observation suggests that Paul also intends this meaning in Romans 1:17—believers become righteous through trust, and therefore live. In the context of the preceding clause, "from faith to faith," one logical interpretation of 1:16–17 is as follows: "I am not ashamed of the gospel, for it is the power of God for salvation for all who trust, for the Jew first and also the Greek. For in the good news, the righteousness of God is breaking into the world from God's faithfulness (or trustworthiness) to human faith (or trust), for as it is written, 'The one who is righteous on the basis of faith will live.'"

But to whose "faith" does Habakkuk 2:4 refer? The Hebrew version of Habakkuk 2:4 says the righteous will live by *his or her* faithfulness; the Greek Septuagint says the righteous will live by *God's* faithfulness. Paul simply omits any possessive pronoun for faith, leaving open the question of whose faith (or faithfulness) is in view. The resulting ambiguity may be intentional: because God's faithfulness generates human faith, the person whose righteousness before God is secured by God's own faithfulness will live—by trusting in God's trustworthiness.

EXCURSUS

Reflections for Preaching and Teaching

Shame

We do not live in an explicitly honor-shame culture like that of the apostle Paul, in which the pursuit of public honor had significant social capital. But we do know quite a bit about shame, and issues of public reputation are intensified by the pervasive influence of internet culture with its curated public identities. For example, current research on internet use among teens in the United States finds that more than 50 percent of young people using the internet experience negative body image and low self-worth associated with spending time on social media. Shame can be a debilitating factor in social formation. Paul's bracing affirmation, "I am not ashamed," thus speaks volumes to issues of pastoral care in the parish and contemporary issues in internet culture.

It is the countercultural good news of Jesus Christ of which Paul is not ashamed, despite much that would be considered shameful in his culture—and ours. Embracing that good news delivers Paul from shame about his own marginal and offensive social location. Jesus was executed as a criminal. He hung out with those whom society considered losers. Paul's churches as well as the Roman congregations were also filled with folks on the bottom rung of Greco-Roman society. Paul himself lived a life that many would consider disreputable: homeless, on the road, relying on the kindness of others. Living on the edges of society, he shows a robust confidence in God, with a corresponding healthy sense of his own call and his own standing in Christ. He simply does not put himself down, even while he puts the spotlight on God's gracious deliverance in Christ. Such preaching counters the destructive power of shame itself, which has no place in Paul's gospel. How do we preach the gospel as an anti-shame message? As we shall see, Paul locates worth, reputation, and glory entirely in God's gift, not in human achievements or appearances. Perhaps we should take a page from Paul's playbook, which is not about self-praise at all—the praise is all toward God—and simultaneously displays a confidence in God that does not have time for (or interest in) being ashamed of oneself. The message is not "I'm OK, you're OK," but "Whether or not we're OK, we are radically loved, here and now."

Power

Paul is sure that the preaching of the good news has the power to save, that is, to deliver people from destructive powers into God's life. His confidence rests in the ancient belief that God's speech does what God says; in this sense Paul surely sees himself in line with the classical prophets of Israel. Dare preachers today do the same? In a time when words are cheap and "alt-facts" are the order of the day, there is a great danger of losing sight of the power of preaching, which is simply the confidence that God speaks through flawed human beings.

Righteousness

"Righteousness" easily brings to mind the negative connotation of "self-righteousness," a smug certainty that one is on the right side of history or morally impeccable, and indeed when human beings claim "righteousness" for themselves or their cause, such smugness seems almost inevitable. As Paul clarifies repeatedly throughout the letter, however,

God's shocking righteousness and justice are demonstrated by Christ's death with and for the nobodies and the wrongdoers, because all have sinned and fall short of God's glory (3:21–23). To know and receive this unmerited divine righteousness entails knowing one's own need of it; such knowledge is the antidote to self-righteousness. Paul will ring the changes on this paradoxical divine righteousness throughout Romans, not least in distinguishing between being in the right through keeping the Mosaic law, and the righteousness that comes from trusting in Christ (10:5–9; cf. Phil 3:9). This divine, undeserved justice without regard to human worth has the power to undercut human judgment and division, and thus underwrites Paul's warnings against judging others (2:1–4; 12:14–18; 14:1–12).

Apocalypse Now

God's intimate involvement in human suffering, sin, and death speaks profoundly to the apocalyptic anxiety that grips today's world. This divine "apocalypse" makes it both necessary and possible to name the horrors that confront human beings every day, both immediately in calamitous personal and familial events, and on a global scale. In dictionary definitions of "apocalypse," catastrophe is listed as a synonym, which is surely what "apocalypse" and "apocalyptic" connote in current discourse—the catastrophic, violent overturning of the existing order. Playing off this meaning of catastrophe, J. R. R. Tolkien coined a new word—eucatastrophe (Tolkien 2000, 100–101). Eucatastrophe is a sudden, unexpected turn to deliverance and joy right in the middle of calamity. Such is Paul's apocalyptic gospel, in which even God's enemies are brought into service to the one Lord of all. To preach this gospel requires "steering toward the pain" in personal lives and in the news, attending to the places of fear and anguish and doubt that most test trust in God, because God in Christ has already entered into those places and ultimately will transform them into places of hope.

"All"

Paul's repeated use of "all" is inclusive, yet without erasing differences. *All* strikes a blow at the human propensity to draw boundaries around communities. There is one defining characteristic of those "in Christ"—faith—yet faith depends on a God who embraces everyone with the gift of grace.

In the Roman Empire, and in Paul's own Jewish heritage, "everyone" meant "Jews and gentiles." In our day, God's inclusive grace requires increasingly diverse expressions in each situation; locating and then subverting existing social barriers is an intrinsic part of preaching and pastoral ministry. This does not mean spouting an easy universalism that claims we are all the same and that can only be viewed as imperialistic and oppressive by those who suffer at the hands of the powerful. Rather, it means the careful, attentive, humble, and patient work of building relationships across differences without minimizing those differences.

Faith

As noted earlier, the Greek word *pistis* can be translated as faith and faithfulness, trust and trustworthiness, and belief. This richness of meaning opens up new ways of preaching about faith. Preaching and pastoral care that flow from the assurance of God's trustworthiness will focus consistently on Christ, rather than on human belief as a condition of salvation. The point is that the more deeply we hear and receive the good news of God's faithfulness, the stronger our trust in God becomes; conversely, the more we try to conjure up faith, whether as cognitive belief in doctrines or as emotional trust and experience, the more we are tempted to doubt. *Pistis* is not an individual human achievement or choice, nor the one requirement from the human side in the divine human relationship, but human trust responding to God's gift of God's self through Christ.

One imaginative way to express this reality is to rephrase the Nicene Creed, which many church traditions say every Sunday: "I trust in God. . . . I trust in Jesus Christ. . . . I trust in the Holy Spirit." As in human relationships, holistic trust in God and cognitive beliefs about God often develop in complex, mutually informed ways. To speak of trust without first requiring assent to a set of doctrinal beliefs can open a way into deeper faith for folks who struggle with doubt about the doctrines of the church.

1:18–3:20. The Human Plight Revealed by the Gospel

Romans 1:18–3:20 begins with the revelation of God's wrath against "all ungodliness and injustice" (1:18) and ends with God's impartial judgment pronounced against all humanity so that "the whole world may be held accountable to God" (3:19). The entire section is bracketed by the apocalypse (1:17) and manifestation (3:21) of the righteousness of God, such that the revelation of God's wrath is enclosed within the larger revelation of God's righteousness and justice and can only be understood within the context of God's saving power (cf. 5:9). Within this context, Paul sets up key issues that continue to be in play throughout the rest of the letter: the relationship between divine and human agency, the relationship between Jew and gentile, the hiddenness and disclosure of God's action in the world, the difference between human and divine judgment.

Paul's grammar and syntax provide a clue to his purpose in these challenging verses, as he leads his listeners on a journey of self-examination. The structure of this section can be set forth as follows:

- 1:18–32 Judgment oracle against all who suppress the truth of God
- 2:1–5 Warning addressed to "you, whoever you are," who judge others
  - 2:5 The day of wrath when God's righteous judgment will be apocalypsed
- 2:6–16 God's impartial judgment according to deeds
  - 2:16 The day when God judges the secrets of human beings through Jesus Christ
- 2:17–27 Warning addressed to "you" who boast in being a Jew
  - 2:17–24 Possession of the law without doing the law dishonors God
  - 2:25–27 Circumcision means nothing apart from doing the law
- 2:28–29 Contrast between human appearances and God's judgment of the heart
  - 2:29 Praise from God
- 3:1–9b Questions and answers about Jewish privilege and divine impartiality
- 3:9b–20 All human beings are under the power of sin
  - 3:10–18 The witness of Scripture
  - 3:19–20 The witness of the law

1:18–32. The Apocalypse of God's Wrath

This challenging section of Romans introduces Paul's depiction of the human plight, which only becomes fully revealed through the gospel. These verses progress through an interplay of human knowledge, leading to culpability, and God's action of "handing over," leading to a situation of cognitive impairment and bondage. Throughout, the motif of cognition is central.

1:18. The Apocalypse of God's Wrath

Several translation issues immediately come to the fore in the announcement of God's wrath in 1:18, which parallels 1:16 in several ways. As in 1:16, the Greek verb translated "revealed" is literally "being apocalypsed" in the passive voice, implying that God is the one revealing both righteousness and wrath; both verses begin with the conjunction "for," linking them to what precedes; in both verses it is *God's* righteousness or wrath that is being revealed. Thus, the reader cannot help but hear an echo linking the dynamic, invasive revelation of God's righteousness with an accompanying revelation of God's wrath. In both cases, the verb is present tense, indicating that this event is happening *now*. As the language of apocalypse and the phrase "from heaven" indicate, this revelation of both righteousness and wrath is something new, not something evolving or built into the status quo. Rather, the revelation of wrath as well as righteousness comes through the gospel of Christ.

This divine wrath is opposed to all "ungodliness and injustice." The Greek word translated "injustice" is *adikia,* which could also be translated as "unrighteousness," just as the Greek word for righteousness (*dikaiosynē*) can also be translated as "justice." God's justice *is* God's righteousness, and vice versa. Thus God's wrath is directed against that which opposes God's righteous justice. Since, as we have seen, God's righteousness is God's life-giving power to save humanity, its opposite is death-dealing resistance to that divine life. Similarly in 2:8, "wrath and fury" will fall on those who "obey not the truth but injustice [*adikia*]."

Contrary to the NRSVue, in the Greek of 1:18 there is no possessive pronoun before "injustice," as if it was only through "their [own] injustice" that human beings "suppress the truth." Yes, humans hold down or suppress truth, but the injustice through which such suppression happens exceeds individual human actions or attitudes. Paul dramatically portrays this cosmic suppression of truth in 7:7–25.

Finally, the theme of *truth,* and by implication its opposite, *falsehood,* here first appears in Romans (see commentary on 1:25; 2:2, 8, 20; 3:4–7; 7:11). As the letter unfolds, it becomes evident that "sin" (which has not yet appeared in Romans) enters human existence through the primal *lie* of idolatry, leading to futile thinking and darkened, debased minds (1:21, 24, 28). The truth, by way of contrast, is the truth of God (3:4, 7), which includes both knowledge *about* God (1:19–21) and God's own character as true and therefore faithful and just (3:3–7). "The truth of God" thus denotes not only God's attribute in God's self, but also the faithful and reliable character of God's dealings with humanity; God is the author of truth.

1:19–22. Human Cognition and Culpability

Paul's repeated references to human knowledge (1:19, 20, 21) establish human culpability for the refusal to acknowledge God as God, because the evidence of God's role as creator is built into the cosmos. Such evidence means that the suppression of the knowledge of God renders human beings "without excuse" (v. 20). This is legal language; the word translated "without excuse" (*anapologētous*) occurs only here and in 2:1 but is common in Greek legal texts. Humanity is in the dock before God, without "apology"—that is, without any alibi for its guilty conduct. The human turn away from creation's witness to God comes in 1:21, in a refusal to honor God or give thanks.

Precisely at this point human understanding becomes compromised: "They became futile in their thinking [*dialogismois*], and their senseless hearts [*kardia*] were darkened." Paul's language includes both rational thought (*dialogismois*) and the heart as a holistic blend of emotion, thought, and action (*kardia*). Up to this point Paul has been speaking of human beings who know about God but refuse to glorify God. But now, again through use of the passive voice, he implies that *God* has darkened human hearts and made their reasoning futile. Verses 22–23 restate human agency in the willful exchange of divine glory for the images of created beings, but with an unintended consequence: "they became fools"—literally, "they were made moronic." The point here is that every aspect of human ways of knowing is compromised and distorted, such that no one can claim to have unimpeded knowledge of the truth. This cognitive impairment is the result of both human self-deception and divine action.

1:23–28. The Primal Exchange

Verse 23 sums up the theme of idolatry and introduces the idea of "exchange" (1:23, 25, 26), echoing significant passages in Israel's

Scriptures: the story of creation and fall in Genesis 3 and the story of the golden calf in Exodus 32, particularly as recounted in Psalm 106:20–23: "They *exchanged* the *glory* of God for the image of an ox that eats grass." Jeremiah 2:11 also describes idolatry as a primal exchange leading to the loss of humanity's original glory in the image of God:

> Has a nation changed its gods,
> even though they are no gods?
> But my people have *changed* their *glory*
> for something that does not profit.

Paul's version of this exchange in Romans 1:23 highlights God as the source of glory and heightens the contrast between God's glory and human facsimiles, through the distinction between God's immortality and the mortality of all created beings. Furthermore, Paul uses the apparently redundant phrase "images resembling"; in other words, that which humans foolishly and ignorantly worship is a copy of a copy, twice removed from the life-giving original, God. "A mortal human or birds or four-footed animals or reptiles" recalls Genesis 1:20–27; this echo of the story of creation in Genesis includes not only Israel's idolatry but all the heirs of Adam and Eve in a sweeping picture of human folly and idolatry.

Adoration of gods in the form of human beings, birds, animals, and snakes was also common in pagan religions, and a stock source of Jewish polemic against gentiles. In particular, Paul seems to echo Jewish mockery of Egyptian idolatry in Wisdom of Solomon 11:15:

> In return for their foolish and wicked thoughts,
> which led them astray to worship irrational serpents and worthless animals,
> you sent upon them a multitude of irrational creatures to punish them,
> so that they might learn that one is punished by the very things by which one sins.

(See also Wis 12:24; 13:10–14; 14:8.)

There are so many resonances between Wisdom 13–14 and Romans 1:18–32 that it seems likely Paul was consciously alluding to Wisdom: the seer in Wisdom points to the evidence in nature for God's identity as creator (13:1–9), then to gentile idolatry (13:10–14:21), and finally to consequent gentile immorality (14:22–31). Similarly, Paul moves from the evidence for God in creation (Rom 1:19–20), to idolatry and its consequences (1:21–28), leading finally to moral depravity (1:29–32). For this reason, Romans 1:18–32 has been read as a typical Jewish judgment oracle directed only against gentiles. But the echoes of Psalm 106:20 and Genesis 1:20–27 argue against narrowing Paul's target to either Jews or gentiles. Rather, the revelation of wrath in Romans 1:18–32 is universal and inclusive; when Paul says *all* (1:18) he means *all.* Nonetheless, his evocation of common Jewish stereotypes of gentiles could set up some of his audience for the pointed judgment in 2:17 on those who claim Jewish identity and privileges.

Throughout 1:23–28, Paul develops the theme of exchange and the claim that God handed humanity over to destructive powers. Three times Paul says human beings "exchanged" one thing for another: "the glory of the immortal God for images resembling a mortal human" (1:23), "the truth about God for a lie" (1:25), and "natural [*kata physis*] intercourse for unnatural [*para physis*]" (1:26). In the first two instances, what is clearly in view is a turn away from worshiping God as creator to worshiping the creature. In the third instance, Paul deploys a particular understanding of human sexual relations as an illustration of the theological claim he has made in the prior statements. The topic of homosexuality is not his point; nonetheless, the history of interpretation and the continued debates around 1:26–27 require further discussion (see commentary below).

Recalling that the apocalypse of God's righteousness circumscribes the apocalypse of wrath, it is fruitful to consider how the good news of Christ illuminates the human situation as one of a primal, lethal exchange. To exchange (*allassō*) something is to substitute one thing for another, to interpose one thing in the place of another. This motif of exchange is not inherent in the human situation per se; rather, it follows from the logic of solidarity and exchange that permeates Paul's understanding of Jesus Christ entering fully into the human condition, even and especially at its lowest point, by undergoing a criminal's death (Phil 2:5–11). Repeatedly in Paul's letters, Christ becomes what we are, that in him we might join in his likeness, in a pattern of interchange and transformation (Gal 3:13; 4:4–7; 2 Cor 5:21; 8:9; Phil 2:6–13). This will become explicit also in Romans 8:3–4. The extremity of Christ's life-giving exchange with humanity under sin exposes the extremity of the human situation as an inverse lethal exchange, which began with culpable idolatry in primal history but now is one of captivity to destructive powers.

1:24, 26, 28. God Gave Them Over

The threefold repetition of "exchange" is accompanied by a threefold repetition of the verb "to give over" (*paradidōmi*), better translated as "to hand over (into another's power)." Whereas human beings are the subjects of the verb "to exchange," God is the one who hands humanity over to the custody of destructive powers. Paul's meaning here is close to Lamentations 1:14:

> My transgressions were bound into a yoke;
> by his hand they were fastened together;
> they weigh on my neck,
> sapping my strength;
> the Lord handed me over
> to those whom I cannot withstand.

Throughout the Old Testament, *paradidōmi* occurs in situations of conflict and judgment: God delivers Israel's enemies and their territory over to Israel (Deut 2:24, 30, 31, 33; 3:2, 3; 7:2, 23, 24; 20:13; Josh 2:14, 24; 6:2, 16; 7:7; 8:18; 10:8, 12). For instance, God hands Jericho over to Israel (Josh 2:14, 24). But God also hands Israel over to defeat and captivity as judgment for its idolatry and disobedience. This is particularly frequent in Jeremiah (Jer 21:10; 22:25; 24:8; 39:28; cf. Ezek 7:21; 11:9; 16:27). Paul uses the verb "to hand over" elsewhere to command the Corinthians to hand an incestuous believer over to Satan (1 Cor 5:5). In each case, the verb "to hand over" has the sense of giving something or someone into another's power or custody (Gaventa 2024, 64–65). In this sense, it resonates with another verb Paul uses to portray God's action toward fallen humanity: "to imprison" or "shut up under the power of another" (*synkleiō;* Gal 3:23; Rom 11:32; see commentary below).

The final "handoff" in verse 28 involves a wordplay employing the verb *dokimazō,* "to see fit, to discern, to consider worthy," and the related adjective *adokimos,* "unfitting, untested, unworthy." Paul says, "Since they did not see fit [*edokimasan*] to acknowledge God, God gave them over to an unfit mind [*adokimon noun*]." The punishment fits the crime, and the result is corresponding actions, doing what is "not fitting." Paul depicts a kind of cognitive impairment, a distorted perception, that leads to distorted and destructive behavior.

Later, and crucially in line with the logic of exchange, Paul will speak of Christ himself as "handed over" to death for our transgressions (Rom 4:25; 8:32; cf. Gal 2:20 and 1 Cor 11:23; see commentary below). The divine judgment and deliverance into captivity that fall on idolatrous humanity also fall on Jesus, who enters into solidarity precisely with those "handed over" in 1:18–32. This divine participation in the human plight, and the consequent assurance of God's love, is critically important for interpreting the threefold "handing over" in 1:24, 26, 28.

1:29–32. Without Brains, Honor, Love, or Pity

Verses 29–32 paint a vivid picture of social relations dominated by an "unfit mind" and improper conduct. Notably, the first word is "injustice" (*adikia*), which echoes 1:18. What follows is a catalog of corrosive attitudes and behaviors that destroy the fabric of human relationships, culminating in 1:31 with a rhyming list denoting the lack of four characteristics deemed essential for civilized society: "without brains, honour, love or pity" is the apt translation of the New Jerusalem Bible. The final wordplay in 1:32 adds insult to injury: those who do such things approve (*syneudokousin*) of others who do them, thereby enacting the judgments of an "unfit mind." Nonetheless, these morally corrupted human agents retain the knowledge of God's righteous decree—a knowledge that renders them without excuse before God's judgment. Such culpability is not limited to either gentiles or Jews, as similar moral instruction can be found in both pagan and Jewish writings of the time. All humanity stands in the dock before God; this is life in the world where the truth of God is suppressed (1:18).

EXCURSUS

Reflections for Preaching and Teaching

Preaching about the Wrath of God

How do we understand and preach "the wrath of God"? Three observations may help us in dealing with this difficult topic. First, Paul simply announces "the wrath of God" and only gradually displays what this divine wrath looks like. What it looks like is God's threefold "handing over" of human beings into the power of sin and death. Just as in Israel's history, here the divine judgment involves deliverance into a situation of captivity that exposes any delusions that humanity can save itself. As also in Israel's history, such captivity is not the last word, but rather a temporary, albeit drastic, chastening. Later in Romans we hear that God has imprisoned all humanity "in disobedience" that God might have mercy on all, suggesting that wrath is not the last word (Rom 11:32; cf. Gal 3:22). So also, in the context of 1:16–3:21, the revelation of divine wrath is enclosed within the larger revelation of God's will and power to save.

Second, the structure of Paul's argument is suggestive for preaching. Paul starts with the good news of God's saving power and only then exposes humanity's desperate need for deliverance, in confidence that God already has rescued humanity from its own idolatry and the disastrous consequences of its failure to honor God. There is both pastoral wisdom and theological insight here: the preacher first emphasizes the certainty of God's love before speaking of God's wrath. Contrary to the preaching dictum, "First you preach 'em down, then you preach 'em up!" the good news comes first; it gives people a foundation of assured love and acceptance from which to confront evil and even to see it rightly. This foundation is especially necessary for recognizing the evil within us. From a theological perspective, because the apocalypse of God's wrath results from the apocalypse of God's righteousness through the death and resurrection of Jesus, we discover the extremity of the problem from the extremity of the solution. If the problem of human existence were simply a human propensity to do wrong occasionally, forgiveness would be adequate. But the crisis facing humanity is a combination of human rebellion and human captivity, which requires a divine rescue mission.

Nonetheless, it is extremely difficult to think of God as wrathful, certainly in much of contemporary Western culture (although some church folks love to talk about God judging other people). Therefore, third, it is crucial to distinguish between human ideas of wrath as emotional rage, and divine wrath as God's unequivocal opposition to all that would destroy God's beloved creation. Ultimately the object of God's wrath is not individual human beings but sin itself, not least in its manifestations of injustice, violence, and abuse. As the French novelist George Sand wrote to her friend Gustave Flaubert, "Humanity is outraged in me and with me. We must not dissimulate nor try to forget this indignation which is one of the most passionate forms of love." Or, as a bumper sticker from the 1980s said, "If you're not outraged, you're not paying attention." God pays attention. God's righteous anger on behalf of God's people is demonstrated all through the history of Israel. The promise of divine justice both gives hope to the oppressed and provides a way to prevent victims from becoming perpetrators. God will repay—therefore it is not our job to repay, not least because human retribution never accomplishes God's justice (cf. 12:14–21).

Without God's judgment, the social cosmos is left in the thrall of retributive violence, reactive rejection of those by whom we feel threatened or judged, and vicious cycles of guilt and rage. The poor suffer injustice, and the wealthy and powerful claim impunity. This is the world we live in, read about in the news every day, and sometimes experience in our families and neighborhoods. Those in positions of privilege *may* be unaware of the need for judgment, although wrong and pain and recrimination infiltrate every part of society. But those who are oppressed and marginalized know that God's judgment is good news. As the prophet Isaiah cried out, "O that you would tear open the heavens and come down!" (Isa 64:1).

The Paradox of Human Culpability and Divine Omnipotence

Three times Paul says, "God handed them over," just as three times he says that humanity exchanged God's truth for a lie and God's glory for created idols. As noted in the commentary, there is a tension between human culpability and human bondage that runs right through Romans. Rather than fitting into a neat logical system, this tension accurately depicts the complexity of human responsibility and enmeshment in destructive, systematic sin, and thus gives us a language to name wrongdoing without demonizing other people. In the wake of humanity's primal refusal to honor God as God, we are in the grip of forces hostile to God and to human flourishing. This knowledge can underwrite compassion toward those whom we would judge—including ourselves. Paul further develops this theme later in the letter, most strikingly in 7:7–25.

Does Paul Teach Homophobia?

Nonetheless, the sensitive preacher and pastor will surely stumble over 1:26–27, one of Paul's best-known and most hated passages. In contemporary Western culture, these two verses often trigger such a reaction that people avoid the rest of Paul's letters and miss the radical grace at the heart of his gospel. In this instance, a few words about the context of these verses in the letter and in Greco-Roman culture may be helpful.

On the one hand, Paul probably did not condone sex between men or between women. On the other hand, that is not his point here. He is far more worried about abusive relationships between people, as verses 28–31 display. To read these verses as saying that "God hates gays" or "Gay people are going to hell" is both to read them outside of their context in the letter and to impose a modern view of sex and gender on the ancient world.

Ancient Romans did not think of gender in terms of inborn sexual orientation, nor even in terms of physical bodies, but rather in terms of the roles taken by sexual partners. They saw "male" and "female" on a spectrum between active (male) and passive (feminine or effeminate) partners, and they assumed that sexual desire (at least for men) could be directed toward either male or female partners. Anyone in the passive role, whether a woman or a man, was seen as inferior. Free males were expected to be virile, even sexually aggressive, and there were no constraints on how they treated those of the lower classes. There is considerable evidence of abusive and manipulative sexual aggression by free men toward enslaved persons and lower-class boys as well as women. In calling the *sexual aggressors* to account, Paul's words may have been welcome to lower-class and enslaved believers, both men and women, in the Roman congregations. Thus, before dismissing Paul as a homophobic killjoy, it is worth pondering what kinds of behaviors Paul might have had in mind in first-century Rome, such as orgies that allowed the abuse of defenseless enslaved persons and children, both male and female.

The pastoral challenge in these verses is to hear Paul's prophetic word against *all* suppression of the truth here, without demonizing any subgroup, especially but not exclusively the LGBTQIA+ community. In fact, to take 1:26–27 as a basis for judging and rejecting gay and transgender folks is to miss entirely Paul's point in the larger section of

1:18–3:30, as Paul immediately makes clear in 2:1: "Therefore you are without excuse, whoever you are, when you judge others." That sharp rebuke speaks directly to contemporary churches that condemn and exclude gay and transgender people. Paul calls his listeners to self-examination, not judgment of others.

2:1–3:20. Human (Mis)judgment and Divine Impartiality

By the end of the judgment oracle in 1:18–32, Paul's listeners in Rome might well have been nodding in agreement. The gentile majority and the Jewish minority in the Roman house churches surely would find points of contact from pagan and Jewish catalogs of vices to avoid. "Yes!" they might say, "such behavior surely deserves God's just condemnation." Paul turns the tables abruptly in 2:1, as he shifts from a third-person description of "those other people" to a direct address in the singular second person: "Therefore *you* have no excuse, whoever you are, when you judge others, for in passing judgment on another you condemn yourself, because you, the judge, are doing the very same things."

Many inconsistencies surface in this section, making it particularly difficult and controversial to interpret. Is Paul contradicting himself? Is he simply incoherent, as some would say? Is he sometimes setting forth opposing points of view in order to debunk some views and promote others? Or is he precisely seeking to render a multifaceted picture of God and humanity that does not fit inside a logical system of thought? What is Paul's overarching aim in this section of the letter, and how does it relate to his goal of strengthening and encouraging the Roman Christians in their faith (1:11–12)?

As we wrestle with these questions, it will be helpful to keep three pointers in mind.

First, as always, we read this section in relationship to the rest of the letter, especially the letter up to this point. Already Paul has emphasized the priority of the Jews in God's redemptive work in history, in the context of a letter written to congregations where gentiles are the majority and Jewish believers are in the minority. This is the context for his concerns with both gentile excuses and Jewish privileges, leading up to his assertion, "all have sinned and fall short of the glory of God" (3:23). As we shall see, however, Paul also here anticipates three subsequent sections of the letter: the power of sin and the limitation of the law (7:7–25), the affirmation of Israel's place in salvation (chaps. 9–11), and specific warnings against judging one's neighbor in the community of faith (chaps. 12 and 14).

Second, it is illuminating to keep our ears attuned to Paul's references to Scripture, both explicit and allusive, as these will illuminate underlying continuities in a text that seems full of contradictions.

Third, the rhetorical structure of these verses clarifies their intended effect on Paul's audience in Rome and their potential effect on us as we read and listen today. In two short diatribes, Paul directly addresses an unnamed conversation partner as "you" (2:1–5, 17–27) when he calls out judgmental behavior. This direct address alternates with descriptive discourses about others who do the good, in which Paul sets out principles of divine impartiality (2:6–16) and Jewish identity (2:28–29). In 3:1–9a Paul again uses a diatribe style to talk with an imaginary Jewish conversation partner, before quoting scriptural passages that establish universal accountability before God. This style of speaking would have been familiar to Paul's Roman audience, so that they would have understood that he was not necessarily speaking directly to them. At the same time, the style of direct address implicitly challenges Paul's audience to put themselves in the scenarios Paul depicts so vividly. In this way, Paul invites his listeners on a journey of discovery, as he creates an imaginative space in which they are confronted with their own tendencies to pass judgment on others while excusing themselves. That Paul intends such an effect is extremely likely, because later in the letter he explicitly exhorts the Roman Christians not to judge one another, using language very similar to 2:1–5 (cf. 14:4, 10–12).

2:1–5. "You Are without Excuse"

In 2:1–5 Paul abruptly turns the tables on his listeners who may have been nodding their heads in agreement while he lambastes unnamed others who "suppress the truth" of God. "You are without excuse" (*anapologētos*) reprises 1:20, but now this accusation shocks Paul's listeners into self-examination. Interpreters who consider 1:18–32 to be a Jewish judgment oracle solely against gentile sinners read 2:1–16 as addressed to self-righteous Jews. But as noted above, in 1:18–32, the echoes of Genesis 1 and Psalm 106:20 in 1:23, when taken together with the Wisdom of Solomon, include both Jews and gentiles in the category of those without excuse. Now in 2:1, Paul turns the tables on these same listeners, "whoever you are." "Whoever you are" is an inclusive term that resists categorizing or convenient finger-pointing at "those other people."

Paul's rhetoric is like that of the prophet Amos, who first announced judgment on Israel's neighbors before turning the tables on his listeners, God's people (Amos 1:2–2:16). It is like that of the prophet Nathan, who described a case of egregious sin to David, and then said, "You are the man!" (2 Sam 12:7). This is a powerful prophetic move, inviting one's listeners into a posture of contempt for "those other people" and then announcing God's judgment on their own pretentious condemnation (cf. Amos 9:10; Jer 2:35; 14:13–16). Words denoting "judgment" appear seven times in Romans 2:1–5, sharply contrasting human and divine judgment (v. 4).

"Repentance" (*metanoia*) is often translated as "a change of mind," but it has an emotional sense as well, as in "remorse" or "grief for wrongdoing." Indeed, in 2 Corinthians 7:9–10, the only other occurrence of *metanoia* in Paul's letters, Paul rejoices that the Corinthians responded to his earlier rebuke of them with a "godly grief" leading to repentance. Such repentance is not a bargaining chip with God but rather a change of mind and heart resulting from an encounter with truth—in this case, the truth of God's patience and kindness, and of one's own wrongdoing seen in the light of divine love. In this sense, repentance is a response to a gift already given. In the Hebrew Bible, to repent is to turn away from wrong and back to God (Wis 11:23; 12:19; Sir 17:24). Paul is calling on his addressees to turn away from judging other people and to submit to God's judgment in the context of God's mercy. Thus, the riches of God's kindness and forbearance and patience stand in stark contrast to human judgment that cancels out other people rather than seeking mutual understanding and reconciliation.

Recalling 1:18, this climactic statement in 2:5 sums up several themes from the intervening verses. "Impenitent" contrasts sharply with the immediately preceding call for repentance. Rather than being led to repentance, those who persist in judging others are unrepentant. The "hard and impenitent heart" of the addressee recalls the senseless and darkened hearts of all who exchange the truth of God for a lie (1:21); indeed, to judge others is to commit the primal idolatry of putting oneself in the place of God. The repetition of "wrath" and the verbal form of "apocalypse" doubly echo and amplify the apocalypse of the wrath of God in 1:18, but now this warning is addressed to the judgmental pious individual, not simply pronounced against human beings in general. Furthermore, whereas in 1:18 the apocalypse of wrath is happening now in conjunction with the apocalypse of God's righteousness through the gospel (1:16–17), in 2:5 the future day of wrath points to the final judgment. The expectation of "the last day" when God will vindicate the righteous and judge the wicked appears in Paul's earliest preaching (1 Thess 1:10; 5:9) and has roots in Jewish apocalyptic expectation (see, e.g., Tob 4:9–10; Zeph 1:15, 18; 2:2–3; 3:8). For "wrath" in Romans as pointing to the Last Judgment, see also 2:8; 3:5; 5:9; 9:22. Indeed, 2:1–3:20 is punctuated with references to God's final judgment that serve as the climax of each subsection (2:5, 11, 16; 3:19–20).

2:6–11. God's Impartial Judgment

At verse 6 Paul switches to the third person to introduce the principle that "God will repay according to each one's deeds [Gk., works]." Verses 6–11 are structured in an ABCCBA pattern, with verse 11 as the punch line:

A 2:6 God will repay according to each one's deeds;
    B 2:7 eternal life for those who do the good,
        C 2:8 wrath and fury for those who do not obey the truth,
        C′ 2:9 anguish and distress for everyone who does evil,
    B′ 2:10 glory and honor and peace for everyone who does the good.
A′ 2:11 For God shows no partiality.

With minor changes, Paul begins by quoting Psalm 62:12, a psalm ascribed to David: "You repay to all according to their work." Taken by itself, this verse seems to contradict Paul's emphasis on justification by grace as a gift (3:24). But the larger context of Psalm 62 expresses David's reliance on God as the one whose power and mercy are the only refuge from human oppressors who "take pleasure in falsehood" (Ps 62:4):

> For God alone my soul waits in silence;
> from him comes my salvation.
> He alone is my rock and my salvation.
> . . . .
> . . . power belongs to God,
> and steadfast love belongs to you, O Lord.
> For you repay to all
> according to their work.
>
> *Ps 62:1–2, 11–12*

In the context of the psalm, God's repayment of human beings according to their works refers to God's judgment on bad behavior, not a reward for good behavior (cf. Rom 12:19). Trusting God's just judgment of all, including enemies, the psalmist waits in silence, in submission, and in hope of mercy.

Verses 7 and 10 of Romans 2 emphasize the promise of "glory and honor" to those who do the good. The word pair develops the double sense of the Greek word for "glory" (*doxa*) as both splendor and reputation, promising a restoration of what humanity lost through exchanging "the glory of the immortal God" for images of mortal creatures, and therefore being given over to dishonor (1:23–24). The repeated references to "doing good" versus doing "evil" anticipate Paul's language in 7:18–21.

In 2:8–9, Paul picks up on the language of 1:18, because those who "obey not the truth but injustice" (cf. Gal 5:7) are like those who suppress the truth in wickedness. The word translated "obey" means "to be persuaded"; Paul here employs a wordplay that translates roughly as "those who resist being persuaded by [*apeithousi*] the truth but are persuaded [*peithomenois*] by wickedness." The judgment of wrath and fury similarly recalls the apocalypse of the wrath of God in 1:18.

Just as in 1:16 the gospel is the power of God for salvation for the Jew first and also the Greek, so now the judgment of God is for the Jew first and also the Greek (2:10). Jewish priority in regard to divine revelation (3:2) does not entail Jewish exemption from judgment—quite the opposite, as the Law and the Prophets testify. On the one hand, Paul always maintains the priority of God's promises to Israel and the irrevocability of Israel's election; on the other hand, God's judgment and redemption are for all humanity.

Therefore, Paul brings this subsection to a climax with the claim, "For God shows no partiality" (2:11). The Greek literally says, "There is no lifting up of the face before God." The image depicts a widespread practice in the ancient world, in which rulers showed favor by lifting up the face of a person prostrated before them. That God does not show such favoritism is a common theme in Hebrew Scripture. For example, Deuteronomy 10:16–17 could well be a subtext for 2:5–11, 29:

> Circumcise, then, the foreskin of your heart, and do not be stubborn any longer. For the Lord your God is God of gods and Lord of lords, the great God, mighty and awesome, who is not partial [Heb., does not lift the face] and takes no bribe. (Cf. 2 Chr 19:7.)

Conversely, in Psalm 82:2 the psalmist complains to God for apparently "lifting up the face" of the wicked, while the weak and the orphan are oppressed. There are many examples of such appeals to God's impartiality in later Jewish texts as well (Sir 35:15; 1 Esd 4:39), usually in the context of judgments against the rich and pleas for justice for the poor within the Jewish community. Paul draws on this tradition but expands the scope of divine impartiality to include God's dealings with gentiles.

2:12–13. No Excuses, No Entitlement

God's equal treatment of all humanity thus sums up the argument of Romans 2:6–11 and is the basis of the argument that follows in verses 12–16. Aware that his balanced treatment of Jew and gentile will raise objections based on Jews' privileged reception of the Mosaic law, Paul now turns to the issue of the law. Again he puts all humanity on equal footing before divine judgment; possession of the Mosaic law functions neither as entitlement nor as an exemption from divine judgment, nor does not having the law (i.e., not being a Jew) excuse one on the basis of ignorance. For Jews, it is not hearing but doing the law that is the basis of being righteous before God. For gentiles, the original knowledge of God's power and deity ("the truth") through creation (1:18–20) renders them equally culpable for wrongdoing. Even though all human beings have been handed over to an unreasoning, undiscerning mind (1:28), they still retain knowledge of God's righteous decree (*to dikaiōma tou theou*), as Paul states in 1:32.

With the first use of the verb "to sin" (2:12), Paul repeats the basic principle of equality before God, following directly from verse 11 but now acknowledging the difference between having and lacking the law. It turns out, however, that with or without the law, all human beings will be judged by God. Romans 2:13 then establishes the principle that will govern the ensuing discussion of the law, culminating in 3:20: it is not hearing the law but doing the law that leads to righteousness before God. Nonetheless, peeking ahead to 3:20 tells us we are in for a bumpy ride in the intervening verses, for there Paul appears to contradict himself: "For no human being will be justified before him by deeds prescribed by the law, for through the law comes the knowledge of sin." If this is where Paul is going, how does he get there?

2:14–16. Gentiles Who Do the Law

Verses 14–16 are among the most contested in Paul's letters, with scholarly debates largely focused on the question, "Who are these gentiles with the law's requirement written on their hearts?" Interpreters generally offer one of three possible answers:

- They are gentiles who do the good, but with bad motives; hence they still "fall short of the glory of God" (3:23). The problem with this view is that Paul does not talk about motives here, but actions.
- They are fictitious ciphers for the purpose of Paul's argument; in theory there could be such people, but in fact there are not. At this point in the letter, however, Paul has given no clues that he considers such people fictitious.
- They are gentile Christians. In view of Paul's affirmations of believers' transformed lives later in the letter (e.g., 6:11–23; 8:4; 13:8–10), this is an appealing proposal, particularly if Paul has the promise of Jeremiah 31:33 in mind. The question is whether it makes sense of Paul's rhetoric and argument in 2:1–3:20.

In 2:14, the word translated "instinctively" in the NRSV is *physei,* which means "by nature." As indicated by the footnote in the NRSVue, "by nature" could mean either "gentiles who do not possess the law by nature" or "gentiles who do by nature what the law requires." The use of the phrase elsewhere in Romans (2:27; 11:21, 24) supports the first option; Paul is referring to gentiles "who do not possess the law by nature." That is, gentiles do not have the law "by nature" because, unlike Jews, they were not born into the covenant people governed by the law. Nonetheless, they still "do what the law requires" (NRSVue). The Greek simply says, "they do the things of the law." Thus, the verse could be translated, "When gentiles, who do not have the law by nature, do the things of the law even though they do not have the law, they are a law to themselves." The puzzling phrases "the things of the law" and "are a law to themselves" become clear in the following verse, where Paul says, "what the law requires [Gk., the work of the law] is written on their hearts." Gentiles who have the law written in their hearts are "a law to themselves." Paul could be alluding to the eschatological promise of Jeremiah 31:33, where the Lord promises a new covenant with Israel, in which he will "put my law within them . . . and write it on their hearts" (cf. Heb 8:10).

Such a reference potentially supports identifying the mysterious gentiles in Romans 2:14 as gentile believers. Nonetheless, there are good reasons to resist such an exclusive identification at this point in the letter. It would be odd for Paul to describe such gentile Christians in a distanced, third-person way when writing precisely *to* gentile believers. Are his listeners meant to recognize themselves in this discourse, and simultaneously see the second-person speeches as directed at "those other people (especially the Jews)"? If this were Paul's intention, it would run counter to all his warnings against judging others (2:1–5), not to mention his warnings against gentile arrogance toward Jews later in the letter (11:13–20). Rather, Paul accuses "you" of judging others wrongly, and exonerates "those others," implying he wants his listeners to examine themselves, not to judge others and be certain of their own righteousness.

Furthermore, the reference to *conscience* "bearing witness" is not typical of Paul's depiction of life in Christ. In 8:16 he speaks of *the Spirit* "bearing witness [*symmartyrei*] with our spirit that we are children of God." If Paul wanted to speak of gentile believers here in 2:14–16, surely he would speak of the Spirit as the divine witness (*extra nos*) operating in and among believers, not of "conscience" operating within the individual.

Finally, to assume that only gentile (or Jewish) *Christians* can do what the law requires goes against Paul's own self-description in Philippians 3:6, where Paul describes his own life prior to conversion as "blameless" with regard to "righteousness under the law." Paul certainly thinks that Jews can keep the law. Hence it seems wisest to resist identifying the law-observant gentiles in these verses specifically as gentile Christians.

Alternatively, perhaps "who are these people?" is the wrong question. Perhaps even to ask the question is to set oneself up in the position of God, who alone knows the secrets of human hearts. That is, perhaps Paul's purpose is not to categorize human beings but to destabilize all human judgment and establish God's absolute and impartial prerogative to judge. If so, then these depictions of people who do the good function to undercut any human judgment, and instead invite Paul's hearers to examine their own hearts and say, "I want to be like those obedient gentiles." (For Paul's subsequent distinction between the righteousness of God through faith and righteousness through the law, see commentary on 3:21; 9:30–10:4. For the pastoral and theological issues involved, see discussion below in the Reflections for Preaching and Teaching.)

Finally, in 2:16 Paul repeats the warning of 2:5, driving home the dominant theme of God's judgment in contrast with human judgment at the last day. In verse 5, "God's righteous judgment will be revealed [Gk., apocalypsed]"; in verse 16, "God through Christ Jesus judges the secret thoughts of all." "Secrets" (*krypta*) does not refer to parts of the person, as in a contrast between hidden motives and public actions, but rather to God's privileged perception of human hearts in contrast with the distorted and limited perceptions of human beings. Only God sees the secrets of the heart and therefore God alone judges both visible actions (vv. 6–10, 13) and what is hidden (v. 16). Taken as a whole, the passage puts a stop to human judgment, including attempts to define who is "in" and who is "out" in relationship to God.

2:17–27. Against Jewish Claims of Spiritual Superiority

In 2:17–27 Paul abruptly switches back to the second-person singular: "if you call yourself a Jew." As in 2:1, the identity of this "you" is elusive. Most scholars view the addressee as a stock stereotype of a self-righteous Jew, so that Paul attacks the use of Jewish identity as a claim to a superior religious status. Such self-importance, like the stance of the self-proclaimed "judge" in 2:1–5, supplants God's prerogative to call, elect, and judge human beings (see commentary on 9:1–18). With carefully crafted rhetoric, in 2:17–24 Paul exposes and deconstructs any such claims to superiority.

First, in 2:17b–18, Paul criticizes smug reliance on five Jewish privileges: the law, access to God, knowledge of God's will, discernment of what is excellent (perhaps better translated as "what really matters"), and instruction in the law. Then in 2:19–20, he calls out five attitudes of superiority in relationship to others: being a guide to the blind, a light to those in darkness, a corrector of the foolish, a teacher of children, and having in the law the embodiment (literally "form") of knowledge and truth. The word translated "are sure" in verse 19 is *pepoithas*, which occurs also in 2:8; here it means "you have persuaded yourself," suggesting that such self-persuasion is an example of being persuaded by unrighteousness rather than truth (2:8). Finally, in 2:21–23 Paul brings home the accusation of such self-righteousness through a series of five questions, which together echo the sense of 2:1: "You, the judge, are doing the very same things." Verse 24 caps this judgment oracle with a slightly modified quotation from Isaiah 52:5. The quotation is ironic: the addressee's claims to Jewish superiority over gentiles in fact end by dishonoring God before the gentiles.

In 2:25–27 Paul continues his controversy with "you who call yourself a Jew," but now in relationship to the topic of circumcision. Taken together, circumcision and the Mosaic law are the two primary markers distinguishing Jews from gentiles; as Paul says in 2:27, Jews have "the written code [*grammatos*] and circumcision." His point is straightforward: circumcision is no substitute for keeping the law, and indeed, transgression of the law undoes the value of circumcision. As in 2:14–15, Paul again points to gentiles (here called "uncircumcised") who keep the law. In Greek, the phrase translated "physically uncircumcised" in verse 27 is "uncircumcised by nature" (*ek physeos akrobustia*), which parallels the description of gentiles in 2:14 as "not having the law by nature" (*physei*).

2:28–29. Of the Heart, by the Spirit

After attacking all self-righteous pretensions of "you who call yourself a Jew," in 2:28–29 Paul sets forth the heart of Jewish identity, which is granted and known by God alone. These provocative verses continue the thematic antithesis between divine and human perception and judgment that threads through this section of the letter. Because they have been interpreted in ways inimical to God's calling of Israel, their translation and interpretation require particular care.

The NRSVue translates 2:28–29 as follows:

> For a person is not a Jew who is one outwardly, nor is circumcision something external and physical. Rather, a person is a Jew who is one inwardly, and circumcision is a matter of the heart, by the Spirit, not the written code. Such a person receives praise not from humans but from God.

The Greek reads:

> For the Jew is not evident [*phanerō*], and circumcision is not evident, in the flesh. But the Jew is hidden [*kryptō*], and circumcision [is] of the heart, by the Spirit, not by the written code [*grammati*]. Such a person receives praise not from human beings, but from God.

Phanerō means visible or evident. Just as in 2:16, there is no contrast between "outward" and "inner" in Paul's words, as if he were talking about different parts of a person and locating "spiritual" reality only in an "inner self." Rather, Paul is contrasting what can be perceived by human beings with what is perceptible only to God, who will judge the secrets (*krypta*) of human beings on the last day (2:16). The "spiritual" identity of the Jew depends on God through the action of the Spirit, not on what is evident to human eyes. In 9:1–18 Paul insists that Israel exists because God called it into being. Here he is saying that Jewish identity is based on God's doing, not self-praise. Paul's emphatic insistence that God alone judges in truth grounds his distinction between what is visible and what is hidden (cf. 1 Cor 4:1–5). That insistence requires Paul to reject any classification of human beings based on markers "in the flesh."

Therefore, despite frequent interpretations to the contrary, here Paul does not contrast "true" or "real" circumcision with an implied "false" circumcision; the words "true" and "false" are not in the Greek text. Rather he contrasts two different agents in the act of circumcision: the Spirit of God and the written code. His use of the same term for "written code" (*grammatos*) in verse 27 clarifies his meaning; he is speaking of the written law, which the Jewish interlocutor claims as a mark of spiritual status. Thus there is an ironic bite to Paul's claims here: uncircumcised gentiles who keep the law count as circumcised, because their circumcision is not accomplished by the written law but by the Spirit of God, who alone creates God's people.

This word pair, "Spirit" and "written code," occurs later in 7:6, where Paul opposes "the newness of the Spirit" with "the oldness of the written code." In 7:6 "Spirit" clearly refers to the Spirit of God (see also 2 Cor 3:6). Possibly Paul's experience of the movement of the Spirit among gentile believers informs his argument in Romans 2:29. Nonetheless, to impose new categories of "believers" versus "unbelievers" at this point in the letter is to miss the main thrust of Paul's argument, which aims to deconstruct human categories and perception, not create new divisions between different groups of people.

Paul caps off his discussion of Jewish identity and circumcision with a final contrast between human and divine praise (*epainos*). Two observations are important here. First, the distinction between human and divine judgment is again in view, as the echo of 2:16 makes clear. Paul develops the same theme in 1 Corinthians 4:3–5, which provides an illuminating commentary:

> But with me it is a very small thing that I should be judged by you or by any human court. I do not even judge myself. I am not aware of anything against myself, but I am not thereby acquitted. It is the Lord who judges me. Therefore do not pronounce judgment before the time, before the Lord comes, who will bring to light the things now hidden [*krypta*] in darkness and will disclose [*phanerōsei*] the purposes of the heart. Then each one will receive commendation [*epainos*] from God.

The fact that God alone can and will judge everyone subverts all human evaluations; human beings simply do not and cannot know another person's standing before God. This is the main thrust of Romans 2, and it radically dismantles human distinctions based on ethnic or religious identity. Such subversion of human judgment extends even to the presumption to "name oneself" as a Jew, because such calling and naming depends on God alone (cf. 9:6–13).

That point leads to the second observation about 2:29—its social outworking in the Christian communities in Rome. Writing to fledgling groups of believers who are experiencing a new form of community that crosses established religious and ethnic boundaries, Paul anticipates the dangers of mutual judgment and secret or overt claims of superior spiritual status. If the Roman believers are to be strengthened and encouraged in the good news of Jesus Christ, all divisive religious categories, which in practice are also social categories, must be subverted by that good news given to all without exception or entitlement. Any community that follows such a radical reconstitution of social groups certainly can expect criticism, not praise, from the surrounding culture (cf. 14:1–13).

3:1–9. A Dialogue about Jewish Privilege and the Character of God

Using a question-and-answer style, in 3:1–9 Paul names Jewish objections to his claims thus far, as he argues with an imagined conversation partner. The dialogue progresses from talking about "Jews" in the third person (3:1–4) to speaking in first-person plural (3:5–9), with a momentary shift to first-person singular (3:7). This style allows Paul to anticipate and answer objections to his preceding statements about Jewish identity. Verse 9 leads into 3:10–20 and sums up Paul's argument in the preceding verses, linking with 3:1 but also reaching back to 1:16–2:29.

A great deal is at stake in 3:1–9. Paul maintains the absolute lack of any human entitlement before God, the impartial judge before whom Jew and gentile stand equally in need of salvation, as becomes clear in 3:9b–20. But he also must maintain God's faithfulness to the Jews as the first recipients of the oracles (*logia,* or "words") of God (3:2), and the divinely called and chosen people. Thus, these verses anticipate the full discussion of Israel in chapters 9–11.

Here we note the three divine attributes at issue in God's dealings with the Jews: the faithfulness of God (3:3), the righteousness of God (v. 5), and the truthfulness of God (v. 7). These attributes reach back to the revelation of the righteousness of God through the gospel, in relationship to faith (1:16–17) and truth (1:18, 25). They also anticipate the climax of the letter in 15:7–13, especially the vindication of God's truthfulness in 15:8 (see commentary). By implication, all three interrelated attributes have no substance, no reality, apart from God. They are "of God"; they come from God, they belong to God, they are inseparable from the being of God. Yet they have been displayed in history through God's dealings with Israel, paradoxically and especially through God's dealings with unfaithful Israel. Indeed, each question poses a theoretical threat to God's attributes, through their opposite in the human interlocutor: divine faithfulness versus human faithlessness; divine truth versus human falsehood; divine righteousness versus human unrighteousness.

In the Greek of 3:2–3, variants of the word for "faith" or "trust" occur four times in two verses. Jews were entrusted (*episteuthēsan*) with God's words. The passive form of the verb points to God as the one who has entrusted Israel with revelation. Israel did not choose God; God chose Israel (cf. 9:4–5). If some fail to respond in trust, does their lack of trust (*apistia*) nullify the trustworthiness (*pistis*) of God? Here again faith connotes a bond of trust and faith toward another. Such faith involves belief in the sense of believing the truthfulness of the one in whom one trusts. It is possible that Paul has in mind Israel's lack of faith in Jesus as the Messiah, but at this point in the letter such an interpretation is not indicated in the text.

In the Septuagint, the Hebrew word for faithfulness (*emet*) frequently is translated as "truth" (e.g., Pss 25:10; 31:5; 89:1, 2, 5, 14, 24, 33, 49). Similarly, Paul moves seamlessly from God's trustworthiness to God's truthfulness, which cannot be undone by human falsehood. "Everyone is a liar" echoes Psalm 116:11, where the psalmist recalls past affliction and mental anguish; the larger context of the psalm as praise to God for deliverance from death echoes the thematic linking of divine righteousness, faithfulness, and "life" in Romans 1:17 and Habakkuk 2:4. That context underlies Paul's confident assertion of the victory of God's faithfulness and truth, despite and even through all human failures and falsehoods, including failure to be persuaded by the truth (Rom 2:8), and false claims of superiority through possessing the embodiment of truth in the law (2:20). In contrast with such falsehood, in 15:8 Paul will proclaim that God's truthfulness is demonstrated precisely through God's faithfulness to the promises to Israel.

A quotation from Psalm 51:4 in Romans 3:4 drives home the point while also introducing the theme of God's righteousness in relationship to judgment. God will "prevail"—the Greek word means "be victorious" or "triumph"—again emphasizing the theme of divine judgment in contrast with human faithlessness, falsehood, and perfidy. Psalm 51 is ascribed to David as his confession after the prophet Nathan condemned his seduction of Bathsheba (2 Sam 11–12). As such, it is the quintessential confession of human guilt before God, anticipating Romans 4:6–8. The immediate context of the quotation emphasizes the culpability of the speaker:

For I know my transgressions,
  and my sin is ever before me.
Against you, you alone, have I sinned
  and done what is evil in your sight,
so that you are justified in your sentence
  and blameless when you pass judgment.
Indeed, I was born guilty,
  a sinner when my mother conceived me.
Ps 51:3–5

Here David confesses not only an egregious deed, but a state of being "in sin" from his birth. Paul does not quote this, focusing rather on God's own justice in pronouncing judgment, but the echo of the psalm aligns with the prophetic turn of Romans 2:1 and anticipates 3:9b and 4:6–8.

Shifting to the first-person plural to speak of "our injustice" (Gk. *adikia,* also translated "unrighteousness"), in 3:5–6 the speaker asks the obvious theological question: if human injustice magnifies and displays God's justice, is it not unfair of God to judge such human failure? The question reaches all the way back to the charge of *adikia* in 1:18 and anticipates 9:14: "Is there injustice on God's part?" Like Job, Paul answers emphatically: God must judge the world.

In 3:7–8 Paul acknowledges a charge that has been leveled at his own ministry: "Let us do evil so that good may come." Here he dismisses such accusations as simply not worthy of discussion, but in 6:1–7:6 he answers them by arguing for the moral transformation of believers.

In 3:9a Paul brings this dialogue to a close with a question that rephrases 3:1: "What advantage has the Jew?" But now his answer is unclear, because the central question in 3:9a may be translated in opposite ways: "Are we any better off?" (NRSVue) or "Are we at a disadvantage?" The answer also may be translated plausibly either as "no, not at all," or "no, not in every respect." These options yield four possible translations:

Are we any better off? No, not at all!
Are we any better off? No, not in every respect.
Are we at a disadvantage? No, not at all!
Are we at a disadvantage? No, not in every respect.

The first translation is the most widespread but has two problems: First, it ascribes an active meaning to a verb that is either passive or middle in form. Although such a grammatical interpretation is possible, there are no other examples of such a translation for this verb. Second, 3:9 then blatantly contradicts 3:1–2.

The second translation avoids the problem of contradiction with 3:1–2 by acknowledging the existence of some Jewish advantages, such as being entrusted with the words of God (3:2).

The third translation reads the verb as a simple passive: rather than asking, "Do we have an advantage?" the speaker asks, "Are we *dis*advantaged?" This is a straightforward translation with no grammatical issues. The question then arises, what could put Jews at a disadvantage? One possible answer is that the very words of God with which the Jews have been entrusted (3:2) pronounce God's judgment and thereby put the Jews at a disadvantage. The citations in 3:10–17 continue this drumbeat of judgment, spoken by "the law" to those under the law (3:19). These verses too are the "oracles of God" entrusted to the Jews and pronouncing judgment on them; as Paul concludes in 3:20: "through the law comes the knowledge of sin." Thus, the questions of 3:5, 7 that attempt to exonerate human wrong by putting God in the dock are to no avail. Hence the logical question: "Having been entrusted with God's words, are we actually at a disadvantage?" The answer then is either "not at all" or "not in every respect." Given Paul's defense of Israel's divine election in chapters 9–11, the translation of the final clause as "not in every respect" seems most likely.

The disadvantage of being entrusted with God's words is that it does not exempt Jews from judgment. The advantage of Jews' possession of the words of God is that they know of God's righteousness, truthfulness, and faithfulness, and they also know their own unrighteousness, falsehood, and faithlessness. In this way, God's words ultimately point to God's mercy for the undeserving.

3:9b–20. The Whole World Is Accountable to God

Paul's claim in 3:9b sums up 1:18–3:9a and anticipates 3:10–20. Paul certainly has not proved that "all are under sin" in his preceding arguments; rather, his assertion explains and interprets the evidence he has assembled thus far, rather like a detective summing up the evidence at the end of a mystery novel. Paul's bold interpretive move centers on "sin" as a power that holds sway over all humanity. The verb, "to sin," appeared in 2:12, and the term "sinner" in 3:7, but here the noun "sin" (*hamartia*) appears for the first time. The short phrase, "under sin," frames the human situation in a distinctive way; Paul is not talking simply about individual sinners or sinful actions, but about something "over" and distinct from human beings, larger than the individual, and global in its oppressive effects (cf. 5:12–21; 7:7–25). The global scope of sin's reign is evident in the plural "all, both Jews and Greeks," referenced previously only in the singular. As a result, concerns about whether Paul is saying *every* gentile or *every* Jew commits adultery or robs temples are misguided; rather, "sin" is evident as an inescapable systemic distortion in human relationships to God and to one another. Caught up in distorted relationships, individuals do indeed do wrong. In 3:10–18, Paul calls on Israel's Scripture, primarily the psalms, to witness to this moral catastrophe.

This collection of quotations divides into two main sections. Verses 10–12 are structured by the repeated phrase "there is no one," which occurs five times. The theme is the absence of righteousness, with a corresponding cognitive decline—"there is no one who has understanding"—and turning away from God. "There is no one who shows kindness" (v. 12) sets the stage for a list of interpersonal vices in the second section (vv. 13–18), which enumerates different parts of the body in relationship to deception, toxic speech, and violence: the throat, tongue, lips, mouth, feet, and eyes. Verse 18, "There is no fear of God before their eyes," links back to verse 10, "There is no one who is righteous, not even one." The collection of scriptural texts corresponds with the vice list of 1:28–32:

3:10 no one is righteous (*dikaios*)	1:29 unrighteousness (*adikia*)
3:11 no one understands (*ho syniōn*)	1:31 foolish (*asynetous*)
3:12 no one shows kindness	1:31 heartless, ruthless
3:13–14 tongues, lips, mouths	1:29–30 gossips, slanderers
3:15 swift to shed blood	1:29 Full of murder
3:18 no fear of God before their eyes	1:32 They know God's decree, that those who practice such things deserve to die—yet they not only do them but even applaud others who practice them.

As the links with 1:28–32 show, gentiles as well as Jews know God's decree and are therefore without excuse before God; now the witness of Scripture speaks to those "under the law" so they also are without excuse (3:19). The phrase "under the law" describes those whose life is lived within the realm governed by the law of Moses—that is, the Jews. The point is not to single out Jews for particular judgment, however, but to include them along with gentiles in accountability before God. Paul's opening phrase in 3:19, "we know," includes his listeners in agreement with what he is saying. Both Jews and gentiles are indicted in the following phrase: "every mouth," indeed the mouths that are full of cursing and bitterness, will be silenced before God. This is the language of a courtroom, with all humanity in the dock. "The whole world" held accountable to God recalls the axiom that God must and will judge "the world" (3:6).

With some adaptations, in 3:20 Paul cites Psalm 143:2, which reads: "No one living is righteous before you." The NRSVue of Romans 3:20 reads, "For no human [*sarx*] will be justified before him by deeds prescribed by the law, for through the law comes the knowledge of sin." Paul adds "by works of the law" at the beginning of the sentence, giving it emphasis and picking up on the double reference to the law in 3:19, where the point is that the law holds all humanity accountable to God. The phrase "through the law comes the knowledge of sin" repeats and develops this theme. Instead of justifying human beings, the law points out their sin and makes them accountable (cf. 5:13; 7:7).

Paul's amplified quotation of Psalm 143:2 links sin and the law, and refocuses on the theme of righteousness. The word translated "justified" is the passive verbal form of righteousness or justice (*dikaiosyne*), restating the gospel as the apocalypse of God's righteousness (1:16). To emphasize this link to righteousness, the verb also can be translated as "accounted righteous," "made righteous," or "rectified." This theme of divine and human righteousness comes to the fore in 3:21–31. But the larger context of Psalm 143 prepares the way for Paul's message. Immediately before the line that Paul quotes, David pleads with God:

> Hear my prayer, O Lord;
> give ear to my supplications in your faithfulness;
> answer me in your righteousness.

> Do not enter into judgment with your servant,
> for no one living is righteous before you.
> *Ps 143:1–2*

Here the righteousness and faithfulness of God give David hope for deliverance from God's just judgment (see Rom 3:3–5) as well as deliverance from enemies: "For your name's sake, O LORD, preserve my life. In your righteousness bring me out of trouble" (Ps 143:11). This understanding of divine righteousness as God's power to save God's people intersects with Paul's opening proclamation of the gospel as the power of God for salvation, through which the righteousness of God is breaking into human history. Now it becomes clear that this history is one in which all human beings, both Jews and Greeks, are captured by sin and in need of deliverance. David witnesses to that human predicament; in Romans 4:7–8 he testifies by name to God's undeserved mercy.

EXCURSUS

Reflections for Preaching and Teaching

If Paul's gospel proclamation in Romans is intended to set his listeners' faith on a firm foundation, how might the complex and difficult proclamation of 1:18–3:20 contribute to that goal? We get some purchase on this question when we recall that at the heart of Paul's gospel is not an argument, nor a set of propositions, but the world-shattering and world-saving power of God's deliverance through Jesus Christ. That power is known through encountering the living God; such an encounter cannot help but demolish human pretensions to know the truth, whether that be the truth about God, about other people, or about oneself. The effect of such pretensions in human interaction is usually judgment directed toward others, and the judgmental impulse runs very deep in human beings. It is perhaps the most egregious display of humanity's culpable suppression of the truth (1:18) and exchange of the truth of God for a lie, worshiping and serving the creature instead of the Creator (1:25). Thus, the contrast between divine and human judgment that runs through 2:1–3:20 displays humanity's bondage to an "unfit" mind (1:28); the vice lists of 1:29–32 and 3:10–18 display the socially destructive effects of human judgment based on falsehoods.

Such an apparently negative message is exceedingly difficult to proclaim, particularly in a nonjudgmental way! Yet at its heart is still the great good news of Paul's gospel, as Paul leads his listeners on a journey of self-examination that will open them to God's grace in ever deeper ways.

A Journey of Discovery

As we have seen, Paul alternates between third-person descriptions of other people and second-person conversations with imaginary conversation partners. By allowing his listeners to "overhear" these conversations, he invites them to locate themselves in situations of judgment without directly accusing them. In the descriptive sections, he depicts different scenarios, again inviting his listeners to reflect on their own lives. Every impulse to judge another person becomes an invitation to self-examination. This invitation leads toward a renewed experience of God's "grace as a gift, through the redemption that is in Christ Jesus" (3:24); it also prepares Paul's listeners to hear Paul's exhortations to mutual welcome and positive regard later in the letter (14:1–15:13).

Paul thus provides a model for preaching that invites congregation members into recognition of their own failures and tendencies to judge, and of the need for increasingly truthful encounters with God, one another, and themselves. Such invitations can happen through the use of humor in sermons, such as self-deprecating stories about one's own judgmentalism, or through telling a story about human failure and then saying, with tongue in cheek, "Of course, that's those other people!" Wise counselors know that when we judge others most harshly, there usually is an element of projection, seeing in others something of ourselves that we would rather repress. This is the psychological insight that anger and judgmental attitudes toward other people are often bound up in guilt and repression regarding similar actions or attitudes in ourselves. Understood in this way, Paul's rhetoric gives liberating insight into the workings of human relationships. Congregational health can be elusive at best; how easily "speaking the truth in love" can become an excuse for emotional venting or even abusive speech. Surrender to God's judgment in the context of God's grace facilitates truthfulness and mutual welcome, the opposite of suppressing the truth. This is Paul's recipe for healthy fellowship in the Roman house churches.

God's Judgment and Mercy Subvert Our Social Categories

By alternating between description and direct address, Paul destabilizes his hearers. We think we know who the bad guys are and who the good ones are, and generally assume we are on the right side of that divide. In her memoir, *All My Knotted-Up Life*, teacher and evangelist Beth Moore puts this winsomely: "All my knotted-up life I've longed for the sanity and simplicity of knowing who's good and who's bad. . . . As benevolent as he has been in a myriad of ways, God has remained aloof on this uncomplicated request" (Moore 2023, 14). Paul plays on our urge to categorize people, and then pulls the rug out from under our feet. First he does this for all who set themselves up as judges ("whoever you are"), then he narrows in on Jews who claim superior status through knowledge of the law of God and the rite of circumcision. In the context of the first-century Mediterranean world, the social divides ran deep between gentiles and Jews, as well as between the educated and the "barbarians" (1:14). But here Paul deploys such distinctions only to undercut them, because he has *seen* the power of God at work among Jews and gentiles, Greeks and barbarians, and because "God is one" (3:30) and therefore Lord of all.

What a powerful and challenging message for deeply fractured societies, particularly when the Bible is used as a bludgeon against others based on race, gender, social class, or political viewpoints! How refreshing that Paul calls out toxic speech, alt-facts, hate-mongering, and smug exceptionalism! How refreshing that he does not allow anyone to hide behind a facade of religiosity of any flavor, and from behind that facade to judge and reject others! The trajectory of 1:18–3:20 torpedoes judgmental attitudes toward those who are different, such that it is a tragic misuse of the text when preachers focus on 1:26–27 in order to exclude gay people from the church. It is also a misuse of the text when a prominent Christian leader is exposed in fraud or adultery and others respond by gloating. Although this passage authorizes preaching that exposes wrongdoing, particularly when wrongdoing is done in the name of God, it also short-circuits any self-righteous judgment and certainly any self-congratulation. Rather, Paul's words invite and indeed compel an encounter with God the judge, who alone has both the inside story and the Google Earth view of human actions.

God's Witness Is Not Limited to Those inside the Church

As we have seen, Paul is frustratingly vague in identifying the mysterious folks who "by patiently doing good seek for glory and honor and immortality" (2:7, 14–15). Rather, the different viewpoints of the text subvert any certainty beyond reliance on God's sole prerogative to judge. Perhaps the truth of God is multifaceted and exceeds human understanding. And perhaps there are gentiles as well as Jews who do what the law requires but do not thereby achieve the righteousness of God. After all, insofar as God's righteousness is God's power to save not only individuals but the entire cosmos in thrall to sin and death, no individual human action can attain to it.

We may take Paul himself as a case study: in Philippians 3:6 he says of his former life that he was "blameless" in regard to righteousness in the law, yet at the same time he was persecuting the church of God. His righteousness in the law was not the same as the righteousness of God—yet it still was performance of the law. Paul's experience demonstrates that it is possible, as a Jew apart from Christ, to do the law. Here in Romans 2:6–16, where Paul wants to establish God's impartiality, he includes gentiles among those individuals who retain knowledge of God's just decree (1:32) and seek to do the good, and whose consciences alternately accuse or excuse them. They too will stand before the judgment of God, and God is the only one who can and will judge them. Paul has no trouble imagining such a judgment in line with the good news of Jesus Christ.

Does this mean that Paul envisions a kind of salvation through good works apart from Christ? Not at all. But it probably does mean that everyone will be surprised on the last day, when those whom we thought far from the fold precede us into the kingdom. Paul is very clear that the entire human race is in desperate straits, and there is no salvation of the individual apart from the salvation of the whole. Such salvation requires the vanquishing of sin and death, which God alone has accomplished through Christ. At the same time, in what may seem to us to be contradictory claims, Paul maintains both the importance of human actions and God's freedom to judge in ways that exceed human understanding: "I will have mercy on whom I have mercy, and I will have compassion on whom I have compassion" (9:15; Exod 33:19). Final judgment belongs to God alone; thanks be to God, we are freed from that burden.

If this interpretation is correct, then we can admit what we experience in daily life; not only are there devout Christians who name the name of Jesus and at the same time defame that name through their (our?) actions. There also are people of other faiths or no faith who display the sacrificial love of God. Does Paul have no place in his understanding for such folks? Or does he commit such individuals to the merciful and truthful judgment of God, while at the same time preaching that through Jesus Christ God is reclaiming the world? If so, then there is room in his theology to honor people of other faiths while maintaining the centrality of Christ.

For example, in Oran, Algeria, on December 8, 2018, the Roman Catholic Church beatified nineteen monks and nuns who were killed during the Algerian civil war of the 1990s. In an icon written for the beatification, all nineteen Christian martyrs appear in haloes. But there is also a young man without a halo, gesturing toward a mosque. This is Mohamed Bouchikhi, the twentieth martyr, who was the bishop's driver and who perished with him in a bomb attack. Explicitly as a Muslim, Mohamed is included among the martyrs of Algeria and honored by the Holy See.

Not long before his death, Mohamed wrote his testimony:

> Before I pick up my pen, I say to you: Peace be upon you. I thank you who will read my diary, and I say to each one of those whom I have known in my life that I'm thankful. They will be rewarded by God on the Last Day. Farewell. To those whom I have harmed, I ask your forgiveness. And may those who have forgiven me find pardon on the Day of Judgment. Forgive me for any time that an evil word has passed my lips, and I ask of my friends to forgive me on account of my youth. Yet, on this day on which I am writing to you, I remember the good that I have done in my life. May God, in all of his power, help me to surrender to him, and grant me his tenderness. (Stephanie Saldaña, "The Martyr in Street Clothes," *Plough Quarterly* 24 [Spring 2020]: 92–93)

As he examines his conscience and alternately accuses and excuses himself, it is easy to hear in Mohamed's words the kind of seeking and "patiently doing good" that Paul attributes to some gentiles. Paul's emphasis on God's judgment of both deeds and the secrets of the heart, over against human judgment that cannot see the heart, opens up a place of mystery and humility toward others, including those outside the faith. God's reign of justice and mercy is not confined to the boundaries of the church, and God's ultimate salvation encompasses the whole world. Surely this was good news for the small, struggling new groups of Christians in Rome; surely it is good news for us as well.

3:21–31. The Revelation of God's Righteousness through Christ, apart from the Law

Paul now restates and expands the thematic statement of the gospel in 1:16–17, thereby enclosing the revelation of the human plight in 1:18–3:20 within the larger revelation of God's saving power and righteousness in the good news of Jesus Christ. This structural observation is crucial for understanding the theology of the letter: God's wrath is a subsidiary of God's righteousness; the human situation of complicity and bondage to sin is revealed only in the context of salvation from sin; we become able to name our faults, our failures, and our wrongs on the way to being freed from them. All of this is bound up in the undeserved gift of salvation through the person and work of Jesus Christ.

3:21–26. Restatement of the Good News

"But now!" With these arresting words, in 3:21 Paul concludes his long exposé of the human plight and announces that God is doing something new, putting right what is so desperately wrong. *Now* the righteousness of God reappears on the scene with saving power, echoing 1:16–17. "But now," signifying a temporal turning point, is typical of Paul's worldview in which time is divided between the past and the new creation inaugurated by Christ (Rom 6:22; 7:6; 1 Cor 15:20). Nonetheless, in human experience, sin's dominion and the new creation in Christ overlap in the present time.

In Romans 1:17, Paul says God's righteousness is "being apocalypsed"; in 3:21 it "has been disclosed." In contrast with human attempts to become righteous through doing the works of the law, in this revelation of divine righteousness God is the one doing the action; God's righteousness does not evolve out of the status quo or human effort but breaks into history through the historical event of the gospel, independently of human accomplishments or failures. In this sense, the manifestation of God's righteousness through Christ is "apart from the law" of Moses.

"And is attested to by the Law and the Prophets." Despite being "apart from law," however, the manifestation of God's righteousness is witnessed to, or attested by, "the Law and the Prophets," which denotes Israel's Scripture as a whole in its revelatory function. Such an affirmation of Israel's sacred writings is foundational for Paul; it repeats his opening proclamation that the gospel was "promised beforehand through [God's] prophets in the holy scriptures" (1:2) and that Jesus is "descended from David" (1:3). In Romans 4, Paul calls David, Abraham, and Sarah as witnesses to God's way of rectifying the ungodly; in chapter 5 he draws on the Genesis account of Adam; in chapters 9–11 he traces the merciful logic of God's dealings with Israel and the gentiles; in chapter 15 he calls on Deuteronomy, psalms, and the prophets to testify to God's glory in the redemption of gentiles and Jews. All of this is the witness of "the Law and the Prophets" to God's righteousness in 3:21.

"Through the faith of Jesus Christ for all who believe" (3:22a). Amplifying 1:16–17, where God's righteousness is apocalypsed in the gospel, Paul now explicitly names the content of the gospel in terms of Christ's faithfulness and human faith. As footnoted in the NRSVue, this verse may also be translated "through faith in Jesus Christ, for all who believe." These different translations acknowledge the varied meanings of the noun *pistis*, which can signify faith, trust, trustworthiness, reliance upon, belief, and allegiance. The verb can mean believe, trust, and have faith. *Pistis* is a relational term, denoting the characteristics of a bond of trust, much more than a simple cognitive term indicating mental assent to a set of propositions. Thus we might translate 3:22 as "through the trustworthiness of Jesus Christ for all who trust."

The translation options in the NRSVue footnote seem to point to an either-or: either Christ is the subject of faith, the one who trusts and is trustworthy, thereby enacting the righteousness of God, *or* Christ is the object of human trust, and the righteousness of God is enacted through human trust in Christ. On the one hand, the first option is preferable both exegetically and theologically. First, if the first clause speaks of human faith in Christ, the second clause is simply repetitive. But if the first clause speaks of Jesus's trustworthiness as demonstrated by his faithful obedience, then that trustworthiness generates and inspires a reciprocal trust on the part of human beings. In this way, this claim further explains the earlier enigmatic "from faith to faith" in 1:17. Furthermore, in 4:12, 16, Paul uses the same grammatical construction to refer to the "faith of Abraham"; it would be nonsensical to translate this as faith or belief or trust in Abraham.

But further nuance is needed, for it is doubtful whether Paul or his Roman audience distinguished between the trustworthiness of Jesus and believers' trust in Jesus. In 3:22 both Christ's trustworthiness and human trust are in view. To contrast Jesus's faith with human faith is to miss the thoroughly relational character of trust, as well as to minimize the reality of the incarnation. To put it simply, Paul sees faith as expressing and arising out of union with Christ, who faithfully shared our human condition and destiny, thereby conquering sin and death. God's righteousness, God's power to save, is breaking into the world through Christ's faithful incarnation, death, and resurrection, and catalyzing human faith in response. We might say that *pistis* denotes a realm or network of saving relations, grounded in the faithful character of God. Christ is the center of this network, exhibiting both trust toward God and trustworthiness toward human beings, and thereby also trusted by human beings. Crucially then, faith never stands on its own, as a generic human attribute or attitude toward God; it always derives from and leads back to Christ. It is not human faith that sets human beings right with God; it is God's faithfulness acting through Christ's faithful death and resurrection that accomplishes redemption. Human trust in response to God's gracious initiative brings the experience and reality of redemption home to us.

The following verses (3:22b–23) summarize the theme of 1:18–3:20. The inclusive "all have sinned" mirrors the inclusive "all who believe" in 3:22a; divine righteousness is for "all who believe" because "all have sinned" and therefore lack God's glory. The believers *are* the sinners; those who are made right through Christ *are* those who have sinned, and the repeated "all" includes all humanity in this promise of redemption. Paul's reference to divine glory echoes 1:23 and, as there, refers solely to God's glory, not to an innate human glory (cf. 4:20; 15:6–9). To say that in the wake of its primal refusal to worship God humanity lacks "glory" is to say that human beings have become disconnected from the purpose for which they were created and in which they find their very being—glorifying God.

The form of the verb "have sinned" implies a distinct action in the past, not a continuing present action. To understand this, it is necessary to think in line with Paul's logic of solidarity. He is not talking about individual sins committed at some point in each person's early life, nor about original sin as a kind of stain infecting each person's character. Rather, looking forward to 5:12–17, he envisions all Adam's heirs participating in Adam's sin: "sin came into the world through one man [Adam], and death came through sin, and so death spread to all so that all sinned" (5:12, author's translation; see commentary).

This is the fourth occurrence of "sin" and its cognates in the letter. The verb first appears twice in 2:12; "sinner" briefly describes a human individual under God's judgment (3:7); "sin" as a noun appears in 3:9 as something that has power "over" all humanity; now the verb reappears with all human beings as the subject: "all sinned." Hereafter the verb "to sin" occurs only once (5:12), again with the inclusive "all"—"all sinned." Similarly, the word translated "sinner" in 3:7 appears only once more, in Romans 7:13, but this time as a descriptor of sin itself, not human beings: through the commandment, sin itself became surpassingly "sinful" (see commentary). "Sin" as a noun, however, dominates Romans 3:9–8:10, appearing no fewer than forty-six times. Sometimes it refers to human sinful actions (3:25), but more often it denotes sin as an independent, personified actor. After chapter 8, "sin" drops almost completely out of the picture in the rest of the letter, reappearing only at 11:27 and 14:23.

In this dense statement of the good news, three terms in 3:24 stand out: "justified," "grace as a gift," and "redemption." The verb translated here as "justified" is the verbal form of the word "righteousness," thus tightly linking this verse with the manifestation of "the righteousness of God" in 3:21–22. Its basic meaning is "to be made right, or righteous," leading to an alternative translation of "rectified." When understood in a legal sense, to be justified has been interpreted as a right standing with God ("to be put in the right" or "accounted righteous"), and Paul does speak in Romans 8:1 of deliverance from condemnation in a legal sense. "To be justified" has a more dynamic meaning as well—to be set right, made righteous, rectified, changed. The verb appears more frequently in Romans 3 than anywhere else in Paul's letters, from the justification or vindication of God (3:4), to the certainty that no flesh will be justified before God by works of the law (3:20), to the affirmation that God justifies human sinners freely, by grace, through the redemption accomplished by Christ. Paul repeats the promise of justification in 3:26, 28, and 30 (cf. also 4:5; 5:1, 9; 6:7; 8:30), linking it with God's own righteousness and with faith (3:21–22, 25–26).

"Grace" (*charis*) means "gift," and Paul piles on the language of "gift" here: God puts human beings right "by his grace as a gift." We owe the centrality of grace in Christian theology and experience to Paul, who appropriates the common Roman practice of gift and benefaction to describe how Christ's self-giving transforms human beings. The language of grace or gift is also part of a widespread and diverse constellation of writings in Second Temple Judaism about God's abundance, generosity, power, and initiative in the creation of the world and the history of Israel. Paul appropriates this language in his preaching to gentiles but gives it a distinctive twist; in both pagan and Jewish writings, human and divine beneficence is for those who are worthy of receiving a gift and likely to reciprocate appropriately. But in Romans 3:24, the first theological explication of *charis* in the letter, Paul highlights his distinctive and shocking understanding of grace—it is given to sinners, to those who are unworthy and undeserving, who are "bad bets" in every way. This gift is a relationship with God characterized by God's righteousness (3:21–22a), given without distinction to those who have sinned and lack God's glory (vv. 22b–23), "through the redemption that is in Christ Jesus" (v. 24).

"Redemption" (*apolytrōsis*) is related to the verb *lutroō*, to redeem or set free. It signifies liberation from a state of bondage; for example, in 8:23 it answers the yearning of all creation for deliverance from "enslavement to decay." The motif of liberation from slavery recalls the situation of all humanity "under the power of sin" (3:9). This sense of "justification" in terms of liberation expands its meaning beyond that of legal acquittal, as it expresses God's righteousness as God's power to save, freeing God's people from oppression by hostile powers. In the Septuagint *lutroō* refers to God's rescue of Israel from Egypt (Deut 7:8) and from captivity in Babylon (Isa 43:1), as well as to God's protection of individuals (Ps 31:5). Redemption also can be linked with the forgiveness of sin, in the sense of deliverance from the captivity resulting from Israel's sin: "I have swept away your transgressions like a cloud, and your sins like mist; return to me, for I have redeemed you" (Isa 44:22). By speaking of the effect of Christ's death in terms of redemption from bondage, Paul reprises

Romans 1:24, 26, 28 as well as 3:9— humanity has been "handed over" by God into the custody of forces inimical to human flourishing. Liberation from those forces comes "in Christ Jesus," indeed through his sacrificial death, as the next verses show.

The word translated "a sacrifice of atonement" (*hilastērion*) in 3:25 refers to the cover over the ark of the covenant (Exod 25:17), which was to be made of pure gold, with a golden cherub at each end. Moses is instructed further: "The cherubim shall spread out their wings above, overshadowing the cover with their wings. They shall face one to another: the faces of the cherubim shall be turned toward the cover. You shall put the cover on the top of the ark, and in the ark you shall put the covenant that I am giving you. There I will meet with you, and from above the cover, from between the two cherubim that are on the ark of the covenant, I will tell you all that I am commanding you for the Israelites" (Exod 25:20–22). Thus the covering of the ark of the covenant was the holiest place in Israel, the place where God met with the people "between the cherubim." According to Leviticus 16:14–16, on the Day of Atonement the high priest was to sprinkle the cover over the ark with the blood of animals sacrificed as a sin offering for the people.

The NRSVue translation, "sacrifice of atonement," reflects this liturgical rite over the cover of the ark, perhaps also influenced by the only other occurrence of *hilastērion* in the New Testament (Heb 9:5). Hebrews 9:1–10 gives a detailed description of the Holy of Holies in the wilderness and the annual ritual of atonement; 9:11–14 depicts Jesus as the high priest of the new covenant, who enters the heavenly Holy of Holies with his own blood as the eternally effective offering for sin. But Hebrews was written much later than Romans, and while it is possible that Hebrews 9:11–14 reflects an earlier creedal statement about Jesus's death, Paul gives it his own distinctive interpretation.

"By his blood" points to the brutal crucifixion of Jesus as God's way of dealing with sin. It is difficult to grasp the shock of this picture: in the inner sanctum of holiness, a tortured and unclean criminal opens the way to God. Later in Romans and elsewhere in his letters, Paul further describes how Christ's death reconciled humanity to God, through Christ's full participation in the human situation of dereliction and death, and the defeat of death in the resurrection (Rom 4:25; 5:6–11; 8:3; cf. 2 Cor 5:19–21). In these later references to the death of Jesus, as here, the cross is not propitiation offered to a vengeful God; rather it overcomes human enmity toward God. Christ's death vanquishes the death-dealing power of sin and liberates humanity from sin's bondage.

Some translations take the short phrase "through faith" as related to "by his blood," so that believers' faith in the blood of Jesus—that is, in Christ's sacrificial death on humanity's behalf—is the way in which redemption is accessed by human beings. But the NRSVue translation gets at the meaning better; "effective through faith" stands alone, in antithesis to works of the law (Rom 3:20–21), as the way in which redemption takes effect in human lives. The subject of "faith" here remains ambiguous and therefore inclusive, in line with the interplay between Christ's faithfulness unto death and human trust in God (3:22).

In the Greek, "to demonstrate his righteousness" occurs in 3:25b and 26a, setting up two parallel claims: Christ's liberating death demonstrated God's righteousness both by dealing with sin and by establishing God's own righteousness, which sets right those who share in the faith of Jesus. In human terms, righteousness usually means the guilty pay the penalty for their sins and the innocent are vindicated. But God's righteousness is something quite different, demonstrated by God's forgiveness of sins and the rectification of sinners (vv. 23–24).

This counterintuitive vindication and public display of God's righteousness—through Christ, apart from the law (v. 21)—completes the vindication of God in 3:4. God's righteousness, God's integrity and power, are not displayed to the world through the good works of those who keep God's holy law, but through the horrific execution of Jesus with and for those with no claims to moral worth—which is to say, with and for all humanity, because "all have sinned." Paul rings the changes on this assertion throughout the next few chapters (4:4; 5:6–10, 15–21; 8:1–4). No wonder Paul's gospel seems to assault basic moral principles; if this is what God's righteousness looks like, the culturally constructed social cosmos is turned upside down.

The phrase "has the faith of Jesus" might appear to suggest that God justifies those who imitate the trustworthiness of Jesus, such that their faith becomes a prerequisite for God's gift of righteousness. As earlier, the relational sense of *pistis* is crucial: Paul speaks of those who live within the domain of Christ's faithful, obedient self-giving, which also demonstrates God's trustworthiness toward human beings, in a reciprocal divine-human interchange of trust and trustworthiness. God's powerful rectification of human sinners happens precisely in this regime of grace, God's free gift of righteousness, where grace exercises dominion (cf. 5:17, 21; 6:14).

3:27–31. The Unity of God and the Law of Faith

Before moving on in the letter, Paul reprises the situation of Jew and gentile before God in light of righteousness through Christ-faith. Boasting is excluded (2:17, 23), not by the law of works, by which no one will be justified by God (3:20), but by the "law of faith" (3:27). What is this law of faith? In Paul's brief restatement of 3:21–22, it is the gift of being made righteous through faith, apart from works of law (3:28). In other words, in the context of God's trustworthiness, the law is not the means of righteousness, but the witness to God's righteousness apart from the law.

Continuing the theme of divine impartiality (2:11; 3:22b), in 3:29–31 Paul pulls out the final proof of his argument for justification for both Jew and gentile on the basis of faith: "God is one." This is the basic affirmation of Jewish belief, the Shema: "Hear [Heb. *shema*], O Israel: The Lord our God, the Lord is one" (Deut 6:4). The unity of God means God is Lord of all humanity, gentiles as well as Jews, and will justify all on the same basis of faith. Furthermore, because the fundamental revelation of the Mosaic law is the unity and sovereignty of God, which must mean that God is the God of gentiles as well as Jews, Paul concludes, "we uphold the law." This is a tour de force. Rather than creating a dividing line between gentiles and Jews, the law unites them under the one God. This unity is possible, however, not through divisive works of the law, but through the law's witness to God's saving power and righteousness in and through Christ. As Paul shows in Romans 4, the stories of Israel's Scripture also witness to the persistence of sin, the centrality of faith, and the power of grace. Ironically, the divine righteousness manifested apart from the law brings Paul more deeply into the unity and omnipotence of God—as revealed in Israel's sacred writings. Thus, Paul's joyful witness to God's work among his gentile converts catalyzes a robust affirmation of his Jewish faith.

EXCURSUS

Reflections for Preaching and Teaching

Living in the Tension between Judgment and Grace

In the structure of Romans 1:16–3:31, God's gift of salvation through Christ, apart from works of the law, brackets and reframes (but does not negate) God's judgment of human beings according to works (2:6–16). There is an undeniable tension between the claim that God judges according to works and the promise that salvation is a gift for sinners without regard to their worth or achievements. Paul does not resolve the tension, and his refusal to do so has both theological and pastoral consequences. Theologically Paul cannot proclaim a God who is indifferent to human suffering and wrongdoing; in the unjust world in which we live, how could such a God be either righteous or trustworthy? On the other hand, Paul cannot deny the free gift of Christ's lavish self-giving with complete disregard for the worth of human recipients.

The pastoral effect of living in this tension between divine judgment and grace is profound. Paul leads his listeners, including today's readers, into deeper self-knowledge in the context of an unbreakable relationship with God through Christ. Surrender to God's judgment, trust in God's justice, and reliance on God's grace together form the foundation of Christian hope and the power for transformation. But the first and last word is always God's unstoppable grace; nothing we can do will make God stop loving us. Judgment makes truthful self-disclosure necessary; grace makes it possible. When preachers know themselves to be the recipients of such undeserved divine self-giving as the ground of their vocation, they discover a robust freedom in ministry (cf. 1 Cor 4:3–4); because they can fail, they need not prove themselves, they need not focus on defending their integrity or making sure they are in the right. The same is true for all believers. It is not the clergy's job to get church people to do things, and certainly not to change them; it is their job to proclaim the gift and power of God. As that good news gets down into people's bones, they begin to change in ways we could never imagine or engineer.

God's Trustworthiness and Human Trust in God

Understanding "faith" as in the first instance a reference to God's faithfulness puts the focus on God, not the believer. It turns our attention away from an inward anxiety about whether or not we have enough faith, and toward God's loving power and mercy. This shift in focus can be liberating for Christians raised in an atmosphere demanding certainty in belief or a particular emotional experience of faith.

The difference is illustrated beautifully by an image from Hilda Prescott's masterpiece, *The Man on a Donkey*, which takes place in Reformation England. One notable character is a morally tortured priest named Gib Dawe, who intellectually believes in God's grace but is unable to accept it for himself. Prescott describes him as he takes to the road, in despair about his own salvation:

> Never could he, a leaking bucket not to be mended, retain God's saving grace, however freely outpoured. Never could he, that heavy lump of sin, do any other than sink, and sink again, however often Christ, walking on the waves, should stretch his hand to lift and bring him safe.
>
> He did not know that though the bucket be leaky it matters not at all when it is deep in the deep sea, and the water both without it and within. He did not know, because he was too proud to know, that a man must endure to sink, and sink again, but always crying upon God, never for shame ceasing to cry, until the day when he shall find himself lifted by the bland swell of that power, inward, secret, as little to be known as to be doubted, the power of omnipotent grace in tranquil, irresistible operation. (Prescott 2008, 2:543–44)

Radical Change and Radical Continuity

In one sentence, Paul announces the dramatic advent of salvation through Christ apart from the law, and yet claims it has been attested by the Law and the Prophets (3:21). Here in a nutshell is one of the theological and experiential paradoxes of Christian faith and life. On the one hand, God in Christ breaks into the disaster of human history and private lives, including the calamities of dysfunctional families and destitute churches and neighborhoods, and makes things new. God is not bound by the past; God's love and power come from beyond all human imagining. There is no determinism in God's way of working in the world, so there can be no preset limits on what God may do in any situation. "But now" invites us to bold visions for the future.

On the other hand, such radical newness does not abandon the past, as if God has not always been present and active in human affairs.

Rather, it forges a new connection to the past, as the full significance of Israel's Scripture is disclosed in Christ. Analogously, the full significance of individual and collective stories gains clarity retrospectively, in the light of the undeserved grace and power of God. In the life of a congregation, such retrospective clarity might mean that the grace of God in Christ creates room for exploring and confessing past wrongs. It might mean that treasured stories and traditions in the church cannot limit visions for the future, but they can ground and enrich them with remembrances of God's gracious provision in earlier times. Rediscovering our need of God's grace teaches us to narrate our past as a story of God's mercy for sinners, not an honor roll of distinguished luminaries. In this way, God acknowledges and sanctifies each and every origin story, in all its complexity and uniqueness, and draws each story into the final purposes of redemption through Christ.

Examples of such continuity and change are as varied as human communities. For example, in a historic church in the American South, a deep dive into the history of slavery associated with the church creates new opportunities for self-examination and repentance, along with new awareness and celebration of the resilient faith of African American individuals who also are part of that church's history. Such experiences of discovery, repentance, and renewed faith will be different for each community, family, and individual. For Paul himself, his encounter with Jesus Christ deepened and radically expanded his understanding of his own Jewish roots.

4:1–25. Abraham, Sarah, and David Witness to the Gospel of Grace

In Romans 4 Paul recalls the stories of Abraham, Sarah, and David to illustrate his paradoxical claim that the Law and the Prophets witness to God's righteousness apart from the law. Abraham and Sarah are key figures for Paul because Abraham received the promise of offspring and land prior to both circumcision and the giving of the law, and Sarah bore Isaac miraculously through God's promise. David exemplifies the repentant sinner who receives undeserved forgiveness. Together Abraham, Sarah, and David testify to God's prior, gracious initiative for the undeserving. The theme of faith, understood as both trust and trustworthiness, runs through the entire chapter (4:3, 5, 9, 12, 13, 14, 16, 17, 18, 19, 20, 24), contrasted with works (vv. 2, 4–6) and aligned with God's grace and promise (vv. 4, 13–14, 16, 20).

4:1–5. Abraham, Father of the Ungodly

Paul begins with a transitional question: "What then shall we say?" (cf. 3:5; 6:1; 7:7; 8:31; 9:30). The verb translated "gained" by the NRSVue is literally "to have found" (*heurēkenai*), so an apt translation would be, "What then shall we say that Abraham, our forefather according to the flesh, has found?" "*Our* forefather Abraham" names Abraham as father of both Jews and gentiles, as Paul says explicitly in 4:16–17. As in relationship to David (1:3), "according to the flesh" carries with it the connection between "flesh" (*sarx*) and sin; Paul's listeners will have 3:20 in their mind, where Paul claims, "No human [*sarx*] will be justified before God by deeds prescribed by the law." That is, Abraham as "our forefather according to the flesh" is Abraham in the realm of sin, subject to sin. This is precisely how Abraham is portrayed in the following verses.

What has this fleshly Abraham "found"? The implied answer in 4:2 is that he cannot have found or gained righteousness through his own works, since God's righteousness is given as a gift apart from the law (3:21). Continuing his criticism of boasting based on works (3:27), Paul removes Abraham from any possible grounds for boasting before God. Rather, Abraham "according to the flesh," Abraham the sinner, has discovered trust in the God who justifies the ungodly as the only basis for standing before God. Paul quotes Genesis 15:6 to make the point: "Abraham believed God, and it was reckoned to him as righteousness" (cf. Gal 3:6–9).

Once again, the foundation of Paul's startling claim is Scripture itself. Paul's reading of Genesis 15:6 goes against the grain of his fellow Jewish interpreters; in much Second Temple Jewish literature Abraham is depicted as a hero of faith precisely *through* his obedience to the law. Strikingly, 1 Maccabees 2:50–52 references Genesis 15:6 to portray Abraham as the first example of zeal for the law: "Was not Abraham found faithful when tested, and it was reckoned to him as righteousness?" Similarly, Sirach 44:20 says Abraham "kept the law of the Most High and entered into a covenant with him; he certified the covenant in his flesh" (a reference to circumcision). Indeed, Abraham's descendants will include "a godly man" (Sir

44:23 NRSV), presumably because Abraham is numbered among the "godly" whom Sirach praises (Sir 44:10 NRSV; cf. Jub. 21:1–3). In shocking contrast with such praise of Abraham, Paul names him as Exhibit A of the "ungodly." The echo of Romans 1:18 is unmistakable; Abraham joins company with the primal "ungodliness" of the first human beings in their refusal to glorify God.

The word translated "reckoned" (vv. 3, 5, 8) is an accounting term for the "crediting" of something to a person's account or for tallying up sums. Paul takes it from Genesis 15:6 in reference to Abraham, and from Psalm 32:1–2, attributed to David. Over against any interpretation saying that Abraham's own obedience or faithfulness were "credited" to his moral account, Paul insists that such "credit" can only be a divine gift. Setting up opposing columns, he aligns faithfulness with divine gift and righteousness, over against works, wages, and boasting. When works result in wages earned, they put human beings on a transactional footing with God, as if God could owe human beings anything (Rom 4:4; cf. 11:35). Not incidentally, a righteousness reckoned by the achievements of individuals excludes the ungodly, whereas the free gift of righteousness allows Paul to proclaim the radical inclusivity of God's redemption through Christ.

4:6–8. David, Forgiven Sinner

If Abraham is Exhibit A of the "ungodly," David is Exhibit B. The citation of psalms attributed to David threads through Romans 2–3, creating a subliminal story line that traces David's journey from self-righteousness to reliance on divine grace. In 2:6 Paul quotes Psalm 62:12, in which David relies on God's mercy precisely because he is confident God will judge his enemies for *their* wrongdoing. In Romans 3:4 Paul quotes from Psalm 51:4, David's confession of guilt after seducing Bathsheba. Paul follows up in Romans 3:20 with a quotation from Psalm 143:2b; the statement immediately follows David's plea for God *not* to judge God's servant (David himself). David has moved from the stance of the righteous one who wants God to judge others, to the sinner who pleads for mercy. Finally, in Romans 4:6–8 Paul quotes David by name, testifying to the blessing David himself has received—the blessing of being reckoned righteous precisely when he does *not* deserve it. The crucial citation is from Psalm 32:1–2. Like Abraham, David points to God's rectification of the ungodly. Through citing the psalms, Paul invites his readers to share in David's movement from self-righteousness to deepening reliance on God's grace for the unworthy.

This is the second mention of David in the letter. In 1:3 Paul names him as the fleshly progenitor of Jesus, in line with the expectation that the Messiah would be the Son of David (cf. Matt 21:9; 22:41–45). One would expect Paul to highlight David's kingship; instead, he highlights David's repentance. Shockingly, Jesus is descended from an adulterer and a murderer, in solidarity with sinners.

4:9–12. Abraham, Father of All Who Trust

Returning to the example of Abraham, Paul links the logic of the undeserved gift with the inclusivity and global reach of God's blessing. Perhaps drawing on his experience in Galatia, where other Jewish Christian missionaries were telling Paul's gentile converts that they needed to be circumcised, Paul bases his teaching on the order of events in Genesis: Abraham received the blessing of being reckoned righteous (Gen 15:6) *prior* to being circumcised (17:10). Therefore, one can be accounted righteous by God without being circumcised; therefore, uncircumcised believing gentiles may be included with believing Jews as heirs of Abraham (cf. Gal 3:6–29).

This timeline grounds Paul's claim that Abraham's circumcision was not a *condition* of being righteous but a sign of a gift already given and received—the gift of righteousness received through trust in God. In Paul's words, the "sign of circumcision" is a seal of righteousness by faith. The word translated "seal" signifies a stamp or mark certifying the veracity of legal documents, just as the word "seal" is used today. Thus, Paul describes circumcision as a sign marking the righteousness of faith as "signed, sealed, and delivered," *not* as a marker determining insiders and outsiders in the community of faith. By emphasizing the priority of faith, Paul is keen to undermine divisions between Jew and gentile created by the requirement of circumcision. Paul is not opposed to circumcision per se, nor indeed to any works of the law; he is opposed to the misuse of works when they become reasons for boasting, divisions between Jews and gentiles, or prerequisites for encountering God. Once again, Paul's emphasis is on *all:* Abraham is father of *all who believe,* whether circumcised or not.

4:13–17a. The Promise Precedes the Law

The theme of Abraham's inclusive paternity continues, but now in relationship to God's promise of progeny (Gen 15:4–5; 17:4–6). The verb "to promise beforehand" occurs in 1:2 with reference to the gospel; in 4:13 the noun "promise" occurs for the first time in the letter. As in Galatians 3:15–29, Paul contrasts God's singular promise to Abraham with the later appearance of the Mosaic law. God made many promises to Abraham and Sarah, including that they would have an infinite number of descendants (Gen 13:16; 15:5; 17:2, 6; 18:18; 22:17) and that these descendants would inherit the land of Canaan (12:7; 13:14–15, 17; 17:8) and bless "all the nations of the earth" (12:2; 18:18; 22:18). In these promises, Abraham's inheritance centers in the exclusive identity of his offspring; later Paul will mention "the promises" (Rom 9:4) that belong to his Jewish kinsfolk. But here, in line with the global scope of God's calling of Abraham, he condenses all the promises into one astonishing claim: Abraham's heirs will "inherit the world." The world (*kosmos*) includes both the social order of all human beings and the entire natural world. In 1 Corinthians 3:21–23 Paul states a similar claim in present terms, as he tells the Corinthians that everything belongs to them because they belong to Christ: "For all things are yours, whether Paul or Apollos or Cephas or the world or life or death or the present or the future—all are yours, and you are Christ's, and Christ is God's." We note how such a stunning and radically inclusive inheritance is bound up with the mutual belonging of God, Christ, and those who belong to Christ. In the present, such an inclusive possession is hidden under paradoxical dispossession and suffering: "as having nothing and yet possessing everything" (2 Cor 6:10).

If this inheritance were only for "the adherents of the law" (Rom 4:14), it would exclude uncircumcised gentiles; because it is through the "righteousness of faith" and rests on grace, it includes all who share Abraham's trust in God (v. 16). Indeed, the law accomplishes wrath because it creates the category of "transgressions"—that is, it draws a line in the sand that marks out actions that cross that line (v. 15). This is why Paul can say in 5:13, "Sin was indeed in the world before the law, but sin is not reckoned when there is no law."

Paul continues to drive home his point in 4:16–17a—the promise given to Abraham depends on grace, the sheer gift of God, and therefore is received by trusting in God, not by accomplishing the deeds of the law. Once again, faith is elicited and sustained by God's initiating call and encompassing grace. Abraham's identity as "the father of all of us" (v. 16) fulfills the promise of Genesis 17:5, "I have made you the ancestor of a multitude of nations [*ethnōn*, gentiles]," which Paul repeats in Romans 4:17a. It is Paul's *experience* of gentile conversions to Christ that generates his understanding of *how* God is fulfilling God's promise to Abraham, through Christ. At the same time, Paul continues to include his Jewish kinsfolk, both those who believe in Christ and those who do not, within God's purposes. In 4:16 "the adherents of the law" denotes law-observant Jews; "those who share the faith of Abraham" includes both gentiles and Jews who trust in God's faithfulness through Christ.

4:17b–25. Trusting the God Who Gives Life to the Dead

In 4:17b–18 Paul interrupts the narrative of promise to emphasize its source in the presence of the God of life. Just as Moses prayed in God's presence (Exod 32:11), Abraham's faith is a response to the divine presence and is upheld by it. The God in whom Abraham trusts is the One "who gives life to the dead." Paul's affirmation about God surely refers to God's identity as the one "who raised Jesus our Lord from the dead" (Rom 4:24; cf. 8:11), but it also affirms a widespread Hellenistic Jewish belief. The Pharisees affirmed the doctrine of the resurrection of the dead, and by the second century CE many Jews prayed daily the Eighteen Benedictions, including, "Blessed be you, Lord, who gives life to the dead" (cf. Wis 16:13; Dan 12:2; 2 Macc 7:23).

The next clause emphasizes God's all-creative power: "and calls into existence the things that do not exist." Again, Paul's words would be familiar to his Jewish contemporaries, sharing with them the bedrock belief in God's creation of everything through the word. For example, God is "the one who from the beginning of the world called that which does not exist" (2 Bar. 21:4); "with the word you bring to life that which does not exist" (2 Bar. 48:8). This unique creative power stands behind the promise of progeny to Abraham and Sarah; Romans 4:18–19 emphasizes the human impossibility of that promise.

Paul's unusual expression in 4:18, "hoping against hope," can also be translated "beyond hope in hope" or "contrary to hope, on the basis of hope." Abraham and Sarah's desire for a child is truly beyond hope, indeed beyond human imagination, due to their great age and Sarah's barrenness. From a human standpoint, the divine promise could only be considered laughable by Abraham (Gen 17:17) and Sarah (18:12). In Romans 4:18, Abraham's aged body is "as good as dead," as is Sarah's womb (the word translated "barrenness" by the NRSVue is *nekrōsin,* "deadness"). Paul's repeated emphasis on death highlights God's power as the one who raises the dead, setting the stage for 4:24–25. But it also evokes the ancient trope of the barren mother, the miraculous women who play a central role in Israel's history. Sarah was the first but not the last such barren mother; she was followed by Rebekah (Gen 25:21), Rachel (Gen 29:31; 30:22–23), Samson's mother (Judg 13), Hannah (1 Sam 1), and last but not least the "mother city" Jerusalem, who miraculously becomes the mother of children (Isa 54:1; cf. Gal 4:26–28). Throughout Scripture, this maternal image portrays Israel's genesis and continued sustenance as derived solely and surely from God's miraculous power calling Israel into being (cf. Rom 9:6–10).

In contrast to being weak in faith (4:19), Abraham "grew strong" in faith (vv. 20–22). The word translated "grew strong" is a passive verb related to Paul's theme of the gospel as the "power [*dynamis*] of God" (1:16); Abraham "was empowered" (*enedynamōthē*). Again, the passive verb implies God is the one doing the action; thus "Abraham was empowered by God in faith." This theme of empowerment also continues Paul's stated goal of strengthening his listeners' faith (1:11; 16:25). Such empowerment accompanies Abraham's glorification of God, in contrast with humanity's refusal to glorify God (1:21).

Paul here presents Abraham as a model of faith that is reckoned as righteousness (4:3; Gen 15:6). The earlier citation crucially sets the context for its appearance here; Abraham's faith is not some heroic effort on his part. Rather, as one who has no prior claim on God, who indeed is "ungodly" in himself (Rom 4:5), Abraham trusts God despite his own moral and spiritual poverty, hoping beyond hope that God will keep God's promise. This relationship of trust happens in the life-giving and empowering presence of God.

Finally, in 4:23–25, Paul brings the focus back to the Roman believers hearing his letter, and to readers today: the words of Genesis 15:6 are not just for Abraham, but also for us, precisely as a source of hope (Rom 15:4). Paul can write his gentile readers into Abraham's story because he reads Abraham's story in relationship to "Jesus our

Lord" (4:24). Abraham trusted in God who brought life out of death by bringing a son from his and Sarah's "dead" bodies; believers trust in God who raised Jesus our Lord from the dead. God's identity and action in raising Jesus from the dead is the bedrock of Paul's preaching (8:11; cf. Acts 3:15; 4:10; 13:30). Thus God, not Christ, is the object of faith here; Christ is the recipient of God's action in two ways: as "handed over to death" and as "raised" (Rom 4:25).

In 1:24, 26, 28 Paul uses the same verb translated "handed over" to say that God "handed over" idolatrous humanity into destructive powers; now he says God "handed over" Jesus to the power of death (cf. 8:32). Handed over to the power of sin and death, Jesus stands with the sinners, sharing the judgment meted out on humanity; in this way his "handing over to death" is "for our trespasses." The passive verb in the following clause, "and was raised for our justification," again points to God's action (Phil 2:9). Here the divine act of resurrection bestows righteousness on human beings, setting the stage for the connections between the gift of righteousness, life, and victory over sin and death in chapters 5–8.

EXCURSUS

Reflections for Preaching and Teaching

Jesus, Friend of Sinners

The justification of the ungodly is the most radically inclusive theological claim possible, because it erases any line between the "righteous" and "unrighteous" and thus between insiders and outsiders. Inclusion is not the same thing as tolerance or easy affirmations or an "everything goes" culture. Neither is it a political point of view masquerading as faith and inevitably excluding those who think differently. Inclusion begins with the recognition that we all are ungodly, and all are beloved. It is a deceptively low bar. It means that the basis on which Christians are to meet each other is God's gracious gift extended to all, regardless of their politics, their race, or their economic status. This is a challenging word for both conservative and liberal churches. Paul's polemic is in line with Jesus's insistence on hanging out with the unclean, the socially marginalized, the public sinners. What does this look like today in the specific context of each local church?

No More Nagging

Like the teachings of Jesus, Paul's gospel is for the have-nots, not for the haves; knowing our own poverty, we share from the abundance of grace freely given to us in Christ. This makes a tremendous difference in preaching, which must deconstruct human pretensions to self-sufficiency while also affirming God's complete sufficiency. It means, in practice, an end to nagging from the pulpit, and an invitation to acknowledge our desperate need of God. Such acknowledgment may be invited in other ways also, ranging from prayers for healing during Sunday worship or midweek services, to small prayer groups, to pastoral counseling, to various aspects of church life. Thus, for example, stewardship is not about offering our riches to God as a favor, but rather recognizing that all that we have—and are—is gifted by God. Vocation is not about offering our strengths and achievements to God, but about bringing our emptiness to God and seeing what God will make of us, just as God acted through Sarah's barrenness and David's abject sin (4:6–8, 19–21). All the activities of the community of faith thus become places where people experience God's unmerited grace on ever deeper levels and in new areas of their lives.

Similarly, preaching and teaching participate in a gracious interplay between teaching about the revelation of God in Christ and experiencing that revelation personally. This is the kind of teaching Paul models as he circles back over the same basic gospel message from different angles and in relationship to different questions. In fact, all his letters aim at the intersection between experience and the gospel message, in very diverse settings but with the consistent goal of grounding his listeners in the trustworthiness of Jesus Christ.

No Airbrushed Heroes of the Faith

Paul's treatment of David, Abraham, and Sarah aligns with his declaration that "all have sinned and fall short of the glory of God" (3:23). It aligns with the complex biblical narratives about the leaders of Israel, which—unlike later retellings of those stories—display the faults as well as the virtues of the "heroes of the faith": Abraham tries to pass Sarah off as his sister when they are in Egypt (Gen 12:11–20); Sarah jealously throws out Hagar and Isaac to die in the wilderness (Gen 21:9–21); David seduces Bathsheba and has her husband killed (2 Sam 11:1–27). At the same time, Abraham and Sarah model trust in the God who brings life from the dead, and David is beloved for his reliance on God's mercy.

Paul embraces these complex narratives, such that Abraham and Sarah and David, not to mention Paul himself, become models of the "ungodly" who are made righteous through divine faithfulness. As such, they in turn model a kind of personal storytelling that is both truthful about failure and deeply hopeful.

One way to model such truth-telling is through thinking about obituaries. From a popular point of view, the purpose of an obituary, like a memorial service, is to sing the praises of the deceased by cataloging their accomplishments. How different, how much more holistic and truthful and ultimately hopeful, to remember another's life as a story of grace and a testimony to the God who will never let us go.

ROMANS 5:1–8:39
The Triumph of God's Love

In stunning imagery, Romans 5–8 lays out the life-changing power of God's gracious gift of redemption through Christ Jesus. From "God's love" that "has been poured into our hearts through the Holy Spirit that has been given to us" (5:5) to the astonishing promise that absolutely nothing "will be able to separate us from the love of God in Christ Jesus our Lord" (8:39), Paul proclaims the key themes of liberation, power, grace, hope, and love. Bracketed by divine love, these chapters form a distinct unit, but they also have strong ties to what precedes and follows them in the structure of the letter. Throughout, God's unmerited grace in and through Jesus Christ is the engine that powers the Christian life.

The pattern of these chapters may be set forth as follows:

- 5:1–11 Peace through the blood of Christ
- 5:12–8:39 Liberation into life
  - 5:12–21 Adam and Christ
  - 6:1–7:6 Life in Christ
    - 6:1–14 Dead to sin, alive to God in Christ
    - 6:15–23 Freed from sin, slaves of righteousness
    - 7:1–6 Freed from the law for new life in the Spirit
  - 7:7–25 The lethal power of sin's use of the law
  - 8:1–39 New life in the power of the Spirit

5:1–11. Peace through the Blood of Christ

These verses function as a transitional section that concludes 1:16–4:25 and introduces Paul's exposition of new life in Christ in 5:12–8:39. The themes of righteousness, salvation, wrath, the blood of Christ, and the death and life of Jesus link this section of the letter with 1:16–18. In 1:16–17 the good news is the power of God for salvation for all who believe and thus the way in which the "righteousness of God" (*dikaiosynē tou theou*) is breaking into the world. In 1:18 "the wrath of God" is breaking into the world. In 5:9 Paul unites the revelation of righteousness with the revelation of wrath: his listeners *have been made righteous* (*dikiōthentes*) through Christ's blood and *will be saved from the wrath.*

There are further links between this passage and earlier parts of the letter: the positive reference to "boasting" in hope and affliction contrasts with Paul's earlier criticism of boasting in human achievement (2:17, 23; 3:27; 4:2); "affliction" (5:3) now joins with the hope of glory, whereas in 2:9–10 Paul speaks of "affliction and distress" for those who do evil, and glory for those who do the good. The reference to "his blood" (5:9) recalls the imagery of "his blood" in 3:25, now illuminated in terms of reconciliation. "While we were enemies" (5:10) picks up on Paul's depiction of humanity's desperate state in 1:28–31, including their depiction as "God-haters" (1:30; cf. 8:7). In 5:12–21 Paul further expounds on the theme of redemption in terms of a reconciled relationship with God.

Several themes in these verses also anticipate their fuller exposition in chapter 8, including affliction, hope, and glory; the present activity of the Spirit in the fellowship of believers; the indissoluble bond of love between God and God's people; and the certain triumph of that love.

5:1–5. Hope in Suffering

Paul begins with one long sentence in which the three main clauses are "we have peace with God," "we have obtained access," and "we boast in our hope of sharing the glory of God" (5:1–2). The first subordinate clause gives the basis for peace with God: "since we are justified by faith." The verb is in the passive voice, again indicating God as the one who justifies, and in the simple past tense, indicating that justification happened at a specific point in time; a literal translation would be "having been justified by faith." "Therefore" links this claim with 4:25, thus telling us when and how such justification happened: Jesus was "handed over [to death] for our trespasses and was raised for our justification." "Justified by faith" thus refers in the first instance to Christ's faithful death and resurrection. When the great Swiss theologian Karl Barth was asked when he was "saved," he answered, "On a hill outside Jerusalem about two thousand years ago." Barth's answer gets at the objective reality of justification, the bedrock of peace with God because it depends on God's action, not human action (cf. 3:21–26). (For the verb "to justify" or "to be made righteous," see commentary on 3:24.)

At the same time, God's redeeming action in Christ does not exclude but rather evokes a human response of trust. As indicated by the footnotes in the NRSVue, textual variants in these verses express an interplay between God's act in Christ and human trust in God: most ancient manuscripts read, "let us have peace" and "let us boast," exhorting the listeners to claim and receive the peace given through Christ and to boast in hope. Some manuscripts also add "by faith" to the claim that "we have obtained access [by faith] to this grace" in verse 2. These variants do not basically change the meaning of the text, but simply emphasize the human response to God's initiative.

The second clause is "we have obtained access" to "this grace in which we stand." The phrase translated "obtained access" often refers to gaining entrance to a ruler such as a king or to a place such as a sanctuary, usually through making offerings or sacrifices. Here, however, the access is to "grace," which is God's gift to the undeserving and unworthy; by definition, such access excludes offerings or bribes. Paul's language is countercultural in the extreme, as "grace" becomes a spatial metaphor depicting a place or arena where human beings are on a firm footing before God entirely without regard to their moral or social worth. God's gift creates a new realm of existence characterized by undeserved welcome, which in turn becomes a new foundation for the self and the community.

The perfect tense of the verb "to stand" indicates a past action with continuing effects; it could be translated "have come to stand." Such "standing" before God draws on ancient images of the people of God, and the Levitical priesthood in particular, standing in God's presence (Lev 9:5; 2 Chr 29:11; Ps 24:3–4). To stand thus before

God requires "clean hands and pure hearts" (Ps 24:4), but in Paul's statement of the good news, this access is given to the "ungodly" who can rely only on God's grace (4:5; 5:6). "This grace in which we stand" may riff on Paul's identification of Jesus as the cover over the ark of the covenant in the Holy of Holies; through Christ's reconciling self-gift, the inner sanctum of holiness becomes the place of encounter between God and all humanity. (For the interpersonal effects of standing in God's grace, see 14:4.)

Finally, Paul says, "Let us boast in hope." The NRSVue adds "our" and "sharing," but the Greek text simply reads, "in hope of the glory of God." That is, the hope of God's glory is not something only for *believers* (2:10); rather it includes hope for the redemption of *all* creation (cf. 8:18–25). Such boasting directed toward God's glory contrasts sharply with boasting in human entitlement or accomplishments (2:17, 23; 3:27; 4:2). Paul's statement recalls Jeremiah's injunction, "Let those who boast boast in this, that they understand and know me, that I am the Lord; I act with steadfast love, justice, and righteousness in the earth" (Jer 9:24; cf. 1 Cor 1:31; 2 Cor 10:17).

"Boasting in hope" maintains a future orientation to Paul's exhortation here; such hope is thematic for the entire letter, already present in Abraham (Rom 4:18; cf. 8:20, 24–25; 15:13). In 5:3–5 Paul describes how believers are habituated into hope as a way of life, as boasting in future hope paradoxically joins with boasting in present sufferings. In 5:3–5, God's paradoxical power moves believers along a trajectory from affliction to endurance, to tested character, to habituation in hope. The word translated "endurance" means long-suffering, patience, fortitude, perseverance. Paul here sees suffering as a school for perseverance and ultimately for hope. Is he appealing to the Roman believers' own experience of formation through suffering? The Greek, which is literally "the afflictions" combined with the verb "we know," implies a positive answer. Paul is talking about his personal afflictions as well as the afflictions undergone by other Christians, potentially including his listeners in Rome. For Paul, "shameful" suffering is the norm when one follows a crucified Lord, and he never hesitates to name the various trials he himself has undergone (cf. 2 Cor 6:3–10). As for the Roman believers, attempts to reconstruct their experiences of affliction can only be speculative; what is clear is that Paul simply assumes they also have suffered. Given the intense persecution that will be visited on the

Roman Christians under Nero in the 60s, his words are particularly poignant.

It is difficult to translate the Greek word *dokimē* ("character"), which signifies something that has been tested and proven to be authentic (2 Cor 2:9; 8:2; 9:13; 13:3–7; Phil 2:23). It appears to be the reverse of a "debased mind" (*adokimon noun*) in Romans 1:28. Tested character does indeed lead to a hope that "does not put us to shame" (5:5), because we learn by experience that God can and will bring us through terrible trials. Just as Paul is "not ashamed of the gospel" (1:16) and boasts in afflictions, so here he is confident that afflictions which, in human terms, would cause shame and even despair in fact may paradoxically strengthen faith.

There is an important social as well as theological aspect to this language of shame that is lost in translation. In Paul's Roman context, affliction and lowly status were deeply shameful; to be one of the suffering masses was to be invisible at best and frequently the butt of contemptuous jokes. Paul's own catalogs of afflictions, including scars on his back from being whipped and stoned, would place him on the lowest rungs of society, among enslaved persons and criminals who were punished in such ways. Even more shameful, inconceivably so, was worship of a crucified "criminal" such as Jesus was. The shocking social reversal at the heart of the good news is what generates hope in situations of dishonorable suffering, affliction, poverty, failure, and marginalization. At the place of social failure and ostracism, God is present and on the move, transforming the "victims" of suffering into robust and hopeful agents (see 1 Cor 1:27–31). Paul boldly brags of his weakness as the place where God's power is most evident (2 Cor 12:5–10).

Paul concludes Romans 5:5 with the basis for hope: "because God's love has been poured into our hearts through the Holy Spirit that has been given to us." This is the first mention of love in the letter. From start to finish, love is the force that sustains and completes the journey from affliction to hope. This is importantly *God's* love mediated through the *Holy Spirit*—love that comes uniquely and surely from God, and that binds believers to God in an enduring embrace, mediated and sustained by the Holy Spirit who "has been given to us." Paul expounds on this gift of the Spirit to the community in chapter 8; here he emphasizes the gift of God's *love* "poured into our hearts." "Our hearts" (*kardia*) refers to the heart as the center of the person, the seat of intelligence, volition, and desire, and therefore the place of encountering God (Gal 4:6). God has unique access to the human heart, as Paul already has made clear in Romans 2:15–16, 29. The verb translated "poured" occurs very differently in 3:15, describing the murderous impulses of those who "shed" or "pour out" blood. Closer to the meaning of 5:5 is Joel 2:28 (cf. Acts 2:16–17): "I will pour out my Spirit upon all flesh."

5:6–11. God's Love for Sinners

In 5:6–8, Paul contrasts human indifference with God's proactive love for the unlovable, through parallel references to Christ's death on behalf of the "weak," "ungodly," and "sinners" (vv. 6, 8) that bracket two exclamations about how rare it is for one person to die for another (v. 7). The cumulative intensification of the human condition emphasizes the depth and countercultural quality of God's self-gift in Christ, which exceeds human love precisely through its action on behalf of those who are *not* good (v. 7). The temporal language displays God's preemptive strike against human dereliction, and therefore the unconditioned priority of grace for the "weak," "ungodly," "sinners," even "enemies" (5:10)—as such, not as the righteous, human beings receive God's costly love.

In the repeated phrase "much more" (5:9–11), Paul employs a rabbinic mode of comparative argument called "from the lesser to the greater" to underscore the assured future guaranteed by Christ's death on humanity's behalf. Again, the temporal markers are key: *now* that we have been "justified by his blood," how much more *will* we be saved from wrath; *now* that we *were* reconciled, much more *will* "we be saved by his life." The future tense and the echoes of 1:18 and 2:5, 16 suggest that "wrath" here denotes the future day of judgment and wrath (cf. 1 Thess 5:1–10 for an exposition of this theme early in Paul's ministry). The past event of Christ's death and resurrection has set human beings right and reconciled them to God, resulting in a present state of peace with God (Rom 5:1) and confidence in God even in affliction. This reality in turn assures a future salvation, which includes both full liberation from the power of sin and death and full transformation into the likeness of Christ (6:5). Such assurance is the content of hope that "does not put us to shame" (5:5); its end point is "boast[ing] in God through our Lord Jesus Christ" (5:11), linking the end of this section to boasting in hope of the glory of God (5:2). That believers will boast in God's glory is the antithesis of humanity's primal refusal to glorify God (1:21–23).

In 5:10, the promise of a future salvation "by his life" occurs in counterpoint to the reference to Christ's death. "By his life" refers to Christ's resurrection in the singular event of the empty tomb, but in this context the phrase surely also refers to the ongoing work and presence of the risen Christ in the life of the community (cf. 8:10–11). To be "saved" through the presence of the living Christ is to be rescued from destructive powers in the present and from the threat of wrath and judgment in the future, confident of God's gracious victory over sin and death.

As a conclusion both to 5:1–11 and to the entire section from 1:16 up to this point in the letter, 5:11 does two important things. First, it restates the theme of boasting. The Greek phrase introducing this sentence exactly repeats the introduction to 5:3: "Not only that, but let us also boast." In 5:3, believers boast in hope of glory, but also in present affliction. In the overarching proclamation of 5:1–11, Paul gathers up this boasting in both hope and affliction by directing all boasting to God: "We boast in God through our Lord Jesus Christ."

Second, the last word in 5:1–11, and indeed the capstone of 1:16–5:11, is "reconciliation." The Greek reads "the reconciliation," as if in reference to a distinct event—the crucifixion and resurrection of Jesus—not simply a general principle. This assurance of reconciliation picks up the theme of "peace with God" (5:1), the overcoming of human enmity toward God (v. 9), and the two appearances of the verb "to reconcile" in the passive voice (v. 10). We "were reconciled," implicitly by God. Therefore "we have received" the reconciliation *from* God, who is the one who accomplishes reconciliation on humanity's behalf, doing for human beings what they are unable to do for themselves. Therefore, "reconciliation" (*katallagē*) is the final word of this section and the word that sums up the effects of Christ's atoning death (v. 11b). The language of "enemies" in verse 10 and the repeated references to reconciliation in verses 10–11 evoke a situation of cosmic conflict. Crucially, God does not need reconciling to disaffected human beings, but rather, human hostility and resistance toward God needs to be dealt with. God has done this in the most humanly unimaginable way possible, by dying *for the enemy* and thereby establishing peace.

Paul's interpretation of Christ's death in terms of reconciliation plays off the meaning of "reconciliation" in Greco-Roman culture. The Greek verb "to reconcile" (*katalassō*) and the related noun *kattalagē* occur rarely in Paul's letters, and nowhere else in the New Testament. The verb is related to verbs meaning "to exchange one thing for another" (*allassō* in 1:23 and *metallassō* in 1:25, 26), which Paul used to describe humanity's primal idolatry of exchanging God's truth for a lie and worshiping the creature rather than the creator. In nonbiblical usage *katallassō* occurs most often in conflict situations, where a mediator persuades warring parties to make peace with one another, often through an offering of goods or people. It also has a financial meaning, in the sense of exchanging goods. "Reconciliation" thus implies an exchange that creates or facilitates peace between opposing parties. So also in Paul's usage: "while we were enemies we were reconciled to God through the death of his Son" (5:10) precisely because God's Son "was handed over for our trespasses and was raised for our justification" (4:25), in an exchange that surpasses and undoes the "handing over" of humanity to destructive powers (1:24, 26, 28). This divine-human "exchange" cancels out the lethal effects of humanity's primal exchange of God's truth for a lie.

As the letter progresses, Paul repeatedly proclaims Christ's saving solidarity and exchange with humanity under sin, culminating in 8:1–4 (see commentary). Elsewhere Paul also riffs on this theme of reconciling exchange, in which God in Christ changes places with humanity in its situation "under sin" (3:9), thereby bringing about both victory over sin and death and reconciliation for humanity. In 2 Corinthians 5:19–21 he summarizes this claim in a nutshell, shocking in the depth of Christ's solidarity and exchange with humanity under sin:

> In Christ God was reconciling the world to himself, not counting their trespasses against them, and entrusting the message of reconciliation to us. So we are ambassadors for Christ, since God is making his appeal through us; we entreat you on behalf of Christ: be reconciled to God. For our sake God made the one who knew no sin to be sin, so that in him we might become the righteousness of God.

Here is the exchange of one thing for another that reconciles humanity with God and calls them to recognize and release their enmity toward God and be at peace (Rom 5:1). In 5:12–21 Paul tells the story of this reconciling exchange as an interchange between Christ and Adam, in which the "free gift" of God in Christ completely surpasses, outweighs, and overturns the effects of Adam's transgression.

EXCURSUS

Reflections for Preaching and Teaching

"We Were Enemies"

It is altogether too easy to miss the shock of Paul's escalating description of his listeners, including himself: "while we were weak . . . ungodly . . . sinners . . . enemies." Paul's words deconstruct human defenses against the gospel of grace, not least by exposing our own latent hostility toward God. We may be more comfortable praying for our enemies than recognizing that we are the enemy, that we are weak, that we need prayer. Paul pulls the rug out from under all such self-reliance and smug piety, because in Jesus's death on the battlefield of human enmity, God made himself the target of *our* rage: our rage at being guilty, at being the target of others' rage, at being put in the hot seat, at being a helpless victim, at our neighbors or the government or family dynamics or unjust oppression; there is an endless list of things to be angry about, and they are not insignificant. In the public sphere we may consider the rise in violence in this country and around the world; the brutal inequities and injustices, the sense of helplessness and hopelessness, the economic costs, the families stuck with each other, the restrictions on freedom of movement, the loss of connection, perhaps above all the fear and loss of control. All of this is ratcheted up by divisive, hate-filled rhetoric, not only locally but around the globe. When disaster strikes, the human response is to look for someone to blame.

In one sense, the cross is God saying, "The buck stops here." Of course, God is not guilty, but only God can bear and deal with the accumulated burden of blame, grief, guilt, and rage that keeps recycling through human histories on every level: families, communities, countries, and regions of the world. This is the situation of "wrath" and conflict in which we live. This is why we need reconciliation. This is what needs to be exposed, interrupted, defused, defeated, and set right. Paul's language of enmity and reconciliation provides opportunities to name the rage and the blame games, not for the purpose of passing judgment, but for the purpose of healing.

Reconciliation and Exchange

How does the exchange of one thing for another accomplish such reconciliation between opponents? It is tempting to talk about this in transactional terms, and sermons that do so are not difficult to find: Christ's blood "bought" our freedom, paid our debts, and assuaged God's wrath. The problem with such accounts is that they do not get at the radicality of Paul's good news. God, the source of all gifts, can never be "bought off" (cf. Rom 11:35). Rather, the reconciliation that Christ accomplished on the cross is one of solidarity, in which God assumed the place and situation of humanity "under the power of sin," thereby establishing the common ground on which we can meet God and each other, "this grace in which we stand."

Elsewhere Paul develops this theme of exchange in relationship to many aspects of human experience, ranging from the alternating place of Jew and gentile in God's economy of salvation (Rom 11:30–32) to an appeal for generosity based on Christ's voluntary poverty (2 Cor 8:9). An interchange of experience is built into the fabric of human identity and society; as a wise children's therapist once said, "We are always taking bits of ourselves and putting them in other people, and we are always taking bits of other people into ourselves." There is in every social structure a constant sharing of habits, attitudes, emotions, and worldviews that shape who we are and who we imagine we can be. Christ enters and transforms the human interchange by defusing the dynamics of fear, blame, and retribution, instead creating networks of relationship grounded in the undeserved gift of God's power and love. This is the reconciliation that Christ accomplished on the cross and that God continues to bring to reality in human interactions mediated by the Spirit.

Cosmic Conflict

Paul now depicts the situation of human culpability before God (Rom 1:18–3:20) in terms of conflict. But because all are "under the power of sin" (3:9), the struggle is complicated by human bondage to sin, such that human beings are not simply free agents. Rather, as will become increasingly evident in 5:12–8:39, the primary perpetrator of wrong is sin itself (7:17, 19, 23; see commentary), and the salvation accomplished by Christ is liberation from slavery to sin and death, which exceeds and reframes the forgiveness of sins. This reframing of the human condition has important implications for understanding the conflict revealed by the language of enmity and reconciliation. Ultimately, the combatants in this cosmic war are not individuals or social groups, nor even God and humanity; rather, the combatants are God and the twinned powers of sin and death. These powers have no real substance or lasting reality, however; at the end of the day, they are bit players in God's drama of salvation, performing their roles in a cosmos that is always held by the purposes of God (cf. 11:28–36).

Sometimes mainline churches are leery of talking about conflict or preaching about it, for fear of evoking the church's history of violence or fanning the flames of war. But this theme of conflict, which is so strong in Paul's letters, makes readers from relatively comfortable middle-class and upper-middle-class backgrounds the most nervous, while those who come from places of struggle and oppression know exactly what Paul is talking about. They know that life is full of struggle and that while the temptation to demonize other people is very real, we also need daily encouragement to persist in finding "strength to love," as Martin Luther King Jr. put it. We neglect preaching about conflict at our peril. Paul teaches us to listen carefully for the resistance points to his radical gospel of grace in our specific congregations and locations. Furthermore, he invites us to talk about how Christ's death on the battlefield of human hostility and fear can absorb and defuse the lethal power of hate without silencing the cries for justice. Peace is not achieved by erasing or suppressing disagreements, but by the love of God poured into our hearts through the Holy Spirit given to God's people.

Hope Grounded in God's Love

The progression from affliction to endurance, to character, to hope, provides rich resources for teaching and preaching about the life of faith, not least because it is the source for "boasting in affliction." As in Paul's time, so also today many if not most kinds of affliction tend to induce shame, particularly when they involve family rifts, economic hardships, low social status, or addiction. The suffering involved in such affliction can be excruciating, and too often it is exacerbated by being hidden from the church's fellowship. God is not absent from any hardship, no matter how shameful by cultural standards, but the church often is. Paul, on the other hand, sees the work of God hidden in suffering, which thus becomes a training ground for hope.

The challenge for church leaders is to ask themselves how their preaching, teaching, pastoring, and leadership either promote or discourage such growth in hope. Do pastors model transparency about their own shortcomings and openness to people's hardships, or do they model a kind of pious perfection that leaves no room to name ruptures and failures? Do they preach the gospel of grace that can survive the failures of the preacher, or do they preach a message of self-righteous piety that will be shamed by their own wrongs? Paul's honesty about his own weakness can be astounding (e.g., 2 Cor 1:8–11). He knows that some church leaders will criticize him because of his "weakness," but he counters that he prefers to boast in his weakness as the place where God's power will be perfected in him, "for whenever I am weak, then I am strong" (2 Cor 12:9–10). Boasting in weakness, boasting in affliction, boasting in things that our culture (like the culture of the Roman Empire) considers shameful—this is the way of hope in the crucified Lord.

Is Suffering a Good Thing?

One danger of Paul's embrace of suffering is the tendency to glorify suffering as an end in itself. Such a misguided exaltation of suffering, sometimes coupled with judgmental attitudes toward people who do not seem to suffer "enough" (whatever that might mean), seriously undercuts the church's calling to *alleviate* suffering wherever possible. The church is called to a ministry of solidarity and hope, through fellowship and mutual sharing with, and practical help for, those who suffer from the sins of racism, injustice, and inequity, as well as illness, family struggles, mental health issues, loneliness, and loss.

We can understand and embrace Paul's words about suffering when we consider the shape of his own life, which was marked by dislocation, a deeply painful rupture with his past relationships and community, poverty, homelessness, physical violence, and continuing hostility toward his ministry. Paul endured great hardships, and he had to make sense of that fact. He made sense of it through union with the suffering of Christ, discovering Christ sharing *all* of his experiences and promising wholeness and life (cf. Rom 8:35–39). Paul did not seek out hardship, but neither did he run from it.

We human beings have a hard time knowing how to narrate affliction. On the one hand, sometimes we minimize and silence the suffering of others (and even ourselves), particularly when we praise the achievements and virtues of exemplary "saints." On the other hand, sometimes we play the "suffering Olympics," in which one person or group of people tries to outdo others in terms of how much they have been afflicted. For example, people share a particularly painful experience, and their listeners respond by telling a personal story of an even *more* painful experience. Or one group of people dismisses the anguish of others by saying, "That's nothing. They have no reason to complain." Or well-meaning Christians make distinctions between "suffering for Jesus" and "suffering because of sin." Paul makes no such distinctions. All affliction, not least Jesus's own torment on the cross, is "because of sin," and through the cross all affliction is taken up by Christ. Therefore, through Jesus's own agony with and for the human race, all human suffering can be an opportunity for meeting God and growing in hope.

5:12–21. Christ and Adam: The Joyful Exchange

In this short but significant passage, Paul further develops the theme of reconciliation (5:10–11) through telling the stories of Christ and Adam, which illustrate the central act of reconciliation as set forth in his earlier Letter to the Corinthians: "For since death came through a human, the resurrection of the dead has also come through a human, for as all die in Adam, so all will be made alive in Christ" (1 Cor 15:21–22). Now, through parallel yet contrasting typologies of Christ and Adam, Paul revisits and deepens his account of the human dilemma, God's redeeming work in and through Christ, and the experience of the new reality of life in Christ.

This section of chapter 5 falls into three subsections: verses 12–14, depicting the reign of sin and death; verses 15–17, contrasting the free gift in grace through Jesus Christ with the lethal legacy of Adam's trespass; verses 18–21, further expounding the contrast between the destinies of Adam and Christ. Adam and Christ are contrasted as representative figures throughout the passage, as each one bears and determines the destiny of "many." The rabbinic logic of "how much more" governs the relationship between Christ and Adam, so that Adam becomes a foil for the superabounding, all-powerful rule of God's grace. Through antithetical parallelism between Christ and Adam, Paul tells the story of the reconciling exchange, the union and reversal accomplished by Christ's entrance into our common humanity.

5:12–14. The Entrance of Sin and Death

Three interpretive issues arise in 5:12: the meaning of "therefore," questions of translation, and the relationship between sin and death. First, "therefore" (in Greek, "for this reason") closely links what follows to 5:1–11, but in what way? The immediately preceding verses highlight Christ's reconciling death for us while we were weak, ungodly, sinners, and even enemies of God. Given the background of reconciliation as an exchange that brings peace in conflict situations, Paul now retells the stories of Christ and Adam to illustrate both the human dilemma and God's redemptive action through Christ. He explains how human beings have come to be sinners and how they have received reconciliation. Furthermore, the language of sin and death recalls 3:9, 23, where Paul claims that all are under sin and all have sinned. Paul thus signals three things: in what follows he will expand on his statements about human bondage and culpability in 1:18–3:20; he will develop the description of humanity as both accountable for acting sinfully and yet also enslaved to sin as a power; and he will tell *how* the reconciling interchange between God and humanity took place.

Second, as commonly translated (NRSVue, RSV, KJV, NAS), this verse appears to be a sentence fragment, with Paul interrupting himself at verse 13. The culprit is the second clause, "and so death spread to all." But the phrase translated "and so" could also be translated, "so also," yielding the following meaning: "Therefore, just as sin came into the world through one man, and death came through sin, so also death spread to all human beings." This is a less frequent translation of the word order Paul uses here, but not impossible, and it coherently links the second clause with the first. This indeed does seem to be Paul's meaning in these verses: sin entered the world and brought death in its wake.

Third, what is the relationship between death and sin? The final clause, translated in the NRSVue as "because all have sinned," implies that continued human sinning is the cause of death. But the Greek is not so clear. Taken literally, it means "on the basis of which," referring to an antecedent cause for the following phrase: thus, "on the basis of which all sinned." The closest antecedent is the phrase "death spread to all human beings." In other words, people sin because they live in a world (*kosmos*) dominated by sin and death. We thus come to a translation of 5:12 as follows: "Therefore, just as sin came into the world through one man, and death came through sin, so also death spread to all human beings, so that all sinned." This translation highlights the nuanced realism of Paul's claim. On the one hand, human beings are not simply victims; they are actors who "sin." On the other hand, they are not free agents, because their actions are constrained by the global reach of sin and death. Continuing the ambiguity implied by "sin" as a ruling power (3:9), and "sin" as a verb with human beings as sinners (3:23; 5:8), Paul depicts human actors as in the grip of sin and death, and therefore unable not to sin (5:19).

Paul was part of a wider conversation in Judaism about the tension between the human *compulsion* to sin and human *culpability* for sin. For example, 4 Ezra, written after the destruction of Jerusalem in 70 CE, portrays Adam as both prone to sin and responsible for a lethal legacy of sin: "For the first Adam, burdened with an evil heart, transgressed and was overcome, as were also all who were descended from him" (41:21). Dating from the same time, 2 Baruch 54:15, 19 puts the responsibility for wrongdoing squarely on each individual: "For although Adam sinned first and has brought death upon all who were not in his own time, yet each of them who descended from him has prepared for himself the coming torment. . . . Adam is, therefore, not the cause, except for himself, but each of us has become our own Adam." Both authors wrote after Paul's death, but they demonstrate the debates about sin and human culpability that were current in the first and second centuries CE.

In Romans 5:13 Paul reintroduces the topic of Mosaic law. His point is straightforward: sin predates the law, but the law "reckons" or keeps track of sin. The verb translated "reckoned" is rare in the New Testament, occurring elsewhere only at Philemon 18, where Paul tells Philemon that if the runaway enslaved Onesimus owes him anything, Philemon should "charge" that amount to Paul's account. Here in Romans 5:13 the law functions to track and keep a ledger of sin (4:15) that holds human actors accountable and perhaps makes them aware of their sin. God does not need a ledger to reckon sin, but human beings do. Significantly, Paul distinguishes between sin's lethal effects, which predate the law, and the law's role in naming sin and, indeed, increasing it (cf. 5:20; 7:7–11).

Nonetheless, even prior to the law, "death reigned from Adam to Moses" (5:14). So also, in light of Paul's claim in verses 12–13, sin reigned. "Sin" is not limited to trackable breaches of the divine law; it precedes and exceeds conscious human actions. The word translated "reigned" means "ruled as a king." In tandem with sin, death lorded it over humanity. Paul repeats this claim about death's oppressive rule in 5:17, and in 5:21 he says, "*sin* reigned in [or through] death." It is important to note that "sin" and "death" are now the subjects of active verbs. They are not simply results of human actions, nor realms of existence; they are active players on the stage of human history.

In 5:14 Paul further introduces Adam in relationship to Christ. Not only is Adam the one through whose primal trespass sin and death entered the world; he also is "a pattern of the one who was to come." Here Paul begins the Adam-Christ comparison that will govern the rest of the chapter. "Pattern" or "type" (*typos*) originally referred to the imprint left in clay or wax by a mold or a signet ring. The imprint is the exact reverse of the original, yet also is closely related to it as a mirror image (cf. Rom 6:17; 1 Cor 10:6; Phil 3:17; 1 Thess 1:7). The logic of Paul's metaphor implies that Adam is Christ's imprint, not vice versa; Christ is the original, Adam is the copy. In this sense, Christ precedes Adam as the divine image in which humanity is created, and Adam is closely related to Christ, just as the imprint of a signet ring in wax is the exact but reverse image of the ring itself. There is both an indivisible kinship between Christ and Adam, and sharp dissimilarity in their effects for the human race: gift versus trespass, grace versus sin, and life versus death. This close kinship, yet sharp contrast, is a key to the logic of solidarity and reversal in Paul's argument.

5:15–17. The Surpassing Power of God's Gift

Paul piles on the language of gift in 5:15, contrasting the deadly outcome of Adam's trespass with the surpassing abundance of the grace of Christ. Three "gift" words appear here in mutual amplification of the message of grace: the word first translated "free gift" in verse 15a is *charisma,* which is closely related to the next word, *charis,* "the grace of God." To drive home the point, Paul adds a third clause with another term for gift (*dōrea*): "the gift in the grace [*charis*] of the one man [*anthrōpos*], Jesus Christ." Both Adam and Christ here carry and determine the destinies of "the many": through Adam's trespass "the many died," and God's gift abounded for "the many." Paul's functional anthropology here is thoroughly interconnected, in that all humanity is constituted and affected through the actions of these two representative figures.

Continuing in 5:16, Paul now expands on the contrast between Adam's sin and Christ's gift; the first leads to judgment (*krima*) and therefore condemnation (*katakrima*); the second overcomes the effects of many trespasses, leading instead to "justification." The Greek word here is *dikaiōma* (cf. 1:32; 8:4), which means "just decree." God's just decree of righteousness through Christ, even and especially in response to "many trespasses," is the counterpoint and antidote to the judgment and condemnation following upon Adam's trespass. That judgment was just, but nonetheless it is countered and overturned by the even greater divine pronouncement of righteousness through Christ.

With a surprising twist, Paul brings home the result of Christ's gift in terms of human agency (5:17). Death ruled like a king through the one human being, Adam (see v. 14), but those who receive God's abounding grace and freely given righteousness will rule like kings, not in death, but in life. Sin and death supplant human agency; grace empowers it, so that when grace "reigns" (v. 21), human beings also "reign in life" (v. 17; cf. 6:1–14). Here the connection between righteousness and life is fleshed out in the lives of God's people. Implicit in Paul's statements is an understanding of human actions as overrun by sin's enslaving grasp, but liberated by God's gracious alliance with humanity over against all that would diminish us and hold us down.

5:18–21. The Dominion of Grace

Through a staccato series of contrasts, in 5:18–19 Paul juxtaposes the effects of "the one" Adam and "the one" Christ: condemnation versus rectification and life; being made to be sinners versus being made righteous. Christ's "act of righteousness" (*dikaiōmatos*) refers to his faithful death and resurrection on behalf of all (4:25), which results in the rectification (*dikaiōsin*) of life. Although the NRSVue reads "justification and life," a more precise rendering of the Greek is "justification [or rectification] *of* life," which highlights the tight connection between righteousness and life. For Paul, to be set right with God is to be delivered from the power of sin and death and therefore to enter into life; conversely, there is no life apart from God's righteousness (5:21). In fact, as he demonstrates in retelling the story of Abraham and Sarah, righteousness is so closely linked to life that the rectification of the ungodly is inseparable from the resurrection of the dead. Paul's favored word "all" here makes clear that "the many" in 5:15, 19 includes all humanity.

In 5:19 Paul clarifies just what "justification of life" is: "the many will be made righteous" so that through them, God's gracious dominion extends God's righteousness through Jesus Christ. Adam's disobedience made many to be sinners; through Christ the many are made to be righteous. We may note two important corollaries to Paul's claim. First, justification is more than a change in our standing before God, as if it simply meant acquittal. It signifies a transformation of human beings, from being sinners to being righteous. Second, here the logic of participatory personhood is on full display, as in 4 Ezra quoted above. Paul simply assumes that Adam's and Christ's actions directly affect all humanity. This is not a notion of original sin as a kind of contagion passed on by sex, but rather the view that sin and death gained entrance to the cosmos through Adam's disobedience and thereafter constrain every human life. Human beings are born into a toxic environment in which sin is inescapable. The same logic obtains in relationship to Christ, whose "obedience" makes people righteous. Christ's union with Adamic humanity makes his death and resurrection effective for us. Again, Paul probably has in mind Christ's obedience unto death (Phil 2:8).

In the Greek, Romans 5:20 says, "Law slipped in, in order to increase the trespass." The first verb, "slipped in," has a pejorative sense. It occurs only here and in Galatians 2:4, where Paul describes "false brothers . . . who slipped in to spy on the freedom we have." The express purpose of the law's clandestine entrance on the human scene was to "increase" the trespass. Given Paul's explicit reference to the law of Moses in 5:13–14, the Mosaic law is also in view here. But what does Paul mean by "increase the trespass"? The law is supposed to control sin, not exacerbate it! Nonetheless, Paul's claim is clear; the law increases sin, and such an increase is intentional; it is not an unfortunate side effect of the law. Paul thus establishes a strong connection between the law and sin, while implying that somehow both sin and the law retain a place in God's larger purposes. In what way this might be so remains to be seen (cf. 7:7–25; 11:32).

At this point, however, Paul's focus is on neither sin nor law, but rather on the overwhelming abundance of grace. He uses a rare word to indicate this superabundance: *hypereperisseusen*, which translates literally as "hyper-abounded" (in 2 Cor 7:4 Paul uses the same word to indicate his overflowing joy in affliction). The verbal tenses suggest that "where sin increased, grace abounded all the more" probably refers to a specific event—likely the crucifixion and resurrection of Jesus. Sin did its worst, and grace triumphed.

Paul's final clause spells out the purpose of God's triumphant gift: just as sin ruled in death, so grace will "reign through justification leading to eternal life through Jesus Christ our Lord" (5:21). The word translated "justification" is *dikaiosynē*, also well translated as "righteousness." This reference to righteousness recalls God's righteousness as God's power to save, in 1:16–17. Grace reigns through God's powerful, saving righteousness acting through the gospel. The verb "to rule" or "to have dominion" (*basileuō*) implies two conflicting regimes of power—that of sin and death (5:14, 17, 21) and that of grace, in which grace reigns and those who receive grace also reign (vv. 17, 21). But the power of the reign of grace is immeasurably greater than that of sin's reign. In the regime of divine gift where believers stand in grace (5:2), they are empowered to live lives characterized by God's abundance. In 6:1–7:6, Paul further develops the ways in which the surpassing power of God's gift in Christ transforms human agency and behavior.

EXCURSUS

Reflections for Preaching and Teaching

Sin as a Power over Human Beings

Paul's arresting image of sin and death invading the cosmos dramatically transforms preaching about sin and redemption. Popular understandings of sin describe it as an action or perhaps an attitude that above all denotes individual personal decisions worthy of condemnation. Paul's language reframes sin on a cosmic scale. Developing the thought of 3:9, he depicts sin as something larger than individuals or even social organizations, which acts in, through, and on human beings, with deadly consequences. This understanding of sin is a powerful resource for preaching about systemic evils such as racism and violence and for describing and addressing the suffering of those who are unjustly oppressed. It also has crucial implications for pastoral care, not least because it distinguishes between sin and human intentions (see commentary on 7:7–25).

By speaking of sin as something that holds humanity captive, Paul explicitly opposes the popular notion that human beings are "free to sin." In common understanding, the idea of free will means that God loves us so much that God gives individuals the freedom to sin. But in Paul's depiction in Romans 5–8, sinful acts are never free; rather, they demonstrate a lack of freedom. Indeed, in Paul's telling, neither the law nor human effort has any innate power to resist sin's deadly effects; rather, Paul announces the power of God's *gift* of righteousness for weak, sinful, and rebellious human beings. Paul as a preacher focuses on *God's* act in and through Christ, not human actions "for Christ," let alone human resistance to sin. Yet this divine action catalyzes and sustains human freedom to act, through a dynamic gracious alliance between God and believers. Such is the effect of the "free gift," which takes center stage in this drama of liberation and reconciliation.

God's Gift as a Power for Human Beings

A theology of abundance undergirds both the contrast between Christ and Adam, and Paul's confidence in the surpassing potency of God's grace. That victorious gift, which ultimately overcomes both sin and death, comes from the presence of the divine Giver as Lord over the cosmos (5:21; cf. 8:39).

We need to hear and preach how countercultural this gift to unworthy recipients is, both in Paul's context and now; the shared popular wisdom is that to give gifts to the wrong people is simply "throwing good money after bad." Society is shaped by a logic of quid pro quo: scholarships go to those who have earned them; loans are given to those who can repay them; good is rewarded; wrong is punished; this is the order of justice in the human cosmos, not without reason. But this order also is inherently competitive and thus also fosters division, distrust, and violence. It has a limited restraining function, but it cannot change people, and it cannot give life. On the global stage, the logic of quid pro quo results in wars of retribution that become self-perpetuating; this is the order of the day in the regime of sin and death.

In utter contrast to this status quo, grace operates through a divinely bestowed bond between humanity and God that in no way depends on the capacities or worth of the recipients. In 5:5, 8, Paul calls this relationship the love of God; in 5:12–21, he characterizes it above all by the language of "the free gift." Constituted by union with Christ, living in union with Christ in an unbreakable relationship of love, those who receive God's freely given grace "will reign in life." We see here a picture of a gracious alliance between the self and God, a relationally mediated strengthening of believers over against the destructive forces of sin. Contrary to the popular saying "more of Jesus, less of me," in fact "more of Jesus" means "more of me," because God's grace and lordship empower and liberate human beings.

Christ and Adam

In opposition to the logic of quid pro quo, God in Christ effects an interchange between derelict humanity and Christ, as Christ takes the place of those "handed over" to destructive powers (1:24, 26, 28; 4:25). This interchange depends on both the contrast between Christ and Adam and the close link between them. The great church theologian Irenaeus spoke of Christ's relationship to Adam in terms of "recapitulation"—Christ as the second Adam recapitulates the experience of the first Adam (which is to say, all humanity in the wake of Adam), and thereby reverses Adam's legacy. As the second Adam, Christ enters fully into our human experience and changes its outcome. The medieval mystic Julian of Norwich put it this way:

> When Adam fell, God's son fell; because of the true union which was made in heaven, God's son could not be apart from Adam, for by Adam I understand all humanity. Adam fell from life to death, into the hollow of this wretched world, and after that into hell. God's son fell with Adam into the hollow of the Virgin's womb—she who was the fairest daughter of Adam—and so to free Adam through that from guilt in heaven and on earth; and through his great might he fetched him out of hell. (Julian 2015, 112)

This solidarity and contrast between Christ and Adam speak powerfully to human suffering, as Christ shares intimately with every aspect of our lives and promises new life at the same time. When he was lying on his deathbed, the English poet John Donne expressed this comfort and hope in his last poem, which ended with these lines:

> We think that paradise and Calvary,
> Christ's cross and Adam's tree, stood in one place;
> look, Lord, and find both Adams met in me:
> as the first Adam's sweat surrounds my face,
> may the last Adam's blood my soul embrace.
>
> *"Hymn to God, My God, in My Sickness"*

6:1–7:6. Life in Christ

In 5:1–5 Paul maps out the experience of life in Christ, in which the hope of God's glory begins a journey involving affliction, perseverance, and tested character, leading to seasoned hope—all experienced in and through the love of God poured into our hearts. In 6:1–7:6 he expands on this experience through the theme of union with Christ, which generates a vigorous expectation that believers may and will live transformed lives. As in 5:1–5, throughout chapter 6 Paul combines statements about the new life given to believers through union with Christ with exhortations to receive and act out this new reality in their bodily existence. Thus, this section of Romans portrays what the promise of 5:17 looks like in practice: "Those who receive the abundance of grace and the gift of righteousness reign in life through the one man, Jesus Christ." Paradoxically, this dominion entails liberation *from* slavery to sin and the law *into* a new obedience to Christ as Lord; it entails a promised deliverance *from* death *through* death with Christ.

The passage divides into three subsections: in 6:1–14 Paul establishes believers' death to sin and awakening to new life through union with Christ in baptism. He outlines the implications of this union for bodily life in 6:15–23, using the metaphor of slavery and freedom. In 7:1–6 Paul develops the implications of freedom in Christ, in relationship to the law. The first two of these sections begin with a question implying a negative answer (6:1, 15), and all three begin Paul's exposition with "do you not know?" (6:3, 16; 7:1).

6:1–14. Dying with Christ, Walking in Newness of Life

With a series of questions in 6:1–3, Paul sharply counters any potential misunderstanding of God's surpassing gift in Christ. The logical trigger for these questions is 5:20: "Where sin increased, grace abounded all the more." Paul's opening gambit, "What shall we say?" frequently introduces a question with a negative answer (3:5; 6:1–2, 15; 7:7; 9:14). Here it introduces the question "Should we continue in sin in order that grace may abound?" The answer, which could be translated colloquially as "No way!" relies on two further affirmations of believers' new reality, also in question form: believers have "died to sin"; they have been "baptized into Christ Jesus" and, through that, "into his death."

The foundation of Paul's argument is believers' participation in Christ's death to sin, based on Christ's redeeming death on behalf of all. As in 5:12–21, Paul's logic assumes the interconnectedness of all human beings across time and space; therefore, in the incarnation Christ fully assumed our humanity, and his death and resurrection affect us now. Paul sums up the key claim in 2 Corinthians 5:14: "One has died for all; therefore all have died."

The phrase "in sin" (Rom 6:1, 2) has a spatial sense, signifying sin as a realm of power or a kind of force field larger than the self; it is the opposite of "this grace in which we stand" (5:2). Similarly, "baptized into Christ" (6:3) implies immersion into union with Christ in death and the promise of union with Christ in resurrection. Paul's letters are our earliest evidence of Christian preaching linking baptism explicitly with Christ's death; the connection recurs in subsequent depictions of Christ's own baptism in the Gospels. For example, Mark's account of Jesus's baptism (1:9–11) prefigures Jesus's death (15:37–39) as the place where Jesus's divine sonship is revealed. Paul reinforces the symbolism of baptism as a kind of death through the image of burial; burial makes unmistakably clear that the death and new life wrought by Christ are irreversible.

In the declarative statement of verse 4, Paul sums up the purpose of baptism into Christ's death: new life. He frequently uses the word "with," as either a prefix or a preposition, to denote union with Christ (6:4, 6, 8; cf. 8:28–30). Believers have died and been buried together with Christ (the term literally connotes burial in a shared grave), and therefore also trust that they will live together with him. This shared destiny is the basis of Paul's confident expectation that "we also might walk in newness of life" (see Phil 3:8–16 for a similar picture of Christian experience).

In Romans 6:5–11, Paul rings the changes on union with Christ's death and resurrection in two parallel subsections. The first subsection, verses 5–8, concerns human assimilation to Christ; the second (vv. 9–11) focuses on Christ himself in his subjection to death and his victory over it.

In Greek, 6:5 reads, "Since we have been joined together in the likeness [*homoiōma*] of his death, so also we will be [in the likeness of] his resurrection." "Likeness" is not equivalence—believers did not literally die on the cross with Jesus—but assimilation to the condition and destiny of Christ in his death and resurrection. The believer's "death" with Christ signifies deliverance from sin as an enslaving power (vv. 6–7, 10–11), and Christ's own death and resurrection signify the end of death's dominion (vv. 9–10). For those baptized into Christ, the hope of resurrection remains in the future (v. 5) but empowers a new way of understanding oneself as alive to God in the present (v. 11). Paul's argument is cosmic in scope and makes sense only in the context of his exposé of sin and death as hostile forces (5:14, 17, 21) that have been overcome by the surpassing power of God's free gift in Christ, and his certain hope for the redemption of all creation (8:18–25). As throughout his letters, Paul assumes that human beings are constituted in relationship to others—here, to God in Christ.

In the following verses Paul begins to discuss bodily existence in relationship to the movement from death with Christ to new life with Christ. "The body of sin" in 6:6 does not refer to physical bodies as intrinsically sinful, a view Paul never espouses, but rather to the physical and social body in the grip of sin, under sin's distorting and destructive ownership. "Body" here has a corporate rather than an individual sense, as indicated by the plural "our" modifying "old self" in the previous clause. "Body of sin" thus denotes the whole structure of embodied human life dominated by sin as a power greater than human beings, which nonetheless operates in and through human systems and relationships. This structure has been abrogated through Christ's death and therefore has no lasting reality. To "die" to it is to be separated from its false systems of worth and controlling values and instead to find one's worth and behavior directed to and by God in Christ Jesus (6:11).

The basis for this assurance of new life is found in Christ's own victory over death (6:9–10). Crucially, Paul emphasizes Christ's temporary subjection to death: "death *no longer* has dominion over him" implies that in Christ's incarnation, death *did* rule over him. Similarly, in the crucifixion Christ "died to sin once for all." Shocking though it may be, Christ entered fully into the realm of human dereliction and in *that place* won the victory over sin and death. The line of movement is from God to humanity; it is Christ's immersive participation in human suffering that forges the bond which in turn lifts the human race out of death into the promise of resurrection. Again, we may think of the baptism of Jesus, wherein Jesus was fully submerged in the sin-saturated waters of the Jordan and in that place was revealed as God's beloved Son.

This divinely initiated solidarity between Christ and humanity empowers a series of imperatives that begins in 6:11. Significantly, Paul's first command is not about behavior but rather about a basic reconsideration of who we now are in union with Christ, a union that renders us both dead and alive—dead to sin, and alive to God.

In 6:12–14, having laid the groundwork of union with Christ, Paul now exhorts his listeners regarding their actual behavior in their "mortal bodies." The governing metaphor here is slavery; in Paul's social cosmos, human beings belong to one master or another: either to sin as a ruthless overlord or to God, the author of life.

Verse 12 begins with a third-person-singular imperative, which does not exist in English grammar and is difficult to translate. The subject of the verb is sin, not the Roman audience. The RSV rightly translates this grammatical construction as "let not sin therefore reign"; the NRSVue mistakenly implies that the Roman listeners are being commanded, "do not let sin reign." In fact, the Greek leaves open the question, Who will keep sin from reigning? In this regard, it is notable that the third-person imperative often expresses a prayer to God for protection from enemies. This is particularly evident in the psalms. For example, in Psalm 35:4–6 the psalmist prays:

> Let them be put to shame and dishonor
> who seek after my life.
> Let them be turned back and confounded
> who devise evil against me.
> Let them be like chaff before the wind,
> . . . .
> Let their way be dark and slippery,
> with the angel of the Lord pursuing them.

(See also Pss 7:9; 9:19–20; 69:13.)

This common use of the third-person imperative as a prayer to God suggests that in Romans 6:12, Paul prays for God to vanquish sin's reign (Marcus 1988). This prayer, with the corresponding promise that "sin will have no dominion over you" (v. 14a), buttresses three further imperatives in 6:13 that command the Roman believers to act out God's victory over sin in their lives: first, negatively ("no longer present your members to sin"), and then positively ("present yourselves to God" and "present your members to God"). "Members" simply means bodily members such as arms, legs, hands, and feet. The word translated "instruments" also means "weapons," which fits the military imagery implicit in Paul's motif of conflict between sin and righteousness. To present one's bodily members as weapons, either to sin or to righteousness, is to recognize that one is involved in a war between God and the forces of evil in which it is not possible to be neutral (cf. 13:12). To "present" oneself or one's body to another is literally to stand beside them, to place oneself at their disposal, in the position of a soldier or an enslaved person awaiting orders.

This subsection culminates in 6:14 with the repeated promise that "sin will have no dominion over you." Such an assurance follows directly from the theme of solidarity with Christ in 6:1–13. But 6:14b springs a surprise on the listener: sin will not dominate you because "you are not under law but under grace." Why this sudden opposition between the law and grace? And why is the law apparently impotent against sin, while grace is powerful? Paul's claim reaches back to 5:20, where he briefly and shockingly says the law came on the human scene in order to increase sin, not to subdue it. If the law multiplies sin, to be "under the law" is to be vulnerable to sin rather than armored against it. Behind this counterintuitive claim lies sin's cooptation of the law, a topic that Paul develops further in 7:7–25. Conversely, to be "under grace" is to be governed by the free gift of God in Christ, which includes the redeeming lordship of Christ present in the community. This is the lordship that Paul proclaims in 6:15–23.

6:15–23. Slaves of Sin or Slaves of God

The rhetorical structure of 6:15–16 precisely matches that of 6:1–3, opening with a question inferred from the immediately preceding statement (v. 14), followed by a negative exclamation—"By no means!"—followed by "Do you not know?" introducing a corrective positive statement. This repetitive pattern implies the beginning of a new subsection in the argument. Thematically, however, 6:15–19 continues the focus of verses 12–14. In both 6:1 and 6:15 Paul corrects a false inference that God's grace leads to dissolute living because sin no longer results in final condemnation. In both verses, he implies that such a possibility is so far removed from reality as to be laughable, not least because it misconstrues the nature of sin and grace as competing masters. Therefore sin is never an expression of free individual choice, but of servile captivity. Why would anyone want to return to such bondage? And freedom from sin does not come from individual autonomy, but from a binding relationship with Christ as Lord.

In line with Paul's stated goal of bringing about "the obedience of faith" (1:5), 6:16–19 contrasts life in bondage to sin with life in obedience to God's new regime of grace. This obedience is the practical expression of belonging to Christ, whose own "obedience" overcame Adam's disobedience and will establish many as righteous (5:19). Resuming the metaphor of slavery, "present your members as slaves to righteousness" picks up on the mixture of military and slavery imagery in 6:13. This imagery would remind Paul's Roman audience of the practice of selling oneself into slavery, whether due to debt, poverty, or a desire to better oneself through belonging to an upwardly mobile master. In any case, once one became enslaved there was no exit from ownership by one's master, except through death or manumission. At the same time, to belong to a new owner is to be freed from any claims by a past master—in this case, sin and death.

Paul's syntax in 6:16–23 is confusing for three reasons. First, he sets up two columns of opposing regimes of power, but whereas the master in one column is consistently named as "sin" (vv. 16, 17, 18, 20, 22, 23), in the opposing column there is a series of "masters" to whom believers offer obedience and to whom they belong: "obedience" itself (v. 16), "the form of teaching" (v. 17), "righteousness" (v. 18), and finally, "God" (v. 22). Paul's shifting depictions of God's "mastery" only make sense as variations on the ways in which believers enact belonging to God—through obedience, teaching, and righteousness leading to increasing holiness (v. 19).

Second, the phrase "the form of teaching [*typos didachēs*] to which you were entrusted" is difficult to interpret, because *typos* can mean imprint, form, or model. As noted above, in 5:14 Adam is a *typos* of Christ in the sense of being an imprint of Christ, who is the image of God. In Philippians 3:17 Paul and his fellow missionaries are *typoi* in the sense of being models of faith; the same obtains for the addressees of 1 Thessalonians 1:7. In all these verses, *typos* refers to a human being. What then does it mean to speak of a *typos* of teaching? Perhaps Paul has in mind the transformation of believers through the inner imprint of teaching about Christ, such that they now bear his image. Such an interpretation builds on the close identification between believers and Christ that undergirds Paul's logic.

Third, the verb translated by the NRSVue as "entrusted" is *paradidōmi,* the same word that depicts God's action in handing disobedient humanity over to destructive forces (1:24, 26, 28), and in handing Christ over to death on behalf of disobedient humanity (4:25; 8:32). Since *paradidōmi* means "delivered into the custody of" another, the implication is that God has committed believers into the care or protection of a form of teaching imprinted on them. The tense indicates a specific event in the past. Perhaps Paul has in mind the event of baptism as immersion into Christ's death, expressing union with Christ; perhaps he assumes the Roman believers have received instruction about Christ. In any case, believers belong in heart, mind, and body to God, and that belonging also entails their own total commitment to a new lordship imprinted within their very being.

By juxtaposing slavery and freedom, Paul's astounding claim in 6:18 boggles the mind. This is the first occurrence in Romans of the language of "freedom," right in the thick of slavery imagery. He repeats the same claim in 6:22. Paul's idea of freedom is very far from modern notions of isolated individual free will, as if individuals were under no distorting or constraining influences. Such isolated individualism simply does not exist in Paul's social imagination. For this reason, freedom is always mediated and expressed through relationships of belonging to powers greater than the self, so a great deal depends on the nature and effects of those powers. Liberated from their old tyrannical master, sin, believers now belong to a new master characterized by love and righteousness, and a new household characterized by God's unmitigated generosity. Since God's righteousness is revealed through God's saving power on behalf of God's people (1:16–17), to belong to that righteousness is to be free indeed.

Therefore, in 6:20–23 Paul concludes by contrasting the outcomes of serving sin or God. In 6:20–21 he depicts the Roman Christians' past life; in verse 22, beginning with "but now," he shifts to their present reality; in verse 23 he concludes with a stunning contrast between sin's "wages" and God's free gift. The tenses are important: Paul is not telling his listeners to choose between two present realities; rather, he is reminding them of their deliverance from their past life of slavery to sin, in contrast with their present fruitfulness and hope of eternal life. In view of 6:18, the statement "you were free in regard to righteousness" (v. 20) must be read as ironic; as the following questions insinuate, what kind of freedom leads to shame and ends in death? The language of shame contrasts with Paul's confident claim, "I am not ashamed" (1:16), and the assurance that "hope does not put us to shame" (5:5). The contrast between "fruit" that ends with death (6:21) and fruit that leads to holiness and eternal life (6:22) anticipates 7:4–5.

In this context, 6:23 does not mean that God repays sin with death, as emblazoned on religious billboards. The word translated "wages" can mean both remuneration and rations: sin is a slave driver who repays his slaves with death, a commander whose soldiers are on starvation rations. In the slave economy and militarized society of Rome, Paul's listeners would be vividly aware of such brutality. In contrast with the zero-sum economy of sin's regime, God is the owner of all creation, who freely gives eternal life, a life bound up with the gracious lordship of Jesus Christ. This is why Paul can equate service to God with freedom.

7:1–6. Dead to the Law, Alive with Christ

In 6:1–23 Paul has painted a picture of believers' death to sin's dominion and liberation to new life through union with Christ in baptism; now he speaks of death to the law (7:4). This section divides into two subsections: in 7:1–4 Paul uses the analogy of marriage to illustrate believers' transformed relationship to the law; in verses 5–6 he spells out the meaning of this analogy. Like 5:1–11, this section functions in a transitional way, as it raises the question of the law's relationship with sin, which Paul will take up in 7:7–25.

Insofar as Paul is writing to primarily gentile churches, his insistence that "you" have died to the law (7:4) is curious and prompts numerous theories regarding his audience and his intentions in these puzzling verses. Since the Roman churches probably began in the synagogues and the first gentile believers would have been God-fearing gentiles who worshiped in the synagogues, we can assume that Paul's words would not have been inappropriate. He certainly assumes considerable knowledge of Israel's Scriptures and stories as he writes to the Romans; he may also assume that many of his listeners there are attracted to the law and see no conflict in their life being determined by law observance along with baptism into Christ. Perhaps also his experience in Galatia is influencing his argument here and he is making a preemptive strike against the teaching that gentile converts need to be circumcised and keep kosher. This is speculative reconstruction of a historical situation beyond our ken; what is clear, however, is that in Paul's view, the law is powerless against sin, and can even become a tool of sin.

Again asking, "do you not know, brothers and sisters," Paul addresses himself to "those who know the law" (7:1). As we have noted, this qualification does not exclude gentile converts who are familiar with Israel's Scripture. Just as death in union with Christ liberates believers from a binding relationship with sin (6:2), so here death severs a binding relationship with the law. Paul immediately illustrates this claim with an analogy drawn from the death of a spouse (7:2–4). The point in the marriage analogy is straightforward: the death of a spouse completely alters the situation of the survivor, including making possible a new relational bond. Furthermore, death as a kind of severance from "the law concerning the husband" means the law cannot condemn the surviving widow who joins with another man. The widow is not under the threat of condemnation, because she has "died to the law" itself (cf. Gal 2:16–19), so the law has no authority over her. There is no reason to think Paul does not have the Mosaic law in mind, as he will clarify the relationship between the divinely given law and sin in Romans 7:7–25.

Nonetheless, the analogy is confusing because first "the husband" dies (v. 3), then believers are said to "have died to the law . . . so that you may belong to another" (v. 4). Paul's meaning seems to be that after the husband's death, the widow is not bound by the law against adultery. Believers have been cast in the role of the wife, now freed from the ownership and law of the husband; nonetheless, it is unclear just who has "died." To further complicate the analogy, Christ (the new "husband") is actually the one who has died, and believers have been baptized into his death. Perhaps it is best not to press Paul's analogy too far in its details and instead focus on the main point: the death of a spouse means the widow or widower is free to remarry; indeed, the surviving spouse may become a new person in relationship to a new partner.

Paul is careful not to say that the law has died. Rather, he says, "*You* have died to the law through the body of Christ." In other words, the law continues to exist, but it no longer dominates or determines the identity and worth of believers. The reference is to believers' union with Christ's own death, so that "the body of Christ" refers to Christ's crucified body. Thus in 7:4 Paul depicts a shift from belonging to the law to belonging to the crucified and resurrected Christ. This new belonging will yield "fruit for God," in explicit contrast with 6:21, where slavery to sin yields shameful "fruit."

The pressing question at this point is why the law has such toxic effects on those whose life it constitutes. Paul begins to take up this question in 7:5–6. First, verse 5 offers a tantalizing answer, at which Paul has hinted in 5:20 and which he will develop in 7:7–12: in the context of "the flesh," the law arouses "sinful passions" that "bear fruit for death." "Sinful passions" is literally "the passions of the sins"; rather than saying that all "passions" are inherently sinful, Paul may be delineating passions as susceptible to sin.

"In the flesh" (*sarx*) denotes a realm of physical existence subject to sin and death. When he wants to speak specifically about physical bodies in a neutral sense, Paul uses a different word, *sōma.* Sometimes Paul uses "flesh" to refer to mortal physical existence (2 Cor 4:11; Gal 3:3; 4:13–14; Phil 1:22, 24) or kinship (Rom 1:3; 9:3), but even in its neutral use, "flesh" has the sense of that which is limited to merely human effort, at best (Gal 4:23); it is bodily enmeshment in sin's domain, and it ceases with death. Paul speaks of the resurrection of the body (*sōma*) but never of the resurrection of the flesh (see 1 Cor 15:35–54). For this reason, the *flesh* signifies a realm of bodily existence subject to death and sin's toxic power (Rom 8:3–9, 12–13; cf. Gal 5:16–24). Here, "while we were living in the flesh" means "while we were still existing in a regime dominated by sin." In this realm, the good law functions counter to its purpose, arousing rather than controlling sinful passions. Repeating 6:21 and in antithesis to 7:4, the outcome of this unholy alliance of sin and the law is "fruit for death."

Finally, in 7:6 Paul links the metaphors of marriage and slavery in a summary of 6:1–7:5. Like the woman who has been "discharged from the law" through the death of her husband, now "we" have been discharged from the law's oversight through becoming "dead to that which held us captive"—that is, sin's use of the law. The result of this new situation is paradoxical liberation for service in the new dominion of the Spirit rather than "the oldness of the written code" (Gk., the oldness of the letter). The sudden opposition between "the Spirit" and "the letter" recalls 2:29, where circumcision is by the Spirit and not the letter (see commentary; cf. 2 Cor 3:1–6). The issue for Paul seems to be one of power; only the indwelling Spirit of the God who raised Jesus from the dead has the power to overcome sin's lethal reign (Rom 8:3). "Written code" denotes the old relational identity and way of life constituted by sin's deadly use of the law, as 7:7–11 will illustrate. "Spirit" names the new realities of an identity and way of life animated and indwelt by the Spirit of God, as 8:4–30 will illustrate. Romans 7:6 thus sets the agenda for 7:7–8:39.

EXCURSUS

Reflections for Preaching and Teaching

Slaves of Sin, Slaves of God?

For some preachers and biblical interpreters today, the metaphor of slavery is so offensive that they deem it unusable. The offense is multiplied exponentially by the historic complicity of Christian churches in the slave trade in Europe and the United States and by the heinous deployment of Scripture to defend the enslavement of human beings as a God-given good. How are we to reckon with this language in contemporary preaching and teaching?

First, it is helpful to recall the historical context of slavery in the Roman Empire. As noted in the introduction, slavery was ubiquitous in the first-century Mediterranean world, and the Roman house churches probably had a large population of enslaved and freed persons. Whereas some enslaved persons might have had relatively high-status positions and considerable social power in large wealthy households, for most of them life was tenuous at best, subject to violent oppression and death, with no legal recourse. To be enslaved was to have no family, no history, no place of one's own, and no future. Paul and his listeners knew this reality intimately; it was built into the fabric of daily life in a rigidly hierarchical social structure. When Paul depicted sin as a tyrannical slave driver that repaid its slaves with death, his listeners would know whereof he spoke.

Furthermore, Paul was not unusual in using slavery as a metaphor for human wrongdoing. For example, the first-century Stoic philosopher Epictetus, who grew up enslaved in Nero's household and gained his freedom as an adult, describes in scathing terms the "handsomest and sleekest slavery" of the senatorial classes (*Discourses* 4.1.40). He sneers at the upper-class young man who boasts of his freedom: "Were you never commanded by your sweetheart to do something you didn't wish to do? Did you never cozen your pet slave? Did you never kiss his feet?" (4.1.17). Compulsions, addictions, desires, habits, fears, all can and do deprive people of their supposed freedom. Epictetus concludes, "No bad man is free" (4.1.5). In this respect, slave owners are every bit as enslaved as their captives.

Contemporary analogies are widespread. Many years ago, I was teaching in a seminary setting, and one student said, "The difficulty with preaching today is that people don't know about sin." I said, "They know about slavery." In my mind was a billboard I passed every day when driving to work. It had a huge black-and-white photo of two cupped hands filled with pills, and three words: "Addiction is slavery." Not only is addiction slavery; abusive relationships, victimization in war, destructive relational patterns, and the endless cycle of aggression and retribution that grips the human race are all symptoms of humanity's bondage to sin.

But what of being "slaves of righteousness"? It is here that modern individualist notions of the person get in our way. For Paul, freedom is not about individual autonomy, as if we could invent ourselves; for Paul, we always exist in the mode of belonging, and our flourishing as well as our suffering are bound up in the network of human and divine connection that holds and sustains us. It is not a matter of slavery versus "free" self-determining individual autonomy; it is a matter of belonging to the one master, God, whose abundant generosity and grace liberate human agents (cf. 5:17, 21). For this reason, Paul introduces himself as "a slave of Jesus Christ" (1:1; cf. Phil 1:1; Gal 1:10). Even more shockingly, he depicts Jesus himself as "taking the form of a slave" and suffering the form of execution reserved for traitors and enslaved persons (Phil 2:7–8). It is this divine solidarity with enslaved persons, in their liminal status at the very bottom rung of Roman society, that sources true freedom.

The metaphor of slavery calls us to ponder the vulnerable, fragile, and essential network of human connection in which we all live. It undercuts any heroic, macho pictures of Christian freedom, along with any individualistic pictures of human well-being. The way to freedom is not solitary self-sufficiency but belonging to a gracious community where truth can be told in the context of love. In this sense, the positive meaning of "slavery to God" is that we belong to One who is greater than we are, who joins us in solidarity at the lowest point of existence, and who wills our flourishing.

Augustine captured this well in his famous prayer:

> O thou who are the light of the minds that know thee, the life of the souls that love thee, and the strength of the wills that serve thee: help us so to know thee that we may truly love thee, so to love thee that we may fully serve thee, whom to serve is perfect freedom.

Gift and Transformation

Paul is supremely confident that God's unmerited grace given to unworthy recipients has power to change human lives. It is easy to miss just how countercultural this claim is. Reward and punishment, threats and promises, carrot-and-stick disciplinary measures do not change human hearts; only love can do that. This is not to say there are no consequences for bad behavior; there certainly are, and necessarily so for the well-being of the community as well as the individual. Nonetheless, grace, not law, brings liberation from sin (6:14). At this point we may note two aspects of the liberating power of God's gift of Christ.

First, Paul expects his listeners to be changed through union with Christ, a union initiated and sustained through Christ's participation in humanity. Through baptism into Christ, believers have undergone a real change in their situation, a real death of their old identity in relationship to sin, and a real newness in relationship to Christ. This transformation involves both God's action and human action in union with Christ through the Spirit. From the human side, the change involves a new cognitive and perceptive reality—to reckon oneself as dead to sin and alive to God in Christ is to know oneself as "reckoned righteous," as one to whom the Lord does not "reckon sin." For this reason, the believer's present and future are not determined by the past (Phil 3:7–14). As Colossians 2:13–14 puts it vividly, God has nailed humanity's rap sheet to the cross.

Second, the regime of life in Christ, under grace, is qualitatively different from the regime of bondage under sin. Under sin's power, human existence is headed for death; in grace, there is no threat of condemnation and the end point is life. To live under the threat of condemnation and rejection is like being on probation in a cancel culture; to live in the realm of assured acceptance is like being a child at home in a loving family.

Bodies Are Where the Action Happens

Body language dominates Paul's discussion of death and new life in Romans 6:5–19. This is not because Paul denigrates bodily existence—far from it! He uses body language extensively because physical experience is where the action is, the very place where God's redeeming work happens. Paul simply cannot conceptualize disembodied existence or the idea of a disembodied "soul" or "mind" as the true center of the self. No, for Paul we are embodied through and through, and therefore we also are connected to other people in social "bodies." This means that the word for "body" (*sōma*) means socially embedded physical existence. Such physical existence is good, it is in the image of God, it is sanctified by God's Son who bore a human body. At the same time, it is vulnerable to decay, abuse, and death. As illustrations of this reality, we may think of the role of physical therapy and massage in treatment for victims of abuse and trauma; as the title of a classic book on trauma puts it, "the body keeps the score" (Van der Kolk 2014). Bodies carry the scars and memories of experience, both in the skin and in the emotions, and therefore transformation inevitably involves bodies. Paul's body language speaks directly to this reality. Liberation and change involve both mental changes, as we are to "reckon" ourselves as dead to sin, and bodily action, as we are to offer our arms and legs and hands and feet to God in the service of the gospel. This is a holistic picture of human transformation in the context of the church community as the body of Christ (cf. 12:1–13).

7:7–25. Sin, the Law, and the Self

In Romans 7:7, Paul abruptly shifts into a first-person performance that continues through the end of the chapter. That performance vividly enacts the experience that Paul describes in 7:5: "While we were living in the flesh, our sinful passions, aroused by the law, were at work in our members to bear fruit for death." Few passages in Paul's letters have instigated more arguments than this audacious depiction of personal anguish over the gap between good intentions and destructive outcomes for human actions. And few passages invite and provoke such identification on the part of Paul's readers; scholars argue about the situation Paul is depicting and the identity of the speaker, but rare (and delusional?) is the person who never identifies with the repeated lament, "I do not understand my own actions. For I do not do what I want, but I do the very thing I hate" (vv. 15, 19).

Two overarching questions dominate the interpretation of this chapter.

First, whose experience is this? Is Paul describing his own past experience as a devout Jew trying to keep the law of Moses? Is he describing the experience of all human beings "under the power of sin" (3:9)? Is he enacting the present experience of Christians who are "in Christ" but still beset by sin? Augustine famously changed his mind on this question; early in his Christian life he thought Romans 7:7–25 depicted pre-Christian experience, but later he came to think it referred to the experience of Christians, a view shared by Martin Luther and John Calvin. On the other hand, the majority of modern scholars (although not all) think Paul cannot be talking about the experience of those who have been baptized into Christ's death in order to walk in newness of life (6:2–4), to whom Paul says, "Sin will have no dominion over you, since you are not under law but under grace" (6:14).

Second, what is the purpose of these verses, precisely at this point in the letter? One common answer is that Paul is defending the goodness of the law. Having spoken harshly about the Mosaic law in the letter up to this point, Paul pauses to distinguish between the law, which is good, and sin as a power that uses the good law to evil ends. As will become evident, however, although this defense of the law is certainly a part of the argument, it is by no means the whole of it. Rather, any attempt to come to grips with 7:7–25 must attend to the style as well as the content of these verses. Written in the first person, shifting from the past to the present tense at 7:14, and full of emotion, this speech affects both Paul's original listeners and today's readers. Paul is writing to a group of Christian believers in a way that invites them to share the experience of someone in the grip of indwelling sin; what does he want this dramatic experience to accomplish in and for them? And how does this passage contribute to his overall purposes in the letter?

Paul's dramatic monologue in 7:7–25 communicates an experience that is well-nigh universal in its scope. The speech *begins* with a question about the law, but it *ends* with a confessional statement by the speaker. In fact, the relationship of sin to the law cannot be understood without also understanding the effects of both sin and the law on the self. In a three-act drama that sets the stage for 8:1–3, the dramatic narrative of 7:7–25 depicts a complex interaction between the law, sin, and the self. In act 1 (vv. 7–13), the focus is on the law in relationship to sin; act 2 (vv. 14–21) displays the relationship between sin and the speaker; in act 3 (vv. 22–25) the spotlight again falls on the law, but this time in relationship to the constitution of the self.

7:7–13. The Law Is Not Sin, but It Is Co-Opted by Sin

As noted earlier, "what shall we say?" often introduces a question that follows from the preceding argument, followed by an emphatically negative answer. Since Paul has made quite a few negative statements about the law (Rom 3:19–21; 6:14; 7:1–6), in 7:7 he asks the logical question, Is the law sin? and answers, "By no means!" This is not the first time in the letter Paul has defended the law; already in 3:31 he asks, "Do we overthrow the law?" and answers, "By no means! On the contrary, we uphold the law." But now he asks the question again with greater urgency and gives a full, passionate, if not precisely clear, answer. For instead of unambiguously upholding the law, Paul continues with a series of statements that further link the law with sin.

First, the law brings the knowledge of sin: "I would not have known what it is to covet if the law had not said, 'You shall not covet'" (7:7). In Greek, "to covet" (*epithymēsein*) could also be translated "to desire." There are two ways to understand this knowledge of sin: the law provides information that something (such as covetous desire) is sinful; the law awakens the desire itself. According to the first interpretation, the law teaches the correct evaluation of actions and attitudes, so that one cannot plead ignorance; in the second, the law acts as a catalyst for covetous desire. These are not mutually exclusive options, and Paul seems to have both interpretations in view; taken together, they disclose a tight interaction between sin and the law. In a classic double bind, the law triggers covetous desire, and the law names that desire as sinful. Paul clearly has the law of Moses in view here, because he cites the tenth commandment (Exod 20:17; Deut 5:21), which is arguably the final summary of the Decalogue.

In Romans 7:8–11 Paul introduces the word "commandment" (*entolē*) in reference to the specific commandment "you shall not covet." Verses 8 and 11 repeat verbatim, "Sin, seizing an opportunity through the commandment," followed by varied but parallel main clauses: sin uses the commandment to generate every kind of desire (*epithymian*) in the speaker; sin uses the commandment to deceive and kill the speaker. The word translated "opportunity" means "staging area," as in a base of operations for a military assault; sin uses the law as a staging area for its assaults on the self, through desire (v. 8), deception, and death (v. 11). This militaristic image of sin's use of the law brackets the central story line (vv. 9–10) in which the "I" is displaced by sin after the coming of the commandment. "I was once alive apart from the law, but when the commandment came, sin revived and I died." The self was alive and sin lay dormant; sin came to life and the self died. Here is a deadly exchange, the precise opposite of Christ's life-giving exchange in which he dies so that we may live.

In Paul's narrative, the commandment against covetous desire merges with the original commandment in the story of Adam and Eve in the garden. Sin plays the role of the serpent who used the commandment against eating from the tree of knowledge to awaken desire and then deceive Eve and Adam, leading to death for humanity's progenitors. Paul draws the conclusion: the commandment promised life but resulted in death (7:10). By casting sin in the role of the serpent, Paul depicts it as the chief actor in this part of the drama; sin is not a verb depicting what human beings do, but rather a hostile and slippery con artist who uses God's good law contrary to its life-giving intention, by triggering destructive desires, deceiving, and ultimately killing human beings, including the speaker who narrates his own demise. Notably, the first appearance of the word "sin" in Genesis is similar: in the story of Cain and Abel, God tells Cain that "sin is lurking at the door; its desire is for you, but you must master it" (Gen 4:7).

This depiction of sin's use of the law is richly allusive, not only echoing the story of the fall and citing the tenth commandment, but also reprising Romans 5:12–20, where Adam is clearly in view. In 7:9 the speaker says, "When the commandment came, sin revived"; in 5:20 Paul says, "The law came in to increase sin." As in 5:12–21 and 6:23, Paul again draws a close connection between sin and death (7:8–11), but now the law enters the picture, and the drama is focused on the experience of the individual speaker. As is typical of the structure of Romans, Paul circles back to themes he has already stated, expanding and deepening them. Here, what he stated in cosmic terms embracing the sweep of human history (5:12–20) he now expresses in personal, experiential language. By evoking his earlier argument, and invoking Genesis, Exodus, and Deuteronomy in support of his claims about sin and the law, Paul also calls Scripture itself to witness to sin's hostile takeover of the law, which subverts the promise that obedience to the law leads to life.

In 7:12, an apparent about-face, Paul suddenly affirms the goodness of the law, as if drawing a conclusion: "So the law is holy." The NRSVue translation smooths out the grammatical difficulty in this verse, which in Greek reads, "So then, on the one hand, the law is holy," as if Paul is beginning to make a comparison; the problem is that he never gets to "on the other hand," which by implication would offer a different statement about the law. Yet in the following verses he clarifies further the enslavement of the self, which ultimately renders the law powerless against sin: "We know that the law is spiritual, but I am of the flesh, sold into slavery under sin" (7:14).

The identity of the speaker who is in such desperate straits is both inclusive and elusive. The citation of the tenth commandment suggests that Paul is speaking in the persona of a devout Jew. The possible echo of Genesis, however, implies the speaker represents Adam or Adam's heirs—that is, all humanity in the wake of Adam's sin. The clear links with Romans 5:12–20 support such a conclusion, but do not thereby exclude a specific reference to Jewish devotion to the law of Moses. Paul also may be drawing on his own experience of devotion to the law, since in Philippians 3:6 he says he was "blameless" concerning "righteousness under the law," but at the same time he was zealously persecuting the church (cf. Gal 1:13–14). This juxtaposition of "blameless" law observance with opposition to the church of God illuminates sin's use of the law to deceive and kill (Rom 7:11).

The different clues to the speaker's identity argue against nailing it down as *either* one or another possibility. Rather, Paul's own experience, references to devotion to the law of Moses, and the universal plight of all human beings under the power of sin (Rom 3:9) paint a broadly inclusive picture of the I who is speaking here.

The more pressing question for many interpreters is whether the speaker represents the experience of believers or of those not yet "in Christ." Given Paul's strong affirmations in chapters 5–6 of believers' liberation from sin, there are good reasons for understanding 7:7–25 as a vivid *retrospective* performance of life apart from Christ. On the other hand, it is important to ponder the effects of Paul's striking rhetoric here. The I who speaks in 7:7–25 is like the I in the Psalter, who speaks both personally and potentially for anyone who identifies with the psalmist's experience. Similarly, Paul's rhetoric catches his listeners up into the experience of the I, even though he is writing to Christians. And that observation suggests that Paul's purpose here is not to make a systematic doctrinal argument about the theological status of believers or unbelievers, but to speak to the experience of his listeners, and in that sense, perhaps to repreach the gospel to them. This is a style of communication that fits the old dictum: if the shoe fits, wear it.

7:14–21. Sin and the Self

In 7:14, Paul very briefly steps out of the persona of the singular I with the startling claim "We know that the law is spiritual." Just as he began this section of the letter with a plural question ("What then shall we say?") in verse 7, so here also he appeals directly to his readers, establishing a shared positive understanding of the law (v. 1). Paul has used the phrase "we know" at two key points earlier in the letter, both of which have important links to 7:7–25. In 2:1–3 Paul emphasizes the judgment of God, which falls on all who practice and do evil; in 7:15–16 and 19–20, the same verbs depict sin itself as the active agent who practices and does evil through the self as its unwilling accomplice. This ascription of agency to sin distinguishes between sin and the self, and between sin and the "spiritual" law that is co-opted by sin. In 3:19–20, Paul uses the formulaic "we know" to refer to the law's role in holding all humanity accountable to God and in bringing about the knowledge of sin. The third occurrence of "we know" in 7:14 emphasizes the law's divine origin and goodness, which paradoxically is demonstrated in the previous verse 13 by exposing sin's utter sinfulness.

When Paul says the law is "spiritual" (7:14) he refers to its divine origin in connection with the Spirit of God. He does not mean that the law is disembodied in contrast with the "fleshly" speaker. Rather, building on 6:16–23, the speaker immediately defines "of the flesh" as "sold into slavery under sin." The self "sold under sin" acts at the bidding of sin, a ruthless master who repays its slaves with death (6:23).

With considerable pathos, the anonymous I now dramatizes the experience of being indwelt and co-opted by sin. In two parallel passages, 7:14–17 and 7:18–20 enact the self's experience of sin's mastery. This repetitive pattern becomes clearer through close attention to the Greek text, as in the following translation and outline:

14 A For we know that the law is spiritual
But I am of the flesh, sold under sin
15 B For I do not understand what I am accomplishing
C For I do not practice what I want, but I do what I hate.
16 D If I do what I do not want, I agree that the law is good.
17 E Now then I am no longer the one accomplishing it, but sin that dwells in me.
18 A′ For I know that the good does not dwell in me, that is, in my flesh.
B′ For to want the good is close at hand, but not to accomplish it.
19 C′ For the good that I want is not what I do, but the evil I do not want is what I practice.

20 D′ If I do what I do not want,
E′ I am no longer the one accomplishing it,
but sin that dwells in me.
21 B″ So I find it to be a law that when I want to do the good, evil
lies close at hand.

With the singular "I know" (7:18), Paul amplifies what he states in the plural "we know" of verse 14. "I know that nothing good dwells in me, that is, in my flesh" further describes "of the flesh, sold into slavery under sin." Enmeshed in the realm of sin and death, which Paul elsewhere calls "the flesh" (7:5; 8:3–13), the I does not have any inner resources for resisting sin. Rather, indwelling "sin" has displaced the good, leaving the person powerless to do the good he truly wants, and twisting the outcome of his actions into what he actually "hates" (7:15, 18–19). The cause of this disaster is not an inner conflict in the self, nor a lack of willpower, but the presence of sin as an alien, hostile invader who has taken up residence and imprisoned the self, intruding between the good that she wants and the outcome of her actions.

The NRSVue translation of 7:18b captures the sense of the Greek, which says, "To want the good lies close at hand, but to enact it does not." The problem is not that the speaker just needs to try harder. Rather, 7:21 sums up the problem: "When I want to do what is good, evil lies close at hand." The issue is not a weakness of the will, nor wrong motives, nor some essential depravity of the self; the issue is the intimate and powerful action of a stronger resident power, which Paul calls "indwelling sin," that intrudes between human intentions and their outcomes. Verse 21 thus sums up the relationship between the self and sin enacted in 7:15–20, but it also introduces the verses that follow.

Given the individualism of modern assumptions about the self, it is difficult to get at Paul's meaning here. As has become clear by this point in the letter, Paul does not see human beings as autonomous individuals who can choose to do good or to do evil. He does not see sin as an individual choice at all; we are not free to sin. Rather, he sees persons as selves-in-relationship to larger social, and indeed cosmic, realities: on the one hand, the realities of sin and death; on the other hand, the greater reality of God's redemption through Christ. In 7:7–15, sin is revealed as a power that acts on and in and through human beings but is not the same as them. Just as in 7:7–13 Paul sharply distinguished between sin and the law, so here he distinguishes between the self, who wants the good, and sin, which sabotages that good desire. One wonders again if Paul's own experience echoes in the background here. In his former zeal for the law, he surely wanted the good, and indeed believed he was serving God, but he discovered, to his horror, that in fact he was opposing God's own people.

7:22–25. Sin, the Self, and the Law

As noted above, 7:21 is a transitional verse linking back to verse 18 and setting the stage for what follows. Verses 22–25 then bring together the earlier dramatizations of the law in relation to sin, and the self in relation to sin, in an exposé of sin's full-blown appropriation of the law for its hostile takeover of the self. These verses are exceedingly dense and difficult. The word "law" appears seven times in the space of five verses; the major interpretive issue is whether it has the same referent in each case, as the law of God, or whether it has at least two different meanings. The verses set forth a series of antitheses, which become clear through a close reading of the Greek text. The repetition of phrases is noted by italicizing and underlining the text at key points:

22 A For I take delight in *the law of God in my inner person*
23 B but I see another law in my members
A′ waging war on *the law of my mind*
B′ and taking me captive to the law of sin which is in my members.
24 Wretched person that I am! Who will deliver me from this body of death?
25a Thanks be to God through Jesus Christ our Lord!
25b A″ So then, on the one hand, I myself serve *the law of God with my mind*
B″ but on the other hand, the law of sin with the flesh.

At first glance it appears that the speaker opposes two different "laws" here: on the one hand, there is the "law of God" in the inner self, which is the same as the "law of my mind"—that is, the law of God that I serve with my mind. Opposed to this law stands the "other law" at work in my bodily members, in "the body of death";

this law is the "law of sin," in stark contrast with the "law of God." These two laws are distinguished by their spheres of action, whether in the mind or in the flesh. If one reads these verses as referring to different parts of the self, 7:25 describes the experience of a divided self that gives God mental devotion while battling bodily sin, and the law of God only operates in the mind.

Within the immediate context of 7:22–25 such an interpretation may seem plausible, but in the larger context of the letter it falls short, for two reasons. First, Paul already has depicted the Mosaic law as used by sin to lethal ends (7:7–11), even while maintaining the goodness of the law (7:12, 14); God's law given through Moses is holy but can be and is used by sin. In this context, "the law of sin" (7:23) is the Mosaic law taken captive by sin. Second, 6:19 and 12:1 undercut any argument that there can be a nonphysical, mental devotion to God apart from bodily practices. Rather, physical bodies are precisely the place where God vanquishes the power of sin, even as those bodies connect believers to the larger social and transcendent body of Christ (12:1–5).

In 7:24, "the body of death" is the body under the control of death, just as "the law of sin" is the law co-opted by sin. The only antidote to the "law of sin" operating in the "body of death" is the far more powerful body of Christ, understood both as Christ's own self-giving on the cross (5:6–10) and the Spirit-indwelt social body of Christ in the church (12:4). For this reason, in 7:25a Paul interrupts this confession of need and futility with a stunning thanksgiving to God, anticipating the restatement of the gospel in 8:1–4. It is as if God, the chief protagonist of the drama, interrupts with a foretaste of the finale, in which the tragedy of 7:7–25 is changed into joyful victory. The order of the verses here is extremely puzzling; what that order does express is the human experience that alternates between human futility and confidence in God.

What then are we to make of Paul's references to "my inmost self," "the law of my mind," and his concluding statement in verse 25: "With my mind I am enslaved to the law of God, but with my flesh I am enslaved to the law of sin"? In light of the distinction between the human intention to do the good and the outcome of human actions (vv. 15–21), Paul's emphatic contrast between "mind" and "flesh" (vv. 22–23, 25) must refer to this gap between wanting and doing, intention and outcome, rather than between different parts of the self. The doing is the matter at hand, and it involves both mind and body. In this context, the concluding statement of verse 25b is not a victory cry, but a confession of futility: "With my mind—that is, in what I want to do—I serve God's good law, but what I actually accomplish in the sin-dominated sphere of bodily existence shows that I am enslaved to sin's use of the law."

The NRSVue translation of verse 25b omits an important emphasis in the Greek, in which "I myself" begins the phrase: it could be translated "of myself" (as in the RSV) or "by myself." The emphatic "I myself" accentuates the hopelessness of attempting to serve God on our own, apart from the indwelling Spirit. That is, "by myself, acting out of my own resources," I want what is good, I want the life that God's law promises, but my bodily actions serve the law used by sin (cf. vv. 8–11). No wonder the speaker cries out, "Who will rescue me from this body of death?" (v. 24).

EXCURSUS

Reflections for Preaching and Teaching

Romans 7:7–25 is an extraordinarily rich resource for preaching and teaching a liberating vision of the gospel. In the context of Paul's cosmic view of sin and death, in tandem with his relational view of the self, these verses yield compassionate insights into human suffering under sin. They prepare the listener to hear anew the good news proclaimed in Romans 8:1–2: "There is now no condemnation for those who are in Christ Jesus. For the law of the Spirit of life in Christ Jesus has set you free from the law of sin and of death." This is a word of promise spoken directly to the anguished speaker who cries out for deliverance from captivity to the law in the hands of sin and the body gripped by death (7:23–24).

The fluid and inclusive identity of the speaker in this drama invites identification on the part of Paul's listeners. To try to nail down the identity of the I is to ask the wrong question; like the psalmist, whose words become prayers of lament and rejoicing for countless readers, the speech of 7:7–25 gives voice to the experience of anyone who identifies with the speaker's dire straits. Paul is not making a systematic argument about the theological status of believers; he is making an experiential appeal intended to strengthen the Roman Christians in their faith and in the quality of their life together. He wants the good news of "no condemnation for those who are in Christ Jesus" to get down into their bones, to become the marrow of their being. He already has affirmed the theological identity of the Roman Christians as baptized into Christ, dead to that which held them captive, reigning in life (5:17), and victorious over sin (6:14). Thus, theologically speaking, the depiction of captivity to sin in 7:7–25 must be a retrospective account of life apart from Christ's redemption. But the account invites a vivid experience of that captivity in the *present.* To what end? To a new and deeper hearing of the gospel. At the same time, if there are any unbelievers overhearing this performance of life under sin and sin's use of the law, they also are invited into this story of the self, and thus into hearing and responding to the promise of 8:1–2.

These observations have several implications for preaching and teaching today.

A Model for Preaching

In the first place, here Paul models a style of preaching that invites people to experience anew their own need of Christ and then receive anew God's provision for that need. New Testament scholar E. P. Sanders (1977, pp. 442–43) argues that Paul's logic moves from "solution to plight," and that is certainly evident in Romans. Paul starts with the good news of the gospel as the power of God for salvation (1:16–17) and only then moves to the desperate situation of humanity and its need for salvation. But Paul's mode of communication alternates between plight and solution, between desolate need and divine deliverance, and he never tires of repreaching the gospel to those who presumably have heard it many times. He does not "move on" to "more advanced" teaching that leaves behind the basics of the faith; rather, he continually redirects his listeners' attention to God's abundant grace in Christ and their utter need of that divine generosity, as the ground of all further ethical guidance. This restatement of the human plight, followed by a repreaching of the gospel, is precisely what we see in Romans 7–8.

A Picture of the Life of Faith

This pattern of teaching not only serves as a model for teaching and preaching today but also discloses an intriguing picture of growth in faith and how it happens. Such growth certainly does not move in a linear progression, any more than the Letter to the Romans develops in a linear fashion. Rather, it oscillates between discouragement and hope, struggle and victory. The puzzling ending of 7:24–25 vividly enacts such fluctuation between hope and resignation, as does the larger letter structure in which 7:7–25 intervenes between the affirmations of 7:6 and 8:1. But what is the goal of such oscillation, and how might it function in the strengthening of faith? Two wise voices from the past may guide our thinking.

The first voice is that of John Chrysostom, who held that Romans 7–8 concerns "the fact that many fall into sin even after baptism." Paul addresses this situation by reminding readers first of their former condition, summed up in 7:25, and then of their incorporation into a fellowship indwelt by the Holy Spirit. In Chrysostom's words, through deliverance from condemnation, believers are being made "invincible for the future." Thus, Paul's reminder of past captivity and present deliverance has one overriding pastoral aim: "This grievous war did the grace of the Spirit put a stop to by slaying sin, and making the contest light to us, and crowning us at the outstart, and then drawing us to the struggle with abundant help" (*Hom. Rom.* 13, 216). In other words, the reminder of believers' former plight magnifies the hope and power of their present deliverance and the abundant help of the Spirit of God.

In a somewhat different vein, Julian of Norwich describes her fluctuation between joy and "feeling depressed, weary of my life, and disgusted with myself." She concludes that the experiences of both joy and desolation are useful for teaching her the constancy of divine love and care: it "is helpful for some souls to feel in this way: sometimes to be comforted, and sometimes to feel failure and be left to themselves. God wants us to know that he keeps us equally safe in sorrow and in joy" (Julian 2015, 13–14). Julian is describing a somewhat different experience than that of the speaker in Romans 7:7–25, but she ends at a similar point, shared with Chrysostom: passing through dereliction and futility, the believer realizes anew, perhaps even more confidently, the foundation of grace and love that is the reality of her life, and that has not changed.

Reframing Pastoral Care and Preaching

We have seen that Paul sharply distinguishes between the self and sin as an insidious, ruthless, and destructive power. The implications of this insight for pastoral care and preaching are radical and liberating. In the first place, Paul has a surprisingly positive view of human beings as fundamentally seeking life, not death, as wanting to do the right thing, as earnestly desiring the good. Nowhere in this chapter, which is the most thorough exposition of sin in all of Paul's letters, does he label human beings as sinners or as depraved. Nowhere does he question the motives of the inner self; indeed, insofar as he talks about what the I wants, its desires are entirely positive. The law exposes sin itself, not human beings, as "sinful beyond measure" (7:13). Paul thus drives a wedge between the person and sin, which opens up a kind of pastoral care in which God is seen as allied with the self, over against whatever form of bondage is at issue, whether that be addiction, destructive family histories, institutional racism, bitterness, violence, materialism, competition for honor, despair—the list goes on. Such divine-human partnership is mediated and enacted in embodied interpersonal relationships, which in turn become a parable of the gospel.

Second, this complex picture of human agency as compromised by sin yields far more nuanced and truthful ways to talk about sin in all its complexity than does a picture of sin as the wrong motives, choices, and actions of individuals. The message that "you're a sinner and you need to repent" or "you need to change" is a double bind, because sin makes it impossible to change oneself. Nor is sin limited to individuals; 7:7–25 lays the groundwork for talking about systemic, socially mediated sin, without demonizing individuals or people groups. As a deceptive and destructive force, sin is like an abusive partner that deceives its victims and diminishes their agency, such that they internalize distorted images of themselves and are unable to break free. On a larger scale, sin is like a colonial power that not only oppresses its subjects but colonizes their subjectivities, so they adopt and replicate the falsehoods imposed on them. Sin is something that is catching, not inherent to the individual, but inevitably internalized from the social matrices into which we are born. Thus internalized, sin shapes people's social imaginations, so that they become perpetrators as well as victims of wrong. Paul's way of talking about sin as a lethal lie that uses even God's good law gives us ways to name the social ills of our time.

Third, Paul may be surprisingly positive about human nature, but he is profoundly pessimistic about the capacity of individuals to choose and accomplish good. This is the shocking and offensive part of preaching from 7:7–25. It can be far less insulting to be accused of choosing to do wrong than to be told we have no choice in the matter. Paul's gospel strikes at the root of free will and self-sufficiency. Sin is not a choice but a deceptive bondage; we are not free to sin, and of ourselves we are certainly not free to choose not to sin. There is no autonomy in Paul's social universe, and hence he does not use the language of decision. He never says, "The choice is yours." To do so would leave intact the corrosive lie that we are the masters of our fate. Preaching in line with Romans 7:7–25 constantly reminds us that we are not independent beings, but creatures who are dependent on God and interdependent with one another.

Fourth, if the matter at issue in 7:7–25 is not an inner conflict in the self, but the whole person in relationship to sin as an external power that operates inwardly, and the whole person in relationship to Christ as known in the body of Christ, preaching and pastoral care become less concerned with individual choices and more concerned with interpersonal relationships. Of course, these cannot be separated in practice. Nonetheless, Paul is remarkably uninterested in an endless excavation of private motives or in drilling down to some presumed essential core of the person. On the other hand, he is excessively concerned with the quality of Christian communities as mediators of transforming grace, and thus with the interpersonal connections in which believers are reconstituted and transformed. In Romans, this concern will come to the fore in chapters 12–15.

8:1–39. Christian Experience and the Victory of God's Love

Romans 8 brings the first half of the letter to a climax, as Paul gathers up the strands of his message thus far and joyfully proclaims the victory of God's love in Jesus Christ. The language of judgment and condemnation in 8:1 picks up on the theme of human culpability and divine mercy in chapters 1–4. The pervasive appearance of the prepositions "in" and "with" signals and strengthens the theme of union with Christ, further developing the claims of 6:1–7:6. This union is possible precisely because in Christ's incarnation, death, and resurrection (8:3–4), God has dealt with the problem of sin; here Paul restates the claims of 3:24–26 and builds on the image of "this grace in which we stand" in 5:1–5. Thus, the promise of "no condemnation" (8:1–4, 32–34) and Christ's saving solidarity with humanity under sin create the conditions for participation in Christ. Freedom from condemnation *results* in transformed lives indwelt by the Spirit, not vice versa. Subsequently, the Spirit, named interchangeably as the Spirit of God, the Spirit of Christ, and the Spirit of the one who raised Christ from the dead (8:9–11), takes center stage in Paul's account of life in Christ.

These beloved verses round out Paul's picture of Christian experience as a journey through affliction to unabashed hope in the certain victory of God's love (5:1–5; 8:38–39). But Romans 8 also restates and develops themes from 1:1–4:25, including the calling of believers (1:7; 8:28), the loss and restoration of glory in the divine image (1:23; 8:17–18, 29–30), the deliverance of Jesus to death on our behalf (3:23–25; 8:3, 32), the rectifying power of God's gracious gift in Christ (3:21–26; 4:4–8; 8:32), and faith as trust in the God who gives life to the dead (4:17–25; 8:34).

Chapter 8 thus is the capstone of the entire first section of the letter, not just chapters 5–8. But it leaves two key issues unaddressed—the destiny of Israel in God's salvation through Christ, which Paul will take up in chapters 9–11, and ongoing tensions among believers in Rome, which he will address in 12:1–15:13. For this reason, chapter 8 is not the climax of the letter. But it *is* a central proclamation of the divine redemption that empowers everything else in the letter: deliverance from sin through the coming of God's Son in the flesh (8:3), and the stunning affirmation that God is "for us" (v. 31)—that is, for *all* creation, and against all that would separate humanity from God's love (v. 39).

The chapter may be subdivided into three sections: verses 1–17, 18–30, and 31–39. In 8:1–17 Paul contrasts the new realm of the Spirit with the old realm of life indwelt by sin, which he calls "the flesh." In 8:18–30 Paul probes the experience of present suffering and unseen hope (vv. 18–25), the intercession of the Spirit, and God's new family (vv. 26–30). The third section, 8:31–39, brings the chapter to a resounding conclusion, as it reiterates deliverance from the double threats of condemnation (vv. 1–3, 31–34) and separation from God through suffering (vv. 19–23, 35–39).

8:1–17. New Life in the Spirit

In 8:1–17 Paul contrasts the new domain of the Spirit with the old domain of life indwelt by sin, which he calls "the flesh." First, he lays the groundwork for life in the Spirit through God's redemption accomplished in Christ (vv. 1–4). Then he contrasts the mindsets of the flesh and the Spirit (vv. 5–8). In 8:9–13 he highlights the Spirit's indwelling in the community, giving life to mortal bodies. Verses 14–17 establish those in the Spirit in a new family system that calls on God as "Father" and shares in both suffering and the hope of glory.

8:1–4. Deliverance through Jesus, God's Son in the Flesh of Sin
"Therefore there is now no condemnation for those who are in Christ Jesus" (8:1). This tremendous declaration speaks good news directly to the situation of bondage depicted in 7:7–25 and thereby opens the door to participation in Christ. "Condemnation" (*katakrima*) is related to the word for "judgment" (*krima*) but not equivalent to it. All humanity, including believers, will stand before God to be judged on the last day (2:2, 5; 3:6–8; 14:10–12), but not all will be condemned. Furthermore, judgment may be disciplinary, as in 1 Corinthians 3:15 and 5:1–5, but condemnation is the final outcome of divine judgment, with no remediation; it is the punishment meted out at a sentencing hearing, not the verdict of guilty at a trial. *Katakrima* is the death sentence passed on Adam's heirs (Rom 5:16–18). In this context, "death" itself is not simply physical demise, but separation from God. The "no condemnation" promised for those "in Christ" means they will never be separated from God. Thus, when Paul again promises that there is no condemnation for those in Christ Jesus (8:33–34), he adds that therefore there is nothing that can separate believers from their Lord (vv. 35–39).

In 8:2 Paul gives the basis for the declaration of "no condemnation," which is grounded in believers' liberation from "the law of sin and of death" by "the law of the Spirit of life." Four issues deserve our attention here. First, as rightly noted by the NRSVue, the majority of ancient texts say, "has set *you* free," although some read, "has set *me* free." The "you" is singular and directly addresses the singular I in 7:7–25. That I is not under condemnation, not still in bondage, but has been liberated by Christ. Here is good news for sinners. As Jesus said, "I have not come to call the righteous but sinners" (Matt 9:13).

Second, here "law" appears in two opposing relational constructs: "the law of the Spirit of life in Christ Jesus" and "the law of sin and of death." Is this the law of Moses? The context points to a positive answer, precisely because Paul has been speaking of the Mosaic law up to this point in the letter. A clue to Paul's meaning, as is often the case, lies in the preposition "of." "Of" can mean many things in Greek, including ownership and origin. Here it means ownership. Paul is contrasting the law "in the hands of" sin and death with the law "in the hands of" the Spirit. In 7:7–25 he has displayed the distorting and deadly results of sin's takeover of God's good law; now he will display the life-giving role of the law deployed by Christ's life-giving Spirit. Crucially, in this new context the law no longer pronounces condemnation.

Third, the preposition "in" in the phrase "in Christ Jesus" can have both a spatial and an instrumental sense. That is, it can refer to a realm of existence in which Christ is Lord, and it also can mean "through Christ Jesus." Both meanings are possible in the context of verses 1–4, for it is in and through the incarnate Son of God that God dealt with sin, undid condemnation, and opened the way to life in union with Christ (v. 3). Thus, verse 2 could be translated, "In and through Jesus Christ, the law of the Spirit of life has set you free from the law in the hands of sin and death."

Fourth, "the Spirit of life" is the Spirit of the God who gives life to the dead (4:17), who indeed raised Christ from the dead (8:11). Paul later calls this Spirit the Spirit of God and the Spirit of Christ, indwelling the Roman believers (8:9–11).

In 8:3 Paul immediately clarifies his picture of the law in the hands of sin and of death by describing the law as "weakened by the flesh"; in the realm of flesh dominated by sin, the law is unable (*adynaton*, powerless) to resist sin, let alone condemn it. Therefore, God has acted to deal with sin not through the law but in a new way, through God's Son.

That God "sent his Son" implies the preexistence of Christ (1:3; Phil 2:6–8; Gal 4:4). Paul simply assumes the divine identity of Jesus without apparently needing to defend it. It is crucial to keep this in mind when interpreting the following clause, "in the likeness of sinful flesh." Although "likeness" (*homoiōma*) can mean merely appearance or similarity, when Paul uses the word elsewhere it usually has the sense of assimilation to the condition and destiny of another without losing one's distinct identity (see commentary on 6:5–11). In Philippians 2:6–8, "human likeness" describes Christ's full participation in the realm of human dereliction, to the point of sharing humanity's destiny. Thus, Christ entered fully into humanity's fleshly existence under the dominion of sin. "Sinful flesh" is literally "flesh of sin," grammatically parallel to "the body of sin" (Rom 6:6) and "the body of death" (7:24). The "flesh of sin" describes human bodily enmeshment in a relational web possessed and ruled over by sin.

Christ has entered this fleshly realm, in solidarity with humanity under sin's rule, as Paul already has stated in a variety of ways: He was "handed over for our trespasses" (4:25); he was subject to death's rule (6:9–10); now, in the "likeness of the flesh under sin's rule," God's Son shares the predicament of the I who cries out, "I am of the flesh, sold into slavery under sin" (7:14). Recalling Paul's use of "likeness" to signify a shared location and destiny, Christ has joined with the condition and destiny of the I in 7:7–25. The scandalous good news is that deliverance of the enslaved comes through Christ's entrance into the same situation of bondage and *in that place,* in "the flesh of sin," becoming the place where sin itself is condemned.

As in 5:12–21, Christ's solidarity and exchange with humanity under sin effects reconciliation. Paul states the same idea succinctly and shockingly in 2 Corinthians 5:21, "For our sake God made the one [Christ] who knew no sin to be sin, so that in him we might become the righteousness of God."

The Greek phrase in Romans 8:3 translated "to deal with sin" by the NRSVue means simply "concerning sin." Because it occurs frequently in the LXX in reference to cultic sin offerings (Lev 4:3, 14, 28, 35; 5:6–13), it sometimes is translated "as a sin offering," although Paul does not explicitly make such a connection. In fact, it is difficult to see how Christ "as a sin offering" in a cultic sense would deal with sin as a power holding humanity captive. Rather, as in Romans 3:25, Paul puts forth Christ's death as the means of reconciliation between God and humanity, without elaborating on any cultic symbolism. In 8:3, however, Paul further develops the saving significance of Christ's crucifixion: God dealt with sin by condemning sin itself in the flesh of Jesus on the cross. Notably, Paul does not say that Christ died in the place of condemned sinners on whom God's judgment has fallen. Rather, it is sin itself on which God's condemnation falls in 8:3. The condemnation of sin in the flesh of Jesus is the reason why there is no condemnation for those in Christ Jesus (8:1).

In 8:4 Paul states the result of God's condemnation of sin in the flesh of Jesus—the fulfillment of the "just requirement [*dikaiōma*] of the law" in us. The goal of God's liberation of humanity from both condemnation and captivity under sin's use of the law is, paradoxically, the fulfillment of the law of Moses! This claim develops the themes of 5:16–21, where Paul promises that those who receive the free gift of righteousness in Christ Jesus will "reign in life" (5:17). Galatians 5:14 provides an illuminating parallel, where the "fulfillment" of the law enacts the commandment of Leviticus 19:18: "You shall love your neighbor as yourself" (cf. Rom 13:8). Freed from being condemned by the law and from sin's lethal rule, believers are liberated for love as the fundamental requirement of the Mosaic law. The passive form of the verb "might be fulfilled" indicates that this is not something believers accomplish on their own but rather something that flows from God's action in Christ. Paul is speaking of the exercise of love operating in and through the fellowship of believers; the final phrase, "in us," would be better translated "among us."

Paul here introduces an antithesis between the flesh and the Spirit that structures 8:5–17. As in 7:5, so also here, "flesh" signifies both a realm of existence, such that human beings can be "in the flesh," and a power that distorts human intentions and actions. As in 6:4 the verb "walk" is a metaphor for a way of living. Paul's use of this metaphor resembles the teachings of the Essene community at Qumran, which says God "created man to rule the world and placed within him two spirits so that he would walk with them until the moment of his visitation: they are the spirits of truth and of deceit" (1QS 3:17–19). For Paul, however, the Spirit and the flesh are not opposing forces within the individual, but rather the Spirit of God and "the flesh" as opposing powers in two conflicting realms of existence.

The paired phrases "according to the flesh" and "according to the Spirit" first appeared in the letter at 1:3–4, where God's Son is both "descended from David according to the flesh" and "declared to be Son of God with power according to the Spirit of holiness" (see commentary). How are these two depictions of Christ as God's Son in the flesh related to the contrast between living "according to the flesh" and "according to the Spirit"? The short answer is that Christ has made it possible for those "in Christ" to walk in newness of life, through the paradoxical power of Christ's own entrance into the realm of sinful flesh and victory over sin and death.

On the one hand, Paul depicts a chasm between life in the flesh dominated by sin and death, and life in Christ freed from sin's dominion (5:17; 6:1–7:6). The contrast between the flesh and the Spirit in 8:4–13 intensifies this divide between two incompatible regimes. On the other hand, through his incarnation and death Christ crossed that chasm, invading sin's regime and setting its minions free by becoming the locus of God's condemnation of sin. Therefore, when read together with 1:3–4 and 7:14, 8:3–4 yields a paradoxical but powerful picture of Christ's full identification with human dereliction and, at the same time, the exchange wrought by that solidarity. Jesus, God's Son, is both "according to the flesh" and "according to the Spirit" (1:3–4), but through his incarnation, death, and resurrection, human beings are liberated to walk in line with God's Spirit and *not* with the flesh (8:3–4).

Thus, despite the incommensurability of the realms of the flesh and the Spirit, Christ is on both sides of that divide—there is no "fleshly" realm of existence where God is absent. At the same time, through Christ's solidarity with those under sin, there is a change of places, what Luther called "the joyous exchange," so that to be in Christ is to be freed from sin's power. Christ became the place where sin was condemned so that there is no condemnation for those in Christ; Christ came in the likeness of sin-controlled flesh so that those who were controlled by the flesh might no longer be under its rule, but rather led by the Spirit.

8:5–8. The Mindset of the Flesh and the Mindset of the Spirit

Pivoting from the image of "walking," with its implicit focus on behavior, Paul now presents a holistic picture of human cognition and emotion, whether in line with the Spirit or the flesh. The Greek verb *phroneō* and its cognate noun, *phronēma*, characterize a blend of emotion, cognition, and volition. The passage is a bit difficult to translate, because Paul intertwines human and suprahuman agencies by using the verb *phroneō* for human thought and the noun *phronēma* for the contrasting mindsets of the Spirit and the flesh. Paul is speaking of ways of knowing and wanting and willing that arise out of relational systems, whether of the flesh or of the Spirit.

Therefore, in 8:5–6, Paul distinguishes between those who "*are* according to the flesh" and those who "*are* according to the Spirit." The verb "live" (NRSVue) is not in the Greek. The meaning seems to be "those who derive the totality of their identity from the values and practices of a world dominated by sin" and "those whose identity comes from the free gift of the Spirit" (5:5). The language of "being" recurs in 8:8–9, again contrasting those "in the flesh" and those "in the Spirit," thus framing the intervening cognitive language.

In 5:5, the experience of God's love is the first evidence of the Spirit's presence in human hearts. Now in 8:5–6 that indwelling divine life issues in a transformed mindset, incorporating perception, discernment, and judgment, that is inseparable from behavior. In 12:1–2 Paul will again speak of a renewal of the mind that approves the will of God. In both chapters 8 and 12, such cognitive renewal issues from—and results in—transformed bodily behavior. As in contemporary understandings of body and brain, so for Paul there is a constant interaction between mind and body, thinking and action.

In 8:6, the NRSVue translation of *phronēma* as "to set the mind on" is misleading, because it implies only human agents are in view. Paul uses the same noun in 8:27 to refer to the "mind" or mindset of the Spirit. So also here, human thinking and feeling are interwoven with the mindsets of the flesh and the Spirit, such that a kind of dual agency is depicted. People either think "the things of the flesh" or "the things of the Spirit" (v. 5b), but their cognition is shaped by the mindset (*phronēma*) of the flesh versus the mindset of the Spirit (v. 6). As noted above, human thought and emotion cannot be divorced from the relational systems that give rise to them, whether that be the distorted realm Paul calls "the flesh" or the life-giving realm of the Spirit.

These realms are opposed to one another (cf. Gal 5:17), as Paul makes clear in Romans 8:7–8. The mindset of the flesh is enmity toward God, which recalls believers' former stance as God's "enemies" (5:10). Without reconciliation, it is not possible (*ou dynatai*) for such a mindset to submit to God, just as it was impossible (*adynaton*) for the law, weakened by the flesh, to overcome sin (8:2). The human inability to submit to God's law corresponds to the law's inability to overcome sin.

8:9–13. The Indwelling Spirit Gives Life

"You" and "we" are plural here and throughout the rest of the chapter, contrasting with the singular "you" in 8:2, which speaks to the singular "I" in 7:7–25. Now Paul enfolds his listeners into a fellowship that together walks "according to the Spirit" (8:4). For the community of those "in Christ," the shared indwelling of the Spirit

(8:9–11) is the powerful antidote to the isolating indwelling of sin in 7:17, 20, 23. Significantly, the Spirit takes up residence between and among believers, not primarily in them as solitary individuals.

The background to this divine presence in the community of faith is probably the motif of God sojourning with the people of Israel: "I will dwell among the Israelites, and I will be their God. And they shall know that I am the Lord their God, who brought them out of the land of Egypt that I might dwell among them; I am the Lord their God" (Exod 29:45–46). This picture of the Spirit abiding among and between the members of the fellowship locates Christian experience in the interaction between people. Rather than looking inward to experience the Spirit in an esoteric and private way, those in Christ are to anticipate the Spirit's working in and through their interactions with others. To say this is not to deny the reality of the Spirit's presence in individuals, but to recognize the interconnectedness of individuals in the community of faith mediated by the Spirit, the "go-between God" (Taylor 2021).

Paul moves seamlessly from writing about being "in the Spirit," as if the Spirit were a realm, to "the Spirit of God" dwelling "in you" (or better, "among you"), as if the Spirit were an active entity, even a person. Such a two-directional use of the preposition "in" is typical of Paul. To grasp this metaphorical language, we can think of the ways relationships both create distinctive environments and shape us from within; children internalize the relational environments in which they grow up, such that adults as well as children hear their parents' voices in their heads, sometimes long after the parents have passed away.

In 8:9, Paul refers to "the Spirit of God" and "the Spirit of Christ" interchangeably. In 8:10–11, "Christ in you" has the same referent as "the Spirit of him who raised Jesus from the dead." Here Paul depicts the reality of union with Christ (6:5–11) as the powerful working of God's Spirit, which is divine being-in-relationship and as such discloses the participatory relational life at the heart of God. The action of God in raising Jesus, the action of Christ on humanity's behalf, and the action of the Spirit making Christ's death and resurrection effective in human lives all disclose this mutuality within the divine identity. It is therefore no surprise that the Spirit animates a communal life of mutuality and interdependence among believers.

"The one who raised Christ Jesus from the dead" (8:11) is one of Paul's preferred ways of naming God's action (4:24; 10:9; 1 Cor 6:14; 2 Cor 4:14). Here the repeated phrase echoes Romans 4:24, where "the one who raised Jesus our Lord from the dead" is the object of believers' trust, modeled after Abraham's trust in the God who "gives life to the dead" (4:17; see 1 Cor 15:22, 36, 45; 2 Cor 3:6). Paul may have these verses in mind in the final clause of Romans 8:11: the same God who "raised" Jesus from the dead "will give life" to our mortal bodies. The resurrection of Jesus guarantees Christian hope, which hopes for nothing less than resurrection life for mortal human beings (for the resurrection of the body, cf. 1 Cor 15:35–57).

In Romans 8:10, however, Paul describes present Christian existence as both "dead and alive" (Barclay 2015, 501–2). Short of the resurrection of the dead, believers live in mortal bodies, just like everyone else (cf. 8:18–25); this mortality is the result of death's entrance into human history through Adam's trespass (5:12–14). Paul's emphasis on human bodies as "dead" (8:10) and "mortal" (v. 11) highlights the impossible, miraculous quality of "life" through the energizing power of God. The apostle expresses this powerful divine life through two parallel phrases: "the Spirit is life because of righteousness" (v. 10) and God will give life "through his Spirit that dwells in you" (v. 11). The basis of this promise of life is both "righteousness"—that is, the rectification of life accomplished through Christ's own death (vv. 33–35)—and resurrection, as 8:11 makes clear. The life-giving Spirit guarantees that although those in Christ will undergo physical death, they will not suffer the "death" of final separation from God (vv. 31–39); indeed, even their mortal bodies will be given life at the resurrection.

Beginning with "so then," in 8:12–13 Paul spells out the consequences of 8:5–11 in terms of bodily practices. The word translated "obligated" has a technical sense in the Greco-Roman patronage system, which obliged recipients of gifts to reciprocate with allegiance and behavior corresponding to the patron's wishes. Paul first emphatically states that his listeners are *not* obligated to "the flesh"—that is, to the whole system of values, relationships, and behaviors that structures life in the present order of society. Such social mores ultimately lead to death, but for believers they cannot determine either their worth or their actions. To be released from obligation to one's surrounding culture is also to be set on a collision course with that culture. But that release does not mean those in Christ have no obligations! Rather, they are obligated to live in accordance with the leading of God's Spirit.

Paul describes such leading in the next verse (8:13): "If by the Spirit you put to death the deeds of the body, you will live." Paul's formulation is paradoxical in the extreme: attempting to live in line with the fleshly status quo leads to death, but killing off the deeds of the body leads to life! The word translated "deeds" means "practices"—Paul is talking about ongoing bodily behavior in the shared life of believers. In the context of Paul's antithesis between flesh and Spirit, one expects him to speak of killing off the deeds of the flesh, not the body. But his body language locates bodily practices and experience as the site of the struggle with sin and the flesh, precisely because, like all creatures, believers live in "mortal" bodies (8:10–11; 6:12–13). Implicit here is Paul's understanding of physical bodies as the means of connection and communication through which human beings are vulnerable to death-dealing powers but also connected to the life of Christ. The body therefore is where the battle with sin rages most fiercely. At the same time, it would be a mistake to read Paul's focus on the body as excluding the mind and heart, which after all are inseparable from the body in Paul's anthropology. Just as one cannot speak of minds apart from bodies, so one cannot speak of bodies without minds.

Paul's concern is with the embodied practices of the community and the way those practices are life-giving or destructive (cf. the communal aspects of the works of the flesh and the fruit of the Spirit in Gal 5:16–26). Paul continues to speak here in the second-person plural. He is not primarily talking about individual believers struggling against sinful desires; rather, he is encouraging church fellowships to resist shared bodily practices that damage the community. Such resistance can be effective only through mutual attention to the guidance of the Spirit. Thus, it is a mistake to interpret Romans 8:13 as a call to radical asceticism or to maltreatment of individual physical bodies. Even when Paul does speak specifically about individual bodily practices (chaps. 12–14), his focus is on building up rather than dividing the fellowship.

8:14–17. Children of God

For the first time in the letter, in these verses Paul introduces familial metaphors. Linked to the preceding exhortation by "for," Paul's language reminds the Roman churches of the context for transformed lives—their new, shared identity as God's beloved children. The translation obscures the richness of Paul's familial imagery in the Greek, in which Paul moves from calling his listeners "sons of God" (8:14) to "children of God" (vv. 16–17). The terminology develops the metaphor of adoption (v. 15) and continues into the following discussion of suffering (vv. 19, 21, 23). To be God's children is to be God's heirs (v. 17), in line with the promise that Abraham and his descendants would "inherit the world" (4:13). Israel's special status as children of God surely lies behind this cluster of kinship, adoption, and inheritance metaphors (Exod 4:22; Deut 14:1; 32:5–6, 19–20; 2 Sam 7:14; Isa 1:2–4; 30:9; 63:8; cf. Hos 1:10, quoted in Rom 9:26). Indeed, shortly Paul will describe his Jewish relatives as those possessing "the adoption" (9:4). Here in 8:14–17 Paul includes his primarily gentile audience in Israel's gifted filiation with God.

Three aspects of Paul's kinship metaphors invite further attention. First, whereas earlier Paul identified those baptized into Christ as slaves of righteousness (6:18) and slaves of God (6:22; cf. 1:1), now he contrasts a "spirit of slavery" with a "spirit of adoption" (8:15). The contrasting phrases do not denote two different spirits, but rather a false versus a true depiction of the action of the one Holy Spirit. The liberating life-giving Spirit of God (8:2) who raised Jesus from the dead, who also indwells and leads the community (vv. 11, 13–14), will not reinstate believers in a state of bondage leading to fear. Rather, that same Spirit guarantees their security and future as God's children in the household of faith.

In 1:1 and 6:18, 22, Paul uses the metaphor of slavery to God to signify belonging and allegiance to the one from whom all creation comes, but now he corrects and modifies it, by distinguishing such belonging from fearful bondage and by transitioning to the metaphors of childhood and inheritance. Given that slavery was indeed a fearful, horrifying state that severed any family bonds, 8:15 is an important guide to the interpretation of 6:17–23, with the emphasis falling on the gift of life (6:22–23). Galatians 4:1–7 expands on the same themes: "While we were minors, we were enslaved to the elemental principles of the world. But when the fullness of time had come, God sent his Son, born of a woman, born under the law, in order to redeem those who were under the law, so that we might receive adoption as children. And because you are children, God has sent the Spirit of his Son into our hearts, crying, 'Abba! Father!' So you are no longer a slave but a child, and if a child then also an heir through God."

Second, the cry "Abba! Father!" was probably widely known in early Christian worship. Writing to churches he has not yet visited, Paul assumes his listeners will know whereof he speaks. This early practice in worship may come from Jesus's own expression of intimate relationship with God through prayer to God as "Father" (Mark 14:36). Corporately indwelt by the Spirit of Christ, believers are inspired by that same Spirit to cry out to God in this intimate, familial way. Paul uses the same verb, "to cry out" (*krazō*), in Galatians 4:6, where it also expresses Spirit-inspired prayer to God as Abba. *Krazō* can denote loud cries, shrieks, the crying of a baby, and particularly crying out in prayers for deliverance (e.g., Pss 18:6, 41; 22:2, 5, 25; 107:6, 13, 19, 28). The same word describes the shrieking of a demoniac (Mark 5:5) and Jesus's own cry from the cross (Matt 27:50). This is not the gentle murmuring of private prayer, but a public expression of intense emotion.

Third, it is not clear who is speaking in this communal prayer. "We" cry Abba (Rom 8:15), but this cry is the "Spirit bearing witness with our spirit that we are children of God" (8:16; cf. Gal 4:6). It is also unclear whether "our spirit" refers to some inner aspect of the self or the Spirit of God indwelling within the community. The difference may be moot. Paul clearly expects the Spirit to inspire and speak in and through believers gathered in worship. He intensifies this sense of a shared agency between God's Spirit and believers by using verbs augmented by the prefix "with" (*syn*) in Romans 8:16–17. The Spirit "witnesses with" (*symmarturei*); God's children are "joint heirs with Christ" (*synklēronomoi*); they "suffer with him" (*sympaschomen*) in order to be "glorified with him" (*syndoxasthōmen*).

This combination of kinship metaphors and compound verbs displays a new family system in which adoption into God's family leads to co-inheritance, co-suffering, and co-glorification—in other words, a shared experience and destiny. Hence those whom the Spirit joins find themselves in a new relational network that exposes and undoes the destructive web of deception woven by sin. This new family system shakes and reshapes the foundations of identity, conflicting with and renarrating other socially constructed identities and creating new social realities "in Christ."

The provision in 8:17, "if we in fact suffer," should be read as denoting a reality already being experienced: "since we suffer with him." Paul assumes believers suffer, as 8:18–25 makes clear; linking suffering and the promise of glory, he restates the assurance of 5:3–4.

8:18–30. Suffering, Solidarity, Hope, and Glory

In this second subset of chapter 8, Paul probes the experience of present suffering, future hope, and the intercession of the Spirit, while developing two intertwined themes from 8:14–17: prayer (vv. 15–16 and 26–27) and the identity of believers as no longer slaves but God's beloved children with a secure future (vv. 16–17 and 28–30). These considerations of prayer and kinship enclose a central section addressing present suffering and future hope, for believers and for all of creation, in verses 18–25.

8:18. Present Suffering, Future Glory

Paul begins in 8:18 with the headline for this entire section: "I consider that the sufferings of this present time are not worth comparing with the glory about to be revealed to us." Picking up the themes of suffering and glory from 8:17, Paul now frames present suffering within a larger temporal and cosmic context. "Glory" belongs to the future, but it is an assured future that even transfigures the present (8:30). This anticipation of a future revelation of glory draws on prophetic promises, notably Isaiah 40:5: "Then the glory of the Lord shall be revealed, and all flesh shall see it together" (cf. Isa 6:3; 60:1–3, 19; Hab 3:3–4; Ps 72:19).

"I consider" is the same verb translated as "reckon" in Romans 4:3–12 and carries the same sense of "tally" or "account"; now speaking in the first-person singular, Paul contrasts the relative weights of present suffering and coming glory. "Not worth comparing" means "not of equal weight." Because God reckons humanity as righteous on the basis of faith (4:4–11, 22–24), believers are to "reckon" themselves dead to sin and alive to God (6:11). These divine and human "reckonings" ground Paul's own certainty that in comparison to the future weight of glory, present suffering is lighter than air.

As in 1:17, the verb "to be revealed" is the verbal form of *apocalypse*. Here it has an eschatological sense, referring to the future, full, and final revelation of God's righteousness, already present in the apocalypse of divine righteousness through the gospel (1:17) but still awaiting fulfillment in the final revelation of glory, which will include the "revealing [*apocalypse*] of the children of God" (8:19).

8:19–21. Creation's Longing for the Apocalypse of the Sons of God

Switching to the third-person singular, Paul declares creation's "eager longing for the revealing [*apocalypse*] of the children of God" (Gk., the apocalypse of the sons of God). This future apocalypse is inseparable from the future apocalypse of God's glory "to us" (v. 18), and therefore it is awaited not only by creation but also by us. Who are these "sons of God"? One possibility is that here they are baptized believers who have received "the Spirit of adoption" (v. 15) and the promise of future glory (v. 17). If so, their longed-for revelation is the unveiling of their presently hidden status as God's children, or perhaps, in view of 8:14, 23, as the redemption of their bodies. It is not clear, however, why creation would await such an event.

On the other hand, in 9:3–4 Paul reminds his listeners that both the adoption and the glory also belong to his Jewish kinsfolk. Indeed, Paul expects that Israel's full redemption will be "life from the dead" (11:15). These observations suggest that the identity of these "sons of God" in 8:19 cannot be limited to those presently baptized into Christ, excluding Israel from that future apocalypse (cf. 9:26). The full redemption of creation is impossible apart from the full redemption of Israel (Eastman 2002), and the awaited apocalypse is the final fulfillment of the apocalypse of God's righteousness through the gospel, as salvation "for the Jew first and also for the Greek" (1:16). Paul's thought moves from suffering to glory, from anticipation to apocalypse, and from adoption as promise to adoption as full redemption, catching up the identity of God's children into an expanding vision of the liberation of all creation. This global vision picks up on the inclusive scope of redemption for "all" in 3:23–24 and anticipates 11:32.

These observations raise a further question: who or what is "creation" (*ktisis*)? In Paul's use of *ktisis* elsewhere he surely has in mind human beings (Gal 6:15; 2 Cor 5:17) as well as nonhuman realities

(Rom 8:39). Furthermore, in Romans 8:20, the unwilling subjection of creation to futility echoes God's judgment on humanity for its primal refusal to honor (*edoxasan,* glorify) God: they "became futile [*emataiōthēsan*] in their thinking" (1:21). In both 8:20 and 1:21, futility is not a chosen or willed condition, but God's unanticipated judgment on idolatry. This is why Paul says that creation was subjected to futility (*mataiotēti*) "not of its own will." All of these observations suggest that in Romans 8:19–23, *ktisis* includes humanity and the natural order.

"Futility" denotes vanity and emptiness, a "chasing after wind." The same word occurs in Ecclesiastes 1:2 (LXX): "Vanity of vanities, says the Teacher, vanity of vanities! All is vanity." The rest of Ecclesiastes displays the utter futility of all human effort in the face of death. There is no reason to think that Paul has Ecclesiastes in mind here in Romans 8:20, but he limns the same sense of futility in the face of death. Paul's focus is on physical decay, as he makes clear in 8:21, where *ktisis* itself hopes for liberation from slavery (*douleias*) to decay (*phthoras*) into "the freedom of the glory of the children of God." At a minimum, "freedom" here signifies freedom from physical dissolution—that is, from physical death or perishability (cf. 1 Cor 15:42, 50; Gal 6:8; Col 2:22), but also freedom from death as separation from God, which by this point in the letter is associated with the dominion of sin (Rom 5:17, 21; 6:23; 7:24). But just as the promise of future glory outweighs present sufferings (8:18), so also "the freedom of the glory of the children of God" is not comparable to present perishability; it is qualitatively different, both in its inclusion of all creation and because it will be nothing less than the restoration of the divine image, the "glory of the immortal God" lost through humanity's primal idolatry (1:23; cf. 2 Cor 3:18).

8:22–25. Suffering and Hoping Together

Just as all creation joins in yearning and hoping for redemption, all creation joins in suffering. In 8:22 Paul introduces a new subsection with his typical "for we know" (2:2; 3:19; 7:14), which appeals to an experience shared with his listeners—in this case, the labor pains of creation. Paul again uses compound verbs beginning with the prefix "with" (*syn*), well translated by the NRSVue: "The whole creation has been groaning together as it suffers together the pains of labor." The verbs recollect the shared suffering and glorification of believers

(8:17), but now they refer to groaning and birth pangs that unite believers with all creation.

Drawing on the physical dangers of childbirth in the ancient world, "labor pains" is an ancient metaphor for extreme anguish and danger. It occurs in the context of suffering in battle (*Iliad* 2.268–72), and in Israel's Scripture it depicts the anguish of both Israel's enemies (Exod 15:14; Deut 2:25; Ps 48:6; Isa 13:8; Jer 50:43) and Israel itself under God's judgment (Jer 4:31; 6:24; 13:21; 22:23; Mic 4:9–10). God even suffers metaphorical labor pains: in Isaiah 42:13 "the LORD goes forth like a soldier," and in the very next verse the Lord says, "I will cry out like a woman in labor; I will gasp and pant." Later texts associate labor pains with the coming Day of the Lord (1 En. 62:6; 1QH XI, 1–13 [III, 1–13]; 4 Ezra 4:42; Mark 13:8; Matt 24:8; 1 Thess 5:3; Rev 12:2). Romans 8:22 also appears to anticipate the Day of the Lord, but with longing and hope rather than fear. Paul includes all humanity and all the natural order in this intense longing and expectation.

"We know that all creation groans and suffers birth pangs together" surely would resonate with Paul's audience experientially as well. Rome was a colonial power and behaved like one, ravaging and stealing from its outlying holdings to enrich the center. The members of the Roman house churches who came from the colonies would know about the environmental and social destruction caused by Rome's wars and rapacious policies (Burroughs 2022). Paul could not have anticipated the present global ecological crisis, but his depiction of creation's yearning for redemption from decay certainly speaks to that crisis. Paul knew that the health of humanity is inseparable from the health of the natural world.

For this very reason, in 8:23 "we ourselves" now join with nature and all humanity in groaning and longing for redemption. This unity in suffering and yearning for a future redemption stands over against any exceptionalism or triumphalism in Christian experience. Such solidarity correlates with Christ's union with all under the dominion of sin and death. The NRSVue translation, "our bodies," is possible but misses the ambiguity of the Greek, in which "our" is plural but "body" is singular. The reference here is not merely to the resurrection of individual bodies but to an inclusive transformation of all bodily existence. "First fruit" refers to the first gleanings at harvest time, which promise an abundant yield. Christian possession of the "first fruits of the Spirit" thus is a down payment on the redemption of all creation, which reaches out to include all humanity and the whole natural order. The imagery thus has a global scope that supports Paul's planned mission to Spain (15:24).

Paul further develops the theme of hope in 8:24–25. "Hope" recalls believers' "hope of the glory of God" (5:2, 5) in a depiction of Christian experience that includes affliction and perseverance. The intervening chapters have deepened and developed the themes of suffering and hope, such that now they include both human and nonhuman futility, together with hope for the liberation of all (8:20). "In hope we were saved" means simply that believers live in hope, which is to say they live awaiting the final liberation of all creation; this is the situation in which salvation comes to the community of faith. If the object of hope were visible, it would be reduced to what human beings can imagine based on their limited human experience (cf. 1 Cor 2:9). Indeed, if the object of hope were visible, hope would not be necessary. This may seem to be stating the obvious, but the reminder functions as encouragement to persevere in the face of contrary evidence, just as Abraham "hoped beyond hope" (Rom 4:18–21). As in 5:3–5, the goal is a way of life trained in perseverance and habituated in hope, which keeps believers open to God's future beyond the confines of their partial and distorted vision (15:13).

8:26–27. Spirit Speech in God's New Family

Verses 26–30 develop key themes from verses 15–25: the role of the Spirit in prayer, the prominence of kinship metaphors, and the glorious destiny of God's children. In 8:26 Paul depicts the Spirit's aid in prayer with another compound verb (*synantilambanetai*). Translated simply "helps us," it means something like "comes to mutual aid, assists in supporting, shares the burden." It also occurs in Luke 10:40, when Martha asks Jesus to tell her sister Mary to share the burden of preparation; in Numbers 11:17, when seventy elders are appointed to share the burden of the people with Moses (cf. Exod 18:22); and in Psalm 89:21 (LXX), when God says of David, "my hand will come to his aid" (author's translation). Here in Romans 8:26 the Spirit comes to the aid of believers in "our weakness," acknowledging our situation of ignorant anticipation (v. 23). "Groanings too deep for words" is literally "unspeakable groaning," echoing the "groaning" of believers together with creation (vv. 22–23). Creation groans, believers groan, and the very Spirit of God joins in and expresses that groaning to God, who searches all human hearts.

The first word of 8:26, "likewise" (or "in the same way"), connects the Spirit's role in prayer with Paul's preceding encouragement to hope for what "we do not see." For Paul and his audience, knowing and not knowing alternate in the present time of waiting for final salvation. "We know" the groaning of creation (8:22); "we do not know" how or what to pray (v. 26); "we know that in all things the Spirit works for good" (v. 28; see below for translation issues). Prayer occurs in the liminal space created by the tension between these two poles of knowledge and ignorance, need and promise. But at the center of this liminal space is *God's knowledge* of the Spirit's mindset (*phronēma*) in intercession (v. 27), and God's foreknowledge of those whom God has called (vv. 28–29). The limitation in what believers know suggests a degree of mystery in the life of faith, which participates in the even greater mystery of worship and prayer as inner-divine speech acts, whether spoken loudly and publicly (vv. 15–16) or with "unspeakable groanings" (v. 26). Whether aloud or silent, such utterances by and through the Spirit are communicative events between the Spirit, God, and believers.

8:28–30. Called and Destined by God

There are different versions of 8:28 in the ancient manuscripts, but the dominant version reads, "We know that all things work together for good for those who love God" (NRSVue). Because in 8:26–27 the Spirit intercedes and acts on behalf of the saints, and in 8:29–30 God is the one who calls and transforms believers, translations often insert either the Spirit or God as the one who "works together" for good. The compound verb "works together" (*synergei*, from which comes the English "synergism") implies this divine working in and through and among believers, as in 8:16–17, 26.

"Love" recalls the first occurrence of "love" in 5:5, 8; there the focus is on God's love for humanity, here on the human response of love for God. "Called" reminds Paul's listeners of their identity as those called to belong to Christ Jesus (1:6) and of God's power as the one who called them and who calls into being the things that do not exist (4:17). This calling is inseparable from God's "purpose" (*prothesin*), which occurs here for the first time in the letter but reappears with reference to God's election of Israel (9:11). Through two rhetorical sequences, Paul further spells out God's purpose for the Roman believers, which is nothing less than the creation of a new family of God.

First, in 8:29, God "foreknew" and "predestined" those called into God's purpose, which is their "conformation" to the image of God's Son, so that he might be firstborn among many brothers and sisters. In 11:2 Paul uses the same language to say that God "foreknew" God's people Israel and will never reject them. As "the firstborn within a large family" (Gk., many brothers), Christ is the head of the family of God, a family in which Jews and gentiles together will "glorify the God and Father of our Lord Jesus Christ" (15:6). Here Paul's kinship language gestures toward that final vision.

Second, in 8:30, God called, rectified, and glorified those whom God predestined. Rather than simply reading these verses as a dogmatic statement about predestination, it is helpful to consider how Paul's words encourage and strengthen his listeners in their faith. Having just named the experience of sharing in suffering, groaning for deliverance, and praying on the threshold between suffering and hope, Paul now reassures believers that they surely are planted in God's purposes, regardless of the vicissitudes of their lives. The past tense of "glorified" is surprising in light of 8:17; perhaps here it functions to certify and seal this future event, already begun but not yet fully realized.

As in 8:14–17, in 8:28–30 kinship metaphors and compound verbs establish believers in relationship to Christ and to each other. It is God's purpose for them to be "conformed" to the image of God's Son (cf. 12:2; Phil 3:10, 21), who is the true image (*eikōn*) of God (2 Cor 4:4; Col 1:15). Christ in turn is the firstborn among many brothers and sisters. In Colossians 1:15–20, which names Christ as God's image and the firstborn, Christ is the "firstborn from the dead" (v. 18), thereby linking his status as firstborn with his resurrection. Here Paul's interest is in the outcome of Christ's identity for those "in Christ"; embedded in a new family system, they are now siblings of Christ and of each other. At the same time, the motifs of divine purpose and foreknowledge anticipate God's redemptive purpose for Israel as well, in Romans 9–11.

8:31–39. The Victory of God's Love

In the conclusion to the first half of the letter, the themes of "no condemnation" (8:31–34) and union with Christ (vv. 35–39) merge in a joyful proclamation of God's all-conquering love. This section is structured by a series of questions beginning with "who" (*tis*), each with an implied negative answer and restatement of how God is "for us": "Who is against us?" (v. 31b); "Who will bring any charge against God's elect?" (v. 33); "Who is to condemn?" (v. 34); "Who will separate us from the love of Christ?" (v. 35). Lists of seven afflictions (v. 35) and ten suprahuman powers (vv. 38–39) develop the potential threats to believers' union with Christ, only to magnify their surpassing victory over anything that would separate them from God's love (v. 37).

8:31–34. No Condemnation

"What then shall we say?" begins a new discourse (4:1; 6:1; 7:7), which is linked to what precedes it by "about these things." The immediate precedent for "these things" is 8:1–30, in particular the promise that there is "no condemnation" for those who are in Christ Jesus (v. 1). But Paul's answer, "If God is for us, who is against us?" also reaches back to the first proclamation of the gospel as saving power (1:1–6, 16–17). In the entire first section of the letter, that gospel has demonstrated that God is indeed "for us" and not against us.

As proof that God is "for us," in 8:32 Paul briefly recaps the theme of rectification through Christ's death (3:21–26) and specifically repeats the interpretation of that death as God's "handing Jesus over" to death (4:25). Early church fathers (Origen, *Homilae in Genesim*; Epistle of Barnabas 7.3) linked "He who did not withhold his own Son" with the story of Abraham's near sacrifice of Isaac (Gen 22:1–19), because in Greek the phrase parallels the angel's words to Abraham: "You have not withheld your son" (22:16). Whether Paul has the story of Abraham and Isaac in mind is difficult to prove, but the link is suggestive for preaching. Paul describes Abraham's faith as trust in the God who both justifies the ungodly (Rom 4:5) and "gives life to the dead and calls into existence the things that do not exist" (4:17). The context is Abraham's trust that Sarah would have a son, not the story of the near sacrifice of Isaac, but Isaac's story does vividly exemplify God giving life from the dead.

The allusion is strengthened by the connection between 8:32 and 4:24–25. Paul's insistence that Jesus's death was "for us *all*" associates the universal scope of God's action in Christ with the inclusive scope of blessings through Abraham's progeny (4:16), as promised in Genesis 22:18. Nonetheless, if there is a connection between Genesis 22:16 and Romans 8:32, there is also a crucial difference: Isaac was not put to death, and his near sacrifice was not understood by Paul's Jewish contemporaries as redemptive for the world, although later rabbinic interpretations did develop the idea of the "binding of Isaac" as vicarious atonement.

That God will "give us everything else" translates *ta panta* ("all things"). Elsewhere Paul tells the Corinthians, "All things are yours, whether Paul or Apollos or Cephas or the world or life or death or the present or the future—all are yours, and you are Christ's, and Christ is God's" (1 Cor 3:21–23). In the context of Romans 8:32 the promise of "all things" refers to believers' status as "heirs of God and joint heirs with Christ" (8:17) and may also recall the promise to Abraham that he would "inherit the world" (4:13).

In 8:33, by referring to gentile as well as Jewish believers as "God's elect," Paul includes gentile believers within God's elective grace revealed in Israel (11:28–29; cf. 1 Chr 16:13; Pss 89:3; 105:6, 43; Isa 65:9, 15, 23).

The second and third leading questions in Romans 8:33–34—"Who will bring any charge against God's elect?" and "Who is to condemn?"—evoke the heavenly court, where humanity stands before the impartial judgment of God. This is legal language that appears only here in Paul's letters; the verb translated "bring a charge" may be translated "impeach." Elsewhere in the New Testament it occurs only in public trials (Acts 19:38, 40; 23:29; 26:2, 7), but it is common in accounts of legal proceedings (cf. Sir 46:19; Wis 12:12). These two leading questions are answered by the twofold action of God as the one who justifies and Christ as the one who died, was raised, and is at God's right hand. Translated as statements in the NRSVue, these affirmations could also be translated as questions with implied negative answers (Jewett 2007, 540):

33 Who will bring any charge against God's elect?
God—who justifies?
34 Who is to condemn?
Christ Jesus—who died; even more so, who was raised, who is at the right hand of God, who actually is interceding on our behalf?

In other words, how absurd to think that God will reject or condemn those for whom Christ died! No, says Paul, God is *for us,* not against us. There is no condemnation (8:1) because God condemned sin in the flesh of Christ (8:3).

Paul's logic and rhetorical style are akin to Isaiah 50:8–9 LXX, which may echo in the background:

> He who vindicates [Gk., justifies] me is near.
> Who will contend with me? Let us stand up together.
> Who are my adversaries? Let them confront me.
> It is the Lord God who helps me; who will declare me guilty?

Whether or not Paul had this prophetic verse in mind, it nicely expresses the pattern of accusation and defense in a courtroom setting. No reference to the last day is necessary for Paul's audience to recognize the back-and-forth between accuser and accused, and to hear the gracious advocacy of Christ on their behalf.

Finally, Paul emphasizes the surpassing authority and power of Christ Jesus through three clauses that rise to a crescendo: he was raised from the dead, he is at the right hand of God, he intercedes for us. "At the right hand of God" appears only here in Paul's undisputed letters, but elsewhere it identifies Jesus with Psalm 110:1, which reads, "The LORD says to my lord, 'Sit at my right hand until I make your enemies your footstool" (Eph 1:20; Col 3:1; Heb 1:3; 8:1; 10:12; 12:2; cf. 1 Cor 15:25). Christ's intercession for believers mirrors the Spirit's intercession (Rom 8:26–27) but now has the sense of interceding with the judge on behalf of the accused. Given such intercession by the one who was handed over by God, has conquered death, and has God's ear, believers are secure from the threat of condemnation.

8:35–39. No Separation

The fourth question beginning with "who" introduces the second major theme of 8:31–39, the victory of God's love over all that would come between believers and their lord. These verses form a chiastic ABCBA structure, with the second half mirroring the first, and a threefold repetition of God's love anchoring the entire passage:

A 8:35a Nothing can separate us from the love of Christ
  B 8:35b–36 List of seven afflictions
    C 8:37 More than conquerors through the one who loved us
  B′ 8:38–39a List of ten suprahuman threats
A′ 8:39b Nothing can separate us from the love of God through Christ our Lord

This repetitive pattern emphasizes the encircling promise of divine love, just as the larger structure of chapters 5–8 begins and ends with God's love (5:5; 8:35, 39). Enfolded and held by this love, believers may flourish as victors despite present struggles and opposition (5:17; 6:14). "More than conquerors" translates *hypernikōmen* ("supervictors"). In 12:21 Paul draws out the behavioral consequences of this victory, using the cognate verb "to conquer" (*nikō*) with reference to his listeners' moral triumph over evil.

Except for "sword," all seven afflictions in 8:35 are physical adversities that Paul himself has suffered (1 Cor 4:10–13; 2 Cor 6:4–5; 11:26–27; 12:10; Phil 4:12). "Hardship" (*thlipsis*) and "distress" (*stenochōria*) also appear in the judgment that God will visit on those who are disobedient (Rom 2:8–9); Paul does not see himself as exempt from such affliction, but of far greater weight is the assurance of God's ultimate victory over all that afflicts humanity (8:18).

Nonetheless, in 8:36 Paul suddenly gives voice to the oppressed, as he quotes from Psalm 44:22. The psalm is a bitter cry of lament from those who have suffered too long under divine judgment at the hand of their enemies. They are being "killed" and "accounted [*elogisthēmen*] as sheep to be slaughtered," a description that immediately follows "the sword" as a reference to capital punishment. Of most importance, the psalmist lays the blame for this horror squarely at God's feet with the emphatic opening statement, "for your sake." "For your sake" means the afflictions of 8:35 come from following a Lord who sets them in conflict with the status quo. The accusatory and angry tone of the lament clashes with the assurances of victory and love in the immediate context of 8:31–39, as if the cry of the oppressed suddenly interrupts a beautiful liturgy. To hear this tension is to begin to know that divine love does not silence the pain of those who suffer unjustly but allows it to be expressed in its raw anguish.

As if recognizing the abrupt shift in tone between the psalm citation and the affirmation of victory, Paul begins 8:37 with a strong adversative, "but" (NRSVue, "no"). The sense is "nevertheless." Nevertheless, *in all these things*—all these terrible afflictions, including innocent suffering—believers are more than conquerors, not through their own strength, but through the one who loved them even to the death. Undergirding this confidence, which is intensified by the cry of lament, is the self-giving of Christ Jesus in his death, resurrection, and intercession (8:34).

Lest his listeners doubt the force of his assurance, in the concluding long sentence of 8:38–39 Paul switches to the first person, "I am convinced." The following list of ten "powers" is divided roughly into pairs of opposites: death nor life; angels nor rulers; things present nor things to come; height nor depth. The pair of "powers" and "anything else in all creation" breaks the pattern but captures its meaning. Nothing in all creation, including suprahuman forces, can separate believers from the love of God in Christ Jesus their Lord.

EXCURSUS

Reflections for Preaching and Teaching

No Condemnation

What a difference the promise of no condemnation makes for the experience of faith! Paul simply removes any threat of rejection hanging over believers' heads. Colossians 2:13–15 expands on the meaning of "no condemnation" in vivid images that also unite the themes of deliverance from condemnation and victory over enemies:

> And when you were dead in trespasses and the uncircumcision of your flesh, God made you alive together with him, when he forgave us all our trespasses, erasing the record that stood against us with its legal demands. He set this aside, nailing it to the cross. He disarmed

the rulers and authorities and made a public example of them, triumphing over them in it.

God is not keeping a running tab of our infractions and failures, no matter how much we may do that to ourselves and to others. They are nailed to the cross and therefore cannot define us anymore. Along with this deliverance from judgment comes freedom from oppression; on the cross God disarmed the very rulers who crucified Jesus, exposing their powerlessness right in the middle of their apparent victory.

Because through Christ's crucifixion sin itself has been emptied of its power to condemn and to enslave, the door has been opened to union with Christ and the transformed life indwelt by the Spirit. The order of events is indeed crucial. It is not that through the indwelling Spirit we can become good enough to escape judgment and rejection. No, the judgment and condemnation have already happened, on the cross. There is still accountability at the coming Day of the Lord, but it is the accountability of a beloved child to a loving parent, not a guilty criminal before a hostile judge. In such a context, believers have the freedom to grow, take risks, fail, and persevere in hope, precisely because all their life is a gift for the undeserving. Here is the key to union with Christ, which flows out of Christ's gracious solidarity and exchange with humanity under sin's power.

This supremely counterintuitive reality may be told through many stories. Paul surely did not know the parable of the Prodigal Son, but it illustrates the shock value of his understanding of grace for the unworthy. Asked how they would act if they were in the father's shoes, parents of teenagers may respond, "I wouldn't let him in the door without a signed contract" or "I would make him pay back what he owed me." But the prodigal father runs down the road with his robes billowing out behind him, throwing all convention and propriety to the wind, for joy at being reunited with his son. Can we imagine God's love like this? It creates the conditions necessary for reconciliation as an ongoing reality in the life of faith and in the *community* of faith.

For Paul's assurance of "no condemnation" also reverberates in human relationships. In a litigious cancel culture amplified by the internet, this is a powerful message indeed and deeply countercultural. In Paul's view, God simply never writes anyone off. This can be a great encouragement for people in the dock in human courts. It does not undo the necessity for confession and truth-telling, but rather makes truth-telling and reparations possible.

No Separation

Paul's assurance that nothing can separate us from God's love implies the existence of opposing forces that threaten to do just that. Paul simply assumes and surely knows by experience that walking in line with the Spirit of the one who raised Jesus from the dead will bring us into conflict with a culture of death. To live faithfully in allegiance to Christ is to be engaged in battle with all that would separate God's children from God's love. This is the reason for Paul's militaristic imagery, a source of consternation for those living comfortable lives, but immediately understandable for those struggling in situations of conflict and injustice. Martin Luther King Jr. knew this; Desmond Tutu knew this; Oscar Romero knew this. Paul's own experience of these forces of death included homelessness, hunger, physical and mental torments, and the threat of capital punishment. Any of these could easily be understood and interpreted as the absence of God, but Paul sees them as a sign of God's presence, *because* God in Christ entered fully into those experiences of suffering.

Furthermore, rather than demonizing other people, Paul moves on to speak of suprahuman forces—"angels" and "rulers"—that operate on and in and through human individuals and institutions. In "all of these things" he can proclaim victory, not as a kind of Stoic indifference to suffering but through the experience of God's love in Christ. This is not to make a cult of suffering, as has happened in Christian tradition in destructive ways, but simply to recognize its inevitability and know that it cannot have the last word.

Giving Voice to Suffering and Lament

Despite the divine love encompassing the Christian pattern of experience, that pattern is punctuated by groaning (8:18–27) and lament (8:36). These cries interrupt any depiction of the life of faith as a straightforward journey from affliction to hope (5:3–5). Rather, despite its trajectory toward final victory, Christian experience cycles between confidence and lament, not only on believers' behalf but on behalf of the entire world. The threefold groaning of creation, believers, and the Spirit ensures that such lament cannot be silenced. To the contrary, there can be no full redemption when some individuals or groups are excluded or left behind; the good of the part and the good of the whole belong together. As Paul's cosmic vision in 8:18–23 makes clear, this means that the good of the church and the good of the whole created order also belong together.

Similarly, the outburst of the oppressed (8:36) demands a hearing, no matter how awkward or disruptive it may be. To invite such voices into the common life of the church may include the retelling of wrongs both done and suffered, lament, intrusive cries of protest, and radical questioning of the goodness and providence of God. All of these have an insistent voice in 8:36, which mandates expressing such difficult realities rather than sweeping them under the rug. Real change requires both the naming of suffering and injustice and the assurance that they do not have the last word, in a communal context held by the gracious love of God in Christ.

Christian Witness in the World: Solidarity and Difference

Believers join in solidarity with the yearning of all creation for redemption, a solidarity that expresses Christ's redemptive participation in human history. Yet they also have a distinct identity and foundation for their lives—"this grace in which we stand" (5:2)—which sources a distinct hope in Christ. Both the solidarity and the difference contribute to the church's role in promoting the good of the social order, as well as the clergy's role in pastoral care. Both require entering into another's experience, yet both also require differentiation and a larger vision of the good.

A brief rabbinic story provides a vivid and entertaining picture of this combination of solidarity and difference. As the story goes, a prince became completely convinced that he was not a person but a chicken: he took off his clothes, sat under a table clucking, and refused to eat anything but chicken feed. Naturally his parents were deeply distressed; they consulted counselors and physicians, but no one could help them. Finally, they turned to an old rabbi for help. He came to the palace, where he took off all his clothes, joined the prince under the table, clucked, and ate chicken feed. After some time, he said to the prince, "This chicken feed tastes terrible; I'm going to have something else to eat. How about you?" And the prince joined him in eating human food. More time passed. Eventually the rabbi said, "I'm cold. Are you cold? Let's put on some clothes." So they did. Finally, the rabbi said, "It's cramped in this narrow space under the table. I'm going to stand up.

Would you like to stand up?" The prince objected, "But I'm a chicken! I'm eating human food and wearing human clothes. If I stand up no one will know I'm a chicken!" The rabbi replied, "You know you're a chicken, and I know you're a chicken. No one else needs to know." So they stood up together (Eastman 2017).

Without joining the prince in his circumstances and perspective under the table, the rabbi could not have helped him. But if that was all the rabbi did, he also could not have helped the prince. Rather, by joining the prince under the table, the rabbi was able to share with the prince a larger horizon, a different imagination of what was possible. In a similar way, clergy who sit with people in their pain earn the right to be heard on Sunday morning. Churches gain authority to speak for reconciliation and hope when they engage with their neighbors in their hardships and struggles. Conversely, clergy and churches that take their cues only from the surrounding culture, without articulating a robust countercultural vision of the good news, have lost their reason for being.

Allied Agency

We have seen that Paul speaks of the flesh and the Spirit both as realms of power, such that one can be "in the flesh" or "in the Spirit," and as entities that dwell among human beings. The result is an overlap between human agency and other agencies, which operate in relational systems that create distinctive environments. Some environments seem to subvert our best intentions; contrary to what we want, we find ourselves saying and doing things that we hate. This is why going home for the holidays can be deadly for some people, and why recovering addicts may need to move to a new neighborhood. Such is the systemic bondage of sin. But the relational system inaugurated and indwelt by the Spirit generates loving attachments in which the agency of believers is strengthened rather than undercut. Paul spells out the communal implications of this new relational system in chapters 12–14. At this point his focus is on the Spirit's actions, which do not silence but rather amplify human voices, and do not replace but rather energize life-giving bodily practices.

Living in Hope, Empowered by Love

Romans 5:2–5 and 8:24–25 highlight hope as a defining characteristic of Christian faith. This is not triumphalist hope, but the kind of hope that climbs an impossible rock wall with the tiniest of finger- and toeholds and avoids looking down. To live in "hope that is not seen" is to remain open to a mysterious future held only by God. It is to be pulled into that future rather than determined by past failures or accomplishments and therefore to have one's daily life undergirded by God's faithfulness rather than our own resourcefulness. It is, in fact, like walking on water.

The French reformer John Calvin spoke poignantly about hope, in words that sum up the experience Paul describes in 8:24–25:

> Though Christ offers us in the Gospel a present plenitude of spiritual blessings, yet the enjoyment of them always lies hid under the custody of hope till we are divested of our corruptible body and transfigured into the glory of Him who is our first-fruits, our forerunner. In the meantime, the Spirit commands us to rely on the promises. Nor, indeed, have we otherwise any enjoyment of Christ any further than we embrace Him, as He is garbed in His promises. By which it comes to pass that He Himself now dwells in our hearts and yet we live like pilgrims at a distance from Him, because we walk by faith and not by sight. (Calvin 1959, 2.9.3)

The promise of 8:28 belongs to this *hidden* hope. It can be quoted in facile and destructive ways to people burdened by great pain: "In all things the Spirit works for good together with those who love God." Attentiveness and care are necessary before saying this to desperate people. For the "good" Paul envisions is not immediate easing of a terrible situation and not always seen in this life; his horizon is cosmic and eternal. The good is conformation to the image of Christ (8:29), who also suffered yet ultimately overcame death. It is the good of knowing, however tenuously, that God is with us and we will be glorified with him (8:17, 30; cf. Phil 3:20–21), and that nothing can separate us from God's love.

Finally, there can be no hope apart from love. Love gets a bad rap in some Christian teaching, only because people confuse it with sentimental counterfeits. This is a grave mistake. As Paul says elsewhere (1 Cor 13), without love nothing else matters. The German theologian and martyr Dietrich Bonhoeffer warned future pastors against an idealistic vision of the church that fails to see and love the real people in the pew (Bonhoeffer 2009). It is tempting for clergy to pride themselves on their sermons, their leadership skills, their organizational strengths, their prophetic vision for the church, but to criticize or neglect the people in their congregations. Especially the difficult ones! But without love, talk of hope, transformation, fellowship, witness, and the church's work in the world will lead to cynicism and despair for people both in the pew and in the pulpit. God's love is "God for us," and God knows how profoundly every human being needs to know that truth.

Part Two: Israel and the Mercy of God

Romans 9:1–11:36

Romans 8 ends with an acclamation of God's love; Romans 9 begins with a huge question mark over that love. If God is for "us" but not for God's beloved people Israel, all talk of divine love rings hollow. If Paul's fellow Jews are excluded from the salvation announced in the gospel, what becomes of the promises to Abraham? What becomes of the divine faithfulness displayed throughout Israel's history and proclaimed by the prophets? Are the flesh-and-blood people of Israel, Paul's Jewish relatives, simply a means to a different end, the salvation of the gentiles? Paul recoils in horror from such a thought. Romans 9–11 is his answer to these questions, which concern not only Israel's destiny but also God's trustworthiness and the inclusive scope of God's power for salvation, "for the Jew first and also for the Greek" (1:16). In this sense, God is the main subject of these crucial chapters in Romans.

THEOLOGICAL THEMES

Romans 9–11 forms a distinctive subsection of the letter, but as will become evident through careful attention to the text, these chapters also are deeply connected with the preceding and following sections. Three key theological commitments undergird and guide Paul's sometimes tortuous and dense arguments. First is "God's purpose of election . . . , not by works but by his call," shown in God's calling of the patriarchs without regard to their accomplishments (9:11–12). This "purpose of election" is inseparable from God's freedom to be merciful, again without regard to human worth, will, or exertion (9:15–16). Paul describes Israel's call by God as a divine gift from the very beginning; it is this divine grace that shines through Israel's history, that now has come to the gentiles, and that will embrace both Jews and gentiles in the culmination of God's redemptive purposes. The pinnacle of this salvation is also the underpinning of God's dealings with both gentiles and Jews at every point: "Who has given a gift to [God], to receive a gift in return? For from him and through him and to him are all things. To him be the glory forever. Amen" (11:35–36). This is the astonishing divine gratuity that sources all human life and all redemption, without exception, and that is expressed by God's creation of Israel as an act of gracious election. As we shall see, the dynamics of this gift, displayed through Christ's solidarity and exchange with humanity under sin (1:3; 8:3), undergird Paul's vision for the outworking of God's purposes for both Jews and gentiles.

The second theological datum is the absolute centrality and lordship of Christ, who is the one toward whom God's dealings with Israel point and the one who accomplishes salvation for all, both Jews and gentiles (10:4–13). Jesus Christ as God's Son is both "descended from David according to the flesh" (1:3) and sent by God into the world "in the likeness of sinful flesh" (8:3). Paul repeats Christ's fleshly solidarity with Israel in 9:5—from Israel comes the Christ, "according to the flesh." Paul never conceives of a separate path of salvation for Israel, nor of gentiles as simply grafted into Israel per se; "there is no distinction" (3:22). Just as all, Jews as well as gentiles, are under the power of sin (1:18–3:20), so all, Jews as well as gentiles, will be saved through Christ (3:21–25). But the way in which that will happen for the Jewish people remains shrouded in mystery (11:26–33).

Paul's third theological commitment is to God's sovereignty over both unbelief and belief; both play a role in God's purposes. As Paul's argument progresses, gentiles and Jews take turns being in the place of disobedience, so that ultimately all receive God's undeserved mercy. In relationship to God, gentiles were once the outsiders and Jews the insiders, but temporarily "a hardening has come upon part of Israel, until the full number of the gentiles has come in" (11:25). In the same way, "just as you were once disobedient to God but have now received mercy because of their disobedience, so also they have now been disobedient in order that, by the mercy shown to you, they also may now receive mercy" (11:30–31). God hardens hearts and God has mercy, all in service of God's unequivocal commitment to save all: "God has imprisoned all in disobedience so that he may be merciful to all" (11:32). The result of this confident assertion is an immensely capacious view of God's power and purposes, surely exceeding human understanding, and inviting trust, humility, and openness to others as the place in which God will show God's mercy.

When threading through the dense argumentation in these chapters, it will be helpful to keep these three theological dicta in mind. Everything in these chapters is debated in the history of interpretation, but these three observations will guide the approach of this commentary.

SOCIAL HISTORICAL CONTEXT

Paul's theological commitments are inseparable from the social realities pressing in upon the apostle and the Roman house churches. Paul's mission to the gentiles has been fruitful, and he has had the joy of planting and nurturing many young communities primarily composed of gentile converts, but also including some Jewish followers of Jesus. Nonetheless, perhaps as the apostle prepares to go to Jerusalem, the question arises: why have not all Jews embraced Jesus as the Messiah? How can Paul make sense of this? Too often and for too long, Christians have blamed the Jews for rejecting Jesus, with disastrous consequences. Paul's understanding of God's calling and mercy will not allow him to do this; as becomes evident through a careful reading of chapters 9–11, Paul lays the responsibility for the present Jewish rejection of Jesus squarely with God. He never blames his Jewish relatives for some kind of failure in belief. And because he so firmly trusts in God's power, he also maintains a robust certainty that God will have mercy on all (11:32).

The second pastoral concern pressing on Paul in these chapters is gentile Christian arrogance toward Jews (11:13–24). Such arrogance could be an issue in communities where gentile converts have come to outnumber the first Jewish followers of Jesus. As becomes evident in chapter 14, there are divisions in the Roman house churches concerning eating practices and observance of holy days; these do not necessarily reflect divisions between Jews and gentiles, but they do indicate conflicting attitudes toward Jewish practices and mutual judgment on differences in practice. Part of Paul's way of addressing this tension is to give a vigorous theological account of Israel's enduring place in God's purposes.

DISTINCTIVE STYLE AND USE OF SCRIPTURE

Romans 9–11 is set off from the surrounding chapters by extensive quotations from Scripture, more than in any other part of Romans or any other Pauline letter. Given the topic, this is not surprising. Paul retells and interprets the Genesis narratives, and he quotes extensively from Deuteronomy, Psalms, and the Prophets, particularly Hosea and Isaiah. Theologically, this saturation with Scripture demonstrates that God's gracious gift of salvation through Christ is entirely consonant with, and indeed inseparable from, the revelation of God in Israel's history. Pastorally, the citations of Scripture educate Paul's Roman audience into the stories and promises of God's long dealings with the Jewish people.

In ways reminiscent of 2:1–3:9 and following on from the style of 8:31–39, Paul also engages in the rhetorical pattern of the diatribe by posing questions and answers throughout these chapters. Each step of his argument raises a question to which the following verses respond, only to raise further questions. Thus, 9:1–5 highlights Israel's status as heirs of God's promises, with the implied but not yet stated question: why has Israel not accepted Jesus as the Messiah? The following verses 6–29 address the unstated question left hanging by 9:1–5: has the word of God fallen short? Paul's response to this question raises further questions about God's justice (9:19), which he addresses but does not fully answer in 9:20–29. Paul asks, "What then shall we say?" (9:30), responding with an exposition about the necessity of faith in Christ (10:1–13). That exposition plants the further question, "How can people believe without hearing the message?" (10:14), implying that Israel simply needs to hear gospel preaching. But then Paul contradicts that inference with further questions: "Have they not heard? Indeed they have!" (10:18–21), leading to another false inference; Israel is simply disobedient and God has rejected his people. Paul raises this as a question (11:1) only to answer with an emphatic "No way!" Yet his "answer" does not satisfy; rather it heightens the problem and again raises a question: "Has Israel stumbled so as to fall?" (11:11). Paul's second emphatic "No way!" leads into his final proclamation of God's ultimately merciful dealings with both Jews and gentiles (11:11–32). Ultimately, this pattern of questions, answers, and further questions takes Paul's listeners into the mystery of God's sovereign mercy.

Nonetheless, it must be said that Paul's argumentation is exceedingly difficult to follow as he leads his listeners into false inferences that he then corrects. Each stage of the argument is rather like a chapter in a mystery thriller, which leaves the reader hanging and compelled to continue reading to find out how the story ends.

STRUCTURE

The structure of Romans 9–11 divides fairly clearly into four major stages. In 9:1–5 Paul introduces his concern for Israel and its status as God's elect. In 9:6–29 he focuses on God's way of calling a people without regard to their merits or lack thereof; Israel's very existence testifies to the priority of God's undeserved mercy. In 9:30–10:21 Christ and faith take center stage, and in 11:1–36 Paul asserts the certainty of redemption for all Israel and the fullness of the gentiles. This certainty culminates in an outpouring of praise to God for God's inscrutable and gratuitous mercy. Throughout, the central actor in this drama is God, and the central theme is God's plenteous mercy and sovereign power on behalf of all God's people.

ROMANS 9:1–5
What about the Jews?

In 1:18–3:20 Paul carefully puts Jews and gentiles on the same footing before an impartial God, whose impartiality indeed derives from the basic tenet of Jewish faith, that God is one (3:30). In 3:21–8:39, he revisits the human dilemma of bondage to sin and God's redemption through Christ. The culmination of this drama is the victory song of 8:38–39, rejoicing that nothing can separate believers from God's love in Jesus Christ. That song of victory raises a question about Paul's Jewish relatives who have not trusted in Jesus as the Messiah—what about them? In 9:1–5 Paul begins to address the question by expressing his personal anguish on behalf of his Jewish relatives.

9:1–2. Paul's Anguish

Paul begins with a striking first-person cry from the heart, expressing his heartache for his kinsfolk with an emphatic claim: "I am speaking the truth in Christ—I am not lying; my conscience confirms it by the Holy Spirit—I have great sorrow and unceasing anguish in my heart." "Conscience" means "knowing together with oneself," such that the conscience can be called as a witness (cf. 2:15); here it joins with "in Christ" and "by the Holy Spirit" in threefold witness to the truth of Paul's exclamation.

That Paul speaks "in Christ" not only authorizes his speech but determines his attitude toward his Jewish kin. He has just claimed that nothing can separate "us" from "the love of God in Christ Jesus" (8:39). But who is included in this "us"? With extreme pathos and irony, Paul's location "in Christ" contrasts with Israel's implied location apart from Christ (9:3)—a location that Paul would gladly inhabit if he could change places with his kinsfolk. Paul's sorrow and grief heighten the importance of what will follow and emphasize his personal involvement in the destiny of his fellow Jews; he reverts to such personal statements at the beginning of each chapter (10:1; 11:1–2).

We should not minimize Paul's genuine distress nor dismiss his passionate language as merely a rhetorical ploy. He cannot conceive of a salvation that excludes his Jewish kinsfolk. At the same time, Paul surely is telling the primarily gentile audience in Rome that he takes Israel's identity as God's chosen people seriously, and so should they, because if Israel is excluded from salvation, God's promises mean nothing for the gentiles either.

9:3. "Accursed and Cut Off from Christ"

The abrupt shift in tone from 8:38–39 to 9:1–2 assaults the mind and might imply that Paul is turning to a completely new topic. Such is not the case. Rather, reading 8:38–39 together with 9:1–2 illuminates the poignancy and logic of 9:3. Immediately after affirming the certainty that nothing can separate believers from God's love, and naming his own location "in Christ," Paul expresses his own willingness to be "accursed and cut off" (*anathema*) from Christ if that would mean his Jewish brothers and sisters would be included. "I could wish" translates "I have prayed"; this is not a hypothetical wish but an ongoing, earnest prayer.

Paul's prayer echoes Moses's plea for God to forgive Israel after its apostasy at Sinai; Moses ends his plea by adding, "but if not, please blot me out of the book that you have written" (Exod 32:31–32). God refused Moses's request, and God has refused Paul's willingness to change places with Jews who do not follow Jesus as the Christ.

Paul not only echoes Moses, however; his impulse toward taking his fellow Jews' place apart from Christ echoes Christ's own interchange with Adamic humanity, in which Christ takes the place of all who have been handed over to destructive forces (Rom 4:25). This is not to say that Paul is a Christ figure or is offering to make atonement, but simply that his impulse toward solidarity and exchange with his fellow Jews is an interpersonal outworking of God's way of salvation; God in Christ joins with those estranged from God and takes their place. As these chapters unfold, we will see this interpersonal outworking of God's way of salvation operative in Paul's vision of Jew and gentile "changing places" in relationship to God, for the ultimate salvation of all.

"My brothers and sisters" is a term Paul usually uses for siblings "in Christ." Regardless of whether his Jewish relatives view him in such a familial way (and they may not; see 2 Cor 11:24), Paul still claims a sibling bond with them. In Greek, the phrase translated by the NRSVue as "my own flesh and blood" is literally "my kinsfolk according to the flesh [*kata sarka*]." "According to the flesh" characterizes Christ's physical descent from David (1:3), Abraham's physical paternity (4:1), and again, the genealogy of Christ as Messiah "according to the flesh" (9:5).

9:4–5. "They Are Israelites"

Paul continues by naming his kinsfolk's history and God-given identity: "They are Israelites" (9:4). "Israel" is the covenant name given to Jacob and his offspring (Gen 32:28; 35:10); when Paul focuses on God's calling and mercy for his own kinsfolk, he uses their preferred self-designations as "Israel" and "Israelite," in distinction from the term "Jews" that he uses in the first eight chapters of the letter. The present tense in Romans 9:4 is significant; the Israelites are *still* God's chosen people; they have not been displaced by the gentile followers of Jesus. They still possess the attributes that belong to their calling, even if gentile believers also now enjoy some of them: the adoption (Exod 4:22; Jer 31:9; Rom 8:15, 23), the glory (8:18), the worship (12:1), and the benefits of "the promises," particularly the promises given to Abraham (4:16). But in other respects, Israel is unique, and it is always "first" (1:16; 2:10), because in Israel's history God first displayed the creative power of divine election and mercy. Israel possesses "the covenants," referring primarily to God's covenant with Abraham, but also surely including the Mosaic covenant in which the law was given. The plural "covenants" indicates Israel's special status as the people whom God has chosen for covenantal relationship.

Notably Paul emphasizes the patriarchs (9:5), whose stories will undergird his argument in 9:6–18. Of most importance is that the Christ, the Messiah, comes from Israel "according to the flesh." The addition of the article "the" (Gk. *ho*) before "Christ" may emphasize "Christ" as a messianic title. Christ's fleshly continuity with Israel guarantees Israel's continuing priority in God's purposes of salvation.

The final doxology raises a major translation issue. Does "God over all" refer to Christ (NRSVue) or is it a separate doxology in which God is distinguished from Christ (RSV)? Grammatically speaking, since "who is God over all" immediately follows "Christ" as the preceding referent, the logical flow of the sentence supports the NRSVue translation. Furthermore, naming Christ as both from Israel "according to the flesh" and "God over all" parallels the dual designation of Jesus as descended from David's seed according to the flesh and designated Son of God in power according to the Spirit of holiness, at the beginning of the letter (1:3–4). Such a claim about the lordship of Christ anticipates 10:9, 12–13 (see also Phil 2:6, 10–11).

EXCURSUS

Reflections for Preaching and Teaching

First-Person Preaching

Paul rarely refers to himself, and even more rarely in such emotional language as in 9:1–3, but he is not afraid to do so when he wants to engage his listeners on a visceral as well as cognitive level. His anguish is real, and he shares it with the Romans, even though he does not yet know them personally. Might his very limited but effective self-disclosure be a model for preaching? As one layperson said of a pastor whom she admired, "He sweats when he preaches." In other words, the preacher had skin in the game. Paul's passionate investment in his flesh-and-blood kin, regardless of their attitude to him, challenges us to a similar involvement with those to whom we preach and with whom we minister.

Changing Places

Anyone who has longed to exchange places with a loved one who is suffering can empathize with Paul's earnest desire to trade places with his estranged fellow Jews, even to be accursed and cut off from Christ if that would guarantee their inclusion. This impulse toward sacrificial love, this story of one person taking the rap for others, is built into the human psyche. In Charles Dickens's masterpiece *A Tale of Two Cities,* Sydney Carton takes the place of Darnay in going to the guillotine; in *The Hunger Games,* when a young girl is chosen for a fight to the death, her older sister steps forward. In *The Narnia Chronicles,* by C. S. Lewis, the great lion Aslan takes the place of the traitor Edmund. These stories, like Paul's own exclamation in Romans 9:3, illustrate the deep logic of solidarity and exchange in the story of the gospel and the way that logic may permeate human relationships on the level of our emotions, desires, judgments, and actions.

ROMANS 9:6–29
The Calling into Being of God's People

Paul has not yet stated the reason for his grief and will not do so explicitly until 9:31, after he has established God's purpose of election regardless of merit. Instead, at this point he addresses the deep theological question implied by his anguish: Has the word of God failed? Paul's response focuses on the character and timing of God's calling of Israel, not on Israel's identity; the point is that God calls and elects without regard to anything people do, whether good or bad (9:11). Such a claim triggers doubts about divine justice (v. 14); to address those doubts Paul calls both Moses and the prophets as witnesses to God's freedom to have mercy and to "harden" (v. 18), and to create whatever God wants, just as a potter can create any kind of pot (v. 21). This divine freedom authorizes God's calling of gentiles as well as Jews (v. 24), even as "children of the living God" (v. 26). Finally, Paul reminds his listeners that God has always promised that Israel will not be totally rejected, but a remnant will be left (vv. 27–29).

Thus Paul's discussion proceeds by the following steps:

- 9:6–18 Election and the mercy of God
  - 9:6–13 God's purpose of election: "not because of works but because of call"
  - 9:14–18 God's mercy and hardening of hearts: "It depends not on human will or exertion but on God's mercy."
- 9:19–29 God's freedom to be merciful
  - 9:19–24 Vessels of wrath and mercy
  - 9:25–26 Children of the living God
  - 9:27–29 The remnant

9:6–18. Election and the Mercy of God

9:6–13. God's Purpose of Election

Paul begins with the theological problem posed by Israel's unbelief—has God's word failed? For a word to "fail" means for it to fail to come to pass, to be proven false, even to fall silent and be ineffective. In the immediate context of 9:4, 8–9, the singular "word of God" refers to the promises to the patriarchs, although it also could denote the gospel itself as "the power of God" (1:16–17) that accomplishes God's purposes. God's faithfulness to the promises is inseparable from God's faithfulness to the gospel. As we read through the following chapters, it becomes clear that the gospel of God's undeserved mercy is already operative in God's promises to Israel. "The promises" conclude the list of Israel's divinely gifted benefits in 9:4 and ground Paul's subsequent exposition of Israel's genealogy through Abraham and Isaac: "the children of the promise are counted as descendants" (9:8). Paul retells Israel's family history to demonstrate how God's word always has been, and continues to be, effective through God's gracious election and not through human achievements. He invokes the scriptural witness to God's modus operandi through election and mercy apart from human merit; this scriptural witness thus supports God's salvation through Christ's gift for the undeserving. In this way, Paul assures his readers that the word of God in the gospel also did not and will not fail.

The translation of 9:6b is both hotly contested and crucial for understanding Paul's argument. The Greek says literally, "for not all who are from Israel, these [are] Israel." The question is whether this terse statement means there is a present division within "Israel," or a distinction among those *descended from* "Israel," such that only some of the descendants are members of the people known as Israel—that is, the Israelites who are recipients of the promises (9:4–5). This commentary takes the latter position, which is well captured by the NRSVue translation: "Not all those descended from Israel are Israelites."

Beginning in 9:7, Paul reads the Genesis stories carefully as he traces out the family tree of Abraham's descendants. Ishmael was the son born through Abraham's physical liaison with Hagar (Gen 16:1–5); Isaac was the child miraculously born to Sarah as a result of God's promise (Gen 21:1–7; cf. Gal 4:22–23 for Paul's emphasis on Isaac as the child of promise). Therefore, Isaac and his descendants are "children of promise," and it is through Isaac, not Ishmael, that Israel's lineage comes. This is not to deny that Ishmael's descendants also trace back to Abraham, a point that becomes important in later dialogue between the three Abrahamic religions. Paul, however, is not concerned with those later issues. His point here is simply to say that the people named Israel came into being through God's promise; therefore, not all of Abraham's descendants are named as Israel, but only those descended from Isaac, the miracle baby (Rom 9:8).

Paul is not making a division within Israel; rather, he is highlighting the way in which God called all Israel into being—through divine promise in the face of human impossibility, not through the "flesh," which in this case signifies merely human effort. God's promise has not failed, because Sarah bore Isaac. The focus is on *how* God called Israel into being, through promise, not on defining *who* Israel is or is not.

The Greek of 9:9 reads, "this is the word of promise," in parallel with "the word of God" in 9:6a; the word of God that came to Abraham and Sarah was indeed a word of promise that came to pass in the birth of Isaac. In Paul's interpretation of the Genesis narrative, "the promises" (v. 4) signify the way God's word (v. 6a) works in history. The general "promises" then are narrowed down to the specific "word of the promise" (v. 9) to Abraham and Sarah (Gen 18:10, 14). This brief reference suggests three further insights. First, God's word and God's promises are not timeless truths, generalized theological claims that may be lifted out of their context; they are specific, historical, and embodied in flesh-and-blood people.

Second, the quotations from Genesis 18:10, 14 recall the story of God's appearance to Abraham by the oaks of Mamre (Gen 18:1–16), when Sarah eavesdrops on the conversation between Abraham and their mysterious visitors and overhears the statement that she will have a son (v. 10). Sarah has never been able to conceive and now is long past childbearing years. She breaks into muffled laughter that is overheard by the divine visitors. The Lord asks, "Why did Sarah laugh?" and goes on to reiterate the promise: "Is anything too wonderful for the Lord?" Between the first and second statements of the promise is Sarah's cynical, entirely understandable laughter. This richly drawn, humorous, and very human story echoes in the background of Paul's insistence that the people Israel owe their existence to God's faithfulness to the promise and to nothing else. That divine faithfulness allows room for Sarah's doubt and laughter.

Third, the mention of Abraham and Sarah recalls Romans 4:13–22, where Paul also highlights the promise of progeny given to Abraham (vv. 13, 14, 16, 20–21), a promise that Abraham trusts despite the deadness of his own body and of Sarah's womb (v. 19). Abraham trusts the God "who gives life to the dead and calls into existence the things that do not exist" (v. 17). This God who calls things into being out of nothing is the God who has called Israel into existence through the promise, in 9:8–9.

If the story of Isaac's miraculous birth through God's promise emphasizes God's generative initiative, in 9:10–11 a second story from Genesis further elaborates on Paul's point. The NRSVue translation fudges a bit on the specific meaning of the Greek, which states that Rebekah became pregnant through one act of intercourse with her husband Isaac. The twins Jacob and Esau not only had the same father; they were conceived at the same time through a single sexual union. Therefore there is absolutely nothing to distinguish the sons of Rebecca and Isaac prior to their birth; they are twins who were not yet born and had done nothing either "good or bad" (9:11). Yet God chose Jacob, not Esau; Esau will serve Jacob (Gen 25:23). Paul then spells out the main point of the story: "so that God's purpose of election might continue, not by works but by his call" (Rom 9:11b–12a). Israel's own genealogy testifies to God's election apart from any human merit. Therefore, "election" displays the action of a God who saves, who calls into being, and who blesses solely because God chooses to do so, without any regard to the achievements or failures of those whom God chooses.

Introduced by "as it is written," the quotation from Malachi 1:2–3 in Romans 9:13—"I have loved Jacob, but I have hated Esau"—adds further scriptural backing for Paul's interpretation of the Genesis story. God calls and chooses whomever God will. The arbitrariness of God's choice naturally raises the question of God's justice. Paul reframes this question in terms of mercy.

9:14–18. Mercy

"What then are we to say?" in 9:14 introduces a possible false inference from the preceding narrative, "Is there injustice on God's part?" (cf. 3:5–7). Anyone who has read the stories of Jacob and Esau will find the same question arising, for Jacob is surely an unsavory character who tricks his brother out of his father's blessing (Gen 27:1–29). There is nothing admirable about Jacob, yet God blesses him and gives him the name Israel (Gen 32:28). As with Abraham and David, Paul does not airbrush Israel's ancestry, but rather gives examples of God's dealings with people purely in terms of mercy and grace (cf. Rom 11:5).

Paul's "answer" to the question is not an answer. That omission has not gone unnoticed by Paul's interpreters, who from patristic times have sought to supply a rationale for God's choice of Jacob over Esau. For example, Ambrosiaster, a fourth-century commentator, says that God's choice of one person over another is based on God's foreknowledge of how people will behave; he glosses 9:15 as "I will have mercy on the one whom I knew in advance . . . that the person will be converted and remain faithful. . . . I will have compassion on the person whom I knew in advance will turn back with an upright heart after straying" (*Commentary* 9:14–16, in Burns 2012, 227). Cyril of Alexandria similarly interprets God's choice as "the grace of election and the gift given on the basis of foreknowledge" (*Commentary* 9:14–18, in Burns 2012, 227). Nonetheless, Paul does not speak of God's foreknowledge; the insistence of these early interpreters on inserting a rationale for God's election simply highlights how perplexing and countercultural God's election of Israel is.

Augustine gets the point:

> The grace, therefore, is from the one who calls; the good works that follow the grace belong to the one who receives it. The grace brings forth the works; the works do not themselves produce the grace. Fire heats because it is hot, not to become hot; a wheel rolls smoothly because it is round, not to become round. In the same way, a person acts well because grace has already been received, not in order to acquire grace. (*To Simplicianus* 1.2.3, in Burns 2012, 224)

Augustine further clarifies Paul's reasoning by recalling Adam's sin, to which both Esau and Jacob are heirs. It is not that Esau deserved mercy that he did not receive; neither Esau nor Jacob deserved anything from the Lord, but the Lord chose to call Jacob. Therefore, Paul was teaching "that anyone being rescued from that lump coming from the first human, to which death was rightly due, owes this salvation not to human merits but to the mercy of God" (*Letter* 186.5.15–6.16, in Burns 2012, 226). Augustine here exposes the unspoken assumption in accusations that God is unjust—the assumption that human beings have a claim to merit and accomplishments that put God in their debt. Paul's final answer to this claim is 11:35–36.

Having retold the Genesis narratives to confirm God's election apart from human deserving, in 9:15 Paul cites a story from Exodus to illustrate God's freedom to have mercy on those who are disobedient. The context is God's theophany to Moses after the golden calf incident, in response to Moses's request to see God's glory (Exod 33:18). It is thus a foundational revelation of God's character, in terms of God's freedom to be merciful and have compassion on whomever God chooses. God's exercise of compassion (*oiktirō*) reappears in Romans 12:1, where God's compassions (*oiktirmōn tou theou*) are the basis of human worship.

In the oracle against human unrighteousness and idolatry in 1:18–32, Paul echoes Psalm 106:20, which retells the story of Israel's idolatrous worship of the golden calf (Exod 32). Now, explicitly referring to the same story, Paul emphasizes Israel's lack of any claim on God beyond God's own trustworthiness. Against such a backdrop, God's freedom to be merciful to whomever God chooses utterly rejects any notion that some people have a greater claim on God than others do.

Yet a third time (Rom 9:16) Paul spells out the point regarding God's action in human history: "It depends not on human will or exertion but on God who shows mercy." The word translated "exertion" is literally "running," anticipating the image of a race in 9:30–31. Here again Paul's argument restates his earlier claims about the priority of God's grace as exemplified in Abraham (4:1–5).

The flip side of God's freedom to be merciful to the undeserving is God's freedom to harden human hearts, as Paul describes in 9:17–18. He names Pharaoh as Exhibit A of this divine hardening, offering a noncontroversial example for Jews as well as gentiles familiar with the story of the exodus (Exod 4:21; 7:3; 9:12; 10:1, 20, 27; 11:10; 14:8). Notably, Pharaoh's resistance to Moses served God's purposes, so that Pharaoh, the symbol of oppression and injustice, was also "raised up" by God as a medium through which God's saving power was demonstrated and God's name (the very name revealed to Moses as "merciful" and "compassionate") proclaimed. "Hardened hearts" also play a role in the revelation of God's power and mercy. Ironically, Paul's depiction of Pharaoh, a quintessential gentile sinner, anticipates his depiction of Israel in Romans 11:1–12. Both Pharaoh and Israel are "hardened" by God, and both ultimately serve God's purpose of demonstrating his mercy through the riches of grace.

9:19–29. God's Freedom to Be Merciful

9:19–24. Vessels of Wrath and Mercy

Paul's response to the question of God's justice (9:14) intensifies the mystery of God's sovereignty over human hearts, which Paul puts in a question addressed directly to himself in verse 19. His answer in verses 20–24 comes from a combination of scriptural texts averring God's right to act as God wishes (Job 9:12; Wis 12:12; 15:7; Jer 18:6; Isa 29:16; 45:9). Human beings are like clay, and God is the potter who makes different pots for different uses (Rom 9:21; cf. Wis 15:7). Some clay vessels are used as wine pitchers, others as chamber pots. The point is straightforward: God the Creator may do whatever God wishes, and every "pot" has its place in God's creative work.

The NRSVue translation of 9:22 as "objects of wrath that are made for destruction" is misleading. The word translated "objects" simply means "vessels"; the context of 9:22–23 shows that they are "of wrath" in the sense that God will demonstrate his wrath and power through them, not that they are targets of God's wrath. The key phrase is "God has endured with much patience," which echoes 2:5, where God's patience is meant to lead to repentance. "Made for destruction" translates a verb meaning "prepared" or "fitted." Following closely after Paul's depiction of Pharaoh, it is Pharaoh, not unbelieving Jews, who is the immediate referent for such "vessels of wrath"; through Pharaoh, God did indeed demonstrate God's wrath and power.

The ultimate point of Paul's metaphor is not wrath, however, but the demonstration of the riches of God's glory for those who receive mercy (9:23–24). Indeed, Paul drops discussion of the destiny of the "vessels of wrath" and focuses completely on the vessels of mercy, as he suddenly switches to first-person plural: "including *us* whom he has called, not from the Jews only but also from the gentiles." By saying "not from the Jews *only,*" Paul maintains the priority of the Jews in the order of salvation (1:16; 2:9, 10; 3:29; 10:12), but now he *includes* gentiles, so that *together with* Jews they will receive mercy and become the way God shows the "riches of his glory" (cf. 10:12; 11:12, 33; 15:7–9; cf. Phil 4:19; Col 1:27; Eph 3:16). At this point, however, Paul's focus is on God's freedom to call gentiles as well as Jews into being as God's people.

9:25–26. "Sons of the Living God"

By writing, "*He* also says in Hosea," in 9:25 Paul names God as the speaker of the prophetic text, divinely confirming the inclusion of the gentiles through the promises spoken through the prophet (Hos 2:1, 25). The Hosea quotation thus functions on two levels. In its original context, it is a promise to Israel that, after a temporary period of rejection when they were called "not my people" and "not beloved," God will restore them to their first and lasting relationship as "children [Gk., sons] of the living God." In this way, the citation anticipates Paul's conclusions in Romans 11:25–32. But in the immediate context of 9:24, God's promise in Hosea addresses gentiles who once were "not my people" and "not beloved," but now also are called "children of God," as indeed Paul has claimed in 8:14–17.

9:27–29. Only a Remnant

Paul explicitly invokes Isaiah to speak to Israel's present condition by quoting a somewhat abbreviated version of Isaiah 10:22 in Romans 9:27–28 and Isaiah 1:9 in Romans 9:29. The image of the "remnant" functions as both a sign of judgment—*only* a remnant!—and a sign of hope; if the Lord had not left a remnant we would have perished utterly. But the Lord *has* left a remnant. The implication from 9:24 is that this present remnant is composed of both Jewish and gentile believers, but Paul does not state this explicitly until 11:1–5. The further implication is that Israel is identified with the vessels through which God demonstrates wrath, even with Pharaoh whose heart was hardened, but again, Paul does not speak of Israel with hardened hearts until 11:7–10, 25.

EXCURSUS

Reflections for Preaching and Teaching

As noted above, preaching from this dense and puzzling section of Romans must always keep in mind the trajectory of these passages, which is toward the salvation of both Jews and gentiles. Any reading that sees Israel or even a part of Israel as excluded from God's salvation runs the risk of ignoring that goal, misrepresenting Paul's gospel, and contributing to the anti-Semitism that is still rampant in the church and in Western culture. Given that warning, some key guidelines for preaching and teaching come to the fore.

Keep the Focus on God's Gracious Initiative

Throughout these verses Paul's primary focus is not on the question of Israel's or gentiles' identity but on God's gracious initiative. In 9:6–18 the apostle is not redefining "Israel" but highlighting key points in Israel's history that demonstrate God's freedom to call, to elect, and to have mercy without any preconditions on the part of human beings (9:11, 16, 18). Similarly, in the difficult metaphor of the potter and the clay, Paul carefully dismantles any sense of entitlement or claim on God's creative molding of the clay. Jesus's parable of the Workers in the Vineyard (Matt 20:1–16) illustrates this principle well; those laborers who come late to the harvest receive the same wage as those who worked all day in the hot sun. God dispenses God's riches indiscriminately, which is why both gentile and Jewish inclusion in God's people is always due to God's merciful generosity alone. Preaching from this text therefore will direct attention to God's freedom to be merciful, rather than using this text to label insiders and outsiders, let alone to distinguish between "true Israel" (a term Paul never uses) and false. All Israel is created and called by God, just as all gentile believers have been called by God's grace (Rom 1:6).

If the Vision Tarry, Wait for It

One reason Romans 9–11 is so difficult to understand is that Paul describes the unresolved status quo without any quick resolution. Indeed, his dialogical style raises questions, only to answer them with further questions that keep intensifying the problems and perplexing the reader. In so doing, Paul gives voice to objections and serious questions about God's justice and trustworthiness. These questions do not admit of sound-bite answers. Rather, to sit with these texts is to learn to live with delayed answers and to be led into a kind of truthful listening that practices waiting on God. By allowing Paul's rhetoric to work on us, we may be habituated into patience and openness and away from rushing to judgment. In today's impatient internet culture, this is a truly radical way of being.

Paul's dialogical style and delayed resolution also teach his listeners to remain open toward one another and toward those who are currently outside Christian faith. As hinted by Hosea, God's ultimate will to save may be hidden under present experiences of division and rejection.

ROMANS 9:30–10:21
Christ and Israel

"What then are we to say?" links what follows with Paul's arguments for the inclusion of gentiles in God's people, and the reduction of Israel's number to a remnant, in 9:24–29. Paul continues with a straightforward declarative statement: gentiles have attained the righteousness that comes from faith, while Israel, pursuing the righteousness that comes from the law, has not reached the goal. Now, for the first time, Paul clearly names the reason for his own grief (9:2–3), which is Israel's lack of trust in Jesus as the Christ (10:3–4). Notably, before turning to this issue, Paul has established God's purpose of election, mercy without regard to human worth, freedom to harden hearts, and mercy toward both Jews and gentiles. Only now does he proceed to the topic of Israel's unbelief.

Paul also reintroduces the topic of the law as a means of righteousness, in contrast with righteousness that comes from faith (9:31–32; cf. 3:21–22). He continues to draw on Isaiah as a witness to this divine righteousness, utilizing the metaphors of a footrace and a stumbling stone (9:30–10:4). Then, in a remarkable tour de force, Paul calls on Moses as a witness to the righteousness from faith, over *against* the righteousness from the law (10:3–13), by citing Leviticus 18:5 and Deuteronomy 30:12–14. Finally, in Romans 10:14–21 he ponders but rejects the possibility that Israel has not believed because it has not heard the gospel (vv. 14–17); Israel *has* heard the gospel, but still has not believed, whereas the gentiles who did not seek God (9:30) have found God (10:20). This section closes with an indictment of Israel for its disobedience (10:21), which sets up the question that begins the next section—has God rejected God's people (11:1)?

This stage of Paul's exposition divides neatly into three subsections, as follows:

9:30–10:4 The metaphors of a race and a stumbling stone
- 9:30–33 The righteousness of law and the righteousness from faith
- 10:1–4 Christ the *telos* of the law

10:5–13 Everyone who calls on the name of the Lord will be saved

10:14–21 Has Israel heard the gospel?
- 10:14–17 Faith comes from the preaching of Christ
- 10:18–21 Israel has heard the preaching, but responded with disobedience

9:30–10:4. The Race and the Stumbling Stone

9:30–33. The Righteousness of Law and the Righteousness of Faith

Using the related metaphors of a race and a stumbling stone, Paul contrasts righteousness based on law with righteousness that comes from faith, building on his claims in the first half of the letter (1:16–17; 3:21–31; 4:1–25).

"Strive" (9:30) translates *diōkō,* which means pursue or seek. It can mean persecution (Gal 1:13), but here it picks up on the sense of pursuit (Rom 9:16) to evoke a common metaphor of life as a race in pursuit of justice (Deut 16:20; Prov 15:9; Isa 51:1; Sir 27:8). In this race, righteousness is the prize for which the runners compete. With extreme irony, Paul depicts gentiles, who are not even in the race, as being awarded the prize, while Israel, running after the righteousness that comes from the law, does not reach the finish line. The contrast is not symmetrical; without being in the race, gentiles receive the righteousness that comes from faith—that is, from trusting in God's trustworthiness. Pursuing the "law of righteousness"—that is, the righteousness that comes from keeping the law—Israel does not reach the law.

The contrast between "faith" and "works" in 9:32a restates the earlier contrast between human accomplishment and divine gift, expressed in terms of faith (3:27–28; 4:4–5), calling (9:11), and mercy (9:16). As will become clear in 9:32b–10:13, faith does not simply signify a general attitude of trust in God, over against works as an attitude of self-reliance, as if Israel never demonstrated trust in God. Abraham and David both exemplify such trust as the bedrock of Israel's relationship with God (4:1–8). Rather, Paul is speaking quite specifically of Christ-centered trust as the decisive enactment of God's trustworthiness and power to save; such trust, including both Christ's trustworthy death and human trust in the God who justifies the ungodly, achieves God's righteousness, whereas righteousness based on the law does not (cf. Phil 3:9).

Continuing the metaphor of a race, in Romans 9:32b–33 Paul explains why Israel has not made it to the finish line; it has stumbled over a stone in the middle of the track. The image of the stumbling stone is drawn from a conflation of Isaiah 28:16 (cf. 1 Pet 2:6) and Isaiah 8:14. Isaiah 28:16 promises that God is laying in Zion a cornerstone, and "whoever trusts in him will not be put to shame." The reference to shame echoes Romans 1:16 and anticipates 10:11. Possibly drawing on an early Christian tradition in which Christ is identified with this cornerstone, Paul adds an adaptation from Isaiah 8:14, which refers to a stumbling stone for both houses of Israel. Thus the stone, identified with Christ, has two contrasting effects: salvation and stumbling. By quoting Isaiah, Paul attributes both outcomes to God's will; God has placed the stone in Israel's path for the temporary purpose of making Israel "stumble," but ultimately for the salvation of both gentiles and Jews (Rom 11:11–12).

10:1–4. Christ the *Telos* of the Law

As in 9:1–3, Paul cannot restrain his prayer for Israel's salvation. He includes the believers in Rome through addressing them as brothers and sisters, passionately informing the primarily gentile Roman house churches that Israel continues to have a place in God's redemption.

Paul's reference to his fellow Jews' "zeal for God" (10:2) recalls his description of his earlier life in which religious zeal led to violence (Gal 1:13–14; Phil 3:6). Such zeal was praised in Jewish traditions of resistance to gentile oppressors (1 Kgs 19:10, 14; 1 Macc 2:48). Here in Romans 10:2–3, however, Paul makes no reference to this tradition of resistance; rather, he says Israel's present misguided zeal is "not based on knowledge" because it is ignorant of the righteousness of God. Again, Paul may be thinking of his own past zeal "for the traditions of my ancestors" (Gal 1:14) that blinded him to God's new work of redemption in Christ. His self-description in Philippians 3:9 parallels his description of Israel here, with a similar contrast between "having a righteousness of my own that comes from the law" and "one that comes through the faith of Christ, the righteousness from God based on faith" (see NRSVue note for this translation).

Curiously, in Romans 10:3 Paul says Israel has "not *submitted* [*hypetagēsan*] to God's righteousness," presumably because it has not accepted the righteousness that comes through Christ. The verb *hypotassō* means "to submit" or "to be subject to" another; in 8:7 the mindset of the flesh does not *submit* to God's law; in 8:20 the creation *was subjected* to futility. But what would it mean to *submit* to God's righteousness? Paul's immediate invocation of Christ in 10:4 provides a clue: righteousness comes through Christ. Furthermore, as Paul makes clear in 10:9, submitting to God's righteousness through Christ entails confessing Jesus Christ as Lord; thus to submit to God's righteousness is to submit to Christ as the embodiment of that righteousness (cf. 1 Cor 1:30). Behind Paul's contrast between the righteousness of the law and the righteousness of faith lies Paul's exposé of the law's weakness in regard to sin (7:7–8:3) and his proclamation of the gospel of Christ as the means through which "the righteousness of God" is breaking into the world with saving power (1:16–17). At this point, Paul's primarily gentile listeners might think that Israel is to blame for not submitting to God's righteousness; later, however, Paul will ascribe Israel's present rejection of the gospel to God's action in "hardening" the unbelieving majority of the Jews (11:7–10).

The translation of 10:4 presents a puzzle, primarily because the Greek word *telos* can be translated as goal, fulfillment, culmination (NRSVue), or termination. These terms are not mutually exclusive, however. As the conclusion of the metaphor of a race, it makes sense to see Christ as the *goal* and *fulfillment* of the law—the one toward whom the law points and who brings to reality the life that the law promised but was powerless to deliver (7:10). Indeed, by this point in the letter Paul has quoted the foundational stories of Israel's calling—Abraham and Sarah and their progeny, the giving of the law at Sinai, the testimony of the prophets—as witnesses to God's way of salvation through Christ. As Paul claimed in 3:21, "But now, apart from the law, the righteousness of God has been disclosed and is attested by the Law and the Prophets."

But because the law testifies to Christ alone as the revelation and source of God's righteousness, Christ also is the *end* of any attempts to gain righteousness through the law. In effect, such attempts deny the power of what God already has done in Christ (8:3) and threaten to put believers back under the power of sin's use of the law (6:14). It is not that doing the law leads one to Christ, but just the reverse.

"For everyone who believes" keeps the emphasis on trust (9:32; cf. 1:16–17; 3:22–28; 4:1–25), leading into the centrality of trust in 10:5–13.

10:5–13. Calling on the Name of the Lord

10:5–7. The Righteousness That Comes from Faith

Very boldly, in 10:5 Paul quotes Moses, the lawgiver of Israel, but in order to contradict him (cf. Gal 3:10–14). Moses writes that practicing the righteousness of the law will bring life (Lev 18:5; cited also in Gal 3:12), but Paul quotes Leviticus 18:5 by way of *contrast* with "the righteousness that comes from faith." In this sense, the law does not lead to Christ, because in Christ the righteousness of God has been revealed apart from the law (Rom 3:21). But in 10:6–7 Paul also calls Moses as a witness to salvation through Christ. These verses thus expand on Paul's double claim about the law in 3:21, through reinterpreting Scripture with reference to the incarnation. In Deuteronomy 30:11–14 Moses speaks of the ease and "nearness" of the commandment itself, which is "not too hard for you, nor is it too far away" (v. 11), because it is "in your mouth and in your heart" (v. 14). But in Paul's appropriation of the text, it is no longer Moses who speaks but "the righteousness that comes from faith." Furthermore, it is not the commandment but Christ himself who has come down and been raised up from the abyss (Rom 10:6–7). The reference to the "abyss" signifies the Hebrew idea of Sheol, the place of the dead (cf. Ps 107:26), thus reinterpreting Deuteronomy 30:11–14 as a reference to the incarnate, crucified, and resurrected Christ.

10:8–10. In Your Mouth and in Your Heart

Thus Jesus himself is now revealed as the content of "the word of faith that we proclaim"—that is, the gospel, which is so near as to be "in your mouth and in your heart" (10:8). Paul's logic presumes both the indwelling of Christ through the Spirit (8:9–10) and Christ's full participation in the human condition through the incarnation. In the image of the word in hearts and mouths, he also may echo the idea of a new covenant in which God will write the law on human hearts (Jer 31:33). Given the quotation from Isaiah 59:20 in Romans 11:26, it is possible that Paul also has in mind here Isaiah 59:21: "This is my covenant with them, says the Lord: my spirit that is upon you and my words that I have put in your mouth shall not depart out of your mouth or out of the mouths of your children or out of the mouths of your children's children, says the Lord, from now on and forever." But Paul makes no mention of Isaiah here; his focus is on Christ as the living word who has descended to the depths and been raised.

Paul's interpretation of Scripture follows from his conviction that Christ is the goal, fulfillment, and end of the law. From Paul's perspective, the word of faith is "near" because it comes through God's gift, God's unqualified redemption in Christ (Rom 10:12), and as the following verses show, it is as intimate as the heart and as close as speech.

Paul further explicates the content of the "word of faith" in terms of trust in Christ's lordship and resurrection. Romans 10:9–10 has an ABBA pattern, as follows:

9 A Confess with your mouth that Jesus is Lord
B *Believe in your heart* that God raised him from the dead
C You will be saved
10 B′ For in the heart belief is evoked, leading to righteousness
A′ And in the mouth confession is evoked, leading to salvation

This translation attempts to convey a shift from active to passive voice in the Greek text. Paul speaks of human beings actively confessing and believing, but then he shifts to the passive voice, implying that such confession and belief are the result of God's action (Jewett 2007, 631) intimately operating in the center of human emotion, thought, and will.

Thus, as rightly noted in the NRSVue, "believe" could also be translated "trust" (*pistis*); the intimate working of God in evoking trust emphasizes the relational quality of faith. Through following the order of Deuteronomy 30:14, in which the mouth precedes the heart, and then reversing it, Paul creates a picture of faith as trust that flows out of the heart, the holistic center of the person to which God has unique access (Rom 2:15–16, 29). God's love has been "poured into our hearts through the Holy Spirit that has been given to us" (5:5). This experiential gift sources belief as trust in the God who raised Jesus from the dead. Similarly, the verbal confession of Christ's lordship arises from the word already placed in believers' mouths and activated by the Holy Spirit (1 Cor 12:3). The familiar saying "My heart was in my mouth," which expresses the experience of agitation in which one's heart pounds so hard it feels like it is in one's mouth, gets at the close connection between heart and speech here. Paul sees faith, trust in Jesus as Lord, in just such an intense, visceral way. It is no disembodied, cool cognitive assent to a set of propositions, but rather total dependence, trust, and surrender.

This verbal confession of Jesus as Lord is the antidote to, and reversal of, human deception, cursing, and bitterness (Rom 3:13–14). It signifies a loyalty oath, a public proclamation of surrender to Christ in allegiance and service. But it is more than this, because in this context "Lord" means Lord of all; Jesus shares the divine identity as the one to whom "every knee shall bow and every tongue confess" (Phil 2:10–11; cf. 1 Cor 12:3; 8:6; 2 Cor 4:5).

At the center of these verses is the promise "You will be saved." Salvation is often in the future tense, as here, denoting the final completion of the redemption accomplished by Christ (Rom 5:9), but that promised future reaches back into the present in the form of confident hope (5:2–5).

10:11–13. No Distinction

Paul sums up the efficacy of trust in Christ with a threefold emphasis on its inclusivity. "All" occurs four times in 10:11–13. Verse 11 repeats the quotation of Isaiah 28:16 that is in Romans 9:33, but with the addition of "all"; the Greek reads, "All who trust in him will not be put to shame." This reference to shame recalls 1:16 ("I am not ashamed of the gospel") and 5:5 ("Hope does not put us to shame"). In 10:12, "there is no distinction" picks up on 3:22, 29–30, with the same meaning; before God there is no distinction between Jew and Greek (1:16; 2:10) because "the same Lord is Lord of all." As in 3:29–30, Israel's confession of the unity of God grounds the claim that God is Lord of both Jews and gentiles and saves both through Jesus Christ.

Finally, in 10:13 Paul quotes Joel 2:32, which further emphasizes the inclusive promise of salvation in Romans 10:9. In its prophetic context, Joel 2:32 follows oracles of divine judgment and redemption for God's people (2:18–27) and the promise that God will pour out God's Spirit on all flesh (2:28–29). Paul does not quote 2:32b—"for in Mount Zion and in Jerusalem there shall be those who escape, as the LORD has said, and among the survivors shall be those whom the LORD calls"—but it echoes suggestively in the background as a reference to the remnant whom God will save. Joel 2:28–32 was important for early Christians, particularly for interpreting their experience of the Holy Spirit (cf. Acts 2:14–21). By quoting it here, Paul signals that the promised Day of the Lord is at hand in the coming of Christ. Following the acclamation "Jesus is Lord" (Rom 10:9), "the name of the Lord" refers also to Christ (cf. Phil 2:9–11).

Up to this point in the letter, God has been the one doing the calling (Rom 1:1, 6, 7; 9:11, 24–26), so that when Paul speaks of human beings calling on God (10:12, 13, 14) it is evident that people call on God because God has first called them (1 Cor 1:2; cf. Joel 2:32). This is the original "call and response" pattern of worship. Thus this central passage on the topic of human trust in Christ is framed by God's initiative in choosing, showing mercy, and calling human beings without regard to their worth. To take Romans 10:9 out of context and quote it with an emphasis on *if,* as if salvation depended on an individual's supposedly autonomous decision to follow Christ, is to misunderstand Paul's meaning. Paul's emphasis is on *God's* initiative, God's gracious election and call and mercy, to which human trust is always a response.

10:14–21. Israel and the Preaching of the Gospel

Paul now turns directly to the problem of Israel's rejection of the gospel, which has been thrown into relief by the expectation of salvation for *all* who believe. In 10:14–17 the apostle links faith with proclamation; in verses 18–21 he quotes Scripture to demonstrate that Israel *has* heard the gospel proclamation but has not responded with obedient trust, in contrast with gentiles who have come to believe.

10:14–17. Proclamation and Belief

An elegant progression of four questions in 10:14–15 culminates in a quotation from Isaiah 52:7 praising those who preach the good news of the gospel. Each question builds on the previous verse, linked by key words: call, believe, hear, proclaim, sent. This entire sequence follows logically from the promise that "everyone who calls on the name of the Lord shall be saved" (Rom 10:13). In the quotation from Isaiah 52:7 in Romans 10:15, the word translated "beautiful" (*hōraioi*) also can be translated as "timely," which would match Paul's conviction that now is the time of salvation (cf. 3:21, 26; 11:5) (Gaventa 2024, 289). The "good news" in Isaiah is the prophet's announcement to Jerusalem that God will redeem her; indeed, "the Lord has bared his holy arm before the eyes of all the nations, and all the ends of the earth shall see the salvation of our God" (Isa 52:10). This promise echoes in the background of Paul's discussion of Israel's present unbelief.

Taken out of context, these verses have inspired countless sermons on evangelism: people need to hear the gospel proclamation in order to believe and call on the name of Jesus; therefore, the church should commission and send out missionaries to preach the good news. This is a misreading of this passage in its context, however, which concerns the specific problem of Israel's unbelief *despite* having heard the message. Israel already has heard the gospel preaching but has not responded by trusting in Christ. Therefore, although Paul's exclamation in 10:16, "But not all have obeyed the good news!" initially seems like a non sequitur, he is correcting a possible misunderstanding on his listeners' part. Paul is not telling his audience to go preach the gospel; he is describing missionary preaching that has not resulted in a response of obedient faith. "All" echoes 10:4, 11–13; "obeyed" ironically recalls Paul's missionary goal of "the obedience of faith" (1:5) and anticipates "obedience from the gentiles" (15:18). Now, however, the issue is Israel's obedience, not that of the gentiles.

"To obey" (*hypakouein*) is cognate with the verb "to hear" (*akouein*), so we could translate Paul's meaning as "not all have listened obediently to our message," or more colloquially, "not all have taken our message to heart." This is precisely the connection that Paul makes in 10:16b, where he quotes Isaiah 53:1 in reference to unbelief. Paul explains Israel's current rejection of the gospel through Isaiah's prophetic word: "*for* Isaiah says, 'Lord, who has believed our message [*akoē*]?'" "*Our* message" suggests a unity between God, the prophet, and Paul in proclaiming the message of salvation. Just as Isaiah announced salvation to Jerusalem but was met with unbelief, so also the gospel preaching to Israel has been met with unbelief. Isaiah 53:1 reminds Paul's listeners just what is at stake: not general calls to evangelism nor even a mission to the Jews, but the problem of Israel's unbelief, and behind that, the question of God's purposes and power.

In Romans 10:17 Paul states the obvious conclusion drawn directly from Isaiah 53:1: "Faith comes from what is heard [*ex akoēs,* which can also be translated 'from the message'], and what is heard comes through the word of Christ." The "word of Christ" is "the word of faith that we proclaim" which is already "near you" (Rom 10:8). But this simply amplifies the problem: If faith comes from hearing the word of Christ, and Israel has indeed heard the gospel message, logically Israel should have faith—but it does not. Israel has indeed heard the message, but Israel has not *hearkened* to it.

10:18–21. Hearing the Message but Not Taking It to Heart

Paul responds to this situation by appealing to the threefold witness of Israel's Scripture (10:18–21): the Writings (psalms), the Law (Moses), and the Prophets (Isaiah). These scriptural witnesses testify to gentile belief and Israel's unbelief. With the repetition of "but I ask" (vv. 18, 19), Paul emphatically poses questions phrased as double negatives, which stress that Israel has indeed heard but not understood (*egnō*) the gospel message. Just as in 10:2–3, where Paul says Israel has a zeal for God but it is not based on knowledge (*epignōsin*), so here also he frames Israel's lack of understanding in terms of ignorant zeal. This threefold testimony demonstrates that Israel's present rejection of the gospel and the gentiles' acceptance of it have been foretold by Scripture.

First, in 10:18 Paul quotes Psalm 19:4, which proclaims all nature's testimony to God; Paul, however, reads the psalm as proclaiming the global reach of the gospel proclamation. "And their words to the ends of the world" allows him to identify nature's pervasive witness to God as creator, with the "word of faith" that reaches to the heavens and even to Sheol and that resides in human hearts (10:6–8). "Their voice" and "their words" refer to the preachers of the gospel.

Next, in 10:19 Paul quotes from the Song of Moses (Deut 32:21), which describes the judgment that will happen when Israel is unfaithful to the Lord, a judgment that Paul sees as coming to pass in the conversion of the gentiles (Rom 11:11, 14). "Not a nation" recalls Hosea 2:23 (cf. Rom 9:25) in reference to gentile believers. The word translated "I will make you jealous" is *parazēlōsō*, which is related to the word for zeal or jealousy (*zēlos*). *Zēlos* may denote simple jealousy, but in Paul's usage more often it denotes violent zeal, as in his depiction of his own past (Phil 3:4–11; Gal 1:13–14). Furthermore, in the two lines of Romans 10:19, "to make jealous" parallels the verb "provoke," which in Greek is "provoke to anger" (*parorgiō*). This parallelism, together with Paul's own history, suggests that such ardent zeal is closer to the meaning of *parazēlōsō* in 10:19.

Paul quotes Deuteronomy 32:21 in a slightly altered version, so that God, speaking through Moses, directly addresses Israel as "you." Thus God is the one who has provoked Israel to zeal, a zeal that Paul earlier connects with rejection of the gospel (Rom 10:2–3). It is a short step from this claim to the argument that God has hardened Israel (11:7–8, 25) just as God "hardens the heart of whomever he chooses" (9:18). At the same time, the implicit reference to the gentiles, in "those who are not a nation," anticipates Paul's expectation that the salvation of the gentiles will make Israel jealous (*parazēlōsō*), leading ultimately to their salvation (11:14). Rather like using the quotation of Hosea 2:1, 25 in Romans 9:25 to refer to the salvation of gentiles but point also to Israel's ultimate salvation, so in 10:19 Paul gestures in both directions, referring to the salvation of the gentiles but hinting at Israel's final redemption as well.

Finally, in 10:20–21 Paul rounds out this discussion of Israel's unbelief with quotations from Isaiah 65:1–2, which reinforce Paul's earlier point in 9:30–31—the gentile outsiders who have no claim to righteousness or even seeking after God have become the place where God has been "found," whereas the Jews who sought righteousness through the law now are identified as "disobedient and contrary." "Contrary" here is *antilegonta,* which means speaking against, contradictory, argumentative. This description of Israel supports interpreting "jealous" in 10:19 as "zealously opposed." Israel is zealously opposed to the gospel message, resisting it, speaking against it. And yet Paul sees God's intention behind Israel's opposition to the gospel (10:19), just as he sees God's action behind gentile belief (10:20). And God, who is the speaker in 10:21 / Isaiah 65:2, continues to reach out to this contrarian people. As Paul reads Scripture, God is involved in both gentile belief and Israel's unbelief, and at the same time God continues to treat Israel as beloved.

Thus, although on the surface the threefold witness of Scripture from the Psalms, the Law, and the Prophets would seem to write Israel off as God's chosen people, that witness also implies that Israel's present situation makes sense in a larger providential context of divine mercy as well as judgment. After all, Isaiah looks forward to a glorious renewal of Israel in which God will "create new heavens and a new earth" (Isa 65:17–25).

EXCURSUS

Reflections for Preaching and Teaching

Christ the Telos *of the Law*

There is a subtle but crucial difference between saying that Christ is the goal of the law, such that human beings attain Christ through performing the law, and saying that the scriptural witness points to Christ. The second interpretation rightly sees the witness of the Law and the Prophets, not least through the stories of the patriarchs and matriarchs, revealing God's modus operandi as one of undeserved mercy, culminating in the gracious salvation accomplished by Christ. In this way, Scripture reveals God as "the God and Father of our Lord Jesus Christ" (15:6). The first interpretation clearly contradicts what Paul says in 3:21–22; 9:31–32; 10:3, 5, but it is remarkably resilient in popular misunderstandings of Christian faith that presume moral effort will bring us closer to God. Christ is indeed the termination of any such mistaken understandings of God's calling and mercy.

What about Evangelism?

Romans 10:5–17 has long been preached as a call to evangelism, focused on the call to confess Jesus as Lord and believe that God raised him from the dead (10:9) and the questions of 10:14. Indeed, Paul has devoted his life to spreading the news about Jesus Christ, which is what evangelism is. On the other hand, as he comes up against the fact that Israel has heard the gospel but has not come to believe in Jesus as the Messiah, Paul deepens his understanding of faith as reliant on God's mercy and broadens his vision of God's will to save all humanity, Jews as well as gentiles. He even begins to see Israel's present unbelief as part of God's will to save all.

This vision arises from two convictions. First, the saving power of the gospel comes from God's action in Christ, not from the personal faith of individual human beings. Second, Paul thinks in corporate terms; here he is not thinking about the faith or unbelief of individual Jews or gentiles, but about Israel as a whole. Above all, Paul is sure of God's power to save all and God's all-encompassing mercy. This assurance does not stop Paul from preaching the gospel—far from it! But it means that the outcome of his preaching is completely in God's hands. For preachers, recognition of this fact is a great antidote to both despair and arrogance.

The God-centered logic undergirding 9:30–10:21 is consistent with Paul's insistence on Israel's election by divine fiat apart from any moral worth (9:11, 16, 18; see also 4:1–8). For Paul, the calling of the gentiles simply expands and deepens the scope and power of that undeserved gift, so that no individuals or groups might think they have a lock on God's mercy (9:32; 10:11–13). This means that preaching from 10:5–13 must focus relentlessly on the priority of God's calling rather than talking about the confession of faith as something individuals do in order to gain salvation. The confession of faith is not a bargaining chip with God but the reception of a gift already given. *God* has brought salvation near through the incarnation, death, and resurrection of Christ (10:6–7); *God* puts the word of faith into human hearts and mouths (10:9–10). Before the preacher says anything, God already has acted, so that sermons participate in a divine-human call and response initiated and sustained by God.

ROMANS 11:1–36
The Triumph of God's Mercy

In this dense chapter Paul draws together the strands of his argument by proclaiming God's elective grace (11:5–6, 29), which emerges with fresh force at this point in the letter. Just as Israel's very existence is due to God's mercy and calling without regard to human worth (9:6–18), so also the conjunction of God's gifts (*charismata*) and call (*klēsis*) secures Israel's future (11:29). From start to finish, the call and redemption of Israel display God's incongruous grace and point to God's gracious self-revelation in Christ (Barclay 2015, 520–61). Thus, although in chapters 9–11 "grace" (*charis*) appears only in these verses, it carries considerable weight from its centrality in the letter to this point (3:24; 4:16; 5:2, 15, 17, 20, 21; 6:1, 14, 15). By now, Paul's audience knows that the central thrust of the good news is God's world-shattering, countercultural self-giving to and for the unworthy, indeed the ungodly, including David, Abraham and Sarah, and their descendants (chap. 4).

In 11:1–36 Paul further develops the themes that surfaced in 9:6–29, in terms that highlight Israel's particular history with God: election (9:11; 11:5, 28), call (9:7, 12, 25–26; 11:29), remnant (9:27, 29; 11:5), mercy (9:15–18; 11:30–32), and the riches of God's glory (9:23; 10:12; 11:12). All these characteristics of Israel's relationship to God demonstrate God's freedom to be merciful to whomever God chooses. Thus, the conjunction of election and grace in 11:5–6 is key to understanding Paul's argument throughout chapters 9–11, and arguably brackets his gospel proclamation in 1:16–8:39 as well.

Indeed, the theme of God's gracious gift ties Israel's destiny to God's undeserved beneficence as the hallmark of God's involvement with all humanity (11:6). It is in this context that Paul speaks of the "hardening of Israel" (11:7–10, 25) as part of God's plan to save both gentiles *and* Jews. Paul thereby expands the "reconciliation" accomplished for believers (5:10–11) to "the reconciliation of the world" (11:15). Therefore, on the way to his confident affirmation that "all Israel will be saved" (11:26), Paul invokes the metaphor of the olive tree to rebuke gentile arrogance toward unbelieving Israel (11:16–24).

Finally, in 11:25–32 Paul sums up the relationship between Jews and gentiles through a pattern of interactive exchange. Israel and the gentiles take turns being "disobedient," but only so that God may have mercy on all. All of this is God's doing. Paul's concluding doxology in 11:33–36 is therefore a paean of praise to the God from whom and through whom and to whom are all things—that is, the creator, benefactor, and gracious redeemer of all humanity. The final doxology is a fitting climax to the entire letter up to this point, and the theological foundation of Paul's gospel.

11:1–10. God Has Not Rejected His People

11:1–4. The Remnant and Israel

Once again raising the obvious question implied by his quotation from Isaiah—"Has God rejected his people?"—Paul again answers with a strident "No way!" Naming himself as "an Israelite, a descendant of Abraham" (Gk., from the seed of Abraham), Paul uses himself as an example of God's continued faithfulness to Israel. Verse 2 repeats the point by quoting a promise that reverberates in Scripture: "God has not rejected his people" (1 Sam 12:22; Ps 94:14; Jer 31:37). In 1 Samuel, the prophet Samuel assures the Israelites that despite their wickedness in demanding a king, "for his great name's sake" God will not cast them off. Psalm 94 affirms God's discipline as evidence of God's lasting commitment to Israel. Jeremiah 31:37 states the same assurance negatively, in the context of the promise of a new covenant with Israel (31:31–37):

> Thus says the Lord:
> If the heavens above can be measured
> and the foundations of the earth below can be explored,
> then I will reject all the offspring of Israel
> because of all they have done,
> says the Lord.

This rock-solid assurance of God's lasting commitment to Israel lies behind the claim, "God has not rejected his people." Paul adds, "whom he foreknew." That God "foreknew" Israel evokes God's intimate knowledge of those whom God calls (Ps 139:1–16; Jer 1:5) and recalls God's foreknowledge and predestination of those who trust in Christ (Rom 8:29).

In 11:2b–4 Paul adds another scriptural witness to God's faithfulness to Israel. When the prophet Elijah argues with God after fleeing from Ahab (1 Kgs 19:9–18), God rebukes him for thinking he is the only faithful Israelite left; rather, there remain seven thousand (with the number seven signifying completion) faithful to the Lord. So also, says Paul, "at the present time," the time inaugurated by Christ (3:26), God has kept a remnant, here referring to a subgroup within Israel—those Jews (like Paul himself) who have come to trust in Jesus as the Messiah.

"Remnant" can signify a reason for despair or for hope. It might name a tiny group that survives when everyone else is destroyed; for example, a remnant of European Jews survived the Holocaust. Or a remnant might function as a guarantee for the eventual restoration of the whole; in light of 11:16, 25–26, this hopeful sense for "remnant" appears to be Paul's meaning here, but it is important to be clear about precisely how this remnant functions. It is not that a remnant of Israel, those who presently believe in Christ, becomes identified with all of Israel, or even with the church, while the rest of Israel is excluded from covenant relationship with God. Rather, just as Paul sees himself as evidence of God's continued faithfulness to *all* Israel, so the small number of Jews who presently trust in Jesus as Messiah is a sign of the ultimate salvation of the whole. Thus, even when distinguishing between the remnant and the rest, Paul names the unbelieving majority as "Israel" (11:7; cf. 11:25–26).

11:5–6. Chosen by Grace

Lest his listeners assume that the remnant owes its status to some virtue (like those who did not bow the knee to Baal), in 11:5–6 Paul highlights "chosen by grace." The Greek has the sense "brought into being by the election of grace." Notably, whereas in 9:32 Paul contrasted works with faith, here the contrast is between works and grace, undercutting any temptation for gentile believers to view their faith as a badge of superiority (11:18).

Contrary to the NRSVue translation, in 11:6 the Greek word translated "no longer" (*ouketi*) has a logical rather than temporal sense: "If it [election] is by grace, it is not on the basis of works; otherwise grace would not be grace." Election has always been by grace, not by works, because grace is a gift that is not based on the recipient's achievements. Paul is not making a new claim here; rather, he is reminding his listeners of Israel's history as a narrative of mercy (9:6–18).

11:7–10 The Hardening of Israel

In 11:7 Paul briefly repeats the image of Israel running a race but not reaching the finish line (9:30–31) and then offers a theological explanation for the unbelief of the majority ("the rest"); they were "hardened" (cf. 11:25), just as Pharaoh was "hardened" by God (9:18). The following collection of texts in 11:8–10, drawing on Deuteronomy 29:4, Isaiah 29:10, Psalm 69:22–23, and Isaiah 6:9–11, explains why most Jews have not followed Jesus as Messiah—once again, Paul relentlessly puts the focus on God's action. Just as gentile believers cannot take credit for their own trust in Christ, neither can they judge Israel for its unbelief; Israel has not failed, it has been "hardened" by God. Thus, although the harshness of Paul's language could suggest that Israel has indeed stumbled irreparably, the Scriptures implying God's agency subvert such a conclusion. Even "a sluggish spirit" is given by God (Rom 11:8). This ascription of Israel's blindness and incomprehension to God's activity also echoes Isaiah 6:9–10, which appears throughout the New Testament writings with reference to Israel's unbelief (Matt 13:14–15; Mark 4:12; Luke 8:10; John 12:40; Acts 28:26–27).

For the third time in the letter (1:3; 4:6), Paul refers to David by name (11:9–10). Given that Romans is the only one of Paul's undisputed letters in which David appears, we do well to pay attention to his role here: first as the ancestor of Jesus (1:3), then as the seducer who is grateful for God's undeserved forgiveness (4:6), now as the one who pronounces divine judgment on Israel itself. The quotation is from Psalm 69:22–23. The "stumbling block" recalls the stone that tripped up Israel on the racetrack (9:33); the reference to darkened eyes repeats the motif of sensory deprivation in 11:8, attributed to divine action in exercising judgment by making his people insensible to God. The conclusion seems to be that the majority of Israel has been judged harshly and cast off by God, blinded so that it cannot see the salvation at hand in Jesus.

11:11–24. Gentiles and Israel in God's Salvation

At this point Paul has argued for the existence of a remnant *within* Israel, but not the redemption of *all* Israel. Once again the question arises, introduced by Paul's emphatic "I ask": "Have they stumbled so as to fall?" (11:11; cf. 11:1). Once again Paul answers, "By no means!" Once again Paul surprises his listeners, now with the claim that gentile believers owe their present salvation to Israel's current unbelief. From a merely human perspective, Paul could say that Jewish rejection of the gospel preaching led him to preach to the gentiles (Acts 13:46–49). As the preceding citations from Scripture demonstrate, however, Paul frames Israel's unbelief in terms of God's action. Therefore, gentile Christians have no basis for lording it over unbelieving Jews as if they are somehow superior because they have come to trust in Christ.

Paul's argument proceeds in two stages: in 11:11–15 he depicts a reciprocal interaction between Jewish and gentile salvation; in 11:16–24 the analogy of the root and the olive tree demonstrates that gentiles are grafted into the unqualified grace that called Israel into being (9:16; 11:6), so that their own election, like that of Israel, "depends not on human will or exertion but on God who shows mercy" (9:16). Taken as a whole, this section shows that gentile believers are doubly indebted to Israel—paradoxically because of Israel's current unbelief, and ultimately because of God's irrevocable promises to Israel.

11:11–15. Trading Places: The Stumbling of Israel and the Salvation of the Gentiles

The structure of these verses is as follows:

11:11 Thematic statement: Israel's trespass means gentile salvation
A 11:12 If Jewish trespass means riches for the gentiles
  How much more will their full inclusion mean!
  B 11:13 Paul's mission to gentiles
  B′ 11:14 Paul's (indirect) mission to Jews
A′ 11:15 If Jewish rejection is the reconciliation of the world
  What will their acceptance mean but life from the dead?

Paul first repeats and intensifies the question: has Israel stumbled so as to fall? Again he answers, "No way!" Now, however, he begins to point a way forward, with the thematic statement: "Through their stumbling [*paraptōma,* trespass] salvation has come to the gentiles, so as to make Israel jealous [*parazēlōsai*]." The image of Israel stumbling recalls the image of Christ as the stumbling stone (9:32–33). By calling Israel's stumbling a trespass, Paul connects it with 4:25 (Christ "was handed over for our trespasses") and the trespass of Adam in 5:15–21. In other words, although the form of Israel's particular trespass is unique, the fact that Israel has trespassed is something shared with all people; gentiles also have trespassed. Paul thus both subverts gentile arrogance and includes Israel with all humanity in both trespass and redemption. This inclusion picks up on the testimony of Abraham and David to their own wrongdoing and God's mercy and justification of the ungodly.

In 11:12, "riches" occurs twice, linking "riches for the world" with "riches for gentiles." "Riches" characterizes God's limitless abundance in relationship to the world, as in "the riches of God's glory" (9:23; Phil 4:19) and "the riches and wisdom and knowledge of God" (Rom 11:33). The phrase translated in the NRSVue as "full inclusion" is simply "fullness, completeness" (*plērōma*), here denoting the completion of Israel's salvation. In 11:25–26 Paul will speak of the "full number" (*plērōma*) of the gentiles together with the salvation of all Israel, suggesting that *plērōma* means "complete" in an all-inclusive sense.

Two aspects of Paul's argument here deserve further emphasis. First, he hints at a pattern of trading places between Jews and gentiles: Jewish trespass and "loss" mean riches for the gentiles; Jewish "acceptance" will be "life from the dead" (11:15). That is, Israel's temporary rejection benefits the gentiles; later Paul will say that when "the fullness of the gentiles comes in" all Israel will be saved. The redemption of Jew and gentile hangs together. Second, this pattern of mutual salvation is sourced by God's superabundant riches, which create a noncompetitive economy of exchange and mutual benefaction.

In 11:13 Paul interjects a direct address to the gentile believers in Rome right into the middle of his vision for Israel's salvation. In Greek, the "you" is placed first, for emphasis: "You gentiles, I'm talking to you!" Paul then explains how he sees his mission to the gentiles in relationship to the salvation of "some" Jews, presumably among the "remnant" of 11:5. He wants his Roman audience to know that even in his own role as apostle to the gentiles, he also has the salvation of his Jewish relatives in view. He hopes that the success of his ministry to gentiles will make his physical relatives (*sarx*) jealous (11:14) and save "some of them." Paul's caution about the limited effects of his own mission may well reflect his experience; he can say with confidence that Jewish rejection of his message led to his apostleship to gentiles, but he cannot say with confidence that a direct mission to the Jews has been successful—quite the contrary.

The verb *parazēlōsō* (to make jealous or provoke to zeal) picks up on 11:11 and recalls 10:19, where Paul sees Scripture foretelling

Israel's rejection of the gospel preaching; here Paul interprets his own ministry to the gentiles as a way to provoke and thus save some of his own people (11:14). It is difficult to know how to interpret these verses. Paul clearly thinks that the salvation of gentiles will have a saving effect on Jews, but in what way? If Paul wants his ministry to make his kinsfolk "jealous," why would Jews be envious of gentile belief in Jesus? If he thinks his ministry will provoke them to religious zeal, as seems most likely in 10:19, why would such zeal lead them to trust in Christ rather than opposing such trust? Does Paul have his own history of zeal and subsequent conversion in mind? If so, it is still difficult to trace a link between conversion and intense opposition to the gospel. Perhaps it is best to sit with this puzzle rather than try to solve it. The conundrum of these verses sets up the mystery of Israel's future salvation; such salvation, like Israel's originating call (and Paul's own conversion), will come by an unpredictable, miraculous divine initiative (11:26–32). Even and perhaps especially, Israel is precisely in the place where God's divine mercy must and will be all and all.

In the structure of 11:12–15, verse 15 parallels and amplifies verse 12, with a "how much more" argument that links Israel's present unbelief with a promise of surpassing, indeed cosmic, salvation. Verse 12 ends with a question that is answered by verse 15, where "if their rejection is the reconciliation of the world" reframes "if their trespass means riches for the world" (v. 12), and "what will their acceptance be but life from the dead?" reframes "how much more will their full inclusion mean!" (v. 12). Paul sees an inseparable connection between the salvation of all Israel and the redemption of the cosmos.

It is not clear who is doing the rejecting and the accepting in 11:15. Paul uses the same verb in 11:1 to say that God has *not* rejected Israel, suggesting that here in verse 15 "rejection" refers to Israel's rejection of the gospel, not to God's rejection of Israel, and "acceptance" (*proslēmpsis*) refers to Israel's future embrace of the gospel. At the same time, this rejection and acceptance ultimately depend on God's mercy. In 14:1, 3; 15:7, Paul uses *proslēmpsis* to denote mutual welcome between Jewish and gentile believers based on God's acceptance of them; he clearly anticipates a community of Jews and gentiles together glorifying God as "the God and Father of our Lord Jesus Christ" (15:6).

The "how much more" argument of these verses parallels 5:15–21 and indeed applies the basic claim of unmerited, superabounding gift to the question of God's dealings with Israel. Just as the free gift and "abounding" grace of God follow "many trespasses" (5:15–16), so here Israel's trespass leads to God's riches. Just as death reigned through Adam on account of Adam's trespass, but "the abundance of grace and the gift of righteousness" will "reign in life" through Jesus Christ (5:17), so Israel's "acceptance" will mean life from the dead. Paul simply cannot conceive of such resurrection life excluding God's chosen people Israel. Nor can he conceive of that gift as given apart from Christ. Furthermore, just as Christ's death and resurrection accomplished "reconciliation" for believers (5:10–11), so now Paul celebrates the "reconciliation of the world" (11:15). Paradoxically, the global scope of reconciliation has come about at least in part through Israel's unbelief and yet remains incomplete until God has mercy on all (11:32).

The cosmic scope of redemption for "the world" and the eschatological promise of life from the dead (11:12, 15) also echo themes in 8:19–21, which limns creation's longing for liberation from decay. As noted in the commentary on 8:19–21, creation's yearning for "the apocalypse of the children of God" includes the salvation of Israel, the first and enduring "adopted sons of God" (9:4; 11:29). In other words, Paul links Israel's full and final inclusion in salvation with the liberating redemption from mortality that all creation awaits.

11:16–24. The Metaphor of the Root and the Olive Tree

Seamlessly continuing his discussion of Jews and gentiles in God's redeeming work, in 11:16 Paul introduces the analogy of the olive tree with two metaphors that are familiar from Israel's Scripture. The first is the image of "first fruits" offered to God as a surety for the whole. "First fruits" could refer to the first gleanings of the harvest or to a portion of a batch of bread, as here. The offering of a portion of the dough sanctifies the whole loaf (Num 15:20–21). The second image draws on common references to Israel as a vine or tree planted by God (Pss 80:8–13; 92:12–15; Isa 60:21; 61:3; Jer 2:21; 11:16–17; 17:8). The "if . . . then" logic of the strictly parallel clauses gets across Paul's point: the whole is sanctified by the part.

The metaphor of the root and the branches dominates Paul's discussion in Romans 11:17–24. Continuing his speech to "you gentiles" (11:13), in verse 17 Paul suddenly shifts into a direct address to a singular "you." This vivid rhetorical device echoes his earlier rebuke of mutual judgment by both gentiles and Jews (2:1–27) and thus sharpens his rebuke of gentile arrogance in the metaphor of the olive tree. The olive tree signifies God's elect people, broken-off branches signify unbelieving Israel, and the wild olive shoot signifies "you" gentile believer who is now graciously included with God's elect (9:24–26, 30). But what is the rich root that nourishes the tree?

Clues to the identity of the root come from Paul's retelling of Israel's family history in 9:6–18. There Paul focuses on the *manner* of God's calling Israel into being, not based on blood descent, but on divine call, election, and mercy: "It is not the children of the flesh who are the children of God, but the children of the promise are counted as descendants" (v. 8). Abraham's family tree demonstrates that "God's purpose of election" continues "not by works but by his call" (v. 11). This gracious election called Israel into being and has sustained it through history. Thus this divine grace is the "rich root" that always has been the source of Israel's identity as God's chosen people, into which gentiles now have been grafted and in which they now "share" as co-participants (*synkoinōs*); like Israel, their attachment to that same root of undeserved mercy is due to God's grace alone.

Having established the source of Israel's existence and gentile salvation in God's undeserved grace and mercy, in 11:18–20 Paul warns his gentile listeners, "do not boast over the branches" that were broken off (vv. 17–18). That is, do not boast in your faith and claim superiority over those Jews who do not share your trust in Christ. Paul briefly articulates the self-referential arrogance of gentile believers who boast that the Jews were cut off so that gentiles could be included (v. 19), but in 11:20–21 he immediately corrects such arrogance by invoking faith. That is, if Jews are temporarily "broken off" due to their unbelief, gentile believers should remember that they "stand on account of belief." The word "stand" (*hestēkas*) recalls "this grace in which we stand" (*hestēkamen*) in 5:2, thereby reminding the gentile believers that their "belief" is not their own achievement but the operation of God's grace in them. Ultimately, they stand by God's trustworthiness, not through any meritorious trust or belief of their own. (For similar warnings, see also 1 Cor 10:12; 15:1–2; 16:13. For assurance that God has power to make believers "stand," see Rom 14:4.) "Do not become arrogant" in Greek is "do not think in an uppity way" (cf. 12:2); "be afraid" introduces the warning of 11:21–22.

The Jews are the "natural branches" (11:21) because they are the first shoots from the cultivated olive tree that grew out of God's gracious calling of Abraham. In ancient Mediterranean agricultural practices, cultivated branches would be grafted onto a wild olive tree, but Paul reverses the image to speak of gentiles in relationship to Israel. His warning is straightforward; if God did not spare the natural branches, God certainly is free not to spare you gentiles. Paul uses the same verb in 8:32: God did "not spare his own Son but gave him up for all of us."

In 11:22 Paul directs his listeners' attention to God and away from their own faith: "Note then the kindness and the severity of God." The question for gentile believers is whether they will "continue in his kindness." There is a central ambiguity in Paul's meaning here; on what basis will the gentiles continue or remain in God's kindness? The implication is that if they focus on, and trust in, the superiority of their own belief, they will stop submitting to God's judgment and risk losing sight of God's kindness. The clause "otherwise you also will be cut off" implies a real threat of exclusion. But the grammatical formulation of the conditional clause implies a likely positive outcome, so that the meaning is "provided you continue (and surely you will!) in his kindness" (cf. Col 1:21–23). Given Paul's earlier references to God's hardening of hearts and God's mercy, the stress lies on God's freedom to be merciful. The warning to the gentiles thus enjoins them to continue to trust in that undeserved mercy, not in their own supposedly superior faith.

Similarly, Paul frames Israel's present exclusion with a confident assurance that they will be regrafted into the root of God's elective grace. As in Romans 11:22, the conditional clause in 11:23 implies the probable fulfillment of the condition: "if they do not continue in unbelief (and they will not)." As repeatedly in the letter to this point, the basis of Paul's confidence is God's will and power to save, demonstrated throughout Israel's history (4:21).

11:25–32. That God May Have Mercy on All

In a sweeping climax that announces the future salvation of "all Israel" and of "the full number of the gentiles," Paul unites the themes of chapters 9–11: election (9:11; 11:5, 7, 28), calling (9:7, 12, 24–26;

11:29), mercy (9:15–16, 18, 23; 11:30–32), and grace (11:5–6, 29). Paul makes three core theological claims: first, that Israel's "hardening" and salvation are within God's redemptive will for all humanity; second, that God's gifts and calling are irrevocable; third, that in God's providence, Israel and the gentiles temporarily trade places, alternating between disobedience and mercy, so that *all,* both gentiles and Jews, will be saved through Christ and solely by God's mercy.

The passage divides into two subsections: the mystery of Israel's salvation (11:25–27) and the relationship between Israel and the gentiles in God's ultimate redemption of all humanity (vv. 28–32).

11:25–27. The Mystery of Israel's Salvation

Paul shifts back to second-person plural in 11:25, with a typical formulaic introduction (literally, "I do not want you to be ignorant, brothers and sisters"). The content of what follows is a "mystery" (cf. 16:25). In 1 Corinthians 15:51 and Colossians 1:27; 2:2; 4:3 the content of "the mystery" is simply Christ; in Ephesians 1:9–10, the "mystery" refers to God's intention in Christ "to gather up all things in him, things in heaven and things on earth." In this way, Ephesians 1:9–10 could be a summary of Rom 11:25, where "mystery" signals God's eschatological way of salvation for Israel and the gentiles, a way that includes, at present, the rejection of the gospel by a part of Israel (cf. 9:27; 11:7, 14, 17). In 11:25 Paul ascribes this rejection to God's action in "hardening" a part of Israel, just as God hardened Pharaoh's heart (9:18). By emphasizing God's agency at work through Israel's unbelief, Paul implies that God's overarching grace and mercy lie behind the predicament of human impiety and unbelief.

But now Paul adds a time limit to this situation: "until the full number [*plērōma*] of the gentiles has come in." In 11:12, "fullness" refers to the final inclusion of all Israel; when 11:12 and 11:25 are read together, *plērōma* denotes the final ingathering of all God's people into God's kingdom. The paradoxical way of this final salvation is also the "mystery" to which Paul refers, a future divine action that is not disclosed in the present. Paradoxically, Paul does not want his listeners to be ignorant of a mystery that is, by definition, at least partially unknowable. To "not be ignorant" of this mystery is also to be aware of the limitations of one's own understanding. The certain promise is that "all Israel will be saved"; the mystery is how God will bring that salvation to pass.

Paul's eschatological vision of gentiles joining in worship of Israel's God was widely shared in prophetic expectation (Isa 2:2–3; 56:6–7; 60:3–14; Mic 4:1–2; Zech 14:16–17). As Isaiah 60:3 puts it, "Nations [LXX gentiles] shall come to your light and kings to the brightness of your dawn." From the perspective of Paul's fellow Jews, the shocking thing in his vision of the ingathering of the gentiles is not their inclusion but that they enter into salvation before the majority of Israel and without becoming Jews through circumcision. Furthermore, Paul does not speak of gentiles worshiping "the God of Israel," but of Jews and gentiles joining in worship of "the God and Father of our Lord Jesus Christ" (Rom 15:6).

Paul means what he says in 11:26: *all* Israel, including both the "part of Israel" that is presently hardened and the "remnant" that believes in Christ, will be saved. Given Paul's consistent use of "Israel" to signify the Jewish people, "all Israel" is not a term for the church composed of Jews and gentiles. Nor does "all" mean most, with some exceptions. "All" means *all* (11:32), and its breathtaking scope depends on God's resurrection power (4:16–17). For "saved," see 5:9–10; 10:9–13; 11:14. Because in 10:9–13 Paul links salvation with "calling on the name of the Lord," the implication is that all Israel will call on the name of Jesus, but the way in which this will happen is beyond Paul's ken. Notably, here Paul does not specifically say, "All Israel will confess faith in Christ," but neither does he say there is a separate way of salvation for Israel apart from Jesus Christ. If there were such a way, Paul would not need to write Romans 9–11!

The scriptural citation in 11:26b–27 merges two passages from Isaiah that promise divine redemption for Israel (Isa 27:9; 59:20–21). Paul has chosen texts that connect Israel's situation and salvation in chapters 9–11 with the gospel in chapters 1–8. The catchwords "ungodliness" and "sins" link Israel with Abraham and David (4:1–8), Adamic humanity (5:6–8), and the "ungodly" on whom God's wrath falls (1:18), but now Israel's sins are contextualized by God's "hardening" of Israel.

Paul makes one significant change in his quotation from Isaiah 59. Isaiah 59:20 says the Deliverer will come *to* Zion, but Paul's citation says the Deliverer will come *from* Zion. This change undergirds two key Pauline claims: first, he links the Deliverer (*ho rhyomenos*) with Christ who comes from David (Rom 1:3) and from the Jews (9:5) "according to the flesh"; second, Christ does not come only to Zion, but to all people. In Isaiah 59:20 the Deliverer is God, but here Paul names Christ as the Deliverer. Similarly, in 1 Thessalonians 1:10, Paul refers to Jesus as the one "who rescues [*rhyomenon*] us from the coming wrath." In Romans 7:24b–25a, the speaker asks, "Who will rescue [*rhysetai*] me from this body of death?" and answers, "Thanks be to God through Jesus Christ our Lord!" For Paul, Christ's rescue mission cannot be separated from God's action through Christ. Rather, the Christ who sets believers free from sin and death (chaps. 1–8) is the one who will deliver Israel from its present insensible condition of impiety and sins. The way of salvation is the same, although the timing is different: just as Christ entered into the condition of the ungodly and therein accomplished the justification of the ungodly, and just as Christ came "from David" according to the flesh, so also Paul is certain that Christ the Deliverer will come on the scene to banish ungodliness and take away Israel's sins.

The promise in 11:26 that the Deliverer will "banish ungodliness" puts Israel in the same situation as Adamic humanity's "ungodliness" (1:18) and suggests that unbelieving Israel will follow in the footsteps of Abraham, who trusted in the God who justifies "the ungodly" (4:5). In line with the action of God who called, sustained, and justified Israel's patriarch, Israel's anticipated salvation through Christ will be its return to the sustaining "root" of elective grace. Nonetheless, Paul does not speak of Israel's trust in God or faith in Christ, nor of anything that Israel will do; his focus is entirely on God's redeeming purpose and future action.

The NRSVue translation of verse 27a reads, "This is my covenant." In the Greek, however, there is no verb, leaving unclear whether the verse refers to a present, existing covenant or a future one. The preceding verse 26 refers explicitly to a future event: "And in this way all Israel will be saved, as it is written, 'Out of Zion will come the Deliverer; he will banish ungodliness from Jacob.'" In this context, it makes the most sense to translate verse 27 with a future sense as well: "This will be my covenant with them, when I take away their sins." Paul is not referring to Israel's past "covenants" (9:4) but to a new covenant yet to take place (cf. Jer 31:31–34). Paul rarely uses the term "covenant" in Romans (only in 9:4 and 11:27); its occurrence here highlights God's enduring commitment to Israel in the past and into the future.

11:28–32. Disobedience and Mercy in God's Cosmic Salvation

In Greek, the two clauses of 11:28 are precisely parallel in their structure: "With regard to the gospel, enemies for your sake; with regard to election, beloved for the sake of the fathers." Paul is again speaking to gentile Christians; the unbelieving Jews are "enemies for your sake." But whose "enemies" and whose "beloved"? The context suggests Paul is speaking of Israel's status before God, occupying two seemingly opposite positions simultaneously, as "enemies" and as "beloved." This paradoxical conjunction recalls 5:8–10, where God's love operated precisely through Christ's reconciling death "while we were enemies." In both 5:10 and 11:28, Paul speaks of enemies in terms of human enmity toward God, or in Israel's case toward the gospel, not as divine enmity toward human beings. Israel's enmity toward the gospel meant that the gospel went to the gentiles; in this way, it was "for your sake." But God's election of Israel stands, because Israel is beloved "for the sake of the fathers." This does not mean that the patriarchs have merit accruing to Israel's benefit, but that from the beginning God graciously elected and called Israel into being, as demonstrated by the stories of the patriarchs and matriarchs (9:6–13).

The irrevocability of God's "gifts" and "calling" in 11:29 provides the basis for Israel's assured status as God's "beloved" in 11:28. "Gifts" is *charismata* in Greek, again clarifying the close link between God's calling of Israel and election as a matter of grace (11:5); in Israel's case, those gifts are the attributes of Israel listed in 9:4–5. "Calling" harks back to God's creative election that called Israel into being (9:7, 11, 24–26). "Irrevocable" is literally "without regret." This is personal, not legal, language. It is not that Israel's election is a contract that cannot be revoked, but that God's love for Israel overrides any possibility of rejection or any divine regret for having called a people that proves so contrary. To get at Paul's meaning, it is appropriate to remember Hosea, where God says, "When Israel was a child, I loved him, and out of Egypt I called my son. The more I called them, the more they went from me. . . . How can I give you up, Ephraim? How can I hand you over, O Israel? . . . My heart recoils within me; my compassion grows warm and tender" (Hos 11:1, 8). This divine love makes God's gifts and calling "without regret."

Paul continues his correction of gentile arrogance in Romans 11:30–31, which forms a neatly constructed argument summarizing the exchange of places between gentiles and Israel, such that all experience disobedience and all receive mercy. Verse 30 chiefly concerns the gentiles, verse 31 concerns Israel, but both share the same experience of disobedience and mercy. Furthermore, that experience is interdependent: gentile reception of mercy is due to Israel's disobedience, but Israel's experience of disobedience and mercy is connected to the salvation of gentiles.

In a discombobulating conclusion, Paul summarizes the theological rationale that runs through his entire discussion of Israel and gentiles, and indeed his gospel preaching in chapters 1–8 as well: "God has imprisoned all in disobedience so that he may be merciful to all" (11:32). The motif of imprisonment in disobedience recalls 1:24, 26, 28 (see also Gal 4:22) and the theme of human bondage in the regime of sin and death (Rom 3:9). "All" runs through the letter like a red thread, with regard both to human culpability and bondage to sin, and to salvation through Christ (1:5, 7, 8, 16, 18; 2:9, 12; 3:9, 12, 19–20, 22–23; 4:11, 16; 5:12, 18; 6:3; 10:11–13; 11:26). Notably, whereas Paul earlier ascribed human bondage to sin's enslaving dominion, now he narrates it in terms of God's overarching purpose of salvation. The cosmic scope of Paul's theological vision is breathtaking.

11:33–36. Concluding Hymn and Doxology

This magnificent paean of praise to God crowns the entire first section of Romans. Its hymnic quality is conveyed by its opening acclamation (11:33), the triadic structure of verses 33–35, and the closing doxology (v. 36).

11:33–35. God's Inscrutable Wisdom and Grace

In 11:33 Paul characterizes the threefold riches, wisdom, and knowledge of God in terms of "depth," which suggests the mysteries of God that elude human understanding (1 Cor 2:10). "Riches" gathers up the motifs of the riches of God's kindness and patience (Rom 2:4), the riches of God's glory (9:23), and the riches of salvation bestowed on all (10:12; 11:12). God's riches are inseparable from the superabundance of God's grace and free gift of righteousness in Christ (5:15–17, 20).

"Wisdom" occurs only here in Romans, and its presence may support the idea that Paul is quoting from a very early Christian hymn. In 1 Corinthians 1:18–2:16, however, Paul does speak extensively about God's wisdom in contrast with human pretension; it is not a divine attribute that is foreign to Paul's thinking, but one with which he would be familiar from Jewish Wisdom traditions that assigned Wisdom a role in creation (Wis 7:22a; Sir 1:4; 24:1–6). With reference to "the knowledge of God," Paul's listeners are back in familiar territory. Paul's meaning here clearly is not human knowledge about God, but God's privileged knowledge of human hearts (Rom 2:16, 29; 8:27, 29–30) and indeed of the destiny of both Jew and gentile.

The depth of divine riches, wisdom, and knowledge is implicit in the "mystery" of God's workings in the world. No wonder God's judgments are unsearchable (2:16) and God's ways inscrutable! This entire verse replays the contrast between human and divine judgment displayed in 2:1–3:9, but now the tenor is one of rejoicing in the assurance of God's victorious mercy.

The triadic pattern of 11:33 continues in 11:34–35, with three parallel questions that correlate with the three divine attributes in verse 33, but in reverse order: "Who has known the mind of the Lord?" correlates with the depth of God's knowledge; "Who has been his counselor?" emphasizes the depth of God's wisdom; "Who has given a gift to him, to receive a gift in return?" expresses the depth of God's riches. The first two questions come from Isaiah 40:13, in an oracle proclaiming God's incomparable majesty and power. The third question echoes Job's dialogue with God, but without an explicit parallel. Job 35:7 may be the closest parallel, although some also note Job 41:3.

The reverse order of the questions in relationship to God's attributes highlights the theme of divine gift, beginning with God's riches and ending with the statement that no one can give a gift to God, because God cannot be indebted to human beings. God is not on a transactional footing with human beings; God is the source of all things. This theological foundation of abundant divine grace and mercy undergirds Paul's gospel throughout this letter, including the community exhortations that follow in chapters 12–15.

11:36. Doxology to God the Giver and Source of All That Is

Therefore, Paul concludes in 11:36 with praise to God the giver of all, from whom and through whom and to whom are all things. The phrasing of this doxology is familiar in Paul's letters: for example, in 1 Corinthians 8:6 Paul speaks of "one God, the Father, from whom are all things and for whom we exist, and one Lord, Jesus Christ, through whom are all things and through whom we exist." This concluding doxology glorifying God reverses humanity's primal failure to give glory to God (Rom 1:21) and anticipates Paul's hope that Jew and gentile together will "glorify the God and Father of our Lord Jesus Christ" (15:6).

EXCURSUS

Reflections for Preaching and Teaching

Solidarity and Exchange as God's Way of Reconciliation

In chapters 1–8 Paul repeatedly displays God's way of salvation through Christ, who shared the predicament of all humanity under the power of sin and death, and in that divine-human union traded places with all humanity to reconcile us to God and liberate us for life in Christ. God in Christ joined with Adam's heirs in solidarity and exchange, a relational pattern that enacts grace in human lives. In chapters 9–11 that same pattern of solidarity and exchange operates in Paul's vision for the salvation of both Jew and gentile. It is as if God's way in the world, God's gracious modus operandi, has saturated Paul's social imagination, so that he sees through a lens shaped by Christ's sacrificial, loving involvement with God's beloved creatures.

This relational dynamic of grace shows up in Paul's attitude toward his unbelieving Jewish relatives, as he yearns to take their place in the situation of separation from Christ. His impulse is toward sharing their condition, not toward rejecting them. We may know something of this experience through the love we feel toward estranged family members or friends. The same interactive pattern governs Paul's vision of the connection between the salvation of the gentiles and that of the Jews. Although on the human level they may be estranged, both gentiles and Jews pass through an outsider position of disobedience and receive mercy as God's beloved. Even more, their redemption requires the redemption of each other. This is a profound and transformative insight: it means that there can be no redemption of one people without the redemption of all. There is no salvation for the Jews without the salvation of the gentiles, and there is no salvation of the gentiles without the salvation of the Jews. Paul sees the way to this salvation through parallel experiences of exclusion and, ultimately, inclusion and mutual welcome. All of this happens in and through God's salvation through Christ, but its final outworking remains shrouded in mystery.

Pondering this mystery suggests radical perspectives on intractable situations in the world today, where reconciliation and peace seem humanly impossible: the ongoing conflicts in the Middle East and around the world; the deep political and social divides in American culture, including in the church; the legacies of hatred and fear from injustice and oppression. Paul's Christ-centered perspective leads to seeing our enemies, like ourselves, as both enslaved by systemic sin and as God's beloved. That means that peace cannot be achieved through the eradication of one side or another, but requires walking in one another's shoes in solidarity and acting in hope of a reconciliation that ultimately only God will bring to pass.

Sin and God's Sovereignty

In Romans 1–8 Paul paints a picture of sin as a power that subjugates human beings, sabotaging their efforts to do the good, deceiving them, and ultimately killing them (3:9; 5:12–14; 7:7–25). Sin is a slave driver that holds humanity captive. In Romans 9–11 "sin" appears only once (11:27), and never as an enslaving power. Rather, Paul speaks of *God* hardening hearts (9:18; 11:8, 25) and imprisoning all humanity in disobedience (11:32). Even sin, disobedience, and unbelief are taken up into God's all-embracing mercy. Sometimes we catch glimpses of this reality, sometimes in hindsight we see how disasters and betrayals have worked together in unpredictable patterns of redemption, but often we have to take it on trust. Nonetheless, the final affirmation of 11:32–36 can be a great comfort and also a liberation from assuming responsibility for what only God can and will do. And such liberation in turn can free us to do what is given to us to do, knowing that we will fall short and leaving the outcome to God. God is in charge, and yet our actions matter.

In time travel novels by the science fiction author Connie Willis, a group of Oxford graduate students find themselves stuck in England during World War II (Willis 2010). They have gone back in time to do original historical research, but their return to the future is mysteriously blocked; they are trapped in wartime England. Although the students know that Hitler lost the war, they worry incessantly that their actions will alter the space-time continuum, creating aberrations that change the course of history. But gradually they realize that everything they do, sometimes heroic, sometimes small acts of service and love, sometimes disastrous failures, is already part of the space-time continuum and has already played its part in the Allied victory. That realization does not mean that they do not need to act, as they muddle their way through confusing circumstances; rather, it frees them to act with confidence and hope. Similarly, the all-encompassing breadth and depth of God's salvation may free us to take risks, act in hope, and keep our lives in perspective.

Israel Is Not a Metaphor for the Church

Romans 9–11 teaches that the flesh-and-blood people of Israel have a present, vital place in God's redemptive purposes for the world. Contrary to many popular interpretations of Romans and a long history of treating "Israel" as a cipher for the church, Paul cannot imagine God abandoning the specific, historical people called Israel. Paul never calls the church by the names Israel or Zion. Even in Galatians 6:16, when Paul prays for mercy on "the Israel of God," he is praying for mercy on the historic people of Israel who do not believe in Jesus (Eastman 2010). Yes, gentile believers share in the blessings given to Israel, but they never replace Israel. Yes, Paul anticipates Israel's final redemption in and through Jesus Christ, but how that will happen is a mystery that remains in God's hands. What is certain is that, just as for the gentiles, just as for Paul himself, Israel's full redemption will be the action of God's unmerited grace for the unworthy. Paul's focus is consistently and insistently on God, whom Paul never calls "the God of Israel," but rather, "the God and Father of our Lord Jesus Christ." For this reason, Jews and gentiles together draw their existence and sustenance from the fat, nourishing root of God's grace through Jesus Christ.

These observations about God's dealings with Israel yield two takeaways for preaching this challenging text. First, God keeps promises to flesh-and-blood people, who are never treated as a cipher or metaphor for some disembodied theological idea. The God who will not abandon Paul's Jewish relatives is the God who will not abandon any people, no matter how egregious or contrary they may be. As Paul recalls key points in Israel's history, he discerns a basic plotline of divine involvement and radical mercy. It is as if, having boldly claimed that God causes all things to work together for good for those who love God and are called according to his purpose (Rom 8:28), Paul sees that same divine modus operandi in God's dealings with Israel. Perhaps recalling God's mercy to him, which broke into his own life precisely when he was blinded by his zeal for the law (Gal 1:13–16), Paul summons hope for the people from whom he is now estranged and yet to whom he is irrevocably committed. Thus, finding a deep logic of divine mercy, solidarity, and exchange in the narrative arc of Israel's history, of gentile belief, and of his own life, when Paul wrestles with Israel's present unbelief he trusts in the God who justifies the ungodly and is faithful to the promises. His retelling of Israel's history and hope thus encourages us to frame our own history and hope through this same lens, trusting in the God who keeps faith despite our faithlessness.

Second, when Paul speaks of Israel, he is not referring to the present nation called Israel, because such a political entity did not exist in Paul's time. He is referring to the Jewish people. His focus is entirely on the history of this chosen people as demonstrating the unmerited mercy and grace of God, from whom and through whom are all things (11:36). Thus it is a mistake to interpret chapters 9–11 as a blueprint for the present country of Israel in any way. Rather, it is important to exercise care in speaking about the nation of Israel in order to avoid either valorizing it with a kind of entitlement, on the one hand, or harshly judging it with a kind of anti-Semitism, on the other hand. In 2:17–29 Paul carefully dismantles any Jewish entitlement or special pleading before God; in 11:25–29 he maintains God's irrevocable commitment to, and love for, Israel as a people. Thus, Paul would abhor and utterly reject hateful speech and actions toward Jews, but he also would feel free to exercise moral judgments regarding the actions of Israel as a nation. In this he is entirely in line with the prophets, who pronounced judgment on Israel for ethical transgressions while passionately maintaining God's love for God's people.

Part Three: Grace in Human Relationships

Romans 12:1–15:13

In the third major section of the letter, Paul limns the outworking of God's grace in human relationships, primarily within the community of faith, but also in regard to the surrounding culture. At numerous points the instructions in these chapters show explicit connections to earlier parts of Romans. As throughout the letter, Paul's visionary goal is a community of Jews and gentiles together worshiping "the God and Father of our Lord Jesus Christ" (15:6). The foundation of this hope remains God's grace and mercy enacted in Jesus Christ, which now are to shape the character of the community in its mutual fellowship as well as interactions with outsiders. Paul's instructions to the Roman churches hint at the social realities they faced and challenge contemporary readers to work out the gift of salvation in the circumstances of their own ministries.

Paul's exhortations may be divided roughly into two main subsections: general guidance for communal life (12:1–13:14) and specific instructions regarding present tensions in the Roman house churches (14:1–15:13). Within this structure, 15:7–13 functions as both a summary of Paul's exhortation to mutual welcome and a climactic conclusion to the main body of the letter.

ROMANS 12:1–13:14
The Outworking of Grace in Community

In 12:1–13:14, Paul appeals to the churches to express in their common life the "mercy" (12:1), "grace" (12:3), and "gifts" (12:6) given so abundantly by God. Thus chapters 12–13 continue the logic of divine gift in 11:36. Now, however, Paul addresses specific issues in human interaction, both within and beyond the bounds of the community of faith. In 12:1–2 he sources the following exhortations in the mercies of God, yielding bodily and cognitive transformation that test out and demonstrate the will of God. Romans 12:3–8 explores the outworking of gifts of service among members of the body of Christ. The instructions of 12:9–21 promote radically countercultural behavior under the heading of "love without hypocrisy" (v. 9). In 13:1–7 Paul addresses thorny questions about relating to governing authorities, and in 13:8–14 he concludes his instructions by framing them within the love command (12:9–10; 13:8–10) and the apocalyptic newness of God's reign, already begun (12:1–2) yet still awaiting its final triumph (13:11–14).

These chapters form a coherent whole in which practical instruction is couched within a larger theological frame that qualifies its meaning; therefore, they should be read together. At the same time, the material is so rich and demanding that the commentary will offer theological and pastoral reflections at the end of each chapter.

12:1–21. Grace Embracing the Community and the Enemy

Beginning with life in the body of Christ, and broadening his instructions to relations with persecutors, Paul limns the countercultural effects of God's undeserved generosity. Chapter 12 divides into three sections: an introductory exhortation (vv. 1–2), corporate life structured by God's grace and gifts (vv. 3–8), and the exercise of "love without hypocrisy" even toward enemies (vv. 9–21).

12:1–2. By the Mercies of God

With a direct personal appeal to his brothers and sisters, Paul begins a new section focused on practical instruction for communal life.

Just as Romans 9:14–18 and 11:30–32 proclaim God's mercy to whomever God chooses, now Paul links his exhortations with the preceding chapters through the phrase "on the basis of God's mercy" (*dia tōn oiktirmōn tou theou*, by the mercies of God). Indeed, Paul understands his own ministry as given by God's mercy (2 Cor 4:1). Precisely in the context of God's abundant generosity that secures the future and forecloses any attempt to manipulate God through ritual sacrifice (Rom 11:35), believers are to present their full, embodied selves to God, who already has given those selves to them. "Present your bodies" expands on 6:12–14 and denotes physical bodies in relationship with other people, in a "sacrifice" that is "living" and "holy" because it is animated by God's holy and life-giving Spirit indwelling God's people (8:10–11). The word translated "acceptable" also means "well-pleasing"; for example, Paul tells the Philippians that their gifts to him are "a fragrant offering, a sacrifice acceptable and pleasing to God" (Phil 4:18). As "worship," this response to God's mercy reverses the disastrous refusal of Adamic humanity to worship and serve the creator (1:18–23). It is "reasonable" (*logikos*) because it is the logical response to the God from whom and through whom and to whom are all things (11:36). Throughout, the pronouns are plural, so that we should think in terms of communal worship and discernment.

The following verse (12:2) fills out this picture of bodily service with reference to cognitive change, using two related words to speak of transformation: "do not be conformed [*syschēmatizesthe*] to this world [*aiōni*, age], but be transformed [*metamorphousthe*]." Both verbs are plural imperatives in the passive voice; they are addressed to Paul's listeners in their life together, and they assume that God will act in and on the Roman Christians, even as they also exhort the Roman believers to act in line with God's transforming power. The first imperative moves believers away from conformity with the visible structure or schema of the present world order that is passing away (cf. 1 Cor 7:31); the second describes change into a new form of life that endures forever. Philippians 3:21 uses both words to describe the final transformation of believers' bodies to be like Christ's glorious body.

Such change comes through a renewal of the mind that accompanies the presentation of the body to God, thereby enacting "reasonable" worship. Like contemporary research in cognitive science,

Paul finds a close link between mind and body. His cognitive language, including "that you may discern what is the will of God," reinforces the reversal of humanity's loss of cognitive capacity and discernment (Rom 1:28). "Discern" may also be translated "prove" in the sense of "testing out" and communally demonstrating God's will. Paul describes this divine will as "good and acceptable and perfect"—that is, mature (*teleion*). Here again, the word translated as "acceptable" by the NRSVue is also "well-pleasing," correlating God's will with the self-offering of believers.

12:3–8. Embodied Community Grounded in God's Gifts

Paul immediately shows what the renewal of the mind looks like in communal practice; it issues in a new mindset toward oneself and others. In verse 3 he uses a fourfold wordplay on "mindset" (*phronēma*), which may be translated somewhat woodenly, "do not be uppity-minded above what one ought to be minded, but set your mind on being sober-minded" (Jewett 2007, 736). The exhortation recalls Paul's contrast between the mindset of the Spirit and the mindset of the flesh in 8:6–7, and his warning against gentile "uppity-mindedness" in 11:18, 20. Notably, here in 12:3 he speaks to "everyone among you"; the singular address echoes earlier singular warnings against arrogance and judging others (2:1–5, 17–24; 11:17–22) and anticipates 14:4, 10. In parallel with the language of mercy in 12:1, Paul speaks "by the grace given to me," emphatically basing the transformation of body and mind on God's unconditioned mercy and grace.

"The measure of faith that God has assigned" may seem to imply that Paul thinks different people are given different amounts of faith. But a reading more in line with the Greek and with the larger context of 12:1–3 suggests that each person is invited to a sober self-assessment in accordance with the fact that each has received faith from God. Such a sober self-assessment flows out of dependence on, and gratitude for, God's grace, rather than comparison with others (Cranfield 1979, 615–16).

Just as the singular "you" in 8:2 is immediately enfolded in the corporate community of Christ in 8:4, so here in 12:4–5 the individual belongs to an interpersonal whole. Paul's focus is on the uniqueness of *each* "member" in the *one* body of Christ. His language is organic, even visceral; the term "member" (*melē*) is the word for bodily limbs (6:13, 19). As in his extended discussion of the motif of the body of Christ in 1 Corinthians 12:12–27, clearly Paul does not think the metaphorical social "body" is disconnected from physical bodies; just the opposite is true. Nor is the body of Christ to be spiritualized as a metaphysical, transcendent concept; Paul is speaking quite emphatically about and to local communities concerning their embodied and socially embedded practices. Their mutual belonging as "members one of another" has a physical component that resonates with contemporary views of human personhood.

In the ancient Mediterranean world, the metaphor of the "body" often denoted social and political entities, such as Greek city-states or the Roman state. For example, Dionysius of Halicarnassus said, "How like a human body is a city. For it is also put together from many different parts" (*Ant. rom.* 6.86.1). In Stoic thought, "body" could also denote the cosmos as the "body of God"; as stated by the Stoic philosopher Seneca, "All that you behold, that which comprises both god and man, is one—we are the parts of one great body" (*Epistles* 95.52). In Greco-Roman culture, the body was conceptualized hierarchically, as was the social structure it represented. Because the crucified Christ turned that hierarchical structure upside down, Paul's appropriation of the common metaphor of the body also subverts its implicit power structures (see, e.g., 1 Cor 12:12–26).

Paul further develops this motif of the body in Romans 12:6–8. Verse 6 is replete with the language of gift: there are different "gifts" (*charismata*) in accordance with the "grace" (*charis*) that was "given" (*dotheisan*) to us. This emphasis on grace highlights the God-given quality of relationships within Christ's body; because the varied and unified common life of the community flows completely from God's undeserved generosity, it cannot be structured in either competitive or conformist ways. In Greek, 12:6 begins with the present participle "having," which links the following verses with the preceding image of belonging to one body. Therefore, the seven "gifts" that follow flow out of this divine beneficence and are enacted in the community that has already been given by God; they are not individual achievements.

Each of the gifts contributes uniquely to the common life of the church. "Prophecy" probably refers to charismatic prophetic utterances in the gathered assembly (cf. 1 Cor 14:1–5). "In proportion to faith" translates the Greek phrase *kata tēn analogian tēs pisteōs,* signifying "in accordance with the faith"—that is, in accordance with the revelation of God's faithfulness in Jesus Christ. "Ministry" is literally "service" (*diakonia*) and could name roles ranging from a food server to a priest to an ambassador representing another entity. For example, Phoebe, who carries Paul's letter to Rome, is a "deacon" or representative of the church at Cenchrae (Rom 16:1), and Paul calls his apostleship to the gentiles his *diakonia* (11:13).

"Teaching" includes instruction in Scripture and in the traditions about Jesus already being handed down in the very early churches. The "encourager" (*parakalōn*) combines encouragement and consolation in the care of souls. Indeed, Paul introduces this section of Romans with the verbal form of the same word; "I appeal to you" is literally "I encourage you" (*parakalō*). "The giver" probably denotes those who distribute the resources of the community among its numerous impoverished members; "the leader" is to be diligent in the work of administration. Finally, "the compassionate" (*ho eleōn*, the one who shows mercy) is to act with "cheerfulness" (*hilarotēs,* from which comes the English word "hilarity"). Paul's language connotes joy in giving, over against glum or grudging generosity (cf. 2 Cor 9:7). That this list of seven gifts for ministry ends with hilarious mercy expresses its happy source in God's abundant generosity, so that ministry is a matter of giving and receiving with Christ (cf. 2 Cor 8:1–5, 9; Matt 25:34–40).

12:9–21. The Countercultural Expression of Divine Beneficence

In 12:9–13 Paul encourages the Roman house churches to express genuine love for all people; in 12:14–21 he shows what such countercultural love looks like in relationship to those who persecute the faithful.

12:9–13. Love without Hypocrisy

The two clauses of 12:9 state the themes of 12:9–21. "Let love be genuine" (*anhypokritos,* without hypocrisy) heads 12:9–13, which begins with brotherly love (*philadelphia*) and ends with love for the stranger (*philoxenia*). Thus, beginning with a focus on communal life, Paul's admonitions move outward to concern relationships with those outside the community. "Hate what is evil; hold fast to what is good" anticipates 12:14–21, which begins with a countercultural blessing on persecutors and ends with the confident command to "overcome evil with good."

Verses 10 and 13 display the outworking of genuine love, first in noncompetitive mutual honor that is the result of familial affection (v. 10) and finally in the couplet "contribute to the needs of the saints; pursue hospitality to strangers" (v. 13). In Greek, "contribute" is "share fellowship" (*koinōnountes*), implying shared economic resources *and* mutual friendship in Christ (15:27; cf. Gal 6:6; Phil 4:15), which is quite different from impersonal charity bestowed by a social superior. Given the poverty among Roman Christians and the rigid social hierarchies of Roman culture, this advice is both practical and countercultural. This call to practical generosity extends beyond the church; a precise translation of "pursue hospitality" would be "seek out [*diōkontes*] opportunities to show love to strangers."

These verses, in which Paul commands his listeners to love Christian brothers and sisters and to reach out in love to strangers who may or may not be believers, bookend a set of exhortations centered on six attitudes (vv. 11–12). Never flagging in zeal, bubbling over with the Spirit, and serving the Lord are closely related, because the life-giving Spirit of God who raised Jesus from the dead moves in and among the faithful (8:10–11). The outflow of this indwelling presence is hope (5:4–5; 8:24–25), patience (5:3; 8:25), and persistence in prayer. These are the experiential "engines" that empower the kind of love and service Paul depicts here and develops further in 12:14–21.

12:14–21. Victory over Evil

Verse 14 is linked to 12:13 by repetition of the Greek word *diōkō*, "to pursue or seek out," but this time with its common meaning, "to persecute"; Paul himself previously persecuted God's people in this way (cf. Gal 1:13; Phil 3:6), and so he writes as one who knows his own need and experience of undeserved mercy (2 Cor 4:1) and grace (1 Cor 15:9–10). The command to bless persecutors anticipates Romans 12:17–21 and may reflect widespread early Christian adherence to Jesus's commandment to "pray for those who persecute you" (cf. Matt 5:44; Luke 6:28; Didache 1.3b). At this point, it is unclear and perhaps moot whether such persecution comes from those inside or outside the fellowship of believers. Paul's exhortation aligns with Jesus's reversal of the *lex talionis*—the law of "an eye for an eye and a tooth for a tooth" (Matt 5:38–42; Lev 24:19–20). At the same time it reflects a strong strand of Jewish tradition enjoining nonretaliation (see commentary below on 12:17).

Remarkably, immediately after telling the Roman believers to bless their persecutors, Paul encourages them to "weep with those who weep" (Rom 12:15). Might such empathetic compassion extend even to enemies? Solidarity in sorrow was a familiar theme in Jewish contexts (cf. Sir 7:34). For example, in the Testament of Joseph, Joseph describes his attitude toward the brothers who first betrayed him and then came to him for help: "Their life was my life, and all their suffering was my suffering, and all their sickness was my infirmity" (T. Jos. 17:7–8). Again, there is no reason to distinguish between believers and unbelievers in this Pauline exhortation to empathize with others. Rather, the close conjunction of this call to empathy with a call to bless persecutors counters the temptation of schadenfreude, the normal human impulse to rejoice when one's adversaries suffer hardship.

With a threefold repetition of the verb "to have a mindset, to think" (*phroneō*, echoing Rom 12:3), once more Paul commends a mindset of unity and humility (12:16). The first clause is literally "be of the same mind [*phronountes*] toward one another" (cf. 2 Cor 13:11; Phil 2:2; 4:2), followed by "do not be uppity-minded" (cf. Rom 11:20; 12:3; Phil 3:19) and "do not be wise-minded in your own estimation" (cf. 1 Cor 1:19–20, 26–31; 4:10). This admonition is concrete, practical, and unexpected within the rigid hierarchies of Roman society, as Paul knew by experience. He frequently counted himself among the "lowly," not in a spiritualized sense but in the social reality of being scorned, ostracized, and marginalized (cf. 2 Cor 4:8–11).

"Repay no one evil for evil" (Rom 12:17) picks up on the admonition to bless one's persecutors and sets the theme for the rest of the chapter. Similar injunctions against retaliation by human beings are so common that Paul may be drawing on a widely shared early Christian tradition emanating from Jesus (1 Thess 5:15; 1 Pet 3:9; Matt 5:38–42; Luke 6:27–36) and reflecting Jewish tradition (cf. Prov 17:13; 20:22; 24:29; Jos. Asen. 28:14). The verb "repay" simply means "give back" and is cognate with the vocabulary of divine gifting and repayment in Romans 11:35 and 12:19.

Rather than indulging in retaliation, believers are to pay attention ("take thought") to what is noble in the sight of all. This cognitive awareness is the corollary of a mind made new rather than conformed to the present order of reality (12:2). Therefore, attending to "what is noble in the sight of all" is not being guided by common opinion in ethical decisions but rather acting ethically as representatives of the gospel to all people. The admonition conveys Paul's practical concern for the public reputation of the vulnerable Roman house churches. Similarly, "so far as it depends on you" shows practical realism about the challenges of attempting to live peaceably with all people. The apparent necessity of such advice demonstrates the real threat of conflict with persecutors (cf. 8:35).

Verse 19 expands the meaning of 12:17 with a balanced antithesis between *human* vengeance, which is to be avoided, and the promise of *divine* vengeance and retribution for oppressors, which gives hope to the oppressed. The quotation from the Song of Moses (Deut 32:35) names a widespread expectation that God will "repay" Israel's enemies for harming God's people; indeed, in Romans 2:6 Paul quotes just such a promise that God will "repay according to each one's deeds" (Ps 62:12). The same verb translated "repay" or "give back" (*antapodidōmi*) occurs in Romans 11:35, so that these verses describe two sides of the same coin: because all things come from God, God cannot be in debt to anyone (11:35), and God alone may rightly inflict "payback" for human injustice. God's unconditioned, abundant beneficence does not negate the role of recompense in divine judgment; rather, the assurance that everyone will be accountable to God at the last day gives hope and voice to those who suffer unjustly.

Believers nonetheless are called to extend unconditioned, mismatching gifts to their enemies by refusing to pay back in kind. This command also has roots in Israel's Scriptures (e.g., Lev 19:18; Sir 28:1–2) and the teaching of Jesus (Matt 5:38–48). Here the distinction between human and divine judgment and prerogatives (Rom 11:33–34) is crucial; believers are *not* to execute judgment in God's name *because* God alone has the wisdom and power to judge humanity rightly. Therefore Christians are to defer to God's "unsearchable" judgments (11:33) and "leave room for [*dote topon,* give place to] the wrath of God" (12:19), a wrath that they themselves would suffer were it not for the reconciling death of Christ (5:9).

To drive home the contrast between divine and human judgment, in 12:20 Paul introduces a quotation from Proverbs 25:21–22 with an emphatic "instead" (NRSVue), which here means "to the contrary." The verses from Proverbs put the negative injunction against paying back evil for evil in positive terms, as practical generosity toward enemies (cf. Matt 5:38–48). This is the third time Paul has made this point (Rom 12:14, 17, 20). Thus heaping "burning coals" on enemies' heads cannot be understood as taking pleasure in another's suffering, tempting though that might be. Rather, in line with 1 Corinthians 3:13–15, it seems likely that "burning coals" signifies purifying, transforming judgment rather than final rejection on the last day. This is the view held by Augustine, Origen, and Chrysostom, among other early church fathers, who argue that generosity toward enemies would reduce believers' desire for vengeance, and that gifts of food and drink could move the enemy toward reconciliation. As Origen puts it, "Perhaps the wild and barbarous souls of the enemies will be moved to compunction of heart by experiencing our help, by being treated with humanity, affection, and piety" (*Commentary* 9.22–24, in Burns 2012, 311).

Paul concludes his guidance with encouragement to claim the victory over sin and evil that Christ has accomplished (Rom 12:21). When the enemy becomes a friend, then truly good has overcome evil. "Overcome" in Greek (*nikō*) is "win the victory, conquer"; here it signals the defeat of sin's power and the victory of divine grace (5:17, 21; 6:14) in human relations of counterintuitive giving and receiving. This is one of the ways believers are "supervictors" amid afflictions (8:37). "Overcoming evil" displays the final, cosmic victory anticipated in 8:39, now extended to include even enemies: nothing "in all creation will be able to separate us from the love of God in Christ Jesus our Lord."

EXCURSUS

Reflections for Preaching and Teaching

Minds Made New in Mutual Belonging

Is it truly possible for human minds to be made new? The question is worth pondering deeply; anyone who has struggled with old "tapes," deeply ingrained familial and cultural habits of thought and behavior, and unresolved hurts, grudges, and addictions, knows how intractable mindsets can be. This is why Paul puts the command to be transformed in negative terms and the passive voice, implying that God is the one who changes our minds and hearts: "*Do not be conformed* to this world." Radical change requires a definitive break from the destructive habits and mindsets of the old status quo. Furthermore the plural verbs establish such change as occurring in community with others; it is not possible in an isolated, individualistic way.

Yet Paul is supremely confident that profound transformation is not only possible but to be expected (cf. 6:1–14). He goes on to describe such change in interpersonal ways, through the interaction of believers as members of the body of Christ and therefore "members one of another," so deeply knit together that an alteration of one part of the fellowship alters the whole. It is not that individuals change by themselves, let alone that the brain can generate new patterns on its own; as recent studies in cognitive development and neuroscience demonstrate, change happens through environmental, interpersonal connections, mediated by bodily actions and interactions. And that means, in turn, that fellowship is exceedingly important for the cognitive and emotional transformation implied by the "renewing of the mind."

For example, in Alcoholics Anonymous, combating "stinking thinking" is a key part of recovery. "Stinking thinking" refers to ingrained negative thought patterns, including resentments, bitterness, grandiosity, and depression, that may lead to relapse. Solitary thought is not powerful enough to combat attacks of stinking thinking because the mind itself is the problem. Rather, AA meetings and the 24/7 availability of sponsors are necessary for overcoming addictive thought patterns and strengthening recovery; becoming a sponsor and helping others maintain sobriety are also part of the process. Furthermore, no one ever arrives at a point where such a network of support is not needed. Can the church be such a community of honesty and support, a fellowship that does not just tell people what they *should* think and do, but shares in the struggle, weeping with those who weep and rejoicing with those who rejoice?

Love of the Stranger

Paul challenges us not simply to be hospitable to those who come to the church for help but to actively seek out those in need; not simply to advertise the church as welcoming and affirming for everyone who makes it through the church doors but to take the initiative in love and service to and with those outside the church. We might recall Jesus's parable of the Great Dinner, in which the host tells the servants to "go out at once into the streets and lanes of the town and bring in the poor, the crippled, the blind, and the lame" (Luke 14:21–23). As Origen puts it: "We are not just to receive the stranger when he comes to us, but actually to inquire after, and look carefully for, strangers, to pursue them and search them out everywhere, lest perchance they may sit in the streets or lie without a roof over their heads" (*Commentary* 9.46, 10–13, in Burns 2012, 302). This is how familial love becomes the love of the stranger and in turn the stranger becomes part of the family of faith, sharing in a *mutual* fellowship of need and provision out of God's abundant love. Each ministry situation will offer distinctive opportunities for such outreach, but in every case Paul's words challenge churches to pay special attention to those outside their walls.

Nonretaliation and Vengeance

Paul's injunction against violent retaliation toward enemies was as countercultural in his time as it is in ours. Among many possible examples, Psalm 92:9, 11 articulates the prevailing view of the righteous religious person:

> For your enemies, O LORD,
> for your enemies shall perish;
> all evildoers shall be scattered.
> . . . .
> My eyes have seen the downfall of my enemies;
> my ears have heard the doom of my evil assailants.

Such retribution is the normal course of affairs in human life and in human expectations of divine justice. Crucially, in Romans 12:19 Paul gives place and voice to that cry for vengeance from the oppressed, but he also reserves final judgment to God alone. Believers are forbidden to enact vengeance on their persecutors, but they are not forbidden to call down God's wrath!

There is great pastoral wisdom in giving voice to this cry; in situations of serious injustice and abuse, it is humanly impossible (and psychologically harmful) to repress the real desire for retribution as a form of justice. On the other hand, human retaliation contributes to an intractable cycle of violence, and when churches embrace vengeance and presume to be God's moral enforcers, they do great damage and drive away hurting people. In fact, such behavior is a form of practical atheism that usurps God's unique prerogative and power. A story from the desert fathers illustrates the point: A monk went to an older and wiser hermit, saying, "I want to get back at a brother who has hurt me." His friend said, "Don't do that, my son. Leave vengeance in the hands of God." But the monk persisted, so the old hermit said, "My brother, let us pray." Standing, he prayed thus: "O God, we have no further need of you, for we can take vengeance by ourselves" (Ward 2003, 173). Notably, in this instance believers are *not* to imitate God but rather to recognize the immense gulf between divine and human judgment. The assurance that God will judge makes it possible not to take revenge on others.

It is worth pondering the implications of such a radical welcome of enemies for the divisive politics of contemporary culture. There is no "cancel culture" in God's kingdom; there can be no one who is not beloved by God and potentially included in God's economy of grace. There can be no demonizing of others when the goal is reconciliation that wins the victory over evil by transforming enemies into friends. Such transformation often is not possible in this life, but to think of it as our destiny surely puts all relationships in a new light and sets us on a trajectory toward reconciliation rather than vengeance.

A towering example of such reconciliation is the late congressman John Lewis, the powerful advocate for desegregation who suffered multiple brutal attacks and imprisonments in the struggle for civil rights. Over the years Lewis became famous for his willingness to extend forgiveness to those who had harmed him. One story concerned a former member of the Ku Klux Klan who had assaulted Lewis at a bus stop in 1961, leaving him bloodied and battered on the ground. Almost fifty years later the man and his son came to Lewis's congressional office to ask forgiveness. As Lewis told the story, "He said, 'Will you forgive me? I want to apologize. Will you accept my apology?' His son started crying. I said, 'I forgive you. I accept your apology.' The gentlemen started crying. I started crying. We hugged. They called me brother. I called them brother" (Myron B. Pitts, "Lewis Recounts Civil Rights Battles, Reconciliation," *Fayetteville (NC) Observer*, July 31, 2014). Lewis frequently said, "Nonviolence and forgiveness is not just an idea. It is a way of living for me." Lewis's commitment to nonretaliation was anything but passive quietism; rather, it was part and parcel of the tremendous moral authority he brought to the struggle for racial justice.

13:1–14. Bifocal Politics

Chapter 13 divides easily into two main sections: verses 1–7 concern relationships with the pagan governing authorities; verses 8–14 enfold Paul's practical instructions in the larger framework of love (13:8–10; 12:9–10, 13) and God's time as the dawning of the Day of the Lord (13:11–14; 12:2).

Because Romans 13:1–7 has been used for centuries to authorize repressive political power, it is among the most challenging of Paul's writings; therefore, some general observations will be helpful for interpreting this passage. First, Paul does not speak directly to governing authorities but rather to everyone who must deal with them. This is not a treatise on government, nor is it a defense of any form of political power; it is specific, practical advice for fragile communities living under the brutal dictatorship of the Roman Empire. Second, Paul never says the authorities are good in themselves; his interest is in how God uses them. Third, Paul is drawing on an ancient and widespread Jewish belief that God can and does use Israel's enemies for God's purposes, both in judgment and in deliverance. Fourth, it is crucial to read this passage in both its historical and literary context.

Historical Context

Because of his specific instructions about payment of taxes, it appears that Paul is addressing a particular situation in Rome during the 50s—unrest over unjust taxation. Although the first five years of Nero's reign were relatively restrained in terms of violent suppression, that did not mean that violence toward the lower classes and enslaved persons was not common; it was. When there was unrest in the Roman suburb of Puteoli, Nero did not hesitate to send in the Praetorian guard to suppress it violently, including terrorizing the populace by public executions (Tacitus, *Annals* 13.48). The expulsion of Jews by Nero's predecessor Claudius was within recent memory, and the future brutal torture of Roman believers under Nero, who used them as scapegoats after the great fire that destroyed much of Rome in 64 CE, is not that far off. Of course, Paul does not know the terrible suffering that awaits the Roman house churches under Nero, but he surely knows that any tiny minority, and any largely immigrant population, including the Jews, is in a vulnerable position in the capital city of the empire. This vulnerability is the context in which 13:1–7 is written (for other early instructions about relationships with pagan rulers, cf. Mark 12:13–17; 1 Tim 2:2; Titus 3:1; 1 Pet 2:13–17).

Literary Context

Although many commentators treat 13:1–7 as a discrete section unrelated to its context, it is a mistake to do so. These verses continue the instructions for human relationships that began at 12:9, but now with a focus on governing authorities and the payment of taxes. Thus they continue the movement in Paul's exhortations from intracommunity concerns to interaction with the larger society. In its literary context, 12:14–13:7 is bookended by commandments to love (12:9–10; 13:8–10) and crowned by the eschatological hope of 13:11–14. As discussed in the commentary, there are also numerous verbal links between 13:1–7 and the larger context of the letter.

13:1–7. Relationships with the Governing Authorities

13:1–5. Subjection to the Governing Authorities

Switching to third person, in 13:1 Paul speaks of "every person" (literally "every soul," an expression common in Hebrew texts) in a general statement about interacting with "governing authorities." The term refers to local officials who have power to impose taxes and enforce compliance with civic order. While the language of subjection is naturally offensive to modern Western ears, it picks up on Paul's earlier statement that the mindset of the flesh does not "submit" to God's law (8:7). Similarly, in 8:20 Paul says creation has been "subjected" (*hypetagē*) to futility; he uses a cognate verb in 13:1 to say authorities have been set in order by God (*hypo theou tetagmenai*). These related texts set the context for interpreting 13:1, by asserting God's authority over all creation, including human social structures. Thus, despite the misuse of 13:1 to support the "divine right of kings," its meaning is quite the opposite; to say that rulers' authority comes from God is also to say that it does not come from anywhere else, including their own claims to power; they are subject to God's authority, and God can withdraw that authority at any time.

This is a frequent claim in Israel's Scripture. Wisdom of Solomon 6:1–3 provides a clear example:

> Listen therefore, O kings, and understand;
> learn, O judges of the ends of the earth.
> Give ear, you that rule over multitudes
> and boast of many nations.
> For your dominion was given you from the Lord
> and your sovereignty from the Most High;
> he will search out your works and inquire into your plans.

Other references from Israel's tradition include Isaiah 45:1–7; Daniel 2:21; Proverbs 8:15; and Sirach 10:4; 17:17; the motif is widespread. Within Romans itself, Pharaoh is a quintessential example of a pagan ruler who means Israel no good, but whom God has "raised up" precisely to demonstrate God's power through the liberation of Israel from captivity (9:17). In the context of 9:6–18, there is nothing exemplary about Pharaoh; he simply is God's unwitting servant (Gaventa 2017).

In line with Israel's confession of God as the "one" Lord over all the peoples of the earth, gentiles as well as Jews (3:29–30), Paul says twice that authority is established "by God" (*hypo theou*). This is one outworking of the logic of 11:33–36, that "from him and through him and to him are *all things,*" including all earthly powers. Thus, God's sovereign power is the theological basis of Paul's counsel to the Romans; hope is its pastoral fruit.

Paul continues in 13:2 with the negative corollary of the positive admonition to "be subject" in 13:1. "Authority" is again "what God has appointed" (*diatagē*). Now the warning of judgment (*krima*) is added to the counsel against resisting authority. Whether Paul has in mind divine or simply human judgment is unclear; the latter is implied by 13:3–7.

Several key terms come to the fore in 13:3–5: fear (vv. 3–4); the sword (v. 4); wrath (vv. 4–5); good and bad (v. 3–4); agent (vv. 3); rulers (v. 3); and conscience (v. 5). Many of these terms pick up on previous appearances in the letter, but with some surprising twists that present serious puzzles for the interpreter.

First, in 13:3–4 Paul says, if you do what is good, you do not need to fear authority, but if you do wrong, "be afraid, for the authority does not bear the sword in vain!" Twice Paul identifies the authority as "God's agent [*diakonos*]," a term that Paul uses elsewhere in reference to himself (11:13), Phoebe (16:1), and those with a ministry of service (12:7); here Paul repeats the phrase to emphasize that the authority represents God and is at God's disposal. "Sword" had immediate and visceral meaning for people in the Roman Empire, as it was a common method of punishment. Like guns today, swords were the weapons worn by law enforcement; they also were used in public executions (including, according to tradition, Paul's own beheading). Such a weapon surely would inspire fear for those who ran afoul of the Roman authorities. Earlier, however, Paul confidently tells the believers that the sword (8:35) cannot separate them from the love of Christ, because in *all* things they are "supervictors" through Christ (8:37). Why then should they fear authorities who bear the sword?

Second, "wrath" elsewhere refers to divine wrath, notably in 12:19, where the context implies God's wrath on behalf of God's suffering people, but it also denotes God's judgment on human disobedience (1:18; 2:5, 8; 3:5; 4:15; 5:9; 9:22). Furthermore, the sword-bearing enforcer of order is "to execute wrath on the wrongdoer" (13:4). In Greek the phrase is "one who avenges for the purpose of wrath" (*ekdikos eis orgēn*). On the one hand, the phrase can simply name one who enforces punishment for a legal judgment; on the other hand, the twofold designation of the authority as "the servant [*diakonos*] of God," both for "good" and for "wrath," suggests that this wrath is in service of God. If so, pagan authorities instituted by God enact vengeance and wrath, precisely what believers are told not to do (12:19).

Third, the repeated contrast between doing "good works" and "bad" echoes earlier verses contrasting "good" and "bad" in human actions (2:6–10; 7:18–19; 12:17, 21). Romans 13:3–5 shares with 2:2–11 the theme of divine judgment, indeed wrath, for wrongdoers, and glory (or praise) for those who do the good. Elsewhere, however, Paul sets forth a distinctly countercultural understanding of "the good." In 12:2 God's will as "what is good and acceptable and perfect" is explicitly contrasted with the form (schema) of the present world order, which surely included the Roman Empire. Ultimately, it is not the governing authorities who can judge what is good, but God, and those who have been called by God into Christ's body (cf. 1 Cor 2:14–16). Furthermore, in 8:28 Paul promises that God causes "all things to work together for good" for those who love God and are called according to God's purpose. This good may not look like human flourishing according to the judgments of the surrounding culture, however; rather, it is conformity to Christ (8:29; 12:2), a transformation that involves suffering with Christ (8:17). How then does such a radical, countercultural picture of what is "good" cohere with the practical advice of 13:1–7—or does it?

Fourth, in 13:3 Paul states that "rulers [*archontes*] are not a terror [*phobos*] to good conduct but to bad." Here the title seems simply to denote authorities in a positive sense. In 1 Corinthians 2:6, 8, however, Paul uses the same term to refer to "the rulers of this age" who "crucified the Lord of glory."

Finally, in 13:5 Paul repeats his injunction to "be subject" to the authorities (13:1) but now links this injunction to "conscience"; not only are believers to submit to those who bear the sword to avoid wrath, they also are to submit in order to have a clean conscience. As in 2:15, Paul seems to assume that conscience acts as a reliable inward guide to good and bad behavior.

These observations certainly raise many puzzling questions about the interpretation of 13:1–7. At the least, they warn us against reading these difficult verses as guidelines for the state or general axioms about political power and governance. Rather, Paul gives his listeners a guideline for interpretation in the short phrase introducing verse 6: "for the same reason." The link tells us that Paul's instructions in 13:1–5 lead up to guidance regarding a specific situation in Rome. That situation is the imposition of taxes that are causing social unrest in the city.

13:6–7. Advice concerning Taxes

Paul does not say, "You should pay taxes," but "you *are* paying taxes"—as you should (v. 7)! He uses two technical terms for taxes in 13:6–7, denoting both direct, routine taxes on property and persons and indirect toll taxes. The social context of this guidance is significant: tax collectors routinely demanded more than was due, intimidated people into paying them, and pocketed the difference. Because there was significant unrest over the payment of taxes, Paul very likely feared that any disturbances could result in harsh crackdowns or even expulsions that would scatter the fledgling Roman churches. Perhaps the earlier expulsion of the Jews, including Jewish

Christians, was not far from his mind nor the minds of his listeners. Nonetheless, Paul calls the authorities ministers of God, a phrase not far from Paul's own self-designation as a "minister of Christ Jesus to the gentiles in the priestly service of the gospel of God" (15:16).

Finally, Paul admonishes his listeners to "pay to all what is due them," followed by a list of four specific obligations: direct taxes, toll taxes (NRSVue "revenue"), respect (Gk., fear), and honor. Fear and honor are flip sides of the attitude toward authorities that Paul urges on his listeners in 13:1–5. The imperative, "to pay," is the same verb translated "repay" in 12:17 and was a common term for paying taxes. Similarly, Jesus said, "Pay to Caesar what is Caesar's and to God what is God's" (Matt 22:21; Mark 12:17; Luke 20:25). We have no evidence that Paul knew this dominical saying, but his instructions are in line with Jesus's teaching about taxation. Readers of the Gospels often note the trick in Jesus's saying, because of course all things belong to God, even what ostensibly belongs to Caesar. So also, for Paul all things are from and for God (Rom 11:36), even taxes. This is a "sword" that cuts both ways; payment of taxes may be a way of honoring Caesar, but God's ownership of all and status as giver of all is far superior to anything Caesar can claim. Like every other creature, Caesar is beholden to God, and so are the governing authorities instituted by God. Believers are to discharge their "debts" in the present age, including taxes and proper fear and honor toward those in power, but this is a minor part of their service to God and therefore subject to change should God require it. Verses 8–14 clarify this overriding allegiance to God.

13:8–14. Love in God's Time

Paul sums up his exhortations regarding relationships within and beyond the fellowship of believers with a reflection on love (vv. 8–10) and on living in the time of Christ (vv. 11–14).

13:8–10. Love Fulfills the Law

"Owe *no one* anything, except to love one another" radically reframes the injunction to pay *all* people what is due (literally, owed) in terms of love as the singular fulfillment of the law (Lev 19:18; Gal 5:14; cf. Matt 22:37–40). This call to love picks up on Romans 12:9–10 and bookends Paul's instructions for human relationships in

12:9–13:7, relativizing the importance of submission to the authorities and taking Paul's admonitions to a higher level: "Yes, submit to the authorities, fulfill your obligations, and thus live peaceably with all—as much as possible! This is how you take thought for what is noble in the sight of all [12:18], in an age that is passing away [12:2; 13:11–14]. But what lasts is the never-ending debt of love inaugurated and fulfilled through Christ [5:4–5; 8:35–38; 12:9–10]." By using the inclusive, nonspecific term "another," Paul extends the love commandment beyond the bounds of the community, in line with his counsel concerning interactions with fellow believers, strangers, enemies, and governing authorities.

The list of commandments concerning human relationships (13:9) shows that Paul has the Mosaic law in mind. Just as 13:1 names God as the sole source of authority and thereby puts pagan governing authorities under God's rule and judgment, so here Paul's invocation of the law of Moses puts all human ordinances under the judgment of that law. At the same time, Paul sums up the Mosaic law through the love command, which implicitly corrects abusive and harmful forms of zeal for the law (cf. Phil 3:6) and focuses on love as the righteous intention of the law. In Romans 13:10 Paul interprets the Mosaic law through a negative statement: "Love does no wrong [*kakon*] to a neighbor; therefore, love is the fulfilling of the law." Love of one's neighbor, that is, is the "good" that not only exceeds but constrains the exercise of governmental power (13:3–4), which at best restrains the bad. In short, when misuse of governmental power does wrong to a neighbor, it contradicts God's law.

13:11–14. Whose Time Is It?

If the Great Commandment reframes the practical counsel of 13:1–7, so does Paul's clarion call to transformed behavior in light of the coming Day of the Lord (13:11–12). Whose time is it? It is God's time, when the day of salvation is drawing near, even while believers still live in the old age (12:2). Therefore, stop sleepwalking, wake up, and get dressed for battle! In 13:11 the verb translated "wake" is a passive infinitive, meaning "to be roused or raised"; elsewhere in the New Testament it refers to Jesus's resurrection by God (Mark 14:28; Matt 16:21; 26:32; Luke 9:22; Rom 4:25; 8:34). Those who are asleep do not rouse themselves; they are awakened and raised up by another. Baptized into Christ's death, believers have been awakened and raised by God into a new life that awaits the final resurrection (6:3–4). Therefore, united with Christ, with bodies given over to God and minds made new (12:1–2), believers are to live in light of the coming day of salvation. Paul's language evokes this new baptismal identity. His vivid images of awakening from sleep, opposing the nighttime to the coming day and darkness to light, also reflect apocalyptic expectation of the imminent Day of the Lord (cf. 1 Thess 5:1–11; Eph 5:14).

In contrast with the weapons of imperial power (the sword), believers are to don the "armor" (*hopla,* weapons, as in 6:13; cf. 2 Cor 6:7; 10:4; Eph 6:10–20) of light. In striking contrast with the literal sword of the governing authorities, 1 Thessalonians 5:8 tells believers to don "the breastplate of faith and love and for a helmet the hope of salvation." Similarly, Ephesians 6:10–17 further develops the imagery of the "whole armor of God," including "the sword of the Spirit, which is the word of God." What an image for powerful, nonviolent conflict with the forces of sin and death!

The verb translated "put on" (*enduo*) in Romans 13:12 means "clothe yourselves" (cf. 2 Cor 5:2–3; 1 Thess 5:8; Col 3:12; Eph 6:11) and has a long lineage. Job 29:14 speaks of "put[ting] on righteousness"; in Isaiah 52:1 the prophet cries out, "Awake; awake; put on your strength, O Zion! Put on your beautiful garments, O Jerusalem." In Romans 13:14 Paul repeats the image in specifically christological terms: "put on the Lord Jesus Christ." In the ancient world, as now, clothing conveyed the identity, social status, and roles of the person. To be clothed in Christ and in the armor of light is to draw one's personhood and the pattern of one's life from the crucified and resurrected Lord (6:3–4). Paul addresses the Roman listeners as a community here; it is in their common life and their shared relationships to their particular social context that this new pattern of life will be worked out and displayed to the surrounding culture.

United with Christ in baptism, clothed with the armor of light, and leaving the darkness behind, Paul's listeners are reminded of who they are and whom they serve—they serve the Lord who holds the future, and their identity and worth come from that Lord and no one else. As such they will necessarily be at odds with the present age (12:2), but they also must navigate wisely and realistically the power structures of this age (13:1–7). Indeed, to do so wisely may witness not only to the goodness of God's new creation in Christ but also to love for one's neighbor, inspired by that same Lord.

Continuing the metaphor of living in broad daylight rather than under cover of night, in 13:13 Paul spells out the ethical implications of the coming day of salvation with the overarching admonition "let us walk decently" (cf. 1 Cor 14:40). Much as this admonition might grate on contemporary ears, here as elsewhere Paul's concern is with the peace and security of Christian communities and their witness to outsiders (Rom 12:17–18; cf. 2 Cor 8:21; 1 Thess 4:12) and reflects the practical realities of living as a tiny and suspect minority in a hostile culture. Only those with the security of high social status can afford to flout accepted moral standards, in Paul's day as in ours.

Hence Paul lists behavior corresponding to "the night" and "the works of darkness" in three couplets, which cumulatively illustrate excesses associated with the nighttime orgies of upper-class young men: reveling and drunkenness, illicit sex and licentiousness, quarreling and jealousy. "Reveling" (*komoi*) were all-night parties, sometimes coming-of-age parties, involving drunkenness and prostitutes. Similarly, "illicit sex" (*koitais,* couplings) and licentiousness refer to sexual excesses. Lest contemporary readers think Paul was simply being prudish, it is important to know that privileged men could sexually and otherwise assault enslaved persons and those of the lower classes without any penalty, and those who were assaulted had no recourse. Later in his reign Nero was infamous for such nocturnal carousing (Suetonius, *Nero* 26).

The final pairing of quarreling and jealousy reflects Paul's concern for the unity of Christian fellowships (cf. Gal 5:19–21; 1 Thess 5:5–8) and may anticipate his instructions in Romans 14:1–15:6. But quarreling and jealousy also accompanied the competitive character of Greco-Roman culture, in striking contrast with Paul's injunction to "outdo one another in showing honor" (12:10).

Finally, as those baptized into Christ, Paul's listeners are to "put on the Lord Jesus Christ" (13:14; cf. Gal 3:27; Eph 4:22–24) and renounce their old life in "the flesh" (cf. Gal 5:17–24). The verb "put on" is the same as in Romans 13:12; the way to be clothed in "the weapons of light" is by being clothed in Christ. Because union with Christ guarantees that nothing can separate believers from their Lord (8:38–39), the link between donning armor and donning a person is richly evocative; clothed in Christ, believers are protected from all that would destroy them. Paul thus sums up his counsel for the outworking of God's grace and lordship in human relationships by reminding believers to whom they belong, what and whose time it is, and who they are in Christ.

EXCURSUS

Reflections for Preaching and Teaching

God Uses Even God's Enemies for God's Purposes

As noted above, Paul tells believers they are not to pay back evil for evil, but rather they are to bless those who persecute them, even to give food and drink to their enemies, because vengeance and retaliation belong to God alone (12:14–21). As recipients of God's surpassing gift of grace, exercising the gifts God has given them, believers are to extend to others the grace they have received. Regarding God's vengeance, all they can and may do is to "leave room for the wrath of God." Conversely, Paul now says that those who wield the sword on behalf of governing authority are God's servants who "execute wrath on the wrongdoer" (13:4). How are we to make sense of this apparent contradiction? It seems that Christians are forbidden to do what is God's prerogative, but the governing authorities have been set in place by God to execute wrath in human affairs.

The contrast is puzzling and provocative. It also continues the logic of God's use of pagan powers, even God's enemies, to do God's will. When Paul says in 1 Corinthians 2:8 that "the rulers of this age" did not understand God's wisdom, for if they had, "they would not have crucified the Lord of glory," he does not mean that the crucifixion was a terrible mistake. Clearly Paul saw the crucifixion, together with the resurrection, as God's way of delivering humanity from sin and death. The rulers of this age unwittingly did God's will. So also, Pharaoh unwittingly did God's will, both in resisting Moses's demand to let God's people go and in finally relenting. Cyrus of Persia did God's will (Isa 45:1–7). The point is not that any of these rulers were good; they themselves are subject to God's judgment, as the prophets make clear. The point is that God is all-powerful; ironically, God even uses oppressors to deliver God's people from those same oppressors, who remain under God's judgment. This is why prayers of lament and imprecation and demands for deliverance rightly address God as the responsible party. It is also why believers are never to praise or swear allegiance to unjust authorities.

But what does this look like in real life? The answers will be as varied and cross-cultural as the multifaceted world in which we live, but the consistent message is hope in a God who is all-powerful, all-just, and all-merciful. Stories, not arguments, are the way forward. Here are two examples:

In 2015, the militant group calling itself Islamic State (ISIS) released a horrifying video of twenty-one Egyptian Copts beheaded on a Libyan beach for the "crime" of being Christian. Many of these men had left an impoverished Egyptian village south of Cairo and gone to Libya to find work. When journalists went to the village to interview the families of these men, they were surprised by what they found. Banners inside and outside the church showed the men who had been killed next to the throne of Jesus. They were portrayed not as passive victims but as martyrs who had chosen to remain faithful to their Lord. The brother of one of the men said: "I prayed for his soul. I heard him calling, 'Oh Jesus' as he was beheaded. I'm happy and I'm proud of him. He is a martyr for Christ" (Liela Fadel, "ISIS Beheadings in Libya Devastate an Egyptian Village," NPR, February 17, 2015). The mother of another victim said, "We thank ISIS. Now more people believe in Christianity because of them. ISIS showed what Christianity is. We thank God that our relatives are in heaven." The wife of another slain laborer said, "ISIS thought they would break our hearts. They did not." (Jonathan Rashad, "Coptic Christian Village Mourns ISIS Victims in Libya," *Newsweek,* March 8, 2015, updated online April 5, 2016).

It is important to recognize the extreme grief and rage that the villagers also expressed in reaction to the brutal murders of their relatives. Grief, rage, and faith were mingled together. This is not quietism, nor is it collusion in systems of oppression. No, it is a radical victory cry, a way of seeing even enemies as used by God. Does this mean these Egyptian Christians are pacifists? Again, the answer is no. These poor, marginalized Copts were not in a position to avenge themselves against ISIS, nor is it clear that they would do so if they could. On the other hand, many of the villagers said they were glad that the Egyptian government sent warplanes to bomb ISIS in retaliation for the murders. Without any claims about the moral integrity of the Egyptian leadership, they still could see it as executing wrath on the wrongdoers (Rom 13:4).

Here is a second example. On August 15, 1937, four years into Hitler's reign of terror, a German pastor and biblical scholar named Ernst Käsemann preached a sermon on Isaiah 26:13, titled "One Lord Alone." He knew it would get him arrested, and it did.

He spoke about the church's culpable quietism during the rise of the Third Reich and the terrible pass to which things had come over the previous four years. Then he said, remarkably,

> Then God entered the field and led us step by step ever deeper into the darkness and taught us to tread with surer steps in the faith that does not long for sight. . . .
>
> Blessed be our enemies! For they teach us, with all their bluster, what right faith, true peace, and eternal joy are! We do not want to change places with them, whatever they want to have, to plan, and to do. "Other lords have ruled over us." Certainly, we know it and discern it afresh every day. But they hold rule over what is merely the dust of the earth. And they themselves clearly know that, and the knowledge makes them furious.
>
> Nevertheless, we confess, in joy and thanks, the eternal Lord and we declare with the whole Christian family: "but we call on You alone and in Your name!" (Käsemann 1999)

Käsemann was a member of the Confessing Church that opposed Hitler; in later years he was bitterly critical of the German Christians for colluding with Hitler's takeover of the churches. He was anything but a compliant quietist. But he also drew strength and hope from a vision of God's power overarching all human events, using even the enemies of the faith to clarify and strengthen the witness of Christian believers.

Christians and Political Powers

The stories above are examples of what we might call "bifocal politics," a way of understanding and interacting with the immediate operations of worldly power while also seeing the ultimate reality of God's gracious rule. In Romans 12–13, as in life, the penultimate realm of earthly power is framed by the ultimate realm of God's rule. The effect is jarring. But both Paul's practical advice for navigating worldly powers and his corrective vision of God's ultimate authority, love, and victory over evil provide resources for preaching and leadership in the church. If

Romans 13:1–7 is divorced from its context, it can be read in support of Christian nationalism, as indeed was the case in Nazi Germany (Eberhard Arnold, "Reading Romans 13 under Fascism," *Plough Quarterly*, March 25, 2020). Therefore, the command to love enemies and fellow believers, and the promise of the Lord's coming day, set crucial limits on the interpretation of Rom 13:1–7. It should not be read out of context as an inflexible guide for how Christians should behave in every circumstance, but as an example of advice for a Christian minority in adverse and tenuous circumstances. In different circumstances the advice will differ as well. But in every circumstance, the source of hope is the conviction that ultimately God is in charge, using both friends and enemies to accomplish "good for those who love God" (8:28). Similarly, in every circumstance, believers need to be reminded that they belong to God and that, no matter what the times are like, they live in God's time.

ROMANS 14:1–15:13
Welcome One Another

In 14:1–15:6, Paul's zeroes in on differences in religious practice that threaten to divide his Roman audience. In 15:7–13 he brings the main body of the letter to a ringing climax celebrating God's welcome of all people, Jew and gentile, into one community of praise. This is some of the most pointed and historically specific advice in the letter, indicating Paul's apparent knowledge of conflict in the Roman congregations between those believers who adhere strictly to Jewish food and worship practices and those who do not. This division may fall primarily along ethnic lines between Jews and gentiles, but not entirely. Paul himself was Jewish but did not feel bound by the Mosaic law in his eating practices (14:14); it is also possible that some gentile believers associated with the synagogues were concerned to avoid eating food that they considered "unclean."

Although Paul warns people on both sides of this conflict not to judge one another, his primary target is contempt toward those who abstain from eating meat; his admonitions are the social outworking of his earlier exhortations *against* gentile arrogance toward Jews (11:13, 18, 25) and *for* a mindset that puts others first (12:3). The central Pauline theme of faith brackets his discussion of Jewish

Torah observance, as Paul characterizes faith that is tied to particular dietary and worship practices as "weak" (14:1–2) and warns against actions that do not proceed "from faith" (14:23).

Historical Context

In Roman society, Jewish customs were well-known and often the subject of snide jokes. For example, Romans could not understand why Jews refused to eat pork; the emperor Augustus famously joked that he would rather be Herod's pig than Herod's son, because the pig would be safe from slaughter. The popularity of the joke indicates the social irritation and judgment directed toward a social group that refused to dine with others, out of what seemed to be unreasonable pickiness about what they ate. The same social judgment might fall on gentiles who chose, for any number of reasons, to abstain from meat; they could be lumped with Jews in the eyes of other gentiles and lose social status as a result. For that very reason, the philosopher Seneca was advised by his father not to abstain from eating meat (Seneca, *Epistulae morales* 108.22). To follow Jewish practices in public meals would expose gentiles to social scorn, along with Jews; conversely, to avoid such practices would cut believers off from continuing to participate in the synagogue.

Whether such scrupulosity about food concerned issues of kosher slaughter or the offering of meat and wine to idols or simply the prohibition of particular foods such as pork is difficult to know, and perhaps moot. Jewish law does not prohibit meat or wine, but any number of concerns might prompt someone to consider certain foods "unclean" in terms of Mosaic law. Believers anxious to keep the law could point to the example of the prophet Daniel, who refused to eat meat or drink wine from the table of King Nebuchadnezzar (Dan 1:8–17). Practices that seemed picayune and silly to outsiders were matters of life and death in Jewish history and practice, and certainly set them off from the surrounding culture.

Jewish observance of the Sabbath was also well-known and the subject of considerable scorn and judgment in Roman society. Jews were thought to be lazy because they rested every seventh day. Under Roman law, however, they had legal protections for meeting on the Sabbath, including exemptions from collecting their weekly food dole on that day and exemptions for collecting money to send to Jerusalem.

Such legal exemptions, however, would not protect them from social ostracism and ridicule. Particularly in view of this minority status, Jews, including Jewish Christians, would be expected to uphold Jewish identity and prerogatives by keeping Sabbath and attending synagogue instruction and worship.

Rhetorical Structure

Romans 14:1–15:13 divides into four subsections addressing issues of mutual judgment in the community: 14:1–12, 13–23; 15:1–6, 7–13. In 14:1–12, Paul urges the Roman Christians not to pass judgment on one another for differing dietary practices and observations of the Sabbath. In 14:13–23, Paul's instructions become more pointed, directed primarily toward those who eat meat without thinking about the destructive social and spiritual impact of their actions on fellow believers. In 15:1–6 Paul develops the categories of "the strong" and "the weak" to name the different dietary practices he has discussed in chapter 14. He immediately puts forth Christ and Scripture as guides for behavior in the community and concludes with the first of three benedictions (15:5–6; 15:13; 16:20).

Because 15:7–13 not only sums up the argument of 14:1–15:6 but also brings the entire letter to a climax, it will be treated here as a separate subsection. Paul's command to "welcome one another" in 15:7 both links back to 14:1, enfolding community guidance within the motif of Christ's welcome of both Jew and gentile, and introduces 15:7–13 as the culmination of the epistle. After the second benediction in 15:13, Paul speaks personally of his reasons for writing the letter, then turns to practical matters about his future travel plans.

14:1–15:6. Food Laws and Holy Days: Navigating Difference in the Community

14:1–12. Do Not Judge One Another

The first paragraph of this section (14:1–4) issues an evenhanded injunction against judging one another, capped by the assurance that God, the master, has power to make each person stand at the judgment day. The second paragraph (vv. 5–9) briefly addresses different practices for observing holy days. Paul concludes with reference to

Christ as lord of all. In the third paragraph (vv. 10–12), Paul returns to the issue of human judgment, again reminding his listeners of the final judgment by God.

14:1–4. Mutual Welcome in Christ

In 14:1 "welcome" (*proslambanesthe*) signifies inviting someone into a circle of belonging; it is the word Paul uses when he commands the slave owner Philemon to "welcome" Onesimus "as you would welcome me" (Phlm 17). This "welcome" is the theme of 14:1–15:6, repeated in 15:7 as a summary of the preceding verses. It is grounded in God's welcome of all, both Jew and gentile (14:3), and is the opposite of judgments and arguments based on different religious practices. The welcome Paul has in mind is not the kind of pseudo-friendliness in which people are invited into fellowship for the purpose of correcting their behavior, but an openhearted embrace of fellow believers regardless of differences.

Turning to the specific issue of dietary practices, Paul begins with the command to welcome those who are "weak in faith" and eat only vegetables (14:1–2). By framing questions about diet in terms of "weak in faith," Paul links this practical issue to the larger theological claims of the letter, in which faith plays a central role (1:17; 3:21–31; 4:1–5:1; 9:30–10:17). In 4:19–21, depictions of faith as "weak" or "strong" characterize Paul's depiction of Abraham's faith, which became strong as he gave glory to God, trusting in God's promise that Sarah would bear a son. In 14:2, "some believe in eating anything" is literally "some have faith to eat anything"—that is, their faith frees them from the necessity of avoiding nonkosher food; they can take it or leave it without damage to their faith.

Those who are "weak in faith," however, cannot separate the exercise of their Christian faith from particular cultural practices—in this case, dietary and calendrical observances. There is nothing wrong with such practices, and throughout the rest of this chapter Paul strenuously defends the dignity and worth of those who adhere to them. But they render personal faith vulnerable to cultural shifts and less able to adapt across cultures. Paul may be keenly aware of such issues precisely because his own missionary work has taken him far outside his own ethnic and religious comfort zone. Similarly, in a passage that significantly parallels 14:1–15:6, in 1 Corinthians 8–10 Paul speaks of "weakness" in relationship to conscience, as he considers faith in connection with cultural norms derived from daily Torah observance.

In Romans 14:3–4, Paul further depicts "welcome" through a carefully balanced admonition against contempt toward those who abstain and judgment on those who eat. This counsel is meant to keep the peace and promote unity without requiring conformity. What it does require, however, is accepting limits on the universal application of Torah. The theological rationale for this limitation is nothing other than shared and exclusive belonging to the Lord who uniquely judges all. Paul does not argue from Torah, nor from a notion of individual rights, but from the accountability of each person to God as God's servant. The word translated "servant" (*oiketēs*) is a technical term that appears only here in Paul's letters. It denotes enslaved persons or servants who were members of the household. Notably, in Leviticus 25:39–55, the term distinguishes enslaved Israelites from other enslaved people (*douloi*): "For to me the Israelites are servants [*oiketoi*]; they are my servants whom I brought out of the land of Egypt: I am the Lord your God" (Lev 25:55 LXX). The point is that Israelites, all of whom belong to God as God's servants and all of whom God liberated from Egypt, must not mistreat those among them who are socially enslaved. Paul's logic is similar here: because all believers belong to God's household, for such household servants to judge or despise one another would be to usurp the Lord's sole authority.

In Romans 14:4, "who are you [singular] who judges" echoes 2:1. Now Paul applies his earlier admonitions against human judgment to the very specific case of disputes about dietary observances in the community. As noted above, there was no Jewish law against eating meat, but scrupulous believers apparently were refusing to eat meat in public gatherings (cf. 1 Cor 8:1–13). Although Paul's warnings are directed at both those who eat and those who do not, his opening admonition shows that his primary concern is those who judge the scrupulously observant.

Paul's exhortation against mutual judgment revolves around both God's welcoming embrace for all and God's power to establish each of God's servants. "The Lord is able" is literally "the Lord is powerful [*dynamis*]." "Lord" denotes the master of the household; here it continues to carry that meaning but also refers to Christ as Lord. The verb "to stand" or "make to stand" appears three times in verse 4 and again in verse 10: "We all will stand before the judgment seat of God." Human judgment pales in comparison with God's power and will to establish each of God's servants securely on the last day (cf. 1 Thess 3:8; 1 Cor 16:14; Phil 1:27; 4:1).

14:5–9. Living and Dying to the Lord

Continuing the theme of judgment, Paul addresses disagreements about holy days (14:5). The present tense implies routine, repeated observances, pointing to Sabbath observance as the most likely issue. Apparently some Jewish, and perhaps gentile, believers insist on keeping Sabbath and attending synagogue services; others do not. Paul, however, speaks in a general way to make the basic point that each person honors God in distinctive ways and has the freedom to do so.

In Greek, the exhortation "let all be fully convinced in their own minds" is in the singular, continuing the pointed advice to individuals in 14:4. In these matters of practice, Paul emphatically honors and trusts the freedom of individual consciences before God. "Mind" recalls the renewal of the mind for the sake of the community (12:2). Therefore this "freedom" of individuals is freedom for relationship, exercised in the context of connection with others and of care for what will contribute to the faith of one's neighbor. "Be fully convinced" (*plērophoreisthō*) is the verb that describes Abraham's faith (4:21): he was "fully convinced [*plērophorētheis*] that God was able [*dynatos*] to do what he had promised." The point is that faith entails such conviction about God's power, whether to fulfill a specific promise, as in Abraham's case, or to establish each person's worth before God (14:4). In 14:6 Paul gives the theological rationale for this individual freedom: widely divergent actions can be done "for the Lord" and therefore in honor of the Lord.

Panning out from specific practices, in 14:7–9 Paul frames this freedom for individual convictions in terms of belonging to one Lord, in life and in death. This is not a "freedom" conceived in terms of individual autonomy, but rather in terms of belonging to one Lord who authorizes diverse practices. It is this membership and therefore service to the same Lord that provides the only check against misguided decisions and division in the community, and the only basis for a unity that is not exclusive or coercive. By reminding his listeners of the earthly parameters of their lives in living and dying to the Lord, Paul puts their individual differences in perspective. Even more importantly, he reminds them that Christ died and lived again for their sake, and this living Christ is Lord over their life and death.

14:10–12. The Judgment Seat of God

Paul's question in 14:10 recalls his question in 14:4, now directed against both those who "despise" Torah-observant believers, and the "weak in faith" who judge those who eat and drink. Believers are not ultimately accountable to each other; rather, "all will stand before the judgment seat of God" (cf. 2 Cor 5:10). The "judgment seat" (*bēma*) was the raised seat on which judges sat, the "bench" before which defendants stood in court. This anticipation of the eschatological judgment at the last day builds on Paul's emphasis on the risen Christ as "Lord of both the dead and the living" (Rom 14:9). It also builds on Paul's contrast between human and divine judgment in 2:1–5, where Paul also calls out individuals who judge others, warning them that they will face "the day of wrath, when God's righteous judgment will be revealed." In 14:10–12, however, Paul's emphasis on the last day is not concerned with wrath; rather, speaking to believers, he has already assured them that "God has welcomed them" and "is powerful to make them stand" at the last day (14:4); indeed, whether they live or die, they belong to the Lord (14:8).

In 14:11 Paul supports this image of standing before the judgment seat of God with a scriptural citation from Isaiah 45:23, introduced by the prophetic formula "as I live, says the Lord" (cf. Isa 49:18; Num 14:28; Zeph 2:9; Jer 22:24; 46:18). In Philippians 2:10 Paul also cites Isaiah 45:23 explicitly in relationship to Christ: "At the name given to Jesus every knee should bend, . . . and every tongue should confess that Jesus Christ is Lord, to the glory of God the Father." At every point, Paul grounds his admonitions explicitly and exclusively on the lordship and final judgment of Christ, which here gives individual believers hope in God's redeeming power and at the same time undercuts mutual judgment. Paul draws the conclusion in Romans 14:12, again in strikingly individual terms: "Each one of us will be held accountable." In Greek, "will be held accountable" is "will give a word" (*dōsei logon*), a phrase used for financial as well as behavioral accountability. At the great assize, the entire self will be subject to God's assessment, with a focus on personal accountability that is typical of Paul's depictions of the Last Judgment (cf. Gal 6:4–5; 2 Cor 5:10).

14:13–23. Don't Be a Stumbling Block!

14:13–14. Mutual Respect, Not Judgment

If God's power functions to make all God's servants "stand" before the only judgment that counts (14:4), the misuse of human judgment can make them "stumble" (v. 13). In 1 Corinthians 8:9–13 Paul shows similar concern lest Christian freedom cause fellow believers to "stumble" by acting against their conscience. The situation in Rome is somewhat different, in that the specific issue in Corinth is idolatry, but the logic is similar (cf. Mark 9:42); Paul is concerned lest the freedom of some believers cause others to act against their faith.

Briefly switching to the first-person singular, in Romans 14:14 Paul identifies with the view that "nothing is unclean in itself." Indeed, he stresses his conviction "in the Lord Jesus," which may imply knowledge of Jesus's teachings (cf. Mark 7:15; Acts 11:9). More to the point, trusting solely in Christ means that dietary practices are irrelevant for one's standing before God, as Paul makes clear in 4:17. So also, in Romans 15:1 he aligns himself with "the strong" (in faith) in contrast with those who are "weak in faith" (14:1)—a "weakness" demonstrated by anxiety about food practices. Nonetheless, here Paul's concern is for anyone who "considers" or "reckons" (*logizomenō*) certain foods to be unclean according to Jewish beliefs. Although in Galatians 2:11–12 Paul harshly criticizes Peter for refusing table fellowship with gentile believers, in Romans 14 he criticizes gentiles and perhaps nonobservant Jews for treating Jewish scruples with contempt. His exhortation is not based on arguments about the religious status of different dietary practices but on concern for the faith of one's neighbors, regardless of their practices.

14:15–21 Walking in Love

Thus, in 14:15–21, Paul tells his listeners to consider what it means to "walk in love" toward their brothers and sisters rather than "distressing" them. He structures his exhortation by inverse parallelism, as follows:

15 A Do not let what you eat cause the ruin of one for whom Christ died
    16 B Do not let your good be slandered
        17 C The kingdom of God is not food or drink, but righteousness, peace, and joy in the Holy Spirit

18–19 B′ This is the way to please God and be approved by others, through mutual upbuilding and peace

20 A′ Do not, for the sake of food, destroy the work of God.

The repeated prohibition against harming fellow believers is the ethical point, but it is built around two concentric concerns: the public display of what pleases God and causes upbuilding and peace, and the central theological claim about the kingdom of God.

Paul uses two words in 14:15 to denote harm: "distressed" (*lupeitai*), which can mean simply "irritated, disgusted, outraged," and "cause the ruin" (*apollue*), which means "destroy" and is intensified by the related word *katalue* (destroy) in 14:20. What might look like distress to the one who eats in fact may destroy the faith of the one who thinks such eating is unclean. Paul emphasizes the heinous nature of such destruction by naming its victim as "one for whom Christ died." His warnings refer to behavior at shared meals in the house churches, where the public consumption of meat could exert considerable social pressure on those who felt compelled to abstain as a matter of faith.

For Torah-observant believers to act against their convictions would not feel like a minor slip but a violation of covenant loyalty. Paul takes the dangers of such violation seriously, not because the believers will be subject to divine judgment but because, insofar as they consider their belief in Christ to be inseparable from Torah observances, they might well remove themselves entirely from the community and abandon their faith. For the meat-eating believer to act with callous disregard toward such a brother or sister is the opposite of "walking in love."

The "good" in 14:16 is the freedom given by the gospel; if it is abused by callous indifference toward fellow believers, it will be "slandered" (*blasphēmeisthō*)—that is, brought into disrepute. That Paul has the public reputation of the gospel in mind is clear from 14:17. Yet it is worth pondering whose opinion matters here. As noted earlier, in line with Roman scorn toward Jewish practices, most pagan Romans would approve the one who eats meat and jeer at the one who abstains. It is the Jews whose opinion matters here for Paul; he does not want the gospel to be "blasphemed" and discredited to his Jewish brothers and sisters.

Nonetheless, the basis for Paul's exhortations does not come from Mosaic law but from God's kingly rule, which is "righteousness and peace and joy in the Holy Spirit" (14:17). Paul rarely refers to the kingdom of God, but when he does, the term is always associated with the quality of fellowship among Christians in view of the present and coming reign of God (1 Cor 4:20; 6:9–10; 15:50; Gal 5:21; cf. Eph 5:5).

In 14:18–19, being "acceptable [*euarestos*] to God" and garnering "human approval" (*dokimos*) echo 12:2, where Paul envisions a renewal of the mind that leads to a public demonstration (*dokimazein*) of God's will, "what is good [*agathon*] and acceptable [*euareston*] and perfect." The pursuit of peace and mutual "upbuilding" further enacts "walking in love." "Upbuilding" (*oikodomēs*) comes from the word for house (*oikos*) and is one of Paul's favorite metaphors for constructing Christian community (1 Cor 3:9–10; 8:1; 14:3–5, 12, 26; 2 Cor 10:8; 12:19; 13:10). As Paul puts it succinctly in 1 Corinthians 8:1, in the context of an argument closely parallel to Romans 14, "Knowledge puffs up, but love builds up [*oikodomei*]."

Romans 14:20 mirrors 14:15 through the repetition of "for the sake of food" and "destroy" (*apollue* in v. 15; *katalue* in v. 20). Now, however, Paul repeats the warning against destroying "one for whom Christ died" as a warning against destroying "the work of God." "The work of God" *is* the fellow believer for whom Christ died, whose faith might be destroyed by making them "fall" or "stumble" (vv. 20–21, 13). These verses sum up Paul's counsel concerning "clean" and "unclean" foods. On the one hand, everything is clean (v. 14), but on the other hand, no believers should be compelled to act against their convictions (vv. 20b–21). Therefore, in deference to the scruples of those who want to avoid potentially nonkosher food, those who "have faith to eat anything" (v. 2) should willingly forgo the exercise of their dietary freedom in favor of a vegetarian menu for communal meals.

14:22–23. Faith and Freedom

In line with 14:20–21, Paul continues to speak primarily to those who "have faith to eat anything." What believers eat in private is between them and God, as 14:22 makes clear. This verse presents a bit of a puzzle to the interpreter. The word translated as "conviction" in the NRSVue is literally "faith" (*pistis*); a close translation would be, "The faith that you have, have (or keep) to yourself before God." In other words: "Keep your faith that you can eat anything between you and God and publicly behave in the most loving way toward your neighbor." Paul here allows a distinction between what individual believers do in private and what they do in public. Furthermore, he tells his listeners that if their public behavior is guided by love for their neighbor, neither they nor their Torah-observant brother or sister need fall into self-judgment over private ethical decisions: "Blessed are those who do not condemn [*krinōn*] themselves because of what they approve [*dokimazei*]."

The closing exhortation in 14:23 speaks primarily about "the weak" who would "have doubts" (*diakrinomenos*) about eating meat. "Have doubts" means "be of two minds," in the sense of wavering between two opinions. Paul's earlier description of Abraham's faith (4:20) clarifies his meaning here. In Greek, 4:20 reads, "He did not waver [*diekrithē*] in unbelief [*apistia*] concerning God's promise, but he was empowered [*enedynamōthē*] in faith as he gave glory to God." Abraham did not waver in trust that God would give him a son, because he trusted God's power. Paul wants the "weak in faith" (14:1) not to waver but to act in accordance with their convictions because they trust in God's welcome of them. The threat of condemnation may refer to God's condemnation (2:1; 1 Cor 11:32), to self-judgment (Rom 14:22), or to both. Paul wants to reassure those with scruples about dietary practices that they may and should follow their conscience in such matters.

"Whatever does not proceed from faith is sin" has long puzzled interpreters. If we understand "from faith" in light of its sense throughout Romans as trust in Christ's trustworthiness (1:17; 3:26, 30; 4:16; 5:1; 9:30, 32; 10:6), the meaning becomes somewhat clearer. Paul wants his listeners to act out of their trust in Christ rather than any other compulsion; they may do this apart from observing kosher and Sabbath laws, or through such observance. What worries Paul is the possibility that, under social pressure, people will act contrary to the faith that they "have before God" (14:22) and thereby deny their own trust in Christ.

15:1–6. The Examples of Christ and Scripture

15:1–3. Following Christ's Example

For the first time, in 15:1 Paul uses the term "the strong" (*dynatoi*) and includes himself in that category, in comparison with the "weak" (*adynatoi*). A literal, somewhat wooden translation of the verse would be, "We who are powerful are indebted to bear the weaknesses of the powerless and not to please ourselves." Each word of this loaded sentence amplifies key Pauline themes and applies them to the specific issue of divergent practices in the community. Paul elsewhere qualifies "strong" (*dynatoi*) in terms of reliance on Christ (2 Cor 12:10; Phil 4:13), which matches his depiction of faith that relies on Christ alone, apart from any distinctive cultural or social supports; by implication, the faith of "the powerless" (*adynatoi*) is dependent on the exercise of particular cultural or ethnic practices. "Indebted" (*opheilomen*) amplifies Paul's earlier command to "owe [*opheilete*] no one anything, except to love one another" (13:8), which is precisely the point of 14:1–15:6. "Bear" (*bastazein*) simply means to carry a burden, both physically and metaphorically; elsewhere Paul says such bearing of one another's burdens "fulfills the law of Christ" (Gal 6:2). Given the contempt with which some Roman gentiles looked on Jewish dietary and Sabbath practices, such bearing of weaknesses has a concrete, social sense. It means sharing with one's fellow believer in bearing ostracism and judgment by the dominant culture. It means "bearing with" one another.

The thrust of Paul's exhortations has been toward the "strong in faith," but in Romans 15:2 "each of us" includes both "the strong" and "the weak" in the call to put one's neighbor before oneself and attend to what makes for mutual upbuilding (cf. 14:19). Paul's singular emphasis continues the individual focus of his exhortations (14:5, 12). Those who can eat everything without compromising their faith (14:2) can honor their fellow believers by refraining from eating meat and perhaps from drinking wine at shared meals; the vegetarians show honor by refraining from judging those with different practices and instead welcoming them as full members in Christ's fellowship.

In 15:3, Christ is the model for neighbor love that bears with others' weaknesses and puts them first (Phil 2:1–13; 2 Cor 8:9). Paul quotes Psalm 69:9b, a Davidic psalm from which he also quotes in Romans 11:9. In 11:9 Paul names David as the speaker of the psalm, but now Paul ascribes the psalmist's voice to Christ. Immediately prior to the quoted line, Psalm 69:9a says, "It is zeal for your house that has consumed me." In other words, the psalmist suffers insults on God's behalf because of his own "zeal." By ascribing these words to Christ, Paul portrays him in solidarity with Jewish believers who are zealous for the law. In this way, Christ models what Paul tells "the powerful" to do—to share in suffering insults and opprobrium for behaving like a Jew in a gentile culture. Perhaps even more than a model, Christ's living voice invites the powerful to share his own suffering with those who are insulted and mocked, for such *koinōnia* is indeed a sharing in Christ's suffering. Thus, the power of the powerful is shown not by lording it over the powerless but by becoming socially weak in solidarity with their fellow believers.

15:4. The Example of Scripture

Paul's claim about Scripture in 15:4 is striking: it was written for "our instruction" (*didaskalion*). Paul immediately explains what he means by instruction: it is not rules about what to do and what not to do, but "steadfastness" (*hypomonē*) and "encouragement" (*paraklēseōs*), which together lead to hope. Scripture thus mediates Christ's voice through the psalm citation, so that what was written "in former days" is now "*our* instruction." "Endurance" and "hope" echo 5:3–5, which set the agenda for Paul's depiction of Christian life in chapters 5–8. Now Paul encompasses the unified fellowship of the strong and the weak within this trajectory of endurance and hope, indeed trusting in the Christ who died for us "while we were still weak" (5:6).

15:5–6. Blessing from the God of Steadfastness and Encouragement

Paul's prayer for divine blessing (15:5–6) identifies God as the source of steadfastness and encouragement, *because* God grants (*dōē*) "harmony with one another." The Greek is "to think the same thing" (*to auto phronein*), recalling Paul's earlier depiction of the renewed communal mindset characteristic of fellowship in Christ (12:16); now he names this shared mindset as God's blessing bestowed on believers. Does this mean that Paul expects the erasure of all differences in practice among his listeners? That would contradict everything he has said regarding the weak and the strong. Rather, Paul qualifies "harmony with one another" by the phrase "in accordance with Christ Jesus." This could mean "following Christ's example," in which case the immediate example at hand is one of solidarity in sharing reproach, not in every aspect of dietary practice. Paul also could mean "in accordance with the will of Christ," which would entail shared prayer and openness to Christ's leading in seeking that will. Both interpretations imply a deepening of fellowship that is not based on forced conformity but rather on attentive openness to Christ and to one another.

Finally, the goal and expression of the shared mindset gifted by God is in fact glorifying God with one voice (15:6). Such united and vocal glorification of God reverses humanity's rebellion against God (1:21) and its toxic speech (3:14, 19). As such, it takes the focus off differences in practice and puts it on the one God who brings together both "weak" and "strong" and indeed both Jew and gentile (3:29–30). In 15:7–13 Paul returns to his passionate hope for present communities of Jewish and gentile followers of Jesus and his eschatological expectation that through Christ, ultimately Jews and gentiles will worship together. This *telos* sources a unity that is not trivial, premature, or forced, because it is based not on conformity or excluding difference but on the God who welcomes all into the kingdom of righteousness, peace, and joy in the Holy Spirit.

In 15:5 Paul names God as "the God of steadfastness and encouragement"; in verse 6 he names God as "the God and Father of our Lord Jesus Christ." In fact, Paul frequently names God in relationship to Jesus Christ, as "God and Father" (1 Cor 1:3; 2 Cor 11:31) and as the one who raised Jesus from the dead (Rom 4:24; 2 Cor 4:14; Gal 1:1). He also names God in relationship to human beings, particularly as "our Father" (Rom 1:7; 1 Cor 1:3; 2 Cor 1:2; Gal 1:3–4; Phil 1:2; 1 Thess 1:3), as the one who calls us (1 Thess 2:12), and as the one who reconciles us through Christ (2 Cor 5:18). As such, God is the "God of steadfastness and encouragement" (Rom 15:5), the "God of hope" (15:13), the "God of peace" (15:33; 16:20), the "God of love" (2 Cor 13:11), and the "Father of mercies" (2 Cor 1:3). All of these names for God describe God's actions for both gentiles and Jews and are the basis of the unity Paul seeks in Christian fellowship.

EXCURSUS

Reflections for Preaching and Teaching

Only God Tells Us Who We Are

"Why do you pass judgment on your brother or sister? Or you, why do you despise your brother or sister? For we will all stand before the judgment seat of God." To judge or despise our fellow Christians is to say that we get to define who they are, what they are worth, and how they must live. This is a key aspect of every form of oppression, whether based on race, ethnicity, gender, social or economic class, or religious practices. It creeps into the church through cultural identity markers and the social capital, or lack thereof, that accompanies them. The expectation of *God's* judgment, over against every *human* judgment, is a powerful antidote to this presumption, not least because only God knows who each of us truly is, and only God will judge. As Paul sees it, the expectation of God's future judgment makes it impossible to pronounce final judgment in the present, and thus creates space for openness to the future and to one another, particularly the pew mates whom we do not understand and with whom we do not see eye to eye.

Furthermore, Paul's insistence on honoring believers' private faith before God (14:22) also honors the mystery of each person. No human being can be captured or reduced or contained in any category. As the old spiritual puts it, "Nobody knows who I am 'til the judgment morning." But God knows, and the promise is that God is powerful to make each person stand before the presence of the Lord and of one another. This is the end of stereotyping, name-calling, and canceling each other out. So white folks don't get to tell Black folks who they are, and Black folks don't get to tell white folks who they are. Progressives can't label and reject conservatives, the right can't label and dismiss the left, Episcopalians can't sneer at Baptists, and so forth. Nor can first-world Christians talk smugly about their fellow Christians in the two-thirds world. Nor can clergy complain about their congregations, with church members returning the favor. All of this is wiped out by Paul's simple question, "Who are you to despise your brother or sister?"

Moral Injury and Destroying One's Neighbor

Paul's warning against behavior that might "injure" and "destroy" one's fellow Christians is notable; we are not used to thinking about the importance of honoring one another's convictions in such extreme terms. Perhaps we are not used to thinking of faith as a matter of life and death, but this is very much how Paul thinks, and his words challenge us to reckon with the soul-sucking, deadening effects of moral, spiritual, and psychological coercion that drives people to act against their faith in Christ. For example, veterans and others who suffer the aftereffects of trauma have an intimate knowledge of the costs of acting contrary to one's deepest beliefs. In treatment for post-traumatic stress disorder (PTSD), the term "moral injury" refers to the distressing psychological, social, behavioral, and spiritual aftermath of behavior that violates moral convictions. Moral injury may lead to debilitating depression, family trauma, social isolation, and suicidal thoughts and actions. The correlation between faith and action *is* a matter of life and death.

Of course, not all pressure to deny one's convictions is so dramatic. Rather, it happens quietly in daily life, in jobs and family interactions, and in churches. Parishioners quietly go elsewhere to worship or stop going to church altogether. And sometimes no one notices. In Paul's view, to pressure another to act contrary to practices that are integral to their faith is to risk driving them completely away from the faith. While this may seem over the top in a culture that says, "It doesn't matter what you believe, as long as you're sincere," Paul operates with a different logic, a logic that says faith in Christ is ultimately all that matters. His counsel for navigating differences in practice, which always entail differences in belief to some degree, shifts our focus from trying to convince others to conform to our norms, to asking, "How can I come to be trusted by another in such a way that we both change?" And perhaps even more challenging, "How can I grow to trust the fellow believers with whom I disagree, so that we both can be changed?" This is a call to love the other people in the pew well enough to know what deeply matters to them. The alternative is a subtle but callous indifference to the spiritual and psychological well-being of our brothers and sisters.

15:7–13. Welcome One Another for the Glory of God

Romans 15:7–13 repeats the pattern of 15:1–6, with an opening exhortation, a reference to Christ, quotations from Scripture, an emphasis on hope, and a concluding benediction. But whereas in verses 1–6 the focus is on believers' mutual welcome to the glory of God, in verses 7–13 the focus turns to Christ's welcoming embrace in fulfillment of the patriarchal promises. Therefore in verse 7 Paul emphasizes Jesus's messianic title as "*the* Christ" ("Christ" in the NRSVue), the anointed one of Israel. "For the glory of God" repeats the encouragement of 15:6.

These verses sum up Paul's teaching in 14:1–15:6. But they also bring the entire body of the letter to a climax with a sweeping vision of all humanity glorifying God together in a powerful reversal of humanity's primal refusal to glorify and honor God (1:21). They proclaim Jesus as the Christ for both Jews and gentiles, God as the God of hope, and the Holy Spirit as the source of power for trust that abounds in hope.

15:7. As Christ Has Welcomed You

Building on his command to welcome the believer whose faith is weak because God has welcomed that person (14:1, 3), Paul now challenges the entire community of gentile and Jewish Christians: "Welcome one another, therefore, just as the Christ [*ho Christos*] has welcomed you, for the glory of God" (15:7). His admonition follows directly from the inclusive benediction of verses 5–6.

15:8–9a. Christ the Servant of the Circumcised

Verses 8–9a form one sentence that is difficult to translate. The first clause (v. 8) is a straightforward description of Christ as a "servant [*diakonos*] of the circumcised." "The circumcised" denotes the Jewish people in distinction from gentiles (3:30; 4:12; cf. Gal 2:7). By naming Christ as "servant," Paul may assume a messianic interpretation of the Servant of the Lord in Isaiah 49:3–6, who not only will raise up the tribes of Jacob but will also be a light to the gentiles. Here "servant of the circumcised" implies belonging and origin: Christ belongs to Israel, and indeed came from the Jews by fleshly descent (9:5) as the Son of David (1:3). "Has become" denotes a past event with continuing action in the present; Christ became and remains a servant of the Jewish people.

Christ's servanthood is on behalf of God's truthfulness, for the purpose of confirming God's promises to the patriarchs. The entire verse 8 echoes 3:1–7, where God's truthfulness and faithfulness persist despite human falsehood and faithlessness. "To confirm" (*bebaiōsai*) can also be translated "to establish" or "to fulfill." "The promises" recalls 9:5; these (plural) promises refer to God's promise to Abraham that he would "inherit the world" (4:13) and become "the father of many nations [*ethnoi*, gentiles]" (4:17). Through the conversion of gentiles as followers of Christ, those promises are indeed being fulfilled. Paul thus insists on both Christ's Jewish identity and the indestructible tie between gentile believers and God's faithfulness to Israel.

Thus far Paul's meaning is clear, but 15:9a can be translated in a variety of ways. If we remove the English punctuation and versification and read verses 8–9a as a whole, with careful attention to the main verbs ("has become," "confirm," "glorify") and the parallel clauses in Greek ("on behalf of God's truthfulness" and "on behalf of mercy"), we arrive at the following translation: "For I say Christ has become a servant of the circumcised for the sake of the truth of God, in order to confirm the promises of the fathers, and in order that the gentiles might glorify God for the sake of his mercy" (Wagner 1997). This translation keeps the close parallelism between God's mercy and truth (cf. Ps 85:10), and the connection between gentile praise of God and the fulfillment of God's promises to Israel.

The conversion of gentile believers not only fulfills God's promise to Abraham that through his offspring he would become the father of many gentiles (4:16–18); it also is integral to the destiny of Israel (11:25–28). Thus, although the patriarchal promises certainly belong to the Jews (9:4), the gentiles also are beneficiaries of those promises. Conversely, gentile believers must remember and honor Israel's priority in God's providential redemption of the world (11:11–24). Ultimately Jewish and gentile believers share the same destiny, through the same operation of God's unfathomable mercy (11:30–32) and gift (11:33–36). All of Paul's argument in chapters 9–11 drives toward this point, which in turn undergirds his plea in 15:7 for mutual welcome, to the glory of God.

15:9b–12. "Rejoice, O Gentiles, with His People"

In 15:9b–12, "as it is written" introduces a series of citations drawn from the three components of Israel's Scripture: the Writings (vv. 9, 11), the Law (v. 10), and the Prophets (v. 12). Paul has chosen texts that highlight the inclusion of gentiles *together with* God's people Israel in the worship of God. In 15:9, an exact quotation of David's words in Psalm 18:49 now expresses the Messiah's praise of God among the gentiles. The psalm itself is David's song of thanksgiving for deliverance from all his enemies (2 Sam 22:50). If Paul has the context of the psalm in mind, he flips its meaning; David extols

God's name among the gentile nations because God has granted him victory over them, whereas Christ extols God for showing mercy to the gentiles. The "enemies" have become fellow worshipers of the one Lord, "the God and Father of our Lord Jesus Christ" (15:6).

In 15:10, Paul quotes from the Greek version of Deuteronomy 32:43, which differs considerably from the Hebrew by adding the phrase "gentiles, with his people." As in Psalm 18, the larger context of Deuteronomy 32 promises victory over gentiles, but Paul extracts and modifies a quotation that speaks instead of gentiles joining with Israel in praising God. This conversion of enemies into fellow worshipers is the ultimate victory for which Paul confidently hopes (cf. 12:21); through Christ's welcome, gentiles will praise God *with* God's people Israel. The following quotation in 15:11 is directly from Psalm 117:1, which explicitly names God's praise by "all you gentiles" and "all the people," referring to the Jews.

Finally, in 15:12, a citation of the Greek version of Isaiah 11:10 brings the catena to a close with a messianic reference to Jesus as the "root of Jesse" (Isa 11:1–10; cf. Jer 23:5–6; 33:15–16; for the Messiah as the root of David, see Sir 47:22; cf. Rev 5:5; 22:16). "The one who rises" may allude to the resurrection of Christ, as Paul uses the same verb (*anistēmi*) elsewhere to allude to resurrection (1 Thess 4:14, 16). These allusions link 15:12 with the beginning of the letter, where Paul says Jesus "was descended from David according to the flesh and was declared to be Son of God with power according to the Spirit of holiness by resurrection from the dead" (1:3–4). The closing reference to "hope" links the entire catena to 15:4; indeed, 15:9–12 demonstrates the "encouragement of the scriptures" that generates hope, precisely by promising that all will join in glorifying "the God and Father of our Lord Jesus Christ" (15:6).

15:13 The God of Hope

The concluding benediction in 15:13 both mirrors 15:5–6 and brings the entire body of the letter to a close under the banner of "the God of hope." Significantly Paul crowns his message to the Roman Christians by emphasizing the power of the Holy Spirit, which God has gifted to the believing community as the conduit of divine love (v. 5). The indwelling Spirit of the one who raised Jesus from the dead moves powerfully among those who belong to Christ and indeed will give life to their mortal bodies (8:11). Paul describes his own ministry as "what Christ has accomplished through me . . . by the power of the Spirit" (15:18–19). From the opening acclamation of the gospel as "God's saving power for everyone who believes" (1:16) to the eschatological miracle of a united humanity glorifying God together (15:13), the power of God's victory over sin and death, mediated through the indwelling Spirit, is the basis of Paul's confident benediction. Indeed, Paul's prayer that the Roman believers may "abound [*perissuein*] in hope" echoes the "abundance [*perisseian*] of grace and the gift of righteousness" they have received through Jesus Christ (5:17). God's overflowing abundance (11:35) sources the peace (cf. 5:1) and joy for which Paul prays.

Finally, hope runs like a red thread through the tapestry of the letter. God is the "God of hope" because God raised Jesus from the dead. Because Abraham believed in the God "who gives life to the dead and calls into existence the things that do not exist," he "hoped against hope" as "he believed that he would become 'the father of many nations'" (4:17–18). Grounded in "this grace in which we stand" and empowered by the experience of God's love through the gifted Holy Spirit, believers rejoice in "hope of sharing the glory of God" (5:2), a hope that grows through suffering, steadfastness, and proven character, and will never be put to shame (vv. 3–5). In solidarity with the yearning of all creation that has been "subjected to futility . . . in hope" of liberation (8:20–21), Paul encourages his listeners as they hope for the redemption of their bodies (8:23). That hope is not yet seen (8:24–25) but is expressed through and with the indwelling Spirit of God (8:26–27). Precisely because "we hope for what we do not see," hope is paired with patient endurance or steadfastness (*hypomonē*; 5:4–5; 8:24; 15:4).

For what do believers hope? Ultimately, they hope for the liberation of all creation from bondage to decay into the "freedom of the glory of the children of God" (8:20–21). Ultimately, they hope for the salvation of all Israel together with the fullness of the gentiles, "for what will [Israel's] acceptance [*proslēmpsis*] be but life from the dead?" (11:15). Paul's exhortation to Jewish and gentile believers to welcome (*proslambanesthe*) one another is a sign of this resurrection hope for all creation. This is the eschatological, all-inclusive horizon of hope.

Yet in the present, eagerly awaiting a hope that is not yet seen, believers also find strength in the midst of struggle, failure, and defeats as well as victories, through the certainty that nothing is wasted because "all things work together for good for those who love God, who are called according to God's purpose" (8:28). The public, cosmic horizon of hope is the eager expectation that God will reconcile and redeem all creation, liberating it from the powers of destruction and death. The personal, more immediate hope that sustains believers in the present is that God will use their afflictions as well as joys to conform them to the image of Christ, so that they too may be glorified with him (8:17, 29–30).

EXCURSUS

Reflections for Preaching and Teaching

The Source and Horizon of Hope

Here at the end of the main body of the letter, Paul expands the horizon of hope to include the reconciliation of all humanity to God and to each other. His designation of God as the "God of hope" means that God grants this all-encompassing vision; it certainly does not evolve out of the status quo. While some experiences may strengthen trust in God in the middle of adversity, others may tempt us to despair. But the breathtaking scope of Paul's hope arrives from an unimaginable future that only God can bring to pass. For this reason, trusting God with the future precludes looking for hope in all the wrong places, whether our own markers of success or human attempts to manipulate events. Sooner or later, in myriad ways, this difficult education in hope happens to each one of us. Jesus faced it in Gethsemane.

In his searing book, *When Breath Becomes Air*, a young neurosurgeon named Paul Kalanithi chronicles the final year of his life as he faces terminal lung cancer (Kalanithi 2016). He writes that he always knew he would die, but now he knew it intensely. In one scene, he describes traveling to Wisconsin to explore a job offer. As he looked out at a beautiful scene overlooking a lake and his host said to him, "All this could be yours," Kalanithi realized that the future for which he had worked for more than a decade was now a fantasy. He had to learn to reimagine hope, to rethink the meaning of his life.

What do we hope for in the face of inevitable death? As we grapple with the reality of death, the nonoptional journey that each of us faces, the question morphs into a new one: not what do we hope for, but rather, in whom do we place our trust? How do we trust God with the lives of those whom we love but must leave? How do we trust God for a future beyond what we can imagine? With Abraham, how do we hope beyond hope?

Joy and Peace in Believing

Shortly after Russia invaded Ukraine in 2022, the Chicago Symphony Orchestra performed Beethoven's Symphony No. 9, which closes with a famous chorale, "Ode to Joy." The conductor, Riccardo Muti, spoke directly to the audience just prior to the performance and dedicated it to the people of Ukraine. He referred to the horrific images of the war on the nightly news, and then said, "Tonight, in the final movement of the symphony, Beethoven, taking the text from [Friedrich] Schiller, he speaks about joy, joy, joy. But we will think in that moment that joy without peace cannot exist." Muti went on to speak of war not only in Ukraine, but throughout the world, concluding, "We are against all that" (https://www.youtube.com/watch?v=b526O61co3k).

In Romans, peace is a keynote that runs from 5:1 to Paul's final naming of God as "the God of peace" (15:33; 16:20); joy, which Paul names as characteristic of God's reign (14:17) and as one of the fruits of the Spirit (Gal 5:22), is what Paul anticipates when he finally is able to come to Rome (Rom 15:32). Muti's words remind us that joy and peace are inseparable and that they require the flourishing of all humanity. In a world consumed by war, violence, and hatred, to speak of peace and joy is to witness to a divine reality that runs clean contrary to the status quo and to believe that it will have the last word. Weeks after the war began, Ukrainian musicians performed Beethoven's "Ode to Joy" in Maidan Square in the middle of Kyiv, surrounded by the rubble of war, as a testament to hope (Sudarsan Raghavan, "Music as Resistance: Kyiv's Orchestra Plays On," *Washington Post,* March 10, 2022). Despite all appearances to the contrary, by the grace and power of the Holy Spirit, joy and peace will have the last word; this is the eschatological "hope beyond hope" that is the lodestar of Christian witness in a divided world.

The Conclusion of the Letter

Romans 15:14–16:27

Travel Plans and Greetings

Romans 15:14–16:27

Paul has concluded the "gift" of his gospel proclamation to the Roman house churches (1:10–15). Now returning to the letter style of 1:1–15, he resumes discussion of his anticipated visit to Rome. This final section of Romans divides into three main subsections: Paul's recapitulation of his ministry and future travel plans (15:14–33); his personal greetings to numerous members of the Roman congregations (16:1–23); and a concluding doxology (16:25–27).

ROMANS 15:14–33
Paul's Mission and Travel Plans

After briefly recapping his purpose in writing to the Roman churches, Paul returns to the topic of his gentile mission and his hoped-for trip to Rome, elaborating on his own calling and ministry so that his audience will be inclined to support him in his planned trip to Spain (15:24). First, he clarifies his calling to preach to the gentiles and speaks in general terms about what Christ has accomplished through him in his travels around the eastern Mediterranean (vv. 14–21). Then he speaks directly about his desire to continue on to Spain by way of Rome (vv. 22–24, 28–29) after his journey to Jerusalem (vv. 25–27). He concludes by requesting prayer for the Jerusalem trip (vv. 30–33).

15:14–21. Paul's Past and Present Ministry

Aware that he has written a lengthy exhortation to churches that he did not establish and over whom he has no authority, Paul again (1:8) compliments the Roman believers on their faith; perhaps he wants to forestall any suspicion that he will trespass on the welcome he hopes to receive from them. Woe unto a guest who lectures his hosts! Hence the politely apologetic tone of 15:14–15. Paul's fulsome description of the Roman believers presumes the empowering effects of the gospel in their midst: in contrast with the idolaters of 1:29, they are *full* of goodness (*mestoi agathōsunēs*), rather than "full of envy" and other evils (*mestous phthonou phonou*); they have been *filled* (*peplērōmenoi*) with all knowledge, rather than filled with every kind of unrighteousness (*peplērōmenous pasē adikia*). Empowered by the gospel as the power of God for salvation (1:16), and in the power of the Holy Spirit (15:13), they are powerfully able (*dynameis*) to instruct one another (cf. 1 Thess 5:14). "One another" emphasizes the mutuality and reciprocity of such admonishment among all believers. By stressing the capability and maturity of those whom he now affectionately calls *my* brothers and sisters, Paul acknowledges that they do not need *him* to tell them how to behave!

The slightly apologetic tone of 15:14 continues in 15:15a; "I have written to you rather boldly by way of reminder" acknowledges that at least some of what Paul has written is already well-known to the Roman Christians. But "on some points" also acknowledges that some of what he has written may be new to them. All of this is polite discourse aimed at defusing any potential insult to the sensibilities of Paul's listeners, thus preparing the way for his restatement of his unique apostolic calling in 15:15b (cf. 1:5).

The foundation of divine grace and gift again surfaces in Paul's depiction of his call "because of the grace [*charis*] given [*dotheisan*] me by God" (15:15b). Paul's emphasis on God's unmerited grace gifted through the gospel is the experiential as well as theological bedrock of his life's mission and passion (1:5; 12:3), which both authorize his message and qualify everything he does in terms of what Christ accomplishes through him (15:18).

In 15:16 Paul continues to link his comments with the letter's opening greetings. He began his letter by introducing himself as "a slave of Christ Jesus . . . set apart for the gospel of God" (1:1), and the purpose of his mission as "the obedience of faith among all the gentiles" (1:5). Now he elaborates on that mission using cultic language. The word translated "minister" is *leitourgos,* related to the English word "liturgy." Although Paul sometimes uses this word to speak in general of service (Rom 13:6; Phil 2:25), in the context of 15:16 the word takes on its cultic meaning as "priest" (Neh 10:39; Isa 61:6; Sir 7:30; Heb 8:2; Phil 2:17). Paul describes himself as a "priest of Christ Jesus to the gentiles" and his mission as "priestly service of the gospel of God" (*hierourgounta*). The word means simply "doing the work of a priest"; Paul's vocation is to be a priest "of the gospel of God" (cf. 1:1), which in practical terms means being a priest of Christ Jesus.

Paul continues the cultic metaphor in the next clause, naming the purpose of his priestly ministry—"that the offering [*prosphora*] of the gentiles may be acceptable, sanctified by the Holy Spirit." The "offering of the gentiles" could refer to the obedience (1:5; 15:18) and worship (15:9–12) which the gentiles now offer to God, even as they present their bodies to God as a living sacrifice (12:1). The phrase also could refer to the gentile believers themselves as an "offering" that will be "acceptable" (*euprosdektos*) because they have been sanctified by the Holy Spirit, continuing the theme of the central role of the Spirit in Christian life. Because Paul later asks for prayers that the financial collection he has gathered from the gentile believers will be acceptable (*euprosdektos*) to the saints in Jerusalem (15:31), possibly he also has this concrete meaning for "the offering of the gentiles" in mind, as practical evidence of the gentiles' "obedience."

With Paul's characteristic conjunction of divine and human action, 15:17–18 sums up Paul's ministry and introduces a detailed description of his missionary travels among the gentiles. He begins by boasting not of his own accomplishments (cf. 3:27; 4:2) but "in Christ Jesus" concerning "what pertains to God." The words "of my work" (NRSVue) do not occur in the Greek. It is not that Paul denies his central role in the gentile mission, including his own words and deeds, but he puts the focus on "what Christ has accomplished through me." Christ acts, and because Christ acts, Paul's own speech and actions are effective. Thus "power" dominates the subsequent depiction of his ministry in charismatic terms: the power of "signs and wonders" (15:19) that display the power of the

Spirit (15:13). "Signs and wonders" denote miracles, and frequently appear together to describe God's miraculous deliverance of God's people (e.g., Exod 7:3, 9; 11:9–10; Ps 135:9; Acts 2:22, 43; 4:30; 5:12). Paul takes it for granted that miraculous manifestations of divine power happen in the churches he has founded (1 Cor 2:4; 12:28; Gal 3:5; 1 Thess 1:5) and demonstrate his own bona fides as an apostle (2 Cor 12:12).

Scholars puzzle over Paul's claim to have "fulfilled the gospel from Jerusalem and as far around [*kyklō*] as Illyricum" (the NRSVue's "proclaimed" is not in the Greek). Nowhere in his letters does Paul speak of preaching in Jerusalem; indeed, in Galatians 1:18–19; 2:1–2 he emphasizes the secrecy of his two visits to Jerusalem. So perhaps he means more generally his central role in the spread of the gospel from Jerusalem, where it certainly began, into the pagan as well as Jewish world. If so, then Paul identifies Jerusalem as the center and origin of gospel proclamation. Such a view of the mother city certainly accorded with Jewish sensibilities. For example, Ezekiel 5:5 LXX identifies Jerusalem as the center of the world: "This is Jerusalem; I have set her in the center of the gentiles and in the circle [*kyklos*] of the nations" (author's translation).

Paul's use of *kyklō* ("round about") may refer to a circle or a circular pattern of travel. Illyricum was the area now known as the Balkans, across the Adriatic Sea from Italy. Paul thus describes the geographic scope of his mission as reaching almost to Rome; now he hopes to complete the journey all the way to Rome and beyond, because in his view he has "fulfilled the gospel of Christ" in the regions he has traversed. Obviously, he has not preached in every corner of the vast area between Jerusalem and the Balkan peninsula; rather, he has established churches in key cities and is confident that the gospel will continue to spread out from the fellowships in these cities.

Paul yearns to preach where Christ has not yet been "named" or known; in 15:20 he puts this negatively, "so that I do not build on someone else's foundation" (cf. 2 Cor 10:15–16). As noted in the commentary on 14:19, "build" (*oikodomō*) is one of Paul's images for founding congregations. On the other hand, at the beginning of the letter Paul says he is eager to preach the gospel to the Roman Christians, implying that on some level they have not heard it, despite their faith in Christ (1:15). Is this not "building on another's foundation"? As noted in the commentary, Paul seems to think that the gospel always bears repreaching even to those who "know" it, precisely for the purpose of strengthening people's faith (1:11; 16:25). Perhaps in Paul's mind, and in his missionary experience, these two purposes and contexts for preaching the gospel are not mutually exclusive. Perhaps also he hopes that his version of the gospel in the letter will encourage the Romans to support his mission to those who have not yet heard it. The citation of Isaiah 52:15 in Romans 15:21 provides the scriptural warrant for this mission. In Isaiah the content of the message is the Servant of the Lord; here as earlier, Paul assumes a messianic interpretation of the Servant as referring to Christ.

Finally, it is worth noting again how Paul uses "God" and "Christ" interchangeably (cf. 8:9–11) in relationship to the "gospel of God" (15:16) as the "gospel of Christ." All of this is sustained by the power of the Holy Spirit. As is often noted, Paul's language is implicitly Trinitarian.

15:22–24. Paul's Travel Plans: Spain via Rome

Paul's presentation of his ministry to this point serves two purposes. It explains why it has taken him so long to get to Rome (15:22; cf. 1:10–13) and it establishes his credentials as apostle to the gentiles. Now, Paul turns to his specific travel plans, which involve trips in opposite directions: first east to Jerusalem (15:25–27) and then west to Spain, stopping in Rome en route (vv. 23–24, 28). He begins and ends with reference to the plans for visiting Rome and going on to Spain.

It is a delicate matter to invite oneself to visit people from whom one hopes to receive support, and Paul pulls out all the stops. He will not impose on them for too long and certainly not take over leadership of the communities, but on the other hand, he eagerly looks forward to a good visit (15:24). Only after a fulsome time of mutual acquaintance and sharing in fellowship (cf. 1:12) will Paul and the Roman believers discuss his plans to travel on to Spain and his hope for support in that endeavor. The verb translated "to be sent on" (15:24) is a technical term for provisioning someone for missionary travels, including providing financial assistance (Acts 15:3; 20:38; 21:5; 1 Cor 16:6, 11; 2 Cor 1:16; Titus 3:13). It is entirely possible that this practical help is, at least in part, the "fruit" that Paul hopes to reap from the Roman churches (1:13), particularly since he refers to the financial collection for the Jerusalem church as "fruit" (15:28).

Why Spain? It certainly was gentile territory, indeed popularly associated with "barbarians" and therefore part of Paul's missionary agenda (1:14). As the westernmost part of the Mediterranean world, it also was thought of as the ends of the earth, and as such would complete Paul's ambition to preach the gospel "not where Christ has already been named" (15:20).

15:25–28a Travel to Jerusalem

Before heading west to Rome, Paul will go east to Jerusalem to deliver the funds he has collected from the gentile churches. "The ministry [*diakonōn*] to the saints" indicates that Paul sees this collection as the gentile Christians' service to the Jewish believers in Jerusalem. The importance to Paul of this offering is clear from his many references to it in earlier letters (Gal 2:10; 1 Cor 16:1–4; 2 Cor 8–9) as well as his firm commitment to make the lengthy and dangerous journey to Jerusalem before setting out for Rome.

Macedonia and Achaia (15:26) include places where Paul has founded churches in Corinth and along the coastline running from Greece to present-day Albania, including Philippi, Thessalonica, and Berea. The fact that Paul does not mention Galatia may indicate that the Galatian believers refused to commit to the collection, but this is impossible to determine. "Share their resources" is literally "make *koinōnia*"; the word certainly includes the sense of sharing financial resources, but beyond that, it implies a reciprocal fellowship of mutual exchange in Christ. The meaning is close to that of 12:13a (see commentary) and signifies a concrete, practical expression of the solidarity that Paul seeks between gentile and Jewish believers. "The poor among the saints" refers to extensive poverty among the members of the Jerusalem church; Paul's commitment to collecting funds for the poor among the saints arises from the agreement he made with the leaders of the church in Jerusalem to "remember the poor" (Gal 2:10). For him, this financial gift is a crucial link between his mission to the gentiles and the "mother church" in Jerusalem.

For Paul there is no contradiction between saying that other gentile churches were "pleased" to contribute to the support of poor Jewish believers in Jerusalem and that they "owe it to them" (15:27).

The language of debt recalls 1:14, where Paul speaks of his own debt or obligation to preach the gospel. Here debt signifies a bond created by the giving and receiving of gifts through mutual fellowship; the gentiles have come to share fellowship (*koinōnia*) in the things of the Spirit, and therefore they are indebted to offer priestly service (*leitourgēsai*) in material, indeed "fleshly" (*sarkikois*) things. This is the language of reciprocity and exchange rather than unidirectional gift; in the context of interaction between Jewish and largely gentile churches, it undergirds a relationship of equality. Through giving to the Jerusalem church, gentile churches acknowledge their debt to Israel as the recipient of the promises and the lineage of the Messiah (9:4–5). Through receiving from gentile churches, the Jerusalem believers will have to acknowledge the gentiles as fellow members of the household of God (cf. Eph 2:19). Such acknowledgment is Paul's great hope for his trip to Jerusalem; whether it will happen, however, is beyond his ken or his control.

15:28b–33 Hopes and Prayers

In 15:28–29 Paul briefly restates his plan to deliver the collection to the church in Jerusalem and then be on his way to Rome and hence to Spain. His terminology, which in Greek is literally "when I have sealed to them this fruit," implies his concern to personally guarantee the delivery and reception of the funds (cf. 2 Cor 8:20–23). Hence his commitment to take the funds to Jerusalem in person, and his (perhaps tenuous) confidence that having done so, he will go on to Rome "in the fullness of the blessing of Christ."

In light of what contemporary readers of Romans know, but Paul and his first listeners did not know, his plans and his request for prayer in 15:30–32 are exceedingly poignant. "I appeal to you, brothers and sisters," is a formal request (cf. 12:1) couched in familial language, followed by two parallel supporting clauses invoking the authority of Christ as Lord and the motivation of love that the Spirit gives (5:5). The Greek word translated simply "join me" is *synagōnisthai,* which occurs only here in the New Testament and derives from military conflicts and athletic contests. Paul urges his listeners to "strive urgently together with me in prayer" (author's translation) because he knows he is going into a conflict situation on two fronts: he asks for "rescue" from unbelievers, and he asks that the Jerusalem believers ("the saints") will accept his ministry (15:31). The verb translated "rescue" appears elsewhere in pleas for deliverance from mortal danger (2 Cor 1:10; 2 Thess 3:2; 2 Tim 4:18) and in the Lord's Prayer: "deliver us from evil" (Matt 6:13; Luke 11:4). By "the unbelievers" Paul means Jews who are not followers of Jesus (Rom 10:21; 11:30–31); indeed, Paul was attacked by a violent mob when he attempted to speak in the temple (Acts 21:27–36). He knows that he will have a target on his back when he goes to Jerusalem.

Paul also does not assume the leaders of the Jerusalem assembly will accept the funds collected from the gentile churches, because to do so would be to accept the (non-Torah-observant) gentiles themselves as fellow believers on an equal footing in the faith. His prayer that "my ministry [*diakonia*] to Jerusalem may be acceptable [*euprosdektos*] to the saints" echoes 15:16, where Paul hopes the offering of the gentiles will be acceptable (*euprosdektos*). His anxiety in this regard corresponds with ancient notions of benefaction, in which the giving and receiving of gifts implies and establishes a bond of reciprocity. In the dynamics of an economy based on benefaction and obligation, it was simply unthinkable to "take the money and run," to accept the gift and reject the giver (Barclay 2015, 24–31).

"By God's will"—everything depends on God's will, including Paul's eventual arrival in Rome (15:32). As it happened, Paul did get to Rome, but in chains. Paul uses a rare word to speak of being "refreshed" (*synanapausōmai*) with the Roman believers. Poignantly, the occurrence of two compound verbs beginning with *syn* ("with")—"strive together in prayer" (15:30) and "be refreshed together" (15:32)—show how urgently Paul seeks a bond of fellowship and support with the Roman Christians as he embarks on the next dangerous phase of his missionary journeys.

Paul concludes his travel plans with a third benediction (cf. 15:5, 13), now invoking God as "the God of peace." He surely here is thinking of God as the one who has established peace between God and humanity through Christ's death and resurrection (2:10; 5:1; 8:6) but also peace between believers (14:19). Considering his anxiety about how he will be received in Jerusalem, "the God of peace" indicates Paul's intense trust in the God who establishes peace between enemies, indeed the God who makes peace between the wolf and the lamb, the leopard and the kid (Isa 11:6). As in 15:13, joy and peace are closely related.

EXCURSUS

Reflections for Preaching and Teaching

Shattered Dreams

In a magnificent sermon titled "Shattered Dreams," Martin Luther King Jr. expounds on Paul's simple statement "I do hope to see you on my journey and to be sent on by you, once I have enjoyed your company for a little while" (King 2010, 87–97). King talks about the reality that so often we do not get to see the fulfillment of our dreams: "Who has not set out toward some distant Spain, some momentous goal, or some glorious realization, only to learn at last that he must settle for much less?" He meditates on the temptations that accompany such disappointments—temptations to bitterness, to withdrawal from life, and to fatalism, all of which damage the soul. Rather than succumb to such temptations, says King, we must ask, "How may we turn this liability into an asset?" The ground beneath this hopeful pivot is nothing less than the promise of Romans 8:28, "All things work together for good for those who love God, who are called according to his purpose." But to experience this transmutation of loss and failure into gain and victory, we also need our vision of the "good" transformed. In King's words, "Almost anything that happens to us may be woven into the purposes of God. It may lengthen our cords of sympathy. It may break our self-centered pride. The cross, which was willed by wicked men, was woven by God into the tapestry of world redemption."

As King also reminds us, when Paul wrote these words in Romans, he already had experienced being whipped and stoned, "on frequent journeys, in danger from rivers, danger from bandits, danger from my own people, danger from gentiles, danger in the city, danger in the wilderness, danger at sea, danger from false brothers and sisters; in toil and hardship, through many a sleepless night, hungry and thirsty, often without food, cold and naked" (2 Cor 11:25–27). When Paul writes about learning hope through the experience of afflictions, endurance, and tested character (Rom 5:1–5), he knows whereof he speaks, as he gives us a way to speak about hope in the face of shattered dreams as well.

ROMANS 16:1–23
Greetings and a Warning

Paul brings the letter to a close with extensive greetings that pave the way for his intended stay in Rome. He begins by commending Phoebe, his emissary and the bearer of the letter (16:1–2). Then he sends fulsome greetings to numerous people by name, praising them and demonstrating that he already is known and trusted by many of the believers in Rome (vv. 3–16). These greetings are followed by a solemn warning against any who might cause divisions in the churches (vv. 17–20). Finally, Paul's fellow workers, his amanuensis who transcribed the letter while Paul dictated, and his hosts in Corinth also send their personal greetings (vv. 21–23).

It would be a mistake to overlook the importance of this final chapter of Romans. As the close of a letter sent to a place where he has not yet visited, the extensive greetings *to* specific people in Rome name potential witnesses who can vouch for Paul and prepare a welcome for him. The greetings *from* "all the churches of Christ" (16:16) as well as specific people in Paul's cohort (16:21–23) create bonds between the churches and invite the Roman house churches to see themselves as valued members of a larger community of faith around the Mediterranean world.

In addition, the names themselves are a trove of information about the demographic diversity of Paul's fellow missionaries and of the churches in Rome. In 16:3–16 Paul sends greetings to twenty-eight people, twenty-six by name plus the sister of Nereus and the mother of Rufus. Among those who are named, eight are women; with the addition of Rufus's mother and Nereus's sister, that makes ten women and eighteen men. In addition, two of the men named are not Christians themselves but rather the heads of households to which Christians belong, as enslaved or freed persons. Almost all of the women are described as having active roles in ministry.

Paul's specific greetings also address believers who have gone to Rome from the east. Some of these people, like Prisca and Aquila, were expelled from Rome by Claudius and subsequently returned under Nero. In addition, because some names are typical of Rome and some more typical of eastern origin, it is possible to speculate that roughly half of those whom Paul mentions immigrated to Rome. Analysis of names in the Roman era suggests that some names were associated with enslaved persons or descendants of enslaved persons, who formed a large percentage of the population. Such analysis applied to Romans 16 indicates a greater percentage of enslaved persons or descendants of enslaved persons than of freeborn persons among those whom Paul greets. It is instructive to note the Jewish identities of some of those to whom Paul sends greetings, as shown by name (Mary), by evidence from Acts (Aquila), and by Paul's greeting of them as kinsfolk (Andronicus and Junia, Herodian, possibly Rufus and his mother). In short, those whom Paul greets and counts as friends and fellow workers for the gospel include a wide swath of Greco-Roman society—women and men, enslaved persons and those freed from slavery, freeborn persons, immigrant and native populations, Jews and gentiles (Lampe 2003, 153–83).

Finally, Paul's extensive greetings are in the second-person plural. He does not say, "I greet so-and-so," nor does he ask individuals to pass along his greetings, as would be common in ancient letters; he asks the entire church to greet the individuals he names, thereby expanding and strengthening the bonds of fellowship among the Roman Christians in the different house churches.

16:1–2. Phoebe

Phoebe was probably a gentile Christian leader in the vicinity of Corinth. Paul introduces Phoebe as "our sister," thereby identifying her as a fellow Christian, and further as a deacon (*diakonos*) of the church at Cenchreae. As in Paul's depiction of Christ (15:8) and frequent self-designation (1 Cor 3:5; 2 Cor 6:4; Col 1:23, 25), here *diakonos* means "minister" in the sense of having a leadership position in the church. Such a meaning is clear in Philippians 1:1, where Paul addresses "all the saints . . . , with the bishops and deacons." Cenchreae was a port city just southeast of Corinth. As there is no archaeological evidence of a separate church there, "the church of Cenchreae" probably refers to a church in Phoebe's house.

Phoebe would have arrived in Rome as the letter-bearer who read it aloud and interpreted it for believers gathered in the different house churches. In this sense she has a double ambassadorial role, preparing the way for Paul's future visit and also proclaiming Paul's understanding of the gospel, his "spiritual gift" to the letter's recipients (1:11, 15).

Paul instructs Phoebe's audience to "welcome her in the Lord" (16:2). The language implies both a verbal welcome and the provision of practical hospitality in terms of lodging and sustenance. By adding "as is fitting [*axiōs*] for the saints," Paul ups the ante; she should be welcomed with dignity and honor. In addition, Paul requests that his addressees help Phoebe in whatever she may require: "for she has been a benefactor [*prostatis*] of many and of myself as well." A *prostatis* was a wealthy patron who underwrote the needs of both individuals and public institutions. Evidence from papyri and inscriptions now demonstrates that women as well as men undertook this role in the patronage economy of the Mediterranean world. It is possible that Paul is introducing Phoebe as the benefactor of his planned trip to Spain; in any case, he certainly identifies her as a past benefactor of himself and others and asks her hosts to aid her in whatever she requires as she prepares the way for his upcoming visit. Clearly Phoebe is a woman of independent wealth and status who has freedom to travel and resources to support the ministry of the church. Paul does not identify her through familial connections such as marriage, but solely in relationship to her leadership role in the church.

16:3–16. Greetings

Not surprisingly, in 16:3–5a Paul begins by sending greetings to Prisca and Aquila, whom he knows from his time in both Corinth and Ephesus. Aquila was a Jewish Christian who had been among those evicted from Rome by the edict of Claudius (Acts 18:2). Prisca and Aquila probably met in Rome and were members of the churches there before being expelled under Claudius. Like Paul, they were craftspeople, and they shared their home and work with Paul when he first came to Corinth (18:3). Furthermore, they traveled to

Ephesus with Paul, where they continued as leaders of the church after Paul moved on (18:18–19). When a Jewish convert named Apollo began teaching in the church in Ephesus, Prisca and Aquila were the ones who took him aside for further instruction (18:24–26). The fact that Paul mentions Prisca first may also indicate her relative prominence in such leadership activities; indeed, Chrysostom identifies Prisca (called Priscilla in Acts) as the one who instructed Apollos (*Hom. Rom.* 31.1, in Burns 2012, 385).

It is unclear just how Prisca and Aquila "risked their necks" on Paul's behalf; perhaps they intervened when he got into trouble with the authorities (e.g., Acts 19:23–31). Like the contemporary expression "put your neck on the line," the metaphor derives from the ancient Roman method of execution by beheading.

As the "first convert in Asia," Epaenetus was probably the first convert in the church in Ephesus led by Prisca and Aquila and perhaps came with them when they returned to Rome. We know nothing about Mary except that she was Jewish, as implied by her name, and that Paul commends her for her extensive work among the believers in Rome (Rom 16:6). Chrysostom says of her, "What is this? Again a woman is crowned and proclaimed victor; we men are once again put to shame, or rather, we are both put to shame and honored. We are praised because the women among us have such outstanding characters; we are put to shame because we men are left so far behind them" (*Hom. Rom.* 31.1, in Burns 2012, 385).

Andronicus and Junia (16:7) are Paul's fellow Jews who at one time were his fellow prisoners. There is no scriptural reference to such a shared imprisonment but that does not mean it did not happen; Paul was used to being arrested and thrown in jail, and it is plausible that he shared that experience with these two early believers or even met them in prison.

Junia is a feminine name, and the history of interpretation demonstrates the level of traditional resistance to acknowledging her high status as a woman among the apostles. One need only note the RSV translation: "my kinsmen . . . ; they are men of note among the apostles." To the contrary, most of the early church fathers recognized Junia as a woman and commented on her identification as an apostle. For example, Chrysostom writes, "Even to be an apostle is great, but also to be prominent among them—consider how wonderful a song of honor that is! But they were of note according to their works, to their achievements. Oh how great is the devotion of this woman, that she should be even counted worthy of the appellation of apostle!" (*Hom. Rom.* 31.2, in Bray 1998, 358–59). Paul claims that Andronicus and Junia were "in Christ before I was." Whereas Paul elsewhere describes himself as one "untimely born," to whom the risen Lord appeared last of all (1 Cor 15:8), his description of Andronicus and Junia potentially puts them with James and "all the apostles" to whom the risen Lord appeared (1 Cor 15:6–7). If so, they were part of the early Jewish Christian movement in Jerusalem and could have been among those who founded the churches in Rome, although this is speculative.

Paul now adds greetings to a list of recipients about whom we know very little, except that they have names commonly given to enslaved persons (16:8–11). Paul identifies Ampliatus and Stachys as "beloved" and Urbanus as a "coworker in Christ"—that is, a fellow missionary like Prisca and Aquila. "Those who belong to the family of Aristobulus" is a bit misleading as a translation; the Greek simply says, "those from Aristobulus," referring to enslaved and freed persons from the household of Aristobulus. Since Paul does not send greetings to Aristobulus himself, he probably was not a believer. It is possible that this Aristobulus is the grandson of Herod the Great, who with his brother Herod Agrippa was educated in Rome and who lived in Rome until his death in the 40s. This supposition may be strengthened by the fact that Paul immediately sends greetings to his fellow Jew Herodian, a name indicating membership in the larger Herodian household, perhaps as an enslaved person. Such speculation is impossible to prove, however. "Those in the Lord who belong to the family of Narcissus" also refers to believers among the enslaved persons in the household of Narcissus. Like Aristobulus, Narcissus himself is not identified as a believer.

Tryphaena and Tryphosa (16:12) are feminine names, denoting two women who are "workers in the Lord." Similarly, Persis is a feminine name, typically for an enslaved person from Persia; Paul identifies her as a "beloved" hard worker in the ministry. Rufus (v. 13) means "redhead." "Chosen in the Lord" indicates distinction among the Roman believers, but it is difficult to determine what this is.

In Romans 16:14–15 Paul adds greetings to the members of a house church, as indicated by "and the brothers and sisters who are with them." He closes with greetings to members of another house church, first by name, then including "all the saints who are with them." The Greek reads "Philologus *and* Julia," probably indicating a husband and wife as leaders of the church. "Nereus and his sister" may be their children or simply other leaders in the church.

Paul frequently tells his listeners to greet each other with a holy kiss (1 Cor 16:20; 2 Cor 13:12; 1 Thess 5:26), so it is not surprising to find him doing so in Romans 16:16. But in view of his instigation of extensive greetings among and between the Roman Christians in different house churches, this call to familial intimacy is striking. When he adds, "All the churches of Christ greet you," he reminds the Roman Christians that they belong to a much larger fellowship than their individual assemblies and draws them into the fellowship of churches he has established around the Mediterranean world.

16:17–20. A Warning and a Promise

With a third urgent appeal (cf. 12:1; 15:30), in 16:17 Paul abruptly pivots to a solemn warning against divisive intruders. Because the tone and vocabulary of these verses differ somewhat from the rest of the letter, some scholars consider this section an interpolation written by someone other than Paul. On the other hand, it appears in all the ancient manuscripts of Romans, and it is not unusual for Paul to interject warnings against potential troublemakers toward the end of his letters (Gal 6:12–13; Phil 3:2–3, 18–19; 1 Cor 16:22). Therefore, we will consider it as an integral part of the letter. Having just sent extensive greetings and a call to mutual welcome with a holy kiss, all intended to unify the squabbling and potentially divided Roman congregations, Paul naturally warns them against anything or anyone who would divide them. This warning is entirely in line with his concern for the unity of the churches. In Romans 16:17 he tells his listeners to "watch out, be on the lookout for" those who create dissension and hindrances (*scandala*) contrary to the teaching that they have learned. Similarly, in 14:13 he warned against putting a "stumbling block" (*skandalon*) in front of a brother or sister. "The teaching" (*didachēs*) they have learned recalls the teaching to which they were committed (6:17), implying that it refers to their prior instruction in the faith, not Paul's own instruction in the letter. "Dissension" is one of the works of the flesh in Galatians 5:20. This is not unusual terminology for Paul; here he apparently has specific people and divisive teachings in mind. Although it is difficult to ascertain what such teachings might be, Paul's language implies that it is teaching contrary to the gospel itself (again, see Rom 6:17), not differences around dietary practices and Sabbath observance that should not divide the church.

Paul immediately gives further reasons why the Roman Christians should avoid people whose teaching is divisive: they do not serve our Lord Christ but their own belly, and they use fair and flattering words to deceive the hearts of the guileless (16:18). The first criticism is similar to Paul's warning in Philippians 3:18–19 against those who "live as enemies of the cross of Christ. . . . Their end is destruction, their god is the belly, and their glory is in their shame." The similarity is striking, in that both theological and perhaps moral considerations are in play in Paul's concern about these unknown interlopers.

The second criticism concerns the dangers of deception. In Greek, "smooth talk and flattery" are rhyming words that usually have positive connotations, as "pleasant words" (*chrēstologias*) and "good words" or "blessing" (*eulogias*); here, however, Paul warns against their use to "deceive" (cf. 7:11, where Paul says that sin uses the law to deceive). Now in 16:19 he praises the Roman believers for their "obedience" (1:5, 8) but cautions them against being deceived (cf. 1 Cor 14:20). "I want you to be wise in what is good and guileless in what is evil" is a call to mature discernment exercised in their common life.

Given his concern to promote unity and mutual welcome, it seems unlikely that Paul is targeting any members of the Roman house churches here. Rather, he may be forewarning his listeners against potential threats from outside, threats that he considers antithetical to the gospel teaching and potentially destructive of Christian fellowship. It is difficult to be sure whom the apostle has in mind; since he is writing from Corinth, perhaps he is thinking of those whom he calls "false prophets, deceitful workers, disguising themselves as apostles of Christ. And no wonder! Even Satan disguises himself as an angel of light" (2 Cor 11:13–14). The motif of deception, including false claims to be followers of Christ, and the reference to Satan, all correlate with Romans 16:17–20. It is possible that Paul is concerned lest those who have threatened to undermine his authority in Corinth will try to sabotage his visit to Rome and his request for support for his further mission to Spain. If so, here he issues a preemptive warning against such divisive teachers invading the Roman churches.

Paul's sudden reference to "Satan" (*satana*) in 16:20 comes as a surprise, at least to modern readers of the letter. *Satana* is a Greek transliteration of the Hebrew word for the accuser who stands against humanity in God's heavenly court (Job 1:6–12; 2:1–7; Zech 3:1–2). By the time of the first century, the figure of Satan as a hostile angelic power is widespread in Jewish literature. Paul's expectation that God will crush Satan is within this strong stream of Jewish thought. In Paul's vocabulary, Satan seems to be a demonic force that sometimes tempts or deceives believers (1 Cor 7:5; 2 Cor 2:11; 1 Thess 3:5) and hinders the reception and progress of the gospel in a variety of ways (2 Cor 4:4; 1 Thess 2:18); such satanic activity can include false "apostles of Christ" (2 Cor 11:13–14). But Satan is also limited by God's power and even sometimes serves God's purposes (1 Cor 5:5; 2 Cor 12:7). Already in Romans 13:11–12 Paul has promised the imminent victory of salvation, saying, "Let us then lay aside the works of darkness and put on the armor of light." His promise in 16:20 that "the God of peace will shortly crush Satan under your feet" is not an aberration from Paul's gospel proclamation in Romans, but the ultimate acclamation of God's certain victory over all that would destroy God's people (cf. 8:37).

But why is such a promise necessary for the recipients of Paul's letter? And why here, just after Paul's warnings against false teachers? Are they to be identified with Satan? The evidence of 2 Corinthians 11:12–15 shows that Paul can indeed identify his opponents as servants of Satan. On the other hand, given the scope of Paul's depiction of sin as that which deceives and kills humanity (Rom 7:11), and his assurance of Christ's victory over sin and death, to limit the meaning of 16:20 to the defeat of some other teachers who are undermining Paul's mission would surely be a mistake. Rather, at the close of his lengthy letter, as Paul contemplates potential threats to his gospel proclamation, he affirms again the solid faith and obedience of the Roman churches (v. 19) and, above all, God's victory over all that would divide and destroy those churches. For God's gift of peace includes vanquishing that which divides human beings from each other as well as from God. In Origen's words, "Satan, then, is the name used for whatever resists and opposes a soul moving toward God, for whatever troubles its peace. This is why he begins the sentence with 'the God of peace,' that is, the God who takes pleasure in peace will crush the one who opposes peace and causes conflicts" (*Commentary*, in Bray 1998, 364).

Finally, Paul concludes this warning with his consistent, insistent blessing of grace. Because Paul usually places the blessing of grace at the end of his letters, it seems out of place here; some ancient manuscripts place it after verse 23. In any case, its presence is significant: every Pauline letter includes "the grace of our Lord Jesus Christ," because grace is the powerful working of the God from whom and through whom and to whom "are all things" (11:36). As Chrysostom puts it, grace is "the greatest weapon, an unbroken wall, an unshaken tower. . . . See what we ought to begin and to end all things with! For in this he laid the foundation of the Epistle, and in this he puts on the roof" (*Hom. Rom.* 32.1, in Burns 2012, 390).

16:21–23. Greetings from Paul's Fellow Workers

By sending greetings from his coworkers, Paul continues strengthening the bonds between his audience in Rome and other believers. Timothy is well-known from Paul's letters, acting as his comrade in arms in all his missionary endeavors (1 Cor 4:17; 16:10; 2 Cor 1:19; Phil 2:19; 1 Thess 3:2, 6). Indeed, Timothy and Sosipater are named among Paul's companions on his final trip to Jerusalem (Acts 20:4). Paul identifies Sosipater, Jason, and Lucius as fellow Jewish believers. Tertius, the amanuensis (scribe) who wrote down the letter while Paul dictated it, now adds his own personal greetings "in the Lord," indicating he is not only a scribe but also a fellow believer (16:22). His name, meaning "third born," was common among enslaved and freed persons.

Finally, in 16:23 Paul passes on greetings from people with positions of authority in the Corinthian church and the city. Gaius was one of Paul's first converts in Corinth and one of the few people he baptized (1 Cor 1:14). As Paul's host and the one in whose house the Corinthian assembly gathers, Gaius appropriately sends greetings to the Roman churches that will host Paul. Paul names Erastus as "the city treasurer" (*oikonomos*). The title could indicate that he was one of many civic officials overseeing public works or a high-level magistrate (*aedile*). Advancement to such high office usually involved public philanthropy. An inscription discovered on a paving stone dating from the middle of the first century says, "I, Erastus, in return for the aedileship, laid the pavement at his own expense." Because Erastus was an uncommon name in Corinth, and because Paul clearly thinks it important to name his public status, this may possibly be the same Erastus. Named simply as "the brother" (NRSVue says "our brother," but this is an interpretive addition), Quartus remains a mystery. He may be the brother of Erastus, but this is not indicated clearly in the Greek; it seems more likely that "brother" identifies Quartus as a fellow believer. Like Tertius, Quartus ("fourth born") was a common slave name; it is worth pondering that the final greeting in this, Paul's longest and most influential letter, is from an otherwise unidentified descendant of enslaved persons who may still be enslaved himself.

EXCURSUS

Reflections for Preaching and Teaching

A Radical Vision of the Church

The diversity of those whom Paul greets in Rome is both revealing and easily overlooked. As noted in the commentary, a high proportion of those whom Paul singles out for attention are women whom he knows from their partnership with him in preaching, evangelizing, and leading nascent fellowships of believers. Paul does not simply name these women, but emphatically praises their ministry, as was recognized by some of the early theologians. As Chrysostom put it, "The women of that time were more zealous than lions, sharing with the Apostles their labors of preaching. For this reason, they also traveled abroad with them and served them in every other way. In a similar way, women followed after Christ, ministered to the disciples from their possessions, and served the Teacher" (*Hom. Rom.* 31, in Burns 2012, 385–86).

Similarly, Paul sends greetings to and from people whose names indicate slave status. That the final two greetings of the letter are from a high-ranking city official and an unknown enslaved person or freedman encapsulates the breathtaking social effects of the gospel preaching.

How, then, should contemporary Christian leaders address inequality in their own fellowships? Paying attention to the actual people whom Paul names and greets is a great resource for addressing diversity and inclusivity in Christian fellowship. Regarding the ministry of women, it is crucial to highlight the actual *practices* of Paul's missionary work, in which women played equal roles with men, in contrast with the later pushback against such equality, as visible in the Pastoral Epistles (1 Tim 3:1–13) and the interpolation in 1 Corinthians 14:33b–36. It is significant that early commentators on Romans recognized the inclusion of women in ministry. Origen writes of Phoebe in 16:1, "This passage teaches that there were women ordained in the church's ministry by the apostle's authority. . . . Not only that—they ought to be ordained into the ministry, because they helped in many ways and by their good services deserved the praise even of the apostle" (*Commentary*, in Bray 1998, 355).

Similarly, the prevalence of enslaved and freed persons in leadership positions demonstrates just how much the gospel of a crucified Lord upends social hierarchies and liberates people from the roles imposed by social, economic, and legal forces. Paul surely would be shocked by the homogeneity of most Christian churches today, particularly in an American context. The actual picture of the churches in Rome and in Paul's letters invites the church today to extend its welcome and to open leadership positions to those marginalized by our culture.

Creating a Network of Mutual Welcome

As noted in the commentary, Paul does not directly greet the many addressees of the letter, but rather asks the church to pass on his greeting and in that way greet one another. Similarly, in the final greetings from his coworkers, he stands out of the way. This is an important and easily overlooked strategy for facilitating networks of mutual recognition and support within the church that are not dependent on, or mediated by, the clergy. Some churches grow through loyalty to the church leaders, which creates serious problems when those leaders fail or leave (or both). Some churches are collections of cliques or fellowships or prayer groups of like-minded folks who are socially akin. Such patterns of relationship neglect the rich possibilities of transformation and growth in faith that come with fellowship between people who otherwise might have nothing in common. Wise leaders encourage the faithful to establish mutual bonds of love across social and religious differences. They also encourage, facilitate, and support pastoral care between members of the congregation rather than assuming all such care is the special prerogative of the pastor. If Paul's listeners follow his encouragement in Romans 16, believers from opposing groups not only will greet each other, they will exchange a "holy kiss." In Paul's context, that includes Jewish and gentile believers, those who abstain and those who indulge, those who keep Sabbath and those who do not, enslaved persons, freed persons, and freeborn, women and men. In our particular contexts, we need to be alert to the social and cultural divides that may subtly fracture the church. By fostering connections across such divisions, the church becomes what theologian Rowan Williams (2004, 235) calls "a moving and expanding network of saving relationship."

Satan and Sin

In some church contexts, Paul's abrupt promise that "the God of peace will shortly crush Satan under your feet" will cause consternation, embarrassment, even revulsion. Surely we modern Christians do not believe in a personal evil force, do we? There is a story that circulates among New Testament scholars about the Swiss theologian Emil Brunner. Not long after the atrocities of World War II, Brunner gave a public lecture at Wellesley College. During the questions afterward, he was asked, "Dr. Brunner, during your lecture you referred several times to 'the devil.' Surely you do not believe in the devil, do you?" Brunner answered, "I speak of the devil for two reasons. First, the New Testament speaks in this way. And second, I have seen him."

Paul quite simply does believe there is a power other than human beings that seeks our destruction. Throughout Romans, particularly in chapters 1–8, he speaks of this power in terms of sin and death, but here at the end he uses the name Satan. We can see the homiletical and pastoral value of this naming when we consider the alternatives. For example, in a perceptive analysis of modernity's loss of language to talk about evil, Andrew Delbanco (1995) describes modern Americans' endless quest to locate evil in other people, in institutions (which is another way of locating evil in other people), and in ourselves. In searching for explanations and ways of naming horrific atrocities, we end up demonizing others and sometimes even ourselves. The Rwandan genocide was fueled by lies about threats from one group against another; the American invasion of Iraq was fueled by claims that Iraq had weapons of mass destruction; the Russian invasion of Ukraine is justified by blatant lies claiming Ukraine is a threat to Russia. All of these lies (Rom 7:11) demonize others in order to justify self-aggrandizing aggression against them.

The ancient and enduring belief in some kind of Satan grapples with this problem of evil that defies the imagination by locating it in a nonhuman entity that can never be fully identified with any human beings. Consequently, other human beings are never "the enemy." This insight yields ways of preaching and teaching in situations of conflict, fear, and hatred, such that we can name wrong but also name other people as God's creation, not the source of evil. For example, South African Bishop Desmond Tutu frequently said that in the struggle against apartheid, the Afrikaans oppressors were not the enemy, because they also were in bondage to a system bigger than them; they also needed liberation. Here at the end of Romans, Paul names the real conflict and the only solution to it; the conflict is between God and the powers of sin and death that hold both oppressors and victims captive, and the solution is the victory of the God who alone can vanquish those powers and bring peace.

ROMANS 16:25–27
Concluding Doxology

There is tremendous variation among ancient manuscripts regarding the placement of these verses, which occur at the end of chapter 14, 15, or 16, and sometimes are omitted entirely. The style of this concluding doxology also diverges quite sharply from that of the rest of the letter. For these reasons, it seems probable that they were added by a very early interpreter of the letter. Whether Paul or an early editor wrote these verses, however, in the final version of Romans they serve as a guide to its interpretation, summing up key themes in a fitting conclusion and doxology.

This entire concluding paragraph is a doxology in praise of God. It begins by reprising Paul's desire to give the Roman Christians a "spiritual gift" to "strengthen" them (1:11), but now attributes that strengthening directly to God, who is "powerfully able [*dynamenō*] to strengthen you" (16:25). The following clause, "according to my gospel," implies such strengthening comes through Paul's gospel proclamation here in the letter itself, the preaching in which Jesus Christ is the one made known (1:15). That this gospel proclamation is a "revelation" (*apocalypsis*) accords with the gospel as the apocalypse of God's righteousness breaking into human history (1:16). That it is a "mystery" accords with the mysterious working of God to redeem all humanity, both Jew and gentile (11:25).

The combination of a distinctive style with familiar themes continues in 16:26, picking up on ideas from earlier in the letter. In 3:21 Paul says the righteousness of God has been manifested (*pephanerōtai*), having been witnessed to by the Law and the Prophets. Now the final doxology says the mystery of the gospel is being disclosed (*phanerōthentes*) and made known through the prophetic writings, just as it was promised through the prophets in the holy writings (1:2). This mystery is inseparable from the obedience of faith for all the gentiles (1:5; 15:18).

The doxology concludes with the glory of God (cf. Phil 4:20), bringing to a triumphant finale the promise of divine glory that threads through the entire epistle. "The only wise God" names the source of the good news, which is the inscrutable wisdom, power, and grace of God (11:33–36): "O the depth of the riches and wisdom and knowledge of God! How unsearchable are his judgments and inscrutable his ways! For who has known the mind of the Lord? Or who has been his counselor? Or who has given a gift to him, to receive a gift in return? For from him and through him and to him are all things. To him be the glory forever. Amen."

EXCURSUS

Reflections for Preaching and Teaching

The Final Takeaway

At the end of Paul's lengthy, theologically rich, and challenging letter, we are given a final takeaway—the promise that Paul's gospel will strengthen us through the preaching of Jesus Christ, to the glory of God. If we ponder the implications for preaching, we might ask ourselves what the takeaway from our sermons is. Paul's consistent concluding benediction of "grace" (16:20b; 1 Cor 16:23; 2 Cor 13:13; Gal 6:18; Phil 4:23; 1 Thess 5:28) in all his letters should give us pause. As far as Paul is concerned, God's unmerited gift, given by the God who surpasses all human imagination or control, is so radically different from the status quo in which his listeners live that it needs to be proclaimed over and over again. It is *this* gospel preaching of Jesus Christ that will strengthen the Roman believers and contemporary congregations as well. Here at the end, as at the beginning, Romans invites us to find in Scripture the witness to God's surpassing plenitude and grace, which alone creates obedient trust in God, fellowships of love, and transformed lives.

BIBLIOGRAPHY

For Further Reading

Adams, Edward, Dorothea H. Bertschmann, Stephen J. Chester, Jonathan A. Linebaugh, and Todd D. Still, eds. 2023. *The New Perspective on Grace: Paul and the Gospel after "Paul and the Gift."* Grand Rapids: Wm. B. Eerdmans Publishing Co.

Barclay, John M. G. 2015. *Paul and the Gift.* Grand Rapids: Wm. B. Eerdmans Publishing Co.

———. 2020. *Paul and the Power of Grace.* Grand Rapids: Wm. B. Eerdmans Publishing Co.

Barrett, C. K. 1957. *The Epistle to the Romans.* Harper's New Testament Commentaries. New York: Harper & Row.

Barth, Karl. 1959. *A Shorter Commentary on Romans.* Richmond, VA: John Knox Press.

Burroughs, Presian, ed. 2018. *Practicing with Paul: Reflections on Paul and the Practices of Ministry in Honor of Susan G. Eastman.* Eugene, OR: Cascade Books.

Byrne, Brendan, SJ. 1996. *Romans.* Sacra Pagina 6. Collegeville, MN: Liturgical Press.

Cranfield, C. E. B. 1975. *Introduction and Commentary on Romans I–VIII.* Vol. 1 of *A Critical and Exegetical Commentary on the Epistle to the Romans.* International Critical Commentary. Edinburgh: T&T Clark.

———. 1979. *Introduction and Commentary on Romans IX–XVI.* Vol. 2 of *A Critical and Exegetical Commentary on the Epistle to the Romans.* International Critical Commentary. Edinburgh: T&T Clark.

Eastman, Susan. 2017. *Paul and the Person: Reframing Paul's Anthropology.* Grand Rapids: Wm. B. Eerdmans Publishing Co.

Gaventa, Beverly, ed. 2013. *Apocalyptic Paul: Cosmos and Anthropos in Romans 5–8.* Waco, TX: Baylor University Press.

———. 2016. *When in Romans: An Invitation to Linger with the Gospel according to Paul.* Grand Rapids: Baker Academic.

———. 2024. *Romans.* New Testament Library. Louisville, KY: Westminster John Knox Press.

Gorman, Michael. 2022. *Romans: A Theological and Pastoral Commentary.* Grand Rapids: Wm. B. Eerdmans Publishing Co.

Käsemann, Ernst. 1980. *Commentary on Romans.* Edited and translated by Geoffrey W. Bromiley. Grand Rapids: Wm. B. Eerdmans Publishing Co.

Keck, Leander. 2005. *Romans.* Abingdon New Testament Commentaries. Nashville: Abingdon Press.

Keener, Craig. 2009. *Romans.* New Covenant Commentary Series 6. Eugene, OR: Cascade Books.

Meyer, Paul. 2004. "Romans: A Commentary." Pages 151–218 in *The Word in This World: Essays in New Testament Exegesis and Theology*. New Testament Library. Louisville, KY: Westminster John Knox Press.

Rutledge, Fleming. 2015. *The Crucifixion: Understanding the Death of Jesus Christ.* Grand Rapids: Wm. B. Eerdmans Publishing Co.

Works Cited

Barclay, John M. G. 2015. *Paul and the Gift.* Grand Rapids: Wm. B. Eerdmans Publishing Co.

Bonhoeffer, Dietrich. 2009. *Life Together.* New York: HarperOne.

Bray, Gerald, ed. 1998. *Romans.* Ancient Christian Commentary on Scripture 6. Downers Grove, IL: InterVarsity Press.

Burns, J. Patout, ed. 2012. *Romans: Interpreted by Early Christian Commentators.* The Church's Bible. Grand Rapids: Wm. B. Eerdmans Publishing Co.

Burroughs, Presian. 2022. *Creation's Slavery and Liberation: Paul's Letter to Rome in the Face of Imperial and Industrial Agriculture*. Eugene, OR: Cascade Books.

Calvin, John. 1959. *Institutes of the Christian Religion*. Translated by Ford Lewis Battles. Grand Rapids: Wm. B. Eerdmans Publishing Co.

Chrysostom, John. 1877. *The Homilies of St. John Chrysostom, Archbishop of Constantinople, on the Epistle of St. Paul the Apostle to the Romans.* 3rd ed. Translated by J. B. Morris. Oxford: Jas. Parker and Co.–Rivingtons.

Cranfield, C. E. B. 1975. *Introduction and Commentary on Romans I–VIII.* Vol. 1 of *A Critical and Exegetical Commentary on the Epistle to the Romans.* International Critical Commentary. Edinburgh: T&T Clark.

———. 1979. *Introduction and Commentary on Romans IX–XVI.* Vol. 2 of *A Critical and Exegetical Commentary on the Epistle to the Romans.* International Critical Commentary. Edinburgh: T&T Clark.

Delbanco, Andrew. 1995. *The Death of Satan: How Americans Have Lost the Sense of Evil.* New York: Farrar, Straus & Giroux.

Eastman, Susan. 2002. "Whose Apocalypse? The Identity of the Sons of God in Romans 8:19." *Journal of Biblical Literature* 121 (2):263–77.

———. 2010. *Recovering Paul's Mother Tongue: Language and Theology in Galatians.* 2nd ed. Eugene, OR: Cascade Books.

———. 2017. *Paul and the Person: Reframing Paul's Anthropology*. Grand Rapids: Wm. B. Eerdmans Publishing Co.

Gaventa, Beverly. 2017. "Reading Romans 13 with Simone Weil: Toward a More Generous Hermeneutic." *Journal of Biblical Literature* 136 (1):7–22.

———. 2024. *Romans.* New Testament Library. Louisville, KY: Westminster John Knox Press.

Glancy, Jennifer. 2004. "Boasting of Beatings (2 Corinthians 11:22–25)." *Journal of Biblical Literature* 123 (1):99–135.

Jewett, Robert. 2007. *Romans.* Hermeneia. Minneapolis: Fortress Press.

Julian of Norwich. 2015. *Revelations of Divine Love.* Translated by Barry Windeatt. Oxford: Oxford University Press.

Kalanithi, Paul. 2016. *When Breath Becomes Air.* New York: Random House.

Käsemann, Ernst. 1999. "One Lord Alone: A Sermon of Protest." Translated by E. Osborn. *Expository Times* 110 (8):249–51.

King, Martin Luther, Jr. 2010. *Strength to Love.* Minneapolis: Fortress Press.

Lampe, Peter. 2003. *From Paul to Valentinus: Christians at Rome in the First Two Centuries.* Minneapolis: Fortress Press.

Marcus, Joel. 1988. "'Let God Arise and End the Reign of Sin!' A Contribution to the Study of Pauline Parenesis." *Biblica* 69 (3):386–95.

Moore, Beth. 2023. *All My Knotted-Up Life.* Carol Stream, IL: Tyndale House.

Morrison, Toni. 2008. *Beloved.* New York: Vintage Classics.

Prescott, Hilda. 2008. *The Man on a Donkey*. 2 vols. Chicago: Loyola Classics, 2008. First published 1952.

Robinson, Marilynne. 2004. *Gilead.* New York: Farrar, Straus & Giroux.

Sanders, E. P. 1977. *Paul and Palestinian Judaism: A Comparison of Patterns of Religion.* Philadelphia: Fortress Press.

Taylor, John. 2021. *The Go-Between God.* London: SCM Press. First published 1972.

Tolkien, J. R. R. 2000. *The Letters of J. R. R. Tolkien.* Edited by Humphrey Carpenter. New York: Houghton Mifflin.

Van der Kolk, Bessel. 2014. *The Body Keeps the Score: Brain, Mind and Body in the Healing of Trauma*. New York: Viking.

Wagner, J. Ross. 1997. "The Christ, Servant of Jew and Gentile: A Fresh Approach to Romans 15:8–9." *Journal of Biblical Literature* 116 (3):473–85.

Ward, Benedicta. 2003. *The Desert Fathers: Sayings of the Early Christian Monks.* London: Penguin.

Williams, Rowan. 2004. *On Christian Theology*. Oxford: Blackwell.

Willis, Connie. 2010. *Blackout / All Clear.* New York: Spectra.